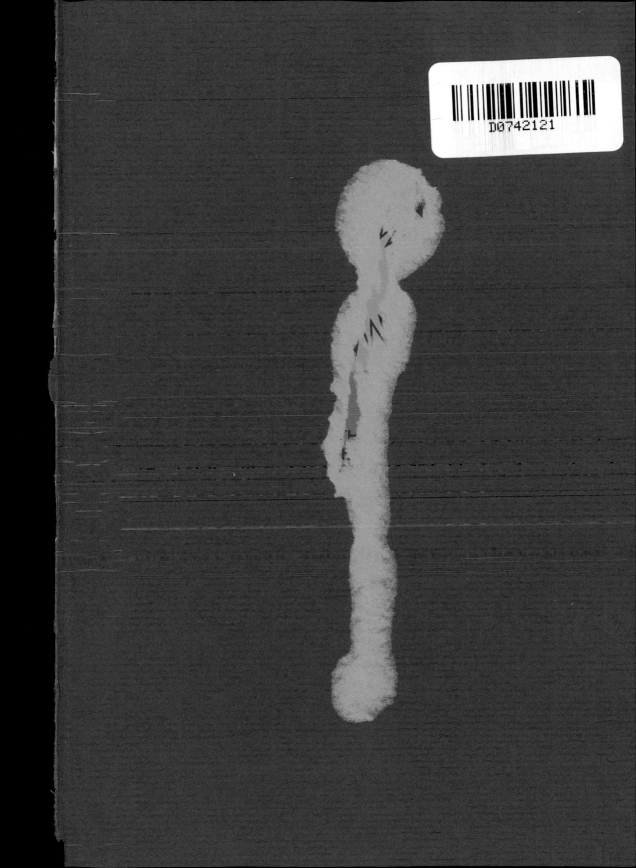

Leigh Hunt and Opera Criticism

The "Examiner" Years, 1808–1821

Leigh Hunt

AND OPERA CRITICISM

The "Examiner" Years, 1808-1821

Theodore Fenner

The University Press of Kansas
Lawrence/Manhattan/Wichita

to Lee

Contents

Illustrations

Preface

LEIGH HUNT'S writings on music have not been entirely neglected by scholars. In this century Edmund C. Blunden was apparently the first to emphasize Hunt's interests in music and to suggest the importance of his criticisms of Mozart's operas.[1] Professor Louis Landré, in his carefully documented study, revealed more clearly the nature and extent of Hunt's musical journalism; he supplied valuable commentary on Hunt's music criticism and discussed the general significance of music in his life and thought. Others have investigated special areas: Dr. Percy M. Young has provided a balanced and competent survey of Hunt's writings on music; Edward D. Mackerness has summarized important features of Hunt's musical journalism; and David L. Jones has compared selected Italian-opera reviews written by Hunt and by William Hazlitt.[2] But none of these articles pretends to deal thoroughly either with Hunt's musical journalism or specifically with his opera criticism.

The present study is an attempt to fill at least part of this gap. Centering on Hunt's opera criticism from 1808 to 1821, it offers only occasional glances at his reviews of other music during this period, and it all but ignores his later musical journalism. But opera occupies a place of primary importance in the *Examiner*. It also provides a convenient context in which to compare Hunt with the other reviewers for the newspaper, especially Henry Robertson,[3] William Hazlitt, and Thomas Barnes. Such comparisons not only help to establish the relative value of the contributions of these writers as opera critics but also furnish a background for viewing the *Examiner* as a cultural force in Regency England.

With few exceptions, the author has not attempted to examine the operas themselves. Such an approach is impracticable in a study involving the criticism of some eighty-five works for the lyric stage and, moreover, largely futile in view of lost plays, librettos, and scores, to say nothing of the unreconstructable "adaptations" that Hunt saw and often complained about. Rather, I have drawn on historians of music and drama for evaluative commentary on works and individuals. I have also cited the views of other contemporaries of Hunt's on points that are relevant to criticisms in the *Examiner*. These comments have been largely confined to the notes for chapters three and four so as to keep the study of Hunt's criticism in the foreground. Details on performances reviewed, composers, playwrights, librettists, and performers have been relegated to the appendixes.[4]

To a considerable extent Hunt's views on opera are presented in his own words. Not only is Hunt eminently quotable (I am not alone in finding that "one cannot write of Leigh Hunt without quoting him at some length"),[5] but little of his opera criticism and none of Robertson's has been reprinted.[6] Moreover, microfilms of the *Examiner* are difficult to read and not readily accessible. All *Examiner* quotations, including Hazlitt's, have been accurately transcribed.[7] The names of people (set in small capitals in the *Examiner*) have been standardized, but the names of characters appear in italics, following the newspaper's practice. Except for a very few typographical errors silently corrected, no other changes have been made. Usage that is now regarded as incorrect but that has historical validity has been retained without comment.

Aside from the *Examiner* itself, the single most useful aid to this study has been Landré's indispensable work. Other sources that should be mentioned because they were frequently consulted are also listed, together with their short forms of citation, at the end of this preface.

To Professor Carl R. Woodring I am greatly obliged for suggestions that led me to investigate this subject and for the encouragement and guidance he gave to my pursuit of this study. To Professor Paul Henry Lang I am especially indebted for a critical reading of the manuscript and for buttressing my deficiencies in matters musicological. (The inevitable errors herein

are of course mine alone.) I also wish to thank him, as editor of
the *Musical Quarterly*, for publishing an article that I wrote,
based on part of the material that became chapter two of this
book. For the services of many libraries and librarians in this
country and in England I am indebted, and wish especially to
mention Vincent J. Sheehey of Columbia University and Frank
Paluka of the University of Iowa, Iowa City. To Virginia Seaver
of the University Press of Kansas I wish to express my appreciation for her keen editorial eye and her many helpful suggestions.
And to my wife, whose typing, proofreading, and editorial assistance indicate only a small measure of her contribution to this
study, goes my deepest gratitude.

Examiner *The Examiner, A Sunday Paper on Politics, Domestic Economy, and Theatricals* (London: 1808–1821).

Autobiography *The Autobiography of Leigh Hunt*, Jack E. Morpurgo, ed. (London: Cresset Press, Ltd., 1948).

Correspondence *The Correspondence of Leigh Hunt*, edited by his eldest son [Thornton L. Hunt, ed.], (2 vols.; London: Elder and Co., 1862).

Poetical Works *The Poetical Works of Leigh Hunt*, H. S. Milford, ed. (London and New York: Oxford University Press, 1923).

Landré *Leigh Hunt: Contribution à l'histoire du Romantisme anglais*, by Louis Landré (2 vols.; Paris: Société d'édition "Les Belles-lettres," 1935–1936).

Nicoll *A History of English Drama, 1660-1900*, by Allardyce Nicoll (6 vols.; London: Cambridge University Press, 1952 [4th ed., I–III], 1955 [2nd ed., IV], 1959 [2nd ed., V; 1st ed., VI]).

Grove's *Grove's Dictionary of Music and Musicians*, Eric Blom, ed. (5th ed.; New York: St. Martin's Press, 1954).

Annals *Annals of Opera: 1597–1940*, Alfred Loewenberg, comp. (2nd ed.; 2 vols.; Geneva: Societas Bibliographica, 1955).

Sears   *Song Index* (New York: The H. W. Wilson Com-
                 pany, 1926) and *Song Index Supplement* (New York:
                 The H. W. Wilson Company, 1934), by Minnie E.
                 Sears.

D.N.B.   *Dictionary of National Biography.*

O.E.D.   *Oxford English Dictionary.*

dle classes, feeling comfortable with a mode of opera that did not
stray too far from the "realistic" conventions of the spoken stage,
generally looked with suspicion on the exotic product imported
by the aristocracy for their amusement. To those of the upper
classes who sought at the opera house more than an idle imitation
of Continental fashions, or a refuge from the boisterous English
playhouses, Italian opera offered an esthetic experience more enriching than the trifles that cluttered the English musical stage.

In England the development of these traditions began with the
introduction of Italian opera as a serious public entertainment
shortly after the turn of the century. At that time the late-Ba-
roque opera seria (serious or tragic opera) was undergoing a slow
transition from the older Venetian type, which employed sophisticated polyphonic and contrapuntal resources and which preferred mythological and pastoral material for its subjects. Its
dramatic form, as in the "Heroic" drama of the Restoration, was
highly episodic and heterogeneous, incorporating elements of
humor, supernaturalism, and fantasy in settings that were primarily serious and elevated.

Responding to more popular influences, the new High Ba-
roque style, which took its inception at Naples, gave to opera
seria a distinctive character during the first half of the eighteenth
century. Its plots, still episodic, were gradually purged of non-
tragic material; its heroes were found primarily in history. The
form derived its popular appeal largely from an emphasis on
melody, to which the accompaniment was completely subordi-
nated. Like the earlier opera, it was sung throughout, but the
recitative underwent further development. There were two general categories. *Recitativo secco,* accompanied only by the "dry"
chords of the harpsichord, permitted rapid and clear delivery of
the "narrative" portions of the drama; *recitativo accompagnato,*
accompanied by the orchestra, marked passages and entire scenes
that carried a heightened emotional intensity.

The newer opera seria also further developed the aria, a kind
of emotional plateau, which projected the dominant mood of the
character at strategic points in the drama. Conceived as action,
operatic drama was brought to a standstill by the aria; conceived

as an exploration of the psychology of character, operatic drama found in the aria its perfect fulfillment. Accordingly, opera seria became bel canto—the singer's opera. The da capo aria, especially, which repeats itself, permitted the prima donna unlimited possibilities for demonstrating the vocal dexterity of her coloratura; in the reprise she was expected to add such improvised embellishments as her agility and artistry could command.

The extemporaneous nature of the performance of opera seria gave it great flexibility and spontaneity, but this also had disadvantages. Singers did not always show good taste when they interpolated airs or indulged in vocal displays. Librettists and composers, working freely with inherited material, could quickly produce viable operas under highly competitive conditions; but sometimes the final product lacked unity. The borrowing of musical or dramatic material was an accepted convention provided the adaptations were imaginative. But borrowings, encouraged by lack of effective copyright laws, became more flagrant as inspiration flagged. The lesser composers, too, failed to achieve a unified musical architecture; this, based on the role of tonal concordances in eighteenth-century Italian opera, the best composers of the period brought to their work. The door was opened for pasticcios—medleys of favorite tunes borrowed from earlier operas (often by different composers) and built into a new libretto—which became more common. By mid century Gluck and others sought to remedy these abuses and bring more musico-dramatic coherence to opera seria.

Opera was Italy's most exportable product. Italian composers, librettists, and performers flocked to cultural centers throughout Europe, carrying their fashionable art with them. Though Venetian opera seria held its popularity for some time at the courts from Madrid to St. Petersburg, the Neapolitan variety gradually supplanted it everywhere else.

Beginning with the second decade of the century, Italian opera was firmly established in London. Its most powerful exponent there was George Frideric Handel (1685–1759). Combining the best of both Venetian and Neapolitan schools, Handel produced

an enormous number of fine operas, which for a time were successful with a certain segment of the English public. In 1720 the
appearance of a successful rival, Giovanni Bononcini (1670–
1747?), eventually created problems for him, which were further
complicated by politics.[2] Handel ultimately lost his opera audiences and turned his attention to the oratorio (see below). But
the opera-seria tradition in London was carried on by others, including another transplanted German, Johann Christian Bach
(1735–1782).

With its bustling prosperity, expanding empire, and consuming interest in the fashionable, England became the most lucra-
tive marketplace for Continental musicians. Opera there depended on public support, which came primarily from the aristocracy. The prosperous middle class, small but growing rapidly,
also patronized it for some years. But even before the first Italian
opera was mounted in 1705, there were signs of revolt against
Italian singers at subscription concerts. One of the characters in
Thomas Baker's *Tunbridge Walks* (1703) speaks of going "to
hear a parcel of Italian eunuchs, like so many cats, squall out
somewhat you don't understand." Three years later the critic
John Dennis, alarmed by attempts to reproduce opera seria in
English, pointed out that the vigorous English language with its
strong consonants "cannot be pronounced without very frequently shutting the mouth, which is diametrically opposite to
the expressing of music"; moreover, as music is not essentially
vigorous, the mind easily becomes slack and "the whole man is
dissolved in the wantonness of effeminate airs."[3]

Resentment towards Italian opera stemmed from numerous
causes: traditional British insularity, displacement of native
musicians by their foreign counterparts, and distrust of the
Machiavellian stereotyped Italian (reinforced, in the days of
the Stuart Pretenders, by a fear of popery and Catholicism). But
the traditional use of castrati for leading roles in Italian opera
did much to further middle-class antagonism towards the medium. The "white" voices of the male sopranos and altos—pure
and unsexed, but powerful and versatile—brought a polish and
perfection to opera that was long admired by aristocratic audi-

ences. The castrati began to disappear by mid century. When the famous Giovanni Battista Velluti (1780–1861) was brought to England in 1825 as something of a curiosity, the tradition had become so completely forgotten that he was detested and maligned.[4] (Hunt's poem "Velluti to his Revilers" [*Examiner,* 7 August 1825] is a moving document in musical humanitarianism.)

The attitude about language, however, as expressed by the playwright and the critic, reveals the most persistent English bias about opera. In most Continental countries the Italian language was more readily accepted, along with other conventions of opera. Attempts to translate Italian opera into English were largely unsuccessful; the English language was unsuited to declamation after the manner of Neapolitan recitative, especially in heroic couplets! In *Dido and Aeneas* (1689) Henry Purcell* had shown how music could be perfectly accommodated to English recitative; nevertheless, the unshakable notion persisted that the English language was basically unmusical. Moreover, the powerful tradition of the English spoken theatre resisted foreign encroachments. The average Englishman had become too accustomed to the power of the word—to the "realism" of the spoken theatre—to accept a native development of operatic conventions or to welcome the imported entertainment that was so fashionable among the upper classes. France, which had a strong stage tradition, also resisted the Italian invasion. Supported by the court, Jean Baptiste Lully (1632–1687) forged a musical idiom perfectly suited to French declamation, and under this musical dictator French serious opera gained a precarious foothold. Still, as in England, its development was thwarted by the strength of the spoken theatre.

Political and social conditions in England, meanwhile, made even an English Lully impossible. There was, to be sure, a "rise of English opera." The so-called first English opera, Sir William D'Avenant's *The Siege of Rhodes* (1656), was something of a historical accident.[5] But the number of operatic types of theatrical performances (often closely related to the masque) that appeared on the Restoration stage testifies to a growing popularity of plays

---

* An asterisk after a person's name at its first incidence in the text indicates that it is listed in an appendix, where there is information about that person.

with varying degrees of musical infusion. Seemingly unconscious
of his unique achievement in *Dido*, Purcell returned to the looser
approach to opera characteristic of the English.[6] At any event,
this great composer died when he was thirty-six, leaving no school
or successor. Into this vacuum stepped Italian opera.

Opera, strictly defined, is determined by the extent to which
the drama is developed and sustained in terms of musical language. Music must become a more substantive medium than
words for communicating dramatic situations. The words present only the skeletal story; the revelation of character and conflict takes place primarily within the musical context. In the
dramma per musica, as the Italians called opera, musical values
had to remain predominant; and it is significant that between
Purcell's *Dido*, Thomas Arne's* *Artaxerxes* (1762), and, say, *The
Mountain Sylph* (1834) of John Barnett (1802–1890)—all of
which are sung throughout—there are few English works of any
importance that musical historians care to call operas.[7] Music
was of course taken seriously in the typical "English opera"—was
indeed the main justification for its popularity as entertainment.
Yet the music—that is to say, the songs—remained essentially a
dramatic embellishment. The Italian *aria* gave the composer
room to develop mood and feeling, and permitted the singer to
reveal inner states of consciousness, to express character through
the feeling of the melodic line. The English *song*, even when on
occasion it furthered dramatic development, was a musical acces-
sory to the dialogue. For English composers were unwilling "to
trespass on the rights of words." Lang says, "In [true] opera there
are situations when music must go its own way, even if it violates
proper prosody, but this the English would not accept." And
Dent affirms that "English poets could never accept the idea of a
normal man expressing himself in song [that is, as in the aria]."[8]

The quantity of music in the English works varied enormously.
Many, having only two or three songs, were of course not operas
under any reasonable definition of the term. It was understood
in general, however, that an English opera would present a sub-
stantial amount of singing. Though much of such music is lost
or inaccessible, the following details from the book of William

Moncrieff's* *Giovanni in London* (1820; see chapter three) are probably indicative of the typical musical: Act I: ten songs and airs, six duets, three trios, four ballads, two glees, three choruses, and one each of air and chorus, stave, sestet, and glee (with grand chorus); Act II: twelve songs or airs, two duets, two trios, and one each of rondeau air, duet and chorus, nocturne, chorus, ballad, and finale.

After the appearance of Italian opera in London, some playwrights recognized the value of the form and attempted to adapt it into English. Joseph Addison, admiring Purcell's achievements, supported recitative in English opera and welcomed a certain Italian infusion in English music. He satirized the absurdities of Italian operas performed in English translation and attempts of Italian singers to cope with English diction.[9] "At length the Audience grew tir'd of understanding Half the Opera," he wrote in the *Spectator* (No. 18), "and therefore to ease themselves intirely of the Fatigue of Thinking, have so order'd it at Present that the whole Opera is perform'd in an unknown Tongue."[10] Stung by the failure of his opera *Rosamond* (1709)[11] and vexed over the great success of Handel's *Rinaldo* (1711), Addison became a bitter enemy of Italian opera in England, and many of his attacks amplify the attitudes previously aired by Baker and Dennis.

Thus the witty gibes of Addison and Steele in the *Spectator* and *Tatler* merely intensified a predisposition against Italian opera that was already latent among the middle classes to whom they addressed themselves. By no means limited to the English, such objections to the conventions of Italian opera found powerful expression among the satirists of England's Augustan Age.[12] In the *Intelligencer* (No. 3) Jonathan Swift denounced the "unnatural taste for Italian music . . . whereby we are over-run with Italian effeminacy, and Italian nonsense." In *The Dunciad* (IV, 47–50) Alexander Pope satirized the "Harlot form":

> Foreign her air, her robe's discordant pride
> In patch-work flutt'ring and her head aside:
> By singing Peers up-held on either hand,
> She tripp'd and laugh'd, too pretty much to stand.

For Dr. Samuel Johnson opera was "an exotick and irrational entertainment" ("Life of Hughes"). Even Lord Chesterfield wrote to his son: "Whenever I go to the Opera, I leave my sense and reason at the door with my half guinea, and deliver myself up to my eyes and ears."

These remarks, which could be multiplied endlessly, referred to "Italian opera," whether sung in Italian, in English translation, or in productions that alternated between the two languages. Meanwhile, "English opera" continued apace. Some of these "operas" come closer to the operatic medium than others, according to their musical importance, which varies considerably. But it must be understood that, with the exceptions previously noted (and a scattering of other, less successful specimens of "true" English opera) these works are not operas, strictly speaking, but are essentially plays with music. They were nevertheless called operas by the English generally, and indeed were regarded by the middle classes as the only operas worth going to. It is in this context, then, that the ensuing discussion of "English opera" is to be considered.

With the première in 1728 of *The Beggar's Opera* by John Gay,* English opera took a distinctive turn and acquired a particular identity and name—ballad opera.[13] The name derives from the fact that the tunes in these operas, already well known to the public, were usually selected from folk ballads; therefore composers were not very important to such productions. Significantly, ballad opera arose as a protest against Italian opera. But Gay's work (probably an outgrowth of the "Newgate Pastoral" that Swift suggested to him) was also a satire on the aristocracy generally and on Robert Walpole's Whig government in particular. Gay himself selected the airs—mostly folk tunes, though some were by Purcell and Handel—writing lyrics that cleverly parodied the original verses.

Perhaps the most popular opera in the eighteenth century, this work gave rise to a school of ballad opera that lasted for ten years or more. But *The Beggar's Opera* was not without its detractors. Scarcely launched, it was denounced by the Reverend Thomas Herring in a sermon at Lincoln's Inn Chapel as immoral, since

London's lowlife is placed on at least as high a plane, morally, as
the aristocracy, and since the rogue anti-hero, Macheath, goes
unpunished. The "immorality" of the opera was debated for
over a century. Although Dr. Johnson, in "Life of Gay," felt the
play safe enough since "highwaymen and housebreakers seldom
frequent the playhouses," he apparently concluded, according to
Boswell's *Life*, that "there is in it such a *labefactation* of all principles as may be injurious to morality." These demurrers probably only added to the work's popularity.

Thus *The Beggar's Opera* served to widen the divergence between the two traditions. Its success helped to ruin the Royal
Academy of Music, where Handelian opera had reigned. While
Italian opera continued its course at the King's Theatre, Handel
turned to the oratorio, which often proved to be highly successful
with the English middle classes. The oratorios were composed
for English texts (Handel had developed a remarkable ear for
the English language) and were based largely on the Old Testament and its stories of heroic leadership with which the English
people had closely identified themselves. The oratorios were
given a highly dramatic treatment and some (*Esther*, for example) were intended to be staged, but the Bishop of London regarded this tendency as blasphemous and banned staged performances. The feeling behind the oratorios was festive, cere-
monial, and consecrational—not religious. Nevertheless, their
Biblical themes and the custom of performing them during Lent,
when both opera and drama were prohibited, encouraged the
nineteenth-century practice of suffusing them with a pseudoreli-
gious character, from which they have not yet escaped.[14] Handel's
oratorio productions offered odes and pastorals as well, and they
included his playing on the organ during intermissions—a popular attraction. The variety thus established in the "oratorio seasons" or "the oratorios," as they were variously called, was further
amplified by John Ashley (?–1805), who started a rival specula-
tion at Covent Garden in 1795 in competition with Dr. Samuel
Arnold's* oratorio performances at Drury Lane. Ashley included
a potpourri of musical numbers, both vocal and instrumental,
which changed the nature and direction of the seasons thereafter.

In his oratorios Handel came close to creating genuine opera in English, though he did not take the final step. Like Purcell, he had no successor, although he placed the stamp of his personality on English music for over a century after his death. English opera, meanwhile, continued to be dominated by the spoken theatre.

Mid-Century Developments

Opera seria and its immediate descendants remained persistent forces well into the nineteenth century, at least in London. But after 1750 tragic opera was slowly displaced by opera buffa—comic opera. Italy also gave rise to this new form, which had its roots in the commedia dell'arte and early-eighteenth-century intermezzi. In opera buffa the recitative-aria sequence and the importance of melody were retained, though the highly mobile *secco* gained on the formal aria. Leading male roles were given to lower voices, especially the basso;[15] concerted numbers appeared, particularly in finales; and other musical effects emphasized the mood of light gaiety. The plots were of course comic, usually farcical though sometimes sentimental as well. And in place of the staid, statuesque characters of Metastasian opera, we find low types, exchanges of repartee, and emphasis on action.[16] A tighter dramatic structure resulted.

Opera buffa reached its first peak in Nicolò Piccinni's popular *La Buona Figliuola* (1760). Succeeding composers, such as Pietro Guglielmi, Antonio Sacchini, Domenico Cimarosa, and Giovanni Paesiello, developed the type in various directions; their operas were highly successful in England.[17] Mozart (1756–1791), like Handel, absorbed the best of the Italian schools: he combined limitless melodic resources with a symphonic musical texture that enriched the characterizations in arias and accompanied recitative without sacrificing the vocal appeal of bel canto. He brought to opera a musico-dramatic intensity that has seldom been equaled.

Along with opera buffa, comic opera of a national character sprang up in Europe. Like English opera, it was written in the vernacular, employed dialogue rather that recitative, and appealed to a more popular audience. The early forms, like the English ballad opera or the Spanish zarzuela, drew on folk airs for melodic material. The German variety, known as singspiel, owed much to English models;[18] it achieved true operatic distinction in the hands of Mozart *(Zauberflöte)* and Beethoven *(Fidelio)*. A parallel development occurred in the French *vaudevilles,* which employed new words to folk tunes for satirical effect.[19] Later the composed songs, called ariettes, were employed, and such types eventually led to the development of opéra comique. By the early nineteenth century the English word vaudeville had roughly the same meaning it had acquired in France—a theatrical piece in which the dialogue was interspersed with rhymed couplets sung to popular melodies of the day.

With the ballad opera, English opera had become wholly comic and satirical. By mid century the mood of satire weakened. As a stepchild of the spoken stage, the lyrical theatre reflected the waning Neoclassic tradition. The growth of the middle classes and the appeal of the sentimental novel brought the impulse of sensibility to the drama. Oliver Goldsmith and Thomas Brinsley Sheridan* attempted to stem the tide, but their efforts were not able to rescue the drama from a steady decline. The lyrical stage increasingly fell heir to melodramatic, farcical, and sensational elements.[20] In *The Duenna* (1775) Sheridan created a superior comic opera that had an extraordinary run of seventy-five performances. It was even translated into Italian and presented at the opera house.[21] But Isaac Bickerstaffe* created the sentimental type that achieved great popularity during the second half of the century.

Like the ballad opera, these later operatic types, which include the burletta and melodrama (see below), were nearly always musical pasticcios. The matter of ascribing credit in such works, for which the playwright wrote many songs to existing tunes and was responsible for the final musical determinations, remains somewhat academic. In that age of the nonspecialist, composers often turned their hands to playwriting, playwrights often composed the songs, and some singers regularly composed the music for

their own roles. The taste for folk airs remained strong, but as
the supply of genuine tunes diminished, playwrights turned increasingly to composers, such as William Shield,* who could
create fine imitations.

Thus the songs in such works ranged from the genuine or the
"composed" ballad types of Scottish, Irish, Welsh, and English
flavor, to sea chanteys and other popular forms suitable to humor-
ous character parts. Concerted vocal numbers and concluding
choruses—found in ballad opera—became more elaborate. For
leading singers, songs of greater complexity were composed or
adapted from Italian operas. Their florid passages and considerable range placed heavy demands on vocal skill. Musically, then,
two styles were apparent: a "simple" style with emphasis mainly
on pathos, and a "scientific" style with emphasis on ornate vocal-
ism—"straight" or burlesqued. Composers and singers adept in
the latter mode were said to have more "science"—that is, musical
dexterity—in their art. The public was divided in its preference
between the one style and the other, but wanted good melodies
whatever their concealed origins might have been.

Some English composers nevertheless achieved a certain distinction. As we have seen, in *Artaxerxes* Thomas Arne composed
a "true" opera seria in English, adapting the libretto himself
from Metastasio's *Artaserse*. Although this opera was enormously
successful, Arne's later attempts in this vein failed, and he devoted his main efforts to music for the English musical stage, for
which his talents were best suited. His settings of Shakespeare's
songs, for example, show melodic gifts and an ear for English
speech. Other notable composers for the stage were: Thomas
Linley (1733–1795), reluctant father-in-law of Sheridan, who for
some years was director of stage music at Drury Lane; Charles
Dibdin the Elder,* who specialized in nautical songs (in his
"Table Entertainments" he appeared simultaneously as author,
composer, singer, and accompanist); Stephen Storace,* who produced some memorable tunes;[22] Dr. Samuel Arnold,* a somewhat superficial but versatile composer; and Shield, the most
gifted but not the most popular of the group.[23] One of the finest
English composers of this period, William Boyce (1710–1779),

wrote little for the stage. "The harmless trifles of Dibdin, Shield, and Storace," declares Grout (pp. 262–63), "are less the flowers of English genius than the somewhat childish pastimes of a people whose real energies were occupied with the growth of industry and the expansion of empire." Great artists these composers certainly were not. Only a few of their songs have claimed the praise of modern historians. Most of their stage works can no longer be considered viable art; they nevertheless had strong appeal for contemporary audiences. A recent recording of Shield's *Rosina* demonstrates to this listener that, at their best, the musical charm of such works remains undiminished after nearly two centuries.

The Nineteenth Century

Of late-eighteenth- and early-nineteenth-century stage composers even less can be said. James Hook, John Davy, William Reeve, Charles Horn, and John Braham, among others, produced many songs during the period, but they have little merit. In their hands "the type of song which the ballad operas had popularized declined in spontaneity and became stiff and pompous."[24] The best of these composers, Henry Bishop,* brought a certain power to the technique of choral writing, long missing from the English stage, and produced some memorable songs; but he often displayed a "feeble sentimentality" in his writing.

These vicissitudes in music and drama were sharply affected by changing conditions in the theatres and audiences. At the beginning of the century only three theatres were considered "legitimate"—Drury Lane, Covent Garden, and the King's Theatre in the Haymarket. Known as "patent" theatres, they jealously guarded their privileges, which they traced to various patents granted by the Crown to their founders during the Restoration and early eighteenth century. Although these claims, vitiated in numerous ways, had precarious legal validity by the end of the century, their traditional force remained strong. They were constantly challenged by a host of London and suburban theatres, known as the "minors," that sprang up early in the nineteenth

century. Some of these soon wrested away certain restricted rights
of performance, but not until 1843 were the ancient prerogatives
of the "majors" legally terminated and the London stage placed
on a freely competitive basis.

English opera was intimately connected with this struggle, for
by 1800 the "patentees had grown envious of every species of
entertainment that in any way resembled a theatrical exhibition."[25] Drury Lane and Covent Garden reserved the right to
all opera except the Italian; sanction for the latter was given to
the King's Theatre—traced to John Vanbrugh's patent of 1704
and confirmed by the "Opera Arrangement" of 1792. Among the
older minors were the Haymarket (also called the Little Theatre
in the Haymarket) and the Lyceum, which had secured a license
to produce offerings during the summer, when the major theatres
were closed. (All London theatres operated under licenses
granted by magistrates or the Lord Chamberlain, and sometimes
these licenses violated what the major theatres considered to be
their royal patents.) Dr. Samuel Arnold was thwarted in an attempt to offer English opera when he rebuilt the Lyceum in 1794.
But when Drury Lane burned in 1809, the company was housed
in the Lyceum until their own theatre could be rebuilt. Through
some complex maneuvering Samuel Arnold, the composer's son,
was able that year to secure a license to perform English opera
during the summer provided it was sung throughout, had at least
five songs, and was limited to three acts (five acts carried the
prestige of "legitimacy"), according to Nicholson (pp. 247–363).

Thus the musical *form* of a work was for a time as much a matter of satisfying a legal technicality as it was a theatrical development. For not only did music become an increasingly important
element in theatrical works as their dramatic importance declined, but the minor theatres were finding it possible to give the
public miscellaneous forms of entertainment with music and
spectacle as the main ingredients.[26] One of the older operatic
forms that played a part in this struggle was the burletta. Originally designating an operatic type that burlesqued both English
and Italian opera as a fashionable entertainment, the term was
soon applied indiscriminately; as early as 1750 it could be con-

strued only as "a kind of poor Relation to an Opera."[27] By the
end of the century the term was found flexible enough to serve
the convenience of the minors, defining any play adapted to the
stage within the legal purviews already mentioned. When Covent Garden announced a performance (c. 1810) of Henry Fielding's *Tom Thumb* as a "burletta," the term was thereby extended to include plays with dialogue—a precedent that the
minors seized upon. Thereafter, musical accompaniment at the
minors diminished sharply; *Othello,* for example, was performed
as a burletta "with an accompaniment that consisted of chords
struck on a piano *every five minutes,* and quite inaudible at
that."[28]

Nevertheless, the demand for musical productions remained
high, and the majors no less than the minors seized upon such "illegitimate" dramatic types as the melodrama to attract audiences.

Like the burletta, the melodrama had its roots in the eighteenth century. Originally a serious stage piece without singing,
in which the action and dialogue were accompanied by music,[29]
its chief appeal, according to Watson (*Sheridan to Robertson,* pp.
349–54), was found in a sensational atmosphere, derived partly
from the music and partly through a specialized plot that "relies
strongly on mechanical contrivance," in which the characters "of
impossible and conventional vices and virtues act with a kind of
mathematical precision. . . . The frank directness with which it
produced its effects made its utter unreality seem real for the
time being and its excessive artificiality seem simple."

More a "spirit" than a type, melodrama underwent numerous
modifications in Germany, France, and England. Combining
Gothic, supernatural, and *Sturm und Drang* impulses, it merged
with a variety of operatic forms and became an important force
in the operas of Mozart, Beethoven, and Weber. Though England did not borrow the name from the French until 1802, elements of melodrama were apparent there by 1770. Lieutenant-
General John Burgoyne, for example, adapted an early opéra
comique by André Grétry, *Richard Coeur-de-Lion* (1784), into
an English melodrama only two years after its première.[30] Many
German and French models served for innumerable English

adaptations in the closing decade of the eighteenth century and
in the early years of the nineteenth, when melodrama became a
major influence on the British stage. Perhaps its most representative expression is to be found in such works as George Colman
the Younger's *The Iron Chest* (1796) and "Monk" Lewis's *The
Castle Spectre* (1797), though melodramatic elements were important, if not paramount, in many works more clearly operatic
in nature.

Other types of drama acquired musical expression in Regency
England. The operatic farce, for example, ranked next to the
melodrama in popularity, though it often was indistinguishable
from comic opera. We need not be concerned with the sixty
dramatic types that Nicoll identifies in this period; but in the
proliferation of these dramatic forms, music and songs often supplied an important ingredient. To be sure, many of these works
have little in common with "English opera" even in its traditional loose usage. But they, too, were called operas by contemporaries, and for better or worse they take their place in the history of the English musical stage. For our purposes it is sufficient
merely to recognize that both the popularity of musical pieces
and their anomalous character were related to the decline of the
"legitimate" drama and the "legitimate" theatres.

That decline was hastened by the majors themselves when, in
1792 and 1794 respectively, Covent Garden and Drury Lane were
rebuilt at nearly double the size of the houses they replaced.[31]
Later alterations ruined their acoustical properties. As a consequence, it became extremely difficult to see or hear the performances. Hence the reliance on spectacular effects, with an inevitable coarsening of the theatrical material. But the cost of such
effects was high: huge sums were lavished on scenic displays even
at the minors.[32] Moreover, the public demanded, and got, their
quantum of entertainment, which began at seven and often continued until after midnight. Typical fare included a three-hour,
five-act play; a pantomime; and a farcical afterpiece.[33] Then
there was a house orchestra to maintain, which provided music
(in the form of overtures and entr'actes to all productions, musical or otherwise) that was popular with the audiences.

The theatre orchestras were larger and more competent than might be supposed. Although Watson (*Sheridan to Robertson,* p. 154) surely exaggerates in asserting that they employed "some two hundred musicians," George Winchester Stone, Jr., has shown that the orchestra at Covent Garden had twenty-one members in 1761 (the same as in 1707) and that Drury Lane in 1778–1779 had an orchestra of at least twenty-three musicians, complete with strings, woodwinds, brass, and timpani of sorts.[34] Musical standards were high, and pay was forfeited for missed rehearsals. Presumably, these forces were further improved and augmented in the ensuing fifty years.

As the nineteenth century progressed, managers had to pay more for stars and could afford less for the plays; consequently, playwrights had to produce more plays and resort to heavy borrowings of plots, foreign and domestic, to make a living.[35] The practice of writing for the stars also cheapened the dramas. Unable adequately to hear or see the performances, audiences became generally unruly and often quite violent. The growing numbers able to afford entertainment enjoyed precisely those sensational effects that melodramas brought to the minors; and the majors, hard pressed, increasingly turned to circus-type entertainments in an attempt to fill their houses. But this atmosphere of rudeness and sensationalism held little attraction for the aristocracy. Though they did not entirely abandon the theatres, it is true that the King's Theatre became the main public amusement of the upper orders, thereby depriving the "legitimates" of that part of the audience that could give the theatres both tone and strong financial support.[36]

Fashion and aristocratic interests did indeed reign at the King's Theatre, where sixty subscription performances were offered on Tuesday and Saturday nights from January to August. For the most part the nobility took their opera *comme il faut,* chatting or finding other diversion during the recitatives but pausing to hear a popular prima donna render a favorite aria.[37] Though their subscriptions were the mainstay of the opera house, it took an unusual event to fill the boxes. Angelina Catalani* was so popular that she commanded the unprecedented sum of £ 5,000 from the King's Theatre in 1807, yet she earned nearly twice that amount the same year from private concerts. The private concerts of the aristocracy often handicapped Italian opera, which had a built-in dependence on the star system.[38] To be sure, such men as Mount-Edgcumbe (1764–1839), although his operatic tastes were old-fashioned, and George Hogarth[39] demonstrated that among the opera regulars were those of the aristocracy and middle classes who had a passion for opera at its best. But the prevailing attitude did little to encourage new productions or high artistic standards.

The nineteenth century opened with an outstanding company at the King's Theatre and a few seasons that offered good productions, including premières of new operas by Peter von Winter,* who was the resident composer there until 1805. By 1807 much had changed. The principals retired, went to Europe, or fled to the playhouses to escape the domination of Catalani! Francis Goold, who had long directed the opera, died that year, and a Mr. Waters, who bought out his shares, attempted to gain control of the house from Goold's former partner, a Mr. Taylor. The Taylor-Waters struggles, which often came before the King's Bench, continued until 1820, seriously handicapping the financial security of the house and antagonizing the patrons. In 1817 William Ayrton[40] took over the management from Waters to "effect administrative reforms," according to Hogarth:

This gentleman, though he failed in his immediate object, produced a great and permanent benefit, by the impulse he gave to the public taste. He was aware that the obstacles to the production and proper performance of the best operas arose, not from the public, but from the performers themselves, whose arrogance and caprice were permitted to over-rule the proceedings of the manager.[41]

The *British Stage* declared in May of that year that there was "not a single box unoccupied" at a *Don Giovanni* performance.[42] At the end of the season it stated that the King's Theatre "is now the common resort, not only of the more exalted ranks of society but of all the middle classes who have the slightest relish for harmony."

This was a gross exaggeration, for even the upper classes failed to support the opera adequately. In 1818 Waters was back, but debts soon forced him out. In 1821 John Ebers (1785?–1830?) took over the management and called on Ayrton to direct that season. But Ayrton's seasons, artistically successful and popular though they were, could not meet the high cost of the productions. In 1821, for example, Ebers (*King's Theatre,* pp. 81–82) says that receipts from the boxes, pit, and gallery of £ 21,516, £ 9,714, and £ 1,017 respectively, still left a debt of £ 7,075 at the end of the season. Of course, expense was not spared on the new operas, though their cost was exceeded by that of the ballets.[43] Moreover, Ebers's management was handicapped by restrictions imposed by the Committee of Nobles (Mount-Edgcumbe was a member) to which he was responsible, and which was something less than efficient.[44] Despite an increased interest in Italian opera by a part of the middle class, that part did not yet have either the numbers or the wealth to exert a sustaining force on the institution.[45] The *Quarterly Musical Magazine and Review* (1818, p. 218) came closer to the truth in asserting that "the persons [of the middle class] who attend the *King's Theatre* are comparatively very few, and they are still fewer who visit the Opera sufficiently often to note and remember the melodies which they there hear."

Artistically, then, Italian opera was in the doldrums for most of the *Examiner* years. There were important exceptions; but the period was generally dominated by third-rate works concocted for Catalani, Teresa Bertinotti,* and other prima donnas. Such operatic fare satisfied the casual taste of the boxholders. In music and the drama the English were often slow in welcoming foreign ideas, and London sometimes lagged twenty years behind the Continent in giving premières to important works (see below, appendix two, and Nicoll, IV, 88).

By the time of Hunt's *Examiner,* then, the two traditions of English opera and Italian opera had become most widely sep-

arated, though they were both close to their nadir and both, in
quite different ways, subject to the whims of fashion. In English
opera especially, that fashion was the product of a fickle taste and
a curiously patronizing view towards music. For although the
middle classes increasingly turned towards music for entertainment in the theatres, they had no respect for music as an art. In
Tudor and Stuart times the English were passionately fond of
music, and a certain accomplishment in the art was considered
desirable in most levels of society. The glees, catches, and rounds
that furnished pleasure to eighteenth-century middle-class homes
gradually fell silent, except in a few circles.[46] Now, even a rudi-
mentary musical training was regarded by the average doughty
Englishman as an effeminate accomplishment. He held musicians in low social esteem, called their heads "as empty as their
fiddles," and proudly admitted that he could not tell one tune
from another.[47] Along with the attractions of "money-getting,"
the Evangelical movement, which achieved wide influence during
this period, did much to quash middle-class interests in music.

Were the English a musical people? The rhetorical question,
raised by correspondents in the columns of the *Examiner*,
prompted vigorous denials so far as contemporary life was concerned. Yet the question was asked. Amid the squabbles of the
pit and the chatter of the boxes, there were voices to protest the
artistic trivialities of the time. Concluding his history with a
passage on English opera, Hogarth wrote:

No man of genius will suffer his poetry to be made the vehicle for
unmeaning sing-song; hence the opera is left in the hands of the
playwrights, and, with few exceptions, is looked upon by people of
sense and reflection as a slight and frivolous amusement, unworthy
of serious notice. . . . There is no want either of dramatic talent
or of musical talent in England. But it requires the co-operation
of these two kinds of talent, in a degree which does not exist at
present, to produce results which will be at all satisfactory to the
growing taste and intelligence of the public.[48]

The public of 1808 gave precious little indication of that
"growing taste and intelligence." But it was precisely to the prob-

lem of public taste that Hunt addressed himself when he began his criticism of the English musical stage that year and when, in his Italian-opera reviews a few years later, he sought to narrow the gap between the two traditions.

2

Leigh Hunt and the *Examiner:* Musical Developments

"We must record Hunt's music in our memories as a constant theme through his biography, together with his Spenser and his Italian poets."—Edmund C. Blunden

HUNT'S WRITINGS on opera can be better understood if we first consider the personal and journalistic contexts in which they were produced. Specifically, it will be useful to look at a profile of his life and accomplishments, with special emphasis on his musical background: the nature of early influences, the extent of his talents, and the importance of music in his social relationships. We need to apprehend the political and cultural force represented by the *Examiner* itself, and the effect it had on the criticism published in it. We need to touch briefly on the backgrounds of other writers whose opera criticisms for the *Examiner* will be compared with Hunt's. And, finally, we should try to assess Hunt's character as opera critic—his limitations, advantages, and predispositions for reviewing the English musical stage and Italian opera during the *Examiner* years.

Hunt's Musical Life and Friends

James Henry Leigh Hunt (1784–1859) narrowly escaped being an American citizen.[1] His father, Isaac (c. 1742–1810), came from a long line of clergymen in Barbados. As a young man he went to the American colonies, where he took his M.A. and settled in Philadelphia to practice law. There, in 1767, he married Mary

Shewell (?–1805), who belonged to a family of seafaring Quakers. Her father, a prosperous merchant, remained a Loyalist during the American Revolution, thereby losing most of his wealth. He once counted among his friends Tom Paine and Benjamin Franklin. The latter offered to teach Mary the guitar, but she was too "diffident" and too much the Quaker to accept.

Soon after the end of the American Revolution, Isaac took his family to England. Of the eight children born to Isaac and Mary Hunt, only five survived childhood; they were all boys, of whom Leigh was the youngest by nine years and the only one born in England. Unable to continue his law practice there, Isaac became an ordained minister in the Church of England. His speculative mind, however, would not permit him to rest secure in the Church's dogmas, and he and his wife later became Unitarians and Universalists. Wandering from parish to parish, he never earned enough to maintain his large family. He obtained assistance from Benjamin West (1738–1820), member of the Royal Academy and the husband of his wife's aunt, whose house, filled with paintings and sculpture, made a lasting impression on young Leigh. The family was also assisted by the Duke of Chandos, who hired Isaac to tutor his nephew James Henry Leigh.[2] Isaac named his son after this nephew and dedicated to him Leigh Hunt's precocious collection of verses, *Juvenilia* (1801).

These connections were not sufficient, however, to prevent acute financial distress, and Leigh's earliest recollection was of a prison room in the King's Bench, where he first heard "a verse of a song, sung out, as he tottered along, by a drunken man, the words of which appeared to me unspeakably wicked." Yet the family survived these ordeals, and at home he heard songs of a more edifying nature. Leigh remembered his mother as "a gentle singer in her way," and one of his earliest memories was of their "poor sitting-room in the year '89 or '90, with my mother in it bidding me sing, Miss C.[3] at the pianoforte—harpsichord more likely, and my little sister, Mary [who died in childhood] . . . wishing me to begin. What a great singer is that little boy to those loving relations." The family sang songs by James Hook as well as by more "fashionable" composers of the day: Oswald,

Boyce, Lampe, Linley, Jackson, Shield, Storace, and the elder
Dibdin. The last three, however, produced "the only genuine
English compositions worth anything at that time."[4] A special
favorite at the Hunt household was the finale of *Inkle and Yarico*
(1787) by the younger George Colman, music by Dr. Samuel
Arnold, with its lines

> Come, let us dance and sing,
> While all Barbados bells shall ring,

for the allusions to Isaac's birthplace. Other songs enjoyed by
the family were airs from operas by such Continental composers
as Paesiello, Sacchini, Piccinni, and Cimarosa,[5] which "wandered
into the streets out of the English operas that borrowed them,
and became confounded with English property." (Hunt's attempts to sort out these early mistaken impressions are evident in
his opera criticism.) The family may have seen the Colman production; otherwise, they seldom if ever attended the theatre. No
ascetics, his parents possibly could not afford that luxury, although they had at least one servant for over thirty years. His
mother would, "as occasion served," attend the fashionable
amusements at Ranelagh and Vauxhall.[6]

In 1791 Hunt was enrolled in Christ's Hospital, a famous
London school for boys from the middle classes. Known as "Bluecoat" boys, their colorful tunics of blue and their yellow stockings gave them a striking appearance. High academic standards
prevailed: the "Classical School" he entered gave a thorough
grounding in Greek and Latin, and provided some training in
English composition and oratory. The school's most outstanding
graduate was the poet Samuel Taylor Coleridge (1772–1834),
who, like Hunt, wrote amusing memoirs of his experiences there.
A more recent graduate was Charles Lamb (1775–1834). Hunt
recalled Lamb's visits to his alma mater before Hunt knew who
Lamb was; later they became great friends, and Lamb contributed criticisms and essays to Hunt's periodicals. Perhaps
Hunt's most famous schoolmate-friend was Thomas Barnes
(1785–1841), who a few years later was to help Hunt in a time of
need and who had an outstanding career in journalism. At

school Barnes and Hunt studied Italian together and enjoyed rural excursions.

During his school days Hunt was ripe for absorbing more sophisticated musical experiences than those available at home. While attending Christ's Hospital he first heard Mozart; that is to say, he heard the band at St. James's Park play a march from *Figaro,* "Non più andrai"; and "with the help of instruments made of paper, into which we breathed what imitations we could of hautboys and clarionets," Hunt "inducted the boys into the 'pride, pomp, and circumstance' of that glorious bit of war." Somewhat later he learned the name of the composer at the Spring Gardens home of a school chum, Papendick, who in after years "became distinguished in private circles as an accomplished musician." The family had a "German passion for music," and Hunt enjoyed his first "musical evenings" there, Papendick and his sister playing the piano and his father the flute. Hunt also became acquainted with his cousins' music master, Dr. John Callcott, whom he later remembered as a scholar and a great reader, and whose appeals for a wider public interest in music he supported.[7]

Hunt nowhere mentions learning to play the piano, but he apparently had some early training on the instrument, which he enjoyed throughout his adult years. While convalescing at school from an injury, he took up the flute at the suggestion of his nurse's daughter. His playing consisted of a few tunes by rote, though his fellow invalids "would have it rather than no playing at all"; his interest in the instrument continued into his mature years. He does not mention any singing at school, though his vocal qualities and training should have made him a welcome chorister. He was at any rate exposed to the good singing standards that prevailed at Christ's Hospital, where Robert Hudson (1731–1815) was music master. Hunt, whose voice was so highly praised in later years for its unusual qualities in speaking and singing, was graduated from school in 1799 as a Deputy Grecian because, like Lamb before him, he suffered from a slight speech impediment—more noticeable in his childhood years but never entirely overcome—which disqualified him for the rank of Grecian and its university privilege.

Out of school at fifteen, Hunt (Bohemian style, complete with a beard of sorts) wrote verses, loafed at bookstalls and music stores, and visited former schoolmates. He early showed a capacity for winning friends (Lamb called him a "perfect fireside companion"). These relationships were marred by occasional jealousies and misunderstandings, which his critics still like to emphasize; but the fact is that many of his early friendships remained undiminished throughout his long life. They rapidly expanded with his growing literary interests to include many budding journalists, most of whom shared a strong interest in music.

Among his earliest and most important friends were the three Robertson brothers, who, with Hunt, called themselves the "Elders"—not through any association with the school (the Robertsons were not Bluecoat boys) but, as Hunt explains, for their liking of elderberry wine. How he made their acquaintance is not clear. He seems first to have known John Robertson, a "pleasant, intelligent, good-hearted fellow" with whom he shared an enthusiasm for books, plays, and music. In 1801 John introduced him to a Miss Elizabeth Kent, who had expressed an interest in the young poet and his verses. But the young poet became more attracted to Bess's sister, Marianne (?–1857), whom he married eight years later. John died in France during the war.[8] It was with Henry Robertson that Hunt was to establish the closest ties, by virtue of his Italian-opera reviews in the *Examiner* (see the next section of this chapter).

Soon after Hunt made the acquaintance of the Kents, their widowed mother married Rowland Hunter, bookseller at St. Paul's Churchyard. Hunter was a man of musical as well as literary interests, through whom Hunt made a number of useful acquaintances. It was at the home of Hunter's music-publishing neighbor and friend, J. S. Button, that Hunt and Bess spent one Friday evening in 1803 or 1804 listening to Barthélemon play some violin solos.[9] Hunt provides scant evidence of the extent to which either Bess or Marianne shared his musical and dramatic enthusiasms. On at least one occasion when he was ill years later, he sent the pair to the theatre to provide him with the details for a review! (*Correspondence,* I, 116–19.)

Hunt's relations with Button soon led to an acquaintance with John Whitaker (see below, chapter three). He was not the first to discover that Hunt's poems were eminently suitable for musical settings; two other songwriters, G. E. Williams and H. Thompson, had already composed Hunt's "The Negro Boy" (from *Juvenilia*) about 1802.[10] But Whitaker was the first to make them popular. About 1809 he composed Hunt's "Silent Kisses" and "Love and the Aeolian Harp," which became such valuable musical property that they were the subject of a lawsuit instigated by Whitaker in 1815. Of the latter song Hunt wrote to Marianne on 19 October 1809 that it was set with Whitaker's "usual taste and feeling"—a comment that, as we shall see in chapter three, probably implied no particular praise. These songs were followed about a year later by "Mary, Mary, List, Awake," which according to Luther A. Brewer was included in popular song books until about 1860. Hunt wrote these three verses for Whitaker; in view of their success as songs, Hunt's compensation was probably inadequate, though he thought otherwise. On 8 January 1811 he wrote the publishers, thanking them for the present of "the numbers of Handel already published. . . . With regard to the little poems which I had the pleasure of writing for you, the information that they had succeeded with the public would have been a quite sufficient return for them at any time."[11] Later he addressed a note to Button from Surrey jail (see below), thanking him and Whitaker for the loan of a lute as "solace to the prisoner."[12]

Released from Christ's Hospital's prohibition on attending plays, Hunt lost no time in going to the theatre. In March of 1800 he saw his first play, Andrew Franklin's comic opera *The Egyptian Festival; An Opera* (music by Florio), at Drury Lane. Enchanted by the scenic effects and John Bannister's* comic portrayal, he was soon attending other productions, becoming acquainted with the actors, and studying their different approaches to the roles. A frequent visitor to school chums still at Christ's Hospital, he "used, in a manner, to act over whole pieces for their amusement, retailing points, & imitating the actors" (*Earliest Sketches,* p. 33). While with the St. James's Volunteers in 1802 he became particularly interested in three "patriot actors" who served with him. Meanwhile, he wrote a tragedy (submitted to Drury Lane), a comedy, and one or two farces to which he solicited Michael Kelly's* attention. But to no avail; they were never produced or printed, and he would have to wait nearly forty years for his "first night."

Perhaps this discouragement turned his attention to criticism. In any event his brother John (1775–1848), who had been apprenticed to the printer Carew Reynell and was assuming increasing initiative in publishing, provided the nine-year-younger Leigh an example of how a would-be writer could earn a living by journalism. In 1804 Leigh was launched on a sort of apprenticeship of his own when he began writing weekly essays for the *Traveller,* for which his recompense was "five or six copies of the paper."

John launched his own weekly, the *News,* in May of 1805, for which Leigh, then clerking at the War Office, agreed to write theatrical reviews. Leigh's judgment ripened rapidly after his first exposure to the playhouses. The stage exerted a magnetic hold over him even though he was seldom impressed with any dramatic quality in the works presented. As he declared in the Preface to his *Critical Essays,* "It was this strange superiority of the mimetic over the literary part of the stage, of organ in fact over its inspirer, that determined me to criticise the actors." As we have seen in chapter one, the actors then offered the greatest rewards to the theatregoer. But the "essays in criticism" that Hunt was beginning to find he had a talent for were not limited to histrionic skills; he went into the details of the pieces as well. Nor was "English opera" neglected. Landré states: "The plays he had to see being often musical, he was soon led to write musical criticisms, without very expert knowledge indeed, but not without taste."[13] Among these were productions of Frederic Reynolds, Thomas Dibdin, Andrew Cherry, and James Cobb (see below, chapter three). Just what critical expertise their works required that Hunt did not already possess, Landré does not explain; but surely the young critic gained valuable experience during this apprenticeship.

In 1808 John and Leigh launched the Sunday *Examiner* under joint editorship, the details of which will be taken up in the next section of this chapter. It was established as a liberal organ, but the editorials became increasingly radical in tone. The *Examiner* spoke out boldly on such issues as military bribes for promotion and military flogging, which resulted in four "informations" being filed against the editors by the conservative Tory government. The Hunts were fortunate in escaping punishment on the first three charges. But in 1812 Leigh went too far, attacking the Prince Regent himself as "a violator of his word, a libertine over head and ears in disgrace, the companion of gamblers and demireps." The editors were found guilty, fined £ 500 apiece, and sentenced to two years in jail. But the *Examiner* was kept alive through the aid of friends, and the Hunts continued to write for it from behind bars.

At Horsemonger Lane jail Hunt was granted special quarters, which he decorated with wallpaper, busts, and trellised ivy. His family was permitted to stay with him, and there his daughter Mary Florimel Leigh was born. There, too, many of his friends and acquaintances came to visit. Yet the confinement was painful, and his health suffered from its effects for several years.

Hunt made literary enemies as well. In 1811 he published a long, satirical poem, *The Feast of the Poets*: Apollo gives the poets a dinner at which many prominent writers of the age are held up to ridicule. Hunt's cavalier approach outraged many of his contemporaries, especially those who were Tories. William Gifford, editor of the *Quarterly Review,* swiftly counterattacked, scoffing at Hunt's "Cockney School of Poetry" in which such "protégés" of Hunt's as John Keats were included. Hunt's poem *The Story of Rimini* (1816) was attacked for its alleged licentiousness in a series of articles by John Gibson Lockhart in *Blackwood's Edinburgh Magazine*.

Against such attacks, and during a period of increasing conservatism in England, Hunt's liberal journalism could hardly succeed. The quarterly *Reflector,* which he established in 1811 and for which he persuaded Lamb to contribute his first essays, failed after a few numbers for lack of support. Likewise the *Indicator,* begun in 1819 to help stem the declining profits from the *Examiner,* soon foundered. Yet Hunt continued to produce a large volume of essays, poetry, and criticism, both for his own periodicals as well as for publication elsewhere. During these years he also enlarged his circle of friends.

Musically speaking, the most important of these was Vincent Novello.[14] It is not clear how or when they were first brought together. Apparently, Hunt was a long-standing friend of Novello when he introduced him to Lamb about 1816. The Hunts, Lambs, and Novellos entertained in rotation—only bread, cheese, celery, and beer to be served, by mutual agreement. Together they attended London theatres and Hampstead picnics.

Novello's interests extended well beyond music. He was an avid reader of fiction, travel, and natural science, and an enthusiastic subscriber to the *Examiner* from its inception. His Catholicism was broad enough to encompass even Shelley's friendship. He had a "simple, undogmatic idealism—very much like that of Leigh Hunt." His friendships with Hunt and Shelley brought him "into sympathy with the liberal movements . . . toward which the Church was politically antagonistic." Although all his children were raised in the faith, Novello believed "not a word" of many of the central tenets of Roman Catholicism. Nor had he any bigotry in music. "His wide-embracing appreciation had love for all really *good* music, whatever its peculiar character."[15] He also showed strong humanitarian interests. Mary Cowden Clarke placed this first among his contributions, declaring that he "has done perhaps more than any other single individual towards spreading a love and cultivation of the best music amongst the least wealthy classes of England."[16] "Least wealthy" is of course an exaggeration, yet Novello's influence was evidenced in his public recitals, in publishing good music in inexpensive editions, and in the example he set by his musical evenings.

These characteristics struck a responsive chord in Hunt. It is

true that he would have kept Catholics and Methodists from the
highest offices of the government.[17] Yet his hatred of bigotry led
him to fight for the emancipation of Catholics as a persecuted
minority. And when he attacked Catholicism, it was as an institution rather than as an expression of faith, for he was never
hostile toward what he considered genuine religious feelings.[18]

In his poetry Hunt paid tribute to Novello's competence:

> And Vincent, you, who with like mastery
> Can chace the notes with fluttering finger-tips,
> Like fairies down the hill hurrying their trips,
> Or sway the organ with firm royalty. . . .

Hunt also wrote two songs "to be set to music by Vincent Novello," which he published in *Foliage.* The first, "When Lovely
Sounds about My Ears," was apparently composed by Novello
sometime after 1818 (*Poetical Works,* p. 332); the second, "His
Departed Love to Prince Leopold," had already been set when it
appeared in the *Examiner* (15 March 1818). Early in 1817, with
the assistance of Novello, he composed a musical piece—a song or
hymn—of his own: "To the Spirit Great and Good." Novello,
who wrote down the tune from Hunt's "singing and playing it to
me," credited him with the bass as well as the melody.[19]

Their most extensive collaboration was "Musical Evenings."[20]
Hunt optimistically wrote Charles Clarke (see below) on 31
August 1821 that he was "putting the finishing touches" on it,
but he had not even completed the first "Evening," of which
there were to have been several, and the project was abandoned,
owing apparently to Hunt's ill health, his pending trip to Italy,
and doubts about the publication itself. In general, the work was
intended to encourage a wider interest in the music of Continental composers. Already fairly well known aria excerpts from such
Italian operas as Mozart's *Cosí fan Tutti, Le Nozze di Figaro,* and
Don Giovanni, and Paesiello's *La Molinara* provided a lure to
which Hunt added less familiar songs. He supplied his own translations and the running commentary that linked the numbers
together, for which he drew heavily on his previously published
translations, on his Italian-opera criticisms, and on the remnants

Engraved by J. C. Armytage from an unfinished miniature by Joseph Severn
From Edmund C. Blunden, *Leigh Hunt, A Biography*

James Henry Leigh Hunt (1820)

Drawn and engraved by Daniel Havell
From Edward W. Brayley, *Historical and Descriptive Accounts of the Theatres of London*

Theatre Royal, Drury Lane (1826)

of older projects (see *Correspondence,* I, 117, 121, 145); but he also added much that was new. Novello's task would have been to provide suitable piano arrangements for the songs. Hunt's comments suggest that some of the scores may have been worked out; if so, they have not been located. The extremely uneven quality of the manuscript is due partly to its unfinished state but even more to Hunt's uncertainties concerning the nature of the work; as a consequence, his incisive observations rest uneasily alongside mawkishly condescending appeals.[21]

The close relationship between these men is indicated in other ways. Novello served as Hunt's intermediary in negotiations with his brother John in the dispute over Leigh's financial interest in the *Examiner.* Leigh gave the name of Vincent to his youngest son, born in Italy in 1823, hoping to assuage Novello's grief over the loss, about 1820, of his favorite child, Sidney. Hunt's birthday that year was celebrated by the Novellos. As Mrs. Novello (Mary Sibella, whom Hunt addressed playfully as "Wilful Woman") wrote him: "Your health *was* drunk *con amore*; and . . . they sang round the table *Beviamo, How sweet is the Pleasure* and many other musical merriments. . . . Indeed, it only rates second to the Twelfth-night [that you once gave]; yet so closely allied, as you well know, are pleasure and pain, that several times, and particularly during the singing of *Ah, Perdona,*[22] many tears were shed by friendly eyes" (*Correspondence,* I, 208–10).

Regarding Lamb as "the greatest critic of all," Hunt was often present at his famous Thursdays from 1815 until he left for Italy in 1822.[23] Lamb's lack of interest in music was a joke that he shared with his friends, although, paradoxically, he included two of the better-known musicians of the day—Novello and William Ayrton—among his closest. He exploited his "defect" in "A Chapter on Ears" (1821)[24]—a retrospective of Novello's musical evenings, where only a draught of "true Lutheran beer" could reconcile him to the "protracted hours" of Haydn, Mozart, Bach, and Beethoven. Hunt admitted that Lamb "is not musical. He will put up with nothing but snatches of old songs. Mozart to him is alien, and Paesiello the Pope of Rome" (4 April 1824).

Lamb and Ayrton enjoyed a close association over many years

despite the former's indifference to music and the latter's indifference to jokes and punning. In 1823 Lamb wrote to Robert Southey that Ayrton was the "last and steadiest left to me of that little knot of whist players." As members of Lamb's circle both Hunt and William Hazlitt (1778–1830) were acquainted with Ayrton. Hazlitt, who apparently first met Hunt at Surrey jail (brought there, most likely, by Lamb), was an accomplished art critic and journalist. He probably intended some condescension in referring to Ayrton as "the Will Honeycomb of our set"[25] as he did in a retrospective, "On Persons one would wish to have seen" (1826), where he makes Ayrton a somewhat obtuse foil for Lamb's wit. In 1824 Hunt described Ayrton as "the most well-bred of musicians, who hates a paradox like an unresolved discord." Despite their friendship with Lamb and their love of Mozart, Hunt and Ayrton seem to have remained strangely distant. Hunt does not mention him once in his *Autobiography*. It is possible that Ayrton was piqued by Hunt's and Hazlitt's unremitting criticism of his brother-in-law Samuel James Arnold, towards whom Lamb was much kinder (see below, chapter three). More likely, the journalists were politically too radical for a former Master of the Royal Chapel.

Another musical friend of this period was Thomas Massa Alsager.[26] Active in amateur musical circles, including Novello's, he could play a number of musical instruments. While in jail Hunt made his acquaintance through Barnes. In 1815 Hunt published a sonnet to Alsager, which he wrote after a visit to his study:

> May peace be still found there . . .
> And never harsher sound, than the fine pleasure
> Of lettered friend, or music's mingling art,
> That fetches out in smiles the mutual soul.

In his *Autobiography* he called him "the kindest of neighbours, a man of business, who contrived to be a scholar and a musician." Whether Hunt was ever invited to any of his famous "private concerts," at which Alsager marshaled forces capable of giving the English première (1832) of Beethoven's *Mass in D* and of a Cherubini *Requiem,* we have no record.

A final group of musical and literary friends, most of whom were somewhat younger than Hunt, remains to be considered.

Charles Cowden Clarke (1787–1877) was to become the most intimate member of the Novello circle by virtue of his marriage, in 1828, to Vincent's eldest daughter, Mary Victoria.[27] The *Examiner* was an early influence at an Enfield academy that was directed by Charles's father, John Clarke, a Baptist of liberal leanings. Charles met Hunt at a musical party in 1812, where he was "dazzled by his jaunty charm."[28] The next year he carried baskets of fruit to the incarcerated editor. Through their visits to the jail Hunt no doubt brought Clarke and Henry Robertson together, for it was during this period that the latter apparently introduced Clarke to the Novellos.[29]

Clarke was already something of a pianist at Enfield, where his playing (c. 1810) had a profound effect upon two of the students, Edward Holmes and John Keats.[30] On others his musical influence was less pronounced; Mary Shelley wrote Hunt on 5 October 1823 that he "puts one out of all patience with his 'charming!' and 'beautiful!' as an accompaniment." But Clarke's musical and journalistic interests brought him into professional associations with Hunt. As early as 1814 Hunt wrote to Clarke from jail regarding a proposed publication on the "songs of Mozart," in which Robertson and Charles Ollier (see below) were to be involved.[31] (In recalling the matter, Clarke was not certain whether Hunt's role was to be that of "translator"; the work apparently never advanced beyond the proposal stage.) In 1828 Clarke and Hunt were for a time coeditors of the weekly *Companion,* and in 1830 Clarke wrote some theatrical reviews for the *Tatler.* Later, Hunt published articles in the *Musical World,* edited for a period by Clarke.

Edward Holmes (1797–1859), probably introduced to Hunt by Clarke, remained a close friend throughout his life. "Bonny" Holmes was Novello's "most eminent pupil" and was received into his home as an intimate.[32] Novello brought Holmes into the Lamb circle and in the late 1820's took him on the "pilgrimage"

to Mozart's sister. Holmes became music critic for the *Atlas* in
the 1830's and later wrote critiques for the *Musical Times*. His
greatest work was the *Life of Mozart* (1845), which Max Graf
calls "the most useful, complete, and trustworthy biography then
in existence."[33] In his *Autobiography* Hunt declared Holmes
"the best musical critic which this nation has yet produced."[34]

In October, 1816, Clarke brought Keats (1795–1821) to Hunt's
Hampstead residence at the editor's invitation, after Hunt had
been profoundly impressed by the "Chapman's Homer" sonnet,
first published in the *Examiner*. It was Alsager's folio edition of
Chapman's *Homer,* loaned to Clarke, that Keats had perused
with him on the famous night of the sonnet's composition the
preceding month. Probably not long after their first meeting
Hunt took Keats to the Novellos, where he enjoyed the musical
evenings and joked with Hunt about the Bach fugues that Novello played on his house organ.[35] By the end of the following year
Keats, exhausted by the recent death of his brother Tom, and
disillusioned with Hunt, found his visits there tedious. "Through
him [Hunt] I am indifferent to Mozart," he wrote to his brother
George (24 December 1818).

Charles Ollier (1788–1859) established a publishing venture
with his brother in 1817, and Hunt assisted them through his
friendship with Keats and Shelley as well as by offering them his
Foliage and other works. Hunt attended Ollier's musical soirée
on 13 May 1815, which prompted "A Thought on Music":

> For not the notes alone, or new-found air,
> Or structure of elaborate harmonies,
> With steps that to the waiting treble climb,
> Suffice a true-touched ear. To that will come
> Out of the very vagueness of the joy
> A shaping and a sense of things beyond us,
> Great things and voices great. . . .

Ollier delighted him with his flute-playing as well as with his
musical evenings, one of which Hunt enjoyed as late as 1851.
Both men died in the same year, but Hunt lived long enough to
write a "Souvenir" of his late friend.

Percy Bysshe Shelley (1792–1822) met Hunt for the first time in 1811, partly through the good offices of Rowland Hunter, but they did not become friends until the end of 1816. From then until Shelley's departure for Italy on 18 November 1818, they often met at Hampstead, London, or Marlow, where they talked politics, morality, literature, and music.[36] Shelley attended musical evenings at Novello's, where he won the admiration of Robertson as well as Novello. He enjoyed "the contribution of his [Hunt's] musical powers" at Marlow in the spring of 1817. Shelley was "persuaded" by his friend Thomas Love Peacock (1785–1866) to attend the King's Theatre in 1817–1818.[37] Hunt was there, in the pit, on at least one of these occasions. Shelley was no stranger to the King's Theatre, however, which he had visited as early as 1809. Like Peacock, Shelley found the behavior of the audiences there more to his liking than those at the playhouses. Peacock, an enthusiast of Italian opera and ballet, wrote many criticisms for the *Globe* and the *Examiner* in the 1830's, some of which have much in common with Hunt's (see below, chapter four).

In Italy the Shelleys continued to attend the opera at Turin, Rome, and Milan, where they found the performances inferior to those at London.[38] From their country retreat Mary Shelley wrote to Hunt (28 August 1819) that the natives sing, "not very melodiously, but very loud, Rossini's music, *Mi rivedrai ti revedrò*"—to the accompaniment of the cicala! Later, from Italy, Hunt wrote to Novello that Mary would "drink in as much Mozart and Paesiello as you choose to afford her" (24 July 1823). Hunt no doubt brought to Italy the three operas of Mozart transcribed for piano and "a collection of the only songs of Winter published in this country," to which he referred in his last letter to Shelley from England (26 March 1822).

These musical friendships indicate an extension of Hunt's musical development rather than being an integral part of it, for his tastes had been largely formed and he was already an experienced opera critic before many of them were established. Indeed, he gave more than he received in these relationships; even Novello's strictly musical influence on Hunt has been overestimated.[39] But they did offer him numerous advantages. At the private concerts and musical evenings of his friends he became exposed to a wide range of influences. In the conversation and recreation of his circle "music usually [formed] a staple in both talk and the diversion."[40] Such exchanges surely enlarged his knowledge of music, while inviting a demonstration of his own talents. Some of these friends also provided him with direct and invaluable resources for opera criticism in the *Examiner*.

These associations reveal not only the breadth and intensity of Hunt's musical interest but also the social value that music had in his life. There is scarcely a friend or acquaintance in whom an interest in music did not furnish some basis for the association—usually it was a vital one. For a man of Hunt's gregarious proclivities, music was more than an asset; it expressed the bond of the social fabric that he created and enjoyed. His early interest in song, enhanced by his natural endowments, contributed much to his socio-musical life. Song and society, in turn, complemented his interest in opera: both are reflected in his opera criticism.[41]

If Hunt the child was a "great singer" to his "loving relatives," others recognized in Hunt the adult a marked degree of musical aptitude. Charles Clarke remembered his "sweet, small baritone" voice, and his talk—"as delicious to listen to as rarest music" (*Recollections,* pp. 16, 45); whereas the highly impressionable Mary Cowden Clarke (a child of eight in 1817) recalled that his "reading aloud was the perfection of spirited perusal. He possessed innate fascination of voice, look and manner" (*My Long Life,* p. 17). Later, when he sang one of Tom Moore's* Irish melodies after his return to England, she wrote, "I was so excited by the sound of his voice after that lapse of time, that I found the tears silently streaming down my cheeks" (*My Long Life,* p. 57). Hunt's son Thornton, stating that his father "was passionately fond of music," gives us a more accurate description of Leigh's voice. It was

of extraordinary compass, power, flexibility, and beauty. It extended from the C below the line [that is, below the bass clef] to the

F sharp above: there were no "passages" that he could not execute; the quality was sweet, clear, and ringing: he would equally have sung the music of *Don Giovanni* or Sarastro [*Magic Flute*]. . . . [He] delighted to repeat airs pleasing or plaintive; and if he would occasionally fling himself into the audacious revels of Don Giovanni, he preferred to be Lindoro or Don Ottavio; and still more, by the help of his falsetto, to dally with the tender treble of the Countess in *Figaro*, or Polly in *Beggars' Opera* [*sic*].[42]

In the absence of supporting evidence one may doubt Blunden's assertion of "the fact that Hunt was a brilliant pianist."[43] The evidence from Thornton suggests otherwise: "Nature had not endowed him with some of the qualities needed for the practical musician,—he had no aptitude for mechanical contrivance, but faint enjoyment of power for its own sake. He dabbled on the pianoforte." "Dabbled" is perhaps used too loosely; Haydon described how Hunt, "going jauntily to the piano," would "strike up, 'Cosi fan tutte,' or 'Addio mi cuore' with a 'Ring the bell for tea.' "[44] In any event a piano was well-nigh indispensable to his ill-furnished establishments. He had one, along with a flute and the borrowed lute, to entertain guests in that strangest of all prison cells. (The lute, difficult to play and all but forgotten since the seventeenth century, was for Hunt probably little more than a curiosity piece, like some of his quaint furnishings.) And when there was no company, he could listen to the "cheerful songs" of the felons and the "gay songs and jolly parties" of the debtors. Without company, though, music was of small solace. Stranded at Ramsgate on his way to Italy, he hired a piano for a month; as he wrote to Mary Shelley, "It is the only pleasure to which I have treated myself, and without . . . [Novello] I find it but a pain" (2 March 1822). Stranded later at Florence without a piano, "with rage and benevolence" in his heart he loaned "to a lady going to Rome" all the new music that Novello had sent (9 January 1824).

Our sketch of Hunt's life after the *Examiner* years must be confined to the highlights of a long and complicated career.

Hunt's decision to go to Italy had several tragic consequences.

Lord Byron (1788–1824), who had visited Hunt in jail and whose
poetry Hunt had praised, was the first to suggest the trip. Byron,
now like Shelley an expatriate living in Italy, proposed to the
poet that they bring Hunt to Italy to edit a new quarterly, the
Liberal, to which all three would contribute, since it was increasingly difficult to find an English publisher for their radical
views. Shelley enthusiastically endorsed the plan, and both poets
urged Hunt to come, agreeing to underwrite all expenses. To
Hunt, Italy was a land of enchantment, promising relief from the
ill health both he and Marianne were suffering at the time.
Moreover, the government was again threatening the editors.
Leigh, who earlier had placed principle before family, wisely
severed "official" ties with the *Examiner* at John's urging. Later,
John spent another year in jail.

Shelley met the Hunts on their arrival in Italy in July, 1822;
but on returning to his summer home at Lerici, he encountered
a violent storm at sea and was drowned. Byron, who became increasingly annoyed with the Hunts, soon departed Pisa for
Greece, placing his wealth at the service of the insurrectionists.
Thus the *Liberal* became another of Hunt's many short-lived
enterprises, and Leigh, Marianne, and their ten children were
stranded in Italy for three desolate years.

They were finally rescued by an advance from a London publisher who wanted Hunt to write a book about Italy. Finally
published in 1828, *Lord Byron and Some of His Contemporaries*
was another disastrous consequence of his Italian journey. Filled
with bitterness over his shabby treatment and betrayal at the
hands of Byron, Hunt thoroughly vilified the poet in his work.
Byron was at the time something of a popular hero in England,
and these harsh memoirs turned the critics against Hunt just
when he was seeking to reestablish himself.

Although Hunt was never again to share the long and modestly profitable relationship he had had with the *Examiner,* his
Victorian years were rich in the production of poems, essays, and
criticism. Most of these appeared in a very wide variety of publications for which Hunt was doing essentially the work of a hack
journalist. His gifts as an editor did not languish altogether,

though the periodicals he edited seldom survived more than a
year of two. (The taint of the Dissenter in Hunt and his contributors was a factor in some cases.) Perhaps the most successful
was the weekly *Indicator* (1819–1821) and the daily *Tatler* (1830–
1832), for which he wrote excellent theatrical criticism. Other
editorial efforts included the *Companion* (1828), *Chat of the
Week* (1830), the *Plain Dealer* (1832), *Leigh Hunt's London
Journal* (1834–1835)—all weeklies—and the *Monthly Repository*
(1837–1838). Hunt included much of his own work in these
periodicals, which were all primarily literary in content, and
from time to time he collected and published his essays and
poems. Longer poems, such as *Bacchus in Tuscany* (1825)—a
translation from the Italian of Francesco Redi—and the satirical
Captain Sword and Captain Pen (1835), he also published separately.

Though Hunt had no aspirations as a novelist, he produced
one, *Sir Ralph Usher*, in 1832; it was not successful. His long-
ings for success as a playwright were finally fulfilled in *A Legend
of Florence,* a tragedy produced at Covent Garden in 1840. His
Lovers' Amazements, a farce, was produced at the Lyceum in
1858. *Imagination and Fancy* (1844) was a popular critical survey of English poetry based on Coleridgian principles. For its
critical acumen, his introduction to *The Book of the Sonnet*
(1867) has enjoyed a certain posthumous fame. Perhaps his most
popular work has been the *Autobiography* (1850, revised 1860),
most of which he adapted from his *Lord Byron,* leaving out the
bitterness. Finally should be mentioned *Christianism, or Belief
and Unbelief Reconciled* (1832), which became the basis for
Religion of the Heart (1852). In these works Hunt set forth his
philosophy of life, a kind of latter-day mystical deism that emphasized Christian charity at the expense of Christian dogma, a
belief in the essential goodness of man. Hunt's humanitarianism,
like Shelley's, owed much to the benevolence of William Godwin's *Political Justice* (1793). It exuded an optimism that harmonized with utilitarianism and a spirituality that embraced
"progress."

Despite the popularity of such anthologized pieces as "Abou

Ben Adam" and "Jenny Kissed Me," Hunt was not a first-rate poet. He was a first-rate essayist and critic, though outshown by Lamb and Hazlitt. He had an uncanny ability to detect outstanding literary talent. During the *Examiner* years he strongly supported Keats and Shelley, whose poems he printed and whose works he praised; for a time he was the only well-known literary critic who thought their poetry significant. Even Hazlitt included no section on Shelley in his *Spirit of the Age* (1825). Hunt also corrected his early mistakes about Wordsworth and Coleridge. During the Victorian years he continued to place his finger on the genius of emerging literary figures: Carlyle, Macaulay, Tennyson, and Browning, among others.

Yet Hunt seldom won the recognition he deserved. His attack on the Queen's uncle was difficult to forget, and the government waited until 1847 to give him a pension for his service to the liberal cause—long after other "radicals" of those pre-Reform days had won their rewards. Hunt's later days were also clouded by a caricature of him that Dickens wrote into the character Skimpole in *Bleak House* (1853). The caricature was grossly inaccurate and scandalously unfair. Unfortunately, Hunt's posthumous reputation has been seriously compromised by generations of readers who take the effete Skimpole for the man.

It is of course the earlier Hunt with whom we are primarily concerned, and our attention should now turn to some of the journalistic developments on which his opera criticism during the *Examiner* years was grounded.

The Challenge of the Examiner

Hunt's reviews in the *News* showed considerable self-confidence and an outspoken manner that was then most unusual in theatrical criticism.[45] It was the latter quality that created the immediate stir. The playwright George Colman the Younger,* for example, wrote a prologue attacking the critic, which the actor John Fawcett* "spoke right in my teeth";[46] Hunt was only amused, looking "upon Mr. Colman as a great monkey pelting me with nuts, which I ate." But Hunt kept his distance, gen-

erally refused to become personally involved with theatre people
(there were some exceptions), and insisted on purchasing his
tickets rather than accepting the usual passes.

Small wonder Leigh and John saw that "independence in
theatrical circles would be a great novelty."[47]

Puffing and plenty of tickets were . . . the system of the day. It
was an interchange of amenities over the dinner-table; a flattery of
power on the one side, and puns on the other; and what the public
took for a criticism on a play was a draft upon the box-office, or
reminiscences of last Thursday's salmon and lobster-sauce. The
custom was, to write as short and as favourable a paragraph on the
new piece as could be; to say that Bannister was "excellent" and
Mrs. Jordan "charming"; to notice the "crowded house" or invent
it, if necessary; and to conclude by observing that "the whole
went off with *éclat.*" [*Autobiography*, p. 155]

In the *News* he had scorned the "haunters of green-rooms" who
provided the "old obliging criticism" for their theatre acquaintances; and in "Rules for the Theatrical Critic of a Newspaper"
he supplied a glossary of commonplace critical phrases from "the
most approved critics," duly translated into the irony of theatrical
realities.

Other sources substantiate Hunt's views. "The reviews of new
pieces or the remarks on the players who played in them had, up
till now [that is, the advent of the *News*], been usually short,"
wrote Alexander Andrews, "—often prepared at the instance of
the parties under review, and not seldom, according to Mr. Reynolds, even written by themselves."[48] Another playwright,
Charles Dibdin the Younger (see Thomas Dibdin*), recalled in
his *Memoirs* (p. 108) his early experiences as a compositor for
London Sunday newspapers (c. 1774–1784); printed Saturday
night, they contained reviews of performances of the same night
at Drury Lane and Covent Garden before they were half over.
None of the London dailies gave much room to theatrical news.
Among the weeklies only the *Weekly Messenger* gave the stage
half a column, while some monthlies, such as the *Monthly Mirror,*[49] carried occasional articles of more than insipid quality:

yet none of this criticism was comparable to that in the *News* (Landré, II, 101).

To be sure, there had been some good stage criticism in the fugitive periodicals of the eighteenth century. Hunt himself seems to have had this in mind in discussing reasons for the decline in theatrical arts, among which he mentioned the public's diversion by politics, the rise of commercial interests, the loss of a class with "small independent fortunes" who had taste, the antipathy of the English to Continental tastes, and the fact that critics had migrated from the pit to the boxes, "where opinions are held in check" (*Reflector*, I, 233–34). George W. Stone, Jr., cites the reviews of John Potter in the *Theatrical Review* (1771–1772) for their close observation of details in the acting but notes that the criticism of the period languished with the waning popularity of Garrick.[50] Indeed, Lucyle Werkmeister, in *A Newspaper History of England, 1792–1793* (pp. 42–44), has explained in detail how political partisanship during the late eighteenth century between newspapers, on the one hand, and theatre managers and even actors and playwrights, on the other, effectively blocked responsible press criticism of Drury Lane, Covent Garden, and Haymarket productions. What was characteristic of theatrical criticism generally was of course applicable to the English musical stage. Some of the late-eighteenth-century monthlies carried brief reviews of English operas, but only three had "any real or intelligent interest," according to Michael Winisanker.[51]

Charles H. Gray finds that towards the end of the century "newspapers in great numbers were publishing regular critical articles about the plays and the acting."[52] He considers some of Thomas Holcroft's critiques for the *English Review* in 1783 to be as vivid as Hunt's *Critical Essays*. "Lively, intelligent criticism," though rare, could be found in the *Times* as early as 1796. Noting Gray's disclaimer on content, one may well agree with his conclusions, after a survey of the period, that the reviews of Hunt in the *News* do not seem "so" revolutionary or epochmaking, as Archer and Lowe claimed, although their judgment (*Dramatic Essays of Leigh Hunt*, p. vii) that Hunt was the first English journalist of genuine importance in dramatic criticism does not appear to be exaggerated. Thornton Hunt wrote in 1860 that with the *News,* Hunt "brought standards of criticism which had before been confined to the lectures of the academies or the library, into the daily literature which aids in shaping men's judgments as they rise" ("Man of Letters," p. 91).

Hunt's reviews appeared in the *News* until the end of 1807. His skill as an experienced critic is clearly evident in *Critical Essays,* with which he culminated his work for that periodical. Its very appearance is testimony to that skill, for theatrical essays were not considered the kind of matter to be distinguished by placing them between hard covers. Yet the work received high praise from the dramatist Richard Cumberland, among others. At the request of another old school friend, Barron Field (1786–1814), who had become dramatic critic for the *Times* in 1805,[53] Hunt wrote two reviews for that newspaper in 1807 with which Field was delighted; one was promptly reprinted by the arch-conservative evening *Courier!*[54]

John and Leigh Hunt, then, were rapidly approaching the point of journalistic independence that was to be achieved when the *Examiner* was established in 1808—a venture in which Leigh shared full partnership with his brother. Leigh was to write most of its "features," while John was to manage the enterprise—a not inconsiderable responsibility in view of Leigh's incredible ineptitude in simple arithmetic, to say nothing of financial or business arrangements. But John provided far more than that. His own liberal instincts, courage, and solid character brought both an example and a stabilizing force to the partnership. John's character has sometimes been praised to the detriment of Leigh's, though John's rather shabby treatment of his brother over his claims on the *Examiner* cannot be entirely mitigated.[55] The fact is, the *Examiner* could never have achieved its success without the diverse talents and complete dedication of both men.

Independent criticism, achieved in the dramatic column of the *News,* was the vital principle in the launching of the Sunday *Examiner.* "As the Public have allowed the possibility of IM-PARTIALITY in . . . [dramatic criticism]," Hunt wrote in the

Prospectus, "we do not see why the same possibility may not be
obtained in POLITICS." The paper "began with being of no
party"; its name was taken from the journal of "Swift and his
brother Tories. I did not think of their politics. I thought only
of their wit and fine writing." Its "politics were rather a sentiment. . . . Zeal for the public good was a family inheritance; and
this we thought ourselves bound to increase." Thus, the *Examiner* stood on the broad premise of "liberality of opinion in general . . . and a fusion of literary taste into all subjects whatsoever"
(*Autobiography,* pp. 173–75).

Hunt's wariness about commitment to party politics is understandable. He had seen how apparently innocuous relationships
vitiated theatrical criticism. In preparing the ground for honest
criticism, "professional" associations had to be eschewed altogether. "In the present day," he continued in the Prospectus,
"we are all so erroneously sociable, that every man, as well as
every journal, must belong to some class of politicians."[56] A year
later, after his zeal had incurred the first "information" against
the *Examiner,* he wrote in the Preface (published 1809) for volume one of the weekly that politics was corrupting everything it
touched in journalism, including style, for no grace could be
found in the writing of the periodicals. "Freedom from party
spirit is nothing but the love of looking abroad upon men and
things, and this leads to universality, which is the great study of
philosophy."

Independent criticism thus leads to philosophical observations,
a practice to be followed in all departments of the *Examiner*:
"As Theatrical Criticism is the liveliest part of a newspaper, I
have endeavoured to correct its usual levity by treating it philo-
sophically; and as Political Writing is the gravest subject, I have
attempted to give it a more general interest by handling it good-
humouredly" (1809 Preface). By treating subjects "philosoph-
ically" Hunt meant not only with freedom from any restraint but
also with a wider range of ideas and values than journalistic
commentators had thought necessary or desirable. Detesting
compartmentalization, he sought to "infuse" his subjects with all
the pertinent imaginative resources at his command. As a result

he brought literature to bear on politics, politics on literature, and politics and literature on the arts, including the theatre and the opera.

In practice, Hunt's credo of independence was sometimes compromised. It was no doubt an inevitable and in some respects a useful development. Hunt boasted that he knew no politicians, whereas in fact he did, and his behavior vis-à-vis his principles was on occasion flagrantly irresponsible.[57] He boasted that he knew no actors or dramatists, whereas he had become acquainted (before 1805, however) with the comedian Charles Mathews* and the playwright Theodore Hook. (If he gave high praise to the actor in the *Examiner,* it was tribute to a talent all London acknowledged as exceptional.) At Thomas Hill's he was much impressed with Hook's improvisations at the piano, where he made a parody (both words and music) "of a modern opera, introducing sailors and their clap-traps, rustics, etc." (*Autobiography,* p. 184). Hunt's admiration survived the attacks Hook would make against him in the administration's *John Bull* (1821 and later), yet he roundly damned Hook's ephemeral stage productions (see below, chapter three). To be sure, Hunt's criticisms—political, literary, and theatrical—were not free from partisanship, which occasionally exercised a deleterious effect on his judgment. But for Hunt "independent" criticism did not mean noncommitment, and if his zeal sometimes overshot the mark, it is no basic contradiction to assert, in the words of Reginald Brimley Johnson, that Hunt's prefaces "not only set forth what he aimed at doing for his readers: but they do actually express what he accomplished."[58]

Independent criticism and the politics of sentiment were mutually complementary aspects in Hunt's thinking and writing. "Both of these aspects are related to his need to rise above purely material preoccupations; they demonstrate his interest in everything that, in his opinion, could contribute to the well-being of humanity" (Landré, II, 99; author's translation). As a journalist Hunt saw his primary role as that of a reformer of taste. Such a role required more than critical independence: it demanded a broad commitment to all the arts, a literary tone and temper unknown to contemporary journalism, and, as he was soon to discover, inevitable conflicts in the arena of party politics. Hunt possessed the intelligence, dedication, taste, and skill for the first two requirements, and the courage if not always the wisdom for dealing with the third.

As a vehicle for that role, the *Examiner* came into being at an auspicious time. The taste of the literate public was perhaps never more in need of mending, yet the *News* had demonstrated the marketability of good criticism. Mere literacy had no doubt accelerated the decay in taste, as Hunt thought (see below), yet the tremendous increase in the number of literate people surely affected that portion of the middle class to whom the *Examiner* directed itself.[59] This growth was paralleled by that of the newspapers.[60] But the *Examiner* handily survived the competition. Achieving sales of 2,200 by November of 1808, in 1812 it led the London weeklies with sales between 7,000 and 8,000. (The *Courier,* the Tory's most powerful voice, had a circulation of 7,000 in 1811.) With their advertising revenues, dailies could make a profit on a circulation of about 2,000, but the government sought to influence the press through the placement of its advertising (Williams, *Revolution,* p. 186), as did the theatre managers (Stone, *London Stage,* Part 4, I, lvi; and Hogan, *London Stage,* Part 5, I, clxxix). The *Examiner,* able to avoid all advertising for several years, had the economic advantage of having a small staff. It carried "news," as did the other weeklies, which was derived almost entirely from secondary sources. Such news was important for those who could not afford a daily as well, but what readers especially sought in weeklies was lively editorial commentary with considerable radical seasoning. The other important dailies (not including those, the majority, that were directed to various commercial interests) were politically conservative with two exceptions: the *Morning Chronicle,* a Whig organ edited by James Perry, which occasionally incurred the government's wrath though its tone was generally restrained; and the *Times,* still no "Thunderer," which was cautiously moving towards a respectably liberal position under the direction of John Walter. These newspapers gave the arts little more than

William Shield

Henry Rowley Bishop

Theatre Royal, Covent Garden (1810), interior view

John Braham (1817)

Charles Incledon as Macheath in
The Beggar's Opera (1818)

Catherine Stephens as Susanna in
Bishop's adaptation of
The Marriage of Figaro

Frances Maria Kelly (1819)

lip service (Landré, II, 101). The weeklies, on the other hand, were for the most part radical and reformist. For Hunt's criterion of critical independence, they were too deeply committed to the political left; in fact, they were generally contemptuous of the arts and cared little for literary polish. Complaining in the 1809 Preface of the paucity of good theatrical criticism, Hunt noted that it was "a department which none of the papers seems inclined to dispute with a person fond of the subject, the daily ones for want of independence, and the weekly for want of care."[61] The most important weekly was William Cobbett's *Register,* established in 1802 when he left the Tory party.[62] Cobbett, supreme at invective, was fined and imprisoned in the military flogging case for which the *Examiner* was prosecuted. Hunt expressed admiration for the political radical, and distaste for Cobbett's vulgarity and pretentiousness; Cobbett reciprocated with bouquets and brickbats.

Against the indifference or the bought opinions of the press towards the arts, the *Examiner* provided its readers with a wealth of varied commentary. "The Political Examiner," the leading article, usually but not always dealt with broadly political considerations. "The Examiner," a much shorter feature, covered nearly everything in subject but was frequently of a topical nature. John Hunt wrote these columns occasionally. (Most but not all of Leigh's work in the *Examiner* can be identified by the "indicator" hand that followed each contribution.) In the "Fine Arts" column Robert Hunt, the youngest of the brothers, proved to be one of the most assiduous, if one of the least brilliant, contributors. (Leigh seldom wrote this feature, though in other columns he made frequent references to the fine arts.) Literature thrust its luxuriant growth into all "departments" of the paper, as well as into the unrubricated interstices, where new poems and other literary matter appeared from time to time. Featured in "Literary Notices," where new publications were reviewed, it often was the subject of "Table Talk" and "The Round Table" essays, to which Hazlitt and others added notable contributions to those of Hunt. But the most popular department was the "Theatrical Examiner," for which Hunt and others supplied

critical reviews of musical and nonmusical productions at the
English patent theatres, with occasional late excursions to the
Olympic "on the Surrey side." After 1813 the column absorbed
Italian-opera criticism, as well. It also included a scattering of
reviews of the Lenten oratorios, performances by the Philharmonic Society, and private concerts; but even *Examiner* readers
were not ready for sustained criticism of this nature.[63] (As with
other subjects, Hunt's occasional references to or commentary on
music appeared elsewhere in the *Examiner* and in other publications.)

While the Hunts were in jail, Thomas Barnes was called upon
to supply the "Theatrical Examiners" and other features. Barnes,
who had joined Hunt and other budding journalists at Thomas
Hill's "open house" gatherings, apparently wrote the dramatic
criticism for the *Times* in 1810 after Field gave up that post to
follow a legal career.[64] The following year Barnes was reporting
on Parliament. In 1812 he wrote a notable series of literary portraits for John Scott's new weekly, the *Champion* (which Hunt
admired). He also wrote "Parliament Portraits" for the *Examiner,* in which he expressed opinions that differed from Hunt's,
and he praised the editor for his tolerance in publishing them
(14 August 1814). In his *Autobiography* (p. 105) Hunt recalled
that Barnes (a notoriously heavy drinker) "might assuredly have
made a name in wit and literature, had he cared much for anything beyond his glass of wine and his Fielding."

After his release from jail, Hunt sought continued assistance
from other writers. This was due partly to ill health, exacerbated
by his long confinement, and partly to his wish to direct the
Examiner towards more literary matters. He turned to Hazlitt,
who had begun his journalistic apprenticeship as Parliamentary
reporter for the *Chronicle* in 1812 and had soon been promoted
to the post of drama critic. Hazlitt wrote other pieces that reflected a politics too radical for Perry's taste; early in 1814 he was
dismissed. He also published drama and art criticism in the
Champion, to which he contributed for about a year; and in
1815 he wrote literary criticism for the *Edinburgh Review.* His

Examiner criticism began in April, 1815, and continued to June, 1816—a period that Baker (*William Hazlitt*, p. 202) calls "perhaps the most febrile and productive of his whole career." Meanwhile, Hunt, whose indicator sign was beginning to reappear beneath some reviews as early as March, 1816, apparently felt well enough to resume his theatrical criticism. Hazlitt moved on to the *Times* for a few months as drama critic, then gave up journalism as a steady employment, though he later made occasional contributions to the *Examiner* and other periodicals.

Beginning with the second issue and continuing with considerable regularity throughout each season, the *Examiner* carried criticism of Italian opera. Until 1813 it was written by Henry Robertson and appeared in the form of a letter-to-the-editor, which was placed close to the "Theatrical Examiner." Under what circumstances he took on the task, whether he was paid for it, and what preparation he had are questions that so far have no answers. We can only ascertain from his reviews that his critical stance showed a marked similarity to Hunt's, that he was already familiar with King's Theatre productions, knew some Italian, and wrote with a certain journalistic competence. Presumably he received some compensation, the letter format notwithstanding; apparently only Ayrton was affluent enough to write gratis reviews.

Very little indeed is known about Henry Robertson. After the time of the "Elders" we hear nothing of him, except for the "Opera Letters," until he visited the Hunts at Horsemonger Lane; following one such visit he wrote a "Sonnet on the Poet's Residence in Surrey Jail."[65] In a later sonnet, "To Henry Robertson, John Gattie, and Vincent Novello: Not keeping their appointed hour" (*Foliage,* 1818), Hunt referred to Robertson as "Harry, my friend, who full of tasteful glee / Have music all about you, heart and lips." Robertson's musical interests and personal qualities drew him into the Novello circle, where he was "as excellent a tenor singer as he was excellent in lively companionship."[66]

Robertson played a subordinate role in the management of Covent Garden Theatre for most of his life. This association may have begun about the time he ceased his regular opera criticism for the *Examiner,* for it is in speaking of this period in the *Autobiography* that Hunt first alludes to the connection. We do know that early in 1823 Charles Kemble, then manager, discharged Brandon, former treasurer of the theatre, and replaced him with Robertson.[67] Charles Clarke in *Recollections* (p. 18) speaks of Robertson as "a Treasury Office clerk, and the appointed accountant of Covent Garden Theatre." The holding of two jobs was fairly common in those days, though Robertson may have relinquished his Treasury post following his appointment as treasurer of the theatre. Possibly not a member of the Lamb circle, Robertson wrote to Mary Lamb on 8 February 1823, in his new capacity, returning a play, *Grandpapa,* with the comment, "not thought to fit this theatre."[68] By mid 1837 Robertson was handling negotiations for the proprietors with Charles Macready regarding the latter's proposed management of the theatre.

Hunt remembered Robertson in his "Wishing Cap Papers" (*Examiner,* 18 April 1824) as "always ready with his tenor, his joke, and his breathing nod of acquiescence." One of Hunt's letters shows Robertson and Novello in company in 1825. In an undated letter (probably 1839) Hunt wrote to Ollier, urging him to come to the new play (no doubt referring to his own), where he would see Novello, Charles Clarke, and Robertson. A final mention comes in a letter Hunt wrote to his daughter Jacintha from his Kensington residence on 21 September 1850: "I have just had an invitation from my old friend Henry Robertson to go and visit him at Chertsey [Surrey], but I cannot yet do it." Though ill at the time, Hunt outlived his friend, for in the posthumous edition of the *Autobiography* he stated that all of the "Elders" were now dead.[69]

Barnes introduced some King's Theatre criticism into the "Theatrical Examiner," but Robertson's "Opera Letter" continued to appear, though far less frequently, until January, 1815. (He returned once again to review a Rossini opera for the "Theatrical Examiner" in 1820.) From 1815 on, first Hazlitt and then Hunt wrote Italian-opera criticism for that column, along with reviews of the English stage. The opera reviews were usually accompanied by critiques of the ballets that interspersed or followed operas produced at the King's Theatre.

The appearance of regular and serious Italian-opera reviews in a weekly—to say nothing of the superb criticism found in the *Examiner*—is in itself remarkable; and the unexpectedness no doubt accounts for the fact that Dennis Arundell's *The Critic at the Opera,* the best available survey of the subject, overlooks this source. Except to illustrate their perfunctory nature, Arundell includes no quotable criticism from the dailies earlier than a few notices of the Mozart London premières of 1811 and 1812. Comparisons of these and later samplings demonstrate the clear superiority of the *Examiner* criticisms. Although some of the middle classes were beginning to find their way into the King's Theatre, editors of the dailies continued to regard Italian opera, along with concerts, generally as primarily of interest to the upper classes and therefore newsworthy only as a social function. Max Graf provides the following sample from the *Morning Advertiser* for 12 March 1792 as typical: "Salomon gave his fourth concert in which Haydn shone with more than his usual lustre. The new Concertante [for violin, cello, oboe, and bassoon] was performed for the first time with admirable effect. The new overture [Symphony in B-flat major] is one of the grandest compositions we ever heard, and it was loudly applauded: the first and last movements were encored. It was 12 o'clock before the concert was over."[70] None of the early-nineteenth-century journals, according to Fuller-Maitland (*English Music,* p. 31), provided a systematic record of the concerts, and even the advertisements were a poor guide.[71]

Leigh Hunt's opera criticism, no production of a journalistic hack for the casual curiosity of *Examiner* readers, was an integral part of a bold and sweeping challenge to the cultural lethargy of Regency England. That challenge was sustained with the help of competent friends, whose support Hunt won largely through his own dedication to the principle of independent criticism. It could not be corrupted by special interests, undermined by the administration, or vitiated by vicissitude.

Illness, persecution, and money problems continued to plague
the Hunts following their release from jail. Leigh suffered from
recurring illness: hypochondria or not, it was debilitating and
seriously impaired his functioning as opera critic at various intervals, especially during the periods 1815–1816 and 1819–1821.
In 1815, overburdened with debt on their release from jail, the
Hunts suffered an added strain when the government that year
raised taxes on newspapers from 3½ d. to 4 d.—half the price of
the *Examiner*. Even opening the last of its eight pages to adver-
tisers could not offset a gradual decline in circulation, which by
1821 reached a level only slightly higher than that at the end of
1808.[72] Moreover, Evangelical and government interests combined in repeated attempts to make the Sunday press illegal.
(The *Examiner* even survived the inept editorship of John's son,
Henry Leigh Hunt, into whose hands it was for a time entrusted.
In 1830 John sold his interests in the newspaper, which continued under various proprietorships until 1881.)

Public opinion was even more restrictive after Waterloo, when
conservative elements regained their prestige throughout Europe
and tried to crush the liberals. "Middle class Radicalism became
quiescent and dispirited; and the *Examiner* was too polished, too
intellectual, and too *dear,* to command the support of the
masses."[73] Bourne observed that the Hunts "found it no easy matter to stand out against the public opinion—the opinion, that is,
of those who could afford to pay the high price the heavy duty
stamp rendered it necessary to charge" (*Newspapers,* I, 370). In
letters to Shelley in mid 1821 Hunt reflected his pessimism. Having resumed his journalism again after a lapse of months "on account of my brother's anxiety for the *Examiner*," he stated that
he had "brought back some *hundreds* of our readers" and ought
to remain "on the spot." "If the paper were going on swimming-
ly," he remarked with unusual cynicism, "the very reputation of
doing so would have too good an effect even upon our 'liberal'
readers—I mean those who would not wait till I was well enough
to amuse them again." Noting that politics different from theirs
was "triumphing all over Europe," he asserted that the trial of
Richard Carlile (whom the *Examiner* had supported—17 and 24

October 1819) had "injured" the paper.[74] "Ours is almost the only journal that is not either dotard or hypocrite on such matters" (*Correspondence*, I, 163–68).

The challenge could be blunted, not quashed. Yet much of its effectiveness was lost as the *Examiner's* early successes became swallowed up in the ground swell of moral and political conservatism. The English playgoing public did not heed Hunt's rhetoric; playwrights and productions were to get worse before they would get better; theatre managers became increasingly committed to the vagaries of public taste; and an English "renaissance" in music appeared at least as remote in 1821 as in 1808. Even the fitful artistic accomplishments at the King's Theatre could not be commercially justified for want of sustained popular support.

In his early opera criticism Hunt occasionally made exaggerated claims of a change in public taste, which he ascribed to the *Examiner*, but such assertions soon gave way to realistic appraisals. In the Prospectus (1810) for the *Reflector* (I, vi) he informed his readers: "The better part of the town have acquired sense enough to despise these things [frivolous theatrical amusements], critically speaking, but if they still continue to be amused by them, they will only be despised in their turn." In the *Examiner* he once observed that only a revolution in the education of the aristocracy would reform its taste in Italian opera; in the *Reflector* (I, 233) he implied that nothing less would do for the middle classes, in which the spread of learning actually contributed to the decline of the stage:

An age, under these circumstances, rather enjoys literature than cultivates it; a taste for books becomes a common part of education; and the consequence is, that while real genius is repressed by it's own fastidiousness, or seeks for the likeness of originality in eccentricity or over brilliancy, mediocrity, less delicate and less ambitious, comes forward with the sole intention to amuse, imposes upon the multitude who have just become critics enough to mistake it, and like a buffoon at court, is endured for a long time by the better sort, who suffer themselves to be amused by what they ought to despise.

But he wasted little energy fulminating against the philistines. Convinced of the ultimate progress of taste and the arts, he gave his rhetoric no pause, though he shifted its emphasis, in acknowledging the public's recalcitrance.

Yet Hunt's *Examiner* criticism had an undeniable effect on some of his contemporaries. If he irritated and provoked playwrights, managers, actors, and the writers for conservative periodicals, he won the praise of others for his critical acumen (Landré, II, 114 ff.). Benjamin Robert Haydon (1786–1846), whose disenchantment with Hunt had recently begun, wrote in his diary on 25 October 1816 that Hunt had already "raised the rank of newspapers" by his example, citing his independence, courage, and disinterestedness and the truth, acuteness, and taste of his dramatic criticism; he had also given "a literary feeling to the weekly ones more especially."[75] In an 1823 review of the periodical press, Hazlitt called the *Examiner* "the ablest and most respectable" of the weeklies. Later historians of journalism have agreed on the leadership exemplified by the *Examiner*. Thus Bourne says, "As a mere literary production it at once took rank above all the other weekly periodicals, and contained such careful and scholarly writing as only appeared occasionally . . . in the best of the daily papers" (I, 338). T. H. S. Escott finds the *Examiner* not only the forerunner but the pattern of high-class weeklies.[76]

Hunt himself was equivocal regarding his influence over contemporary journalistic criticism. After giving up his early notion that a conscientious British press might revolutionize public taste, he vacillated between assertions that criticism in periodicals had improved (sometimes claiming as credit the example set by the *Examiner)* on the one hand, and continuing complaints, on the other, of their lack of critical independence. These views are to be found in his opera criticism as well as in his prefaces. Regarding theatrical criticism he stated in the Prospectus to the *Reflector* (I, vi–vii): "Magazines, generally speaking, have always been the unambitious and unthinking followers of the Daily Papers . . . . It is true, the Newspapers themselves at last begin to be ashamed of praising writers, who have become bye-words for nonsense, and they dismiss the subject, if not with their former panegyrics, with a flippant indulgence half-ashamed of itself." In the Prospectus to the *Plain Dealer* (22 January 1832) he was more assured: "As there really have been, and are instances of independence in stage criticism, the reader may believe us when we tell him, that we mean to be one of them." Judging from his scattered comments and the occasional appearance of serious Italian-opera criticism in the dailies in 1811 and after, it seems likely that criticism in periodicals did improve. But until these sources are scrutinized, such changes and Hunt's possible relation to them remain largely conjectural.

The *Examiner* music criticism probably had no direct effect on the monthly or quarterly reviews, though some good ones appeared after 1816. According to Graf (*Composer and Critic,* p. 165) the *Quarterly Musical Magazine and Review* (1818–1828), edited by Richard Mackenzie Bacon (1775–1844), was the first English journal to achieve a position of authority. Bacon, who according to Fuller-Maitland (*English Music,* p. 32) displayed "a remarkable critical faculty," wrote in the first number (p. 4) that occasional articles in the *Chronicle,* the *Times,* and the *Literary Gazette* (founded in 1817 by William Jerdan) were exceptions to the rule, but that generally they were too "vague and loose." Again, somehow, the *Examiner* was overlooked. For the judgments expressed in the *Quarterly Musical* correspond surprisingly well with Hunt's, as will be seen. But the reviews for 1818–1820 nowhere match the critical insights or incisive style to be found in the *Examiner,* and on occasion they display the grossest triteness. The *British Stage* (1817–1819), edited by Thomas Kenrick, though rather pedestrian, often contained sound critical evaluations of performances of both English and Italian opera. The appearance a few years later of several important musical publications testifies to a growing popular interest in music.[77] But they belong to another period.

Hunt As Opera Critic

These musical and journalistic developments in Hunt suggest something of his character as an opera critic. In attempting here

a fuller rendering of his attributes (many details will of course
be explored in the following chapters), we need first to consider
certain misleading opinions about Hunt that have a direct bearing on his stance as a critic.

Charges of excessive severity brought against him during the
Examiner years and earlier, principally by manager-playwrights,
are understandably exaggerated. But later critics have perpetu-
ated the charge. Thus William Archer, an early editor and critic
of Hunt, found him "a trifle inhuman in the persistence and
virulence of his attacks" on the playwrights Dibdin, Cherry, and
Cobb. Towards Thomas Dibdin especially, Archer found Hunt
guilty of "sheer truculence."[78] Even Landré (II, 104, 116) remarks on Hunt's "pompous" manner in the *News* and the "in-
transigence" of his early criticism, citing as authority the *Autobiography* (pp. 155–56): "Good God! To think of the grand
opinion I had of myself in those days . . . ." But Hunt is often
not the best witness in his own behalf (see Blunden, *Leigh Hunt,*
p. 238).

Now brashness is a quality requisite to one who could hope to
challenge the mediocrity of Regency taste: a mordant wit is an
inevitable concomitant. Yet even in Hunt's more trenchant reviews, personal attacks are extremely rare, and in these instances
the obvious target is not the man but the institution he represents.[79] Hunt reinforced this view by the apologias—sometimes
but not always naming individuals—that he occasionally introduced in his *News* and *Examiner* criticism. No doubt he was
sometimes harsh towards playwrights, but bad opera vehicles,
then as later, were the real target, as he tooks pains to make clear.

Other critics have been prompted to emphasize the dilettante
in Hunt (always with the pejorative meaning)—a view that is
often associated with his supposed cavalier attitude towards
"facts."[80] Thornton himself has been called upon to testify
against his father:

He had no aptitude for material science, and always retained a
very precarious grasp of mere dry facts; which, indeed, in proportion
as they tended to the material or the hard, he almost disliked:

the result was, that he viewed all things as in a mirror, and chiefly as they were reflected in books or illuminated by literary commentary.

It is a necessary consequence of such a habit of mind that he often failed to see realities directly as they were . . . . ["Introduction," p. ix]

But Thornton, observing his father with the eyes of a mid-Victorian realist, had Leigh's money problems and other practical considerations in mind. With respect to Leigh's literary world, Thornton complained of his overscrupulous work: "Seldom have writers so conscientiously verified all their statements of fact," he wrote in the "Introduction" (p. xv); and in "Man of Letters" (pp. 88–89) he emphasized Leigh's "hair-splitting anxiety to be precise."

Although the principle of separation of function has not proved itself an unmixed blessing to society, an age bastioned by specialization looks with amused condescension on the dilettante. Hunt was, of course, a dilettante, but only in the sense that he derived pleasure from a variety of cultural interests. Those pleasures, never solipsistic, merely furthered his zeal for reform. According to Woodring, in his introduction to the *Political Essays* (pp. 40–41), Hunt "went far beyond any of the major Romantic poets in welcoming the Utilitarianism of Jeremy Bentham," though, unlike Bentham, he regarded "poetry, music, the plastic arts, and a rural outing as ends, not means." No less was he a "popularizer" in the sense that he was sincerely convinced of the necessity of forming the taste of the public. An "infusion of literary taste into all things whatsoever" could not be attempted without incurring dangers. Yet Hunt's bold probings along the cultural front were no cheap exploitations, nor was he a mere proselytizer of the arts, according to Landré: "Literature, music, and the fine arts offered their treasures, whose beauty, value, and interest he well knew how to interpret and explain; his commentaries solicited the sympathy of others for the masterpieces that he loved and understood" (I, 102; II, 449; author's translation). Nonsystematic in mode, his criticism is nevertheless suffused with thought. For he deeply distrusted an analytical or systematic approach towards criticism. Indeed, he saw a threat to thought itself in rigidly doctrinaire systems inherited from a "mechanical" century.

From that century, however, Hunt derived ideas and attitudes that are apparent in his comments on the arts in general and on music in particular. In asserting these views he reveals himself most clearly as a man of letters, sincerely dedicated to the fine arts, to be sure, but concerned lest the superiority of poetry be eroded by them. Moreover, he often placed painting before music, though it is undoubtedly true, in the long view, that of all the arts music interested him most, as Landré claims (II, 136). He establishes his hierarchy in two passages from *Critical Essays.* In the first (p. 55) he wrote: "I have always thought it an argument for the superiority of poetry over the other polite arts, that it is more productive of polite manners than either painting or music. There is not a poet whose life is recorded by Dr. Johnson, nor indeed any great poet, with whose private history we are acquainted, who did not bear the character of a gentleman* [in a footnote Hunt cites Addison's *Spectator,* No. 314]; we cannot say this of painters, and certainly not of musicians." Later Hunt would indeed take exception to the characters of some of those poets—Swift and Pope particularly—just as he would come to regard Addison as too much the gentleman and prefer, rather, "open-hearted" Steele. In addition to this traditional view, which in part reflects the low social scale generally occupied by musicians during the eighteenth century, Hunt's attitude is also related to the loose reputation of performers, a problem with which he was concerned in his criticism of English opera.

In the second passage from *Critical Essays* (pp. 51-53), speaking of imagination as "the great test of genius" (elsewhere he calls that test "invention"), since "that which is done by imagination is more difficult than that which is performed by discernment or experience," he concludes:

Thus a great painter is a finer genius than a great musician, because he displays more imagination and consequently more of the *poetical*; Handel, who rises to the sublime in music, is a more *poetical*

genius than Reeve [see below, chapter three], who deals in the
quirks and jollities of the humourous ballad; and the lowest
musician is a more *poetical* genius than the maker of a musical
instrument, because . . . the latter is a mere manufacturer.

To be sure, Hunt is concerned about the decline of English
music since the time of Handel. But his literary bias is self-
evident. He equates poetry with the imagination, which is the
most difficult mode to effect; and he finds the other arts are
comparable only to the extent that they share what poetry has
achieved! Here, no doubt, he is thinking of "poetry" as an imaginative ideal, in the same sense that Coleridge, in his 1811 lectures, was to include music and painting under "the great genius
of poetry." But, aside from the patent absurdity of the comparisons, Hunt's implication that music is an "easy" art had its ante-
cedents among eighteenth-century writers. Oliver Goldsmith, for
example, to whom the young journalist was attracted, had written in the dedication of the *Traveller* (1764): "Poetry makes a
principal amusement among unpolished nations; but in a country verging on the extremes of refinement, Painting and Music
come in for a share. As these offer the feeble mind a less laborious entertainment, they at first rival Poetry, and at length supplant her."

Hunt occasionally shifted his emphasis somewhat on the relative merits of the "sisters" in his hierarchy. (The term "sisters"
representing the arts he of course derived from the eighteenth
century.) There is no doubt that he showed an increase in respect for composers upon further acquaintance with Mozart's
operas. Eventually, music would achieve an uneasy par with
poetry, but as late as "Musical Evenings" he could write, con-
descendingly enough, that "Poetry speaking of Music, is like one
generous sister talking of the merits of another"; painting took
second place, and music came in for show: "Thought itself is not
necessary to her."[81]

Among the older writers, Charles Burney probably exerted the
strongest influence on Hunt, who shows evidence of having read
carefully not only the *History of Music* but Burney's other works
as well, which he cites in his criticism and elsewhere (see *Cor-*

respondence, II, 279). Hunt seems to have found in Burney not only a mine of musical knowledge but also a broadly inquiring spirit solidly grounded on middle-class interests not unlike his own.

As a man of letters, Hunt "pretend[ed] to judge music only from the feeling of a sister art." In fact, despite his personal acquaintance with musicians, he was generally distrustful of the profession, at least as it existed in his time. In a *Tatler* article (5 September 1831) he expressed contempt for musicians who were in the profession because of "trade, accident, necessity, vanity, ignorance, and presumption," having in mind, apparently, the performing musicians and hack composers. But he was no less distrustful of the "professors"—music teachers and writers of technical articles on music for the magazines. He even criticized his friend Holmes in a review of his *A Ramble among the Musicians of Germany* (London, 1828). Noting that the subject had not been handled "these fifty years" (a reference to Burney's *The Present State of Music in Germany* published in 1773), Hunt wrote: "[Holmes] has been accused of being too learned in his musical taste, and redolent of the dust of cathedrals. We apprehend something of the kind ourselves, and yet hardly know why; except that musical professors, whatever they may feel, seem to think themselves bound to be supra-learned, when they come to criticise" (*Companion* [21 May 1828], pp. 277–84).

Hunt's demurrer rests on two principles that he regarded as essential to valid music criticism: it must be responsive to sense impressions ("whatever they may feel" denies this premise), and it must avoid the pedantry of the specialist—a narrowness of spirit that tends to sever the critic from his own valid sense responses or to impede their communication to the public. "There is no such person in English literature," Hunt continued, "as a good musical critic; and if he [Holmes] has any ambition to set the example of one, we think he may do it, and write books which poets and painters will be glad to read, as well as musicians; which is the only proper way; for the business in these things is to extend enjoyment, and show the links of art and nature one with another, in as universal a spirit as possible." Some years later, in welcoming the first number of the *Musical Magazine,* which was "copious, various, amusing, liberal, and cheap" and which contained "accurate and impartial criticism," Hunt warned that too many such endeavors had failed, having been initiated by those who were unsuccessful in their own profession. He attributed the failures to their appeal to a clique among music professors rather than to the public, and he cited the need for a publication that could keep the interests of the art in view, in which public and professors alike are included.[82]

The ability to share one's enjoyment was, for Hunt, an essential attribute in the music critic, far outweighing a technical understanding of the medium.[83] Likely he held such an understanding to be desirable, if not in fact essential, for one who lays claim to the office. (He certainly regarded a fondness for music as highly desirable in the critic of literature, observing, anent Dr. Johnson, that "a writer, who by his own confession was insensible to Painting and Music, has at least very suspicious claims to become a critic" [29 March 1812].) But Hunt himself, aside from his philosophical misgivings about the "professional," was temperamentally undisposed to achieving a disciplined mastery over any craft save writing. He never took the pains to familiarize himself with the technical aspects of any of the fine arts (Landré, II, 133). No doubt he lost something thereby. If nothing else, it would have served as a corrective for the literary bias in his own music criticism. Some passages exhibit insecurity, misguided or clumsy explanations, and just plain ignorance resulting from a lack of training in music. Such passages are rare, however, for he seldom departed from those sensuous and intuitive resources that were the touchstone of his critical response.

On the one hand, Hunt's lack of technical knowledge of music liberated his criticism from the narrow and jejune approach characteristic of articles occasionally written by "Professors" for general periodicals. On the other, because of his broad interests he was able to illuminate his reviews with a rich infusion of literary and cultural ideas.[84] Moreover, Hunt's catholicity of taste freed him from bias against the aristocracy in his Italian-opera criticism.[85] "Angry young bourgeois" though he was, he did not per-

mit the politics of sentiment that set him strongly against aristocratic interests in the "Examiner" columns to seep into his King's
Theatre reviews. He seldom permitted his sensory responses to
become seriously blunted or distorted by philosophical or social
predispositions; thus, he was able not only to avoid prevailing
cant attitudes towards opera but also freely to use his imaginative
resources in bodying forth those perceptions.

Hunt's esthetics was therefore sense-oriented without being
sense-bound. A strong vein of sentiment that was his natural
inheritance, closely linked to the appeal of the senses, is also apparent in his criticism. Yet he recognized the limitations of
sentimentality as a mode of response. This is perhaps nowhere
better expressed than in his reference to the songs of his childhood—songs at which we may smile today, as Landré has observed. Amused by the Strephons and Delias (stereotyped lovers)
that abounded in them, Hunt admitted that "the association of
early ideas with that kind of commonplace, has given me more
than a toleration for it." But, he continued,

I think of the many heartfelt smiles that must have welcomed love
letters and verses containing that sophisticate imagery, and of the
no less genuine tears that were shed over the documents when
faded; and criticism is swallowed up in those human drops. . . .
The feeling was true, though the expression was sophisticate and a
fashion; and they who cannot see the feeling for the mode, do the
very thing which they think they scorn; that is, sacrifice the greater
consideration for the less. [*Autobiography,* pp. 41-42]

In the *Examiner* years, at any rate, precious little of Hunt's criticism was swallowed up in tears. Yet his remarks of 1828 suggest
a duality revealed in that criticism: a distaste for the musical
commonplaces of the age of sentiment and an unusual attraction
for the feelings communicated in its songs.

For Hunt also exhibited strong elements of rationalism that
had their roots in Neoclassic thought. This dualism in his nature
found expression in his writings as well as in his moral development (Landré, I, 43). In his opera criticism sometimes one tone
predominates, sometimes the other. At his critical best, both ele-

ments work well together; the carefully modulated tension between thought and feeling generates a compelling dynamic energy in countless passages. At his critical worst, these elements become separated or work incongruously. At such moments, fortunately rare, Hunt the sentimentalist appears constrained to demonstrate the power of feelings not genuinely apprehended, and a certain mawkishness of tone becomes evident. Or Hunt the rationalist, absorbed by some dominating abstraction, attempts a sustained argumentation that is often no more than a series of rationalizations. In either case, he often finds a corrective in a renewed appeal to direct sense perceptions.

Usually, however, Hunt was quite capable of dealing successfully with general ideas not directly related to sense perceptions. His penetrating intelligence, his broad scholarly interests, and his concern for preserving and cultivating traditional values, all furnish a sustaining power against the caprice of merely sense-responsive critiques. As he threads his arguments through the years, Hunt's ideas, despite a lack of system, present a clear continuum to the student of his opera criticism. For he brought to that criticism a coherence of outlook that stands up remarkably well against the vagaries of time and circumstance.

Nor did he seek to avoid difficulties and conflicts in his criticism, which is perhaps most vital when it reveals the critic wrestling with new musical experiences. When these run counter to his basic impulses and conditioned responses, he attempts to accommodate instinct to experience. For his "self-doubts" and pragmatic commitment exerted a powerful influence that challenged tradition or habitual predispositions. Such conflicts often ensue in a kind of interior debate, and since Hunt seldom takes refuge in an entrenched dogmatic position, they take on a dramatic life of their own, even when they extend intermittently over a period of years, as they sometimes did where basic issues were involved. On certain issues, to be sure, his ambivalence is never fully resolved, and he reaches a critical impasse. More often, his capacity to reexamine enables him to accept new experiences, and he moves toward sounder and more comprehensive judgments.

These judgments and issues are fully discussed in the succeeding chapters and need not detain us here. But in concluding this
preview of Hunt as opera critic, some general characteristics of
his *Examiner* reviews are worth noting.

A disproportionate amount of attention was bestowed on the
performers, especially in reviews of the English musical stage, for
reasons already discussed. Hunt was initially drawn to the theatre
by the "mimetic" superiority of the performer. The extraordinary critical attention he directed to the art of the opera singer
demonstrates the perennial appeal it held for him. There were
also many critiques on revivals of old favorites, familiar enough
to readers of the *Examiner,* in which the main interest centered
on how some new performer measured up in this role or that.

It follows that Hunt would give scant treatment to English
opera vehicles. Yet he seldom failed to comment on their many
inadequacies or occasional virtues. Avoiding the dull plot sum-
maries usually recorded faithfully by the best reviewers in other
periodicals, he gave just enough to illustrate their inanities.
When, on occasion, he discussed the better works that were revived, he usually pointed out the ways in which managers, playwrights, composers, or performers had mangled the original in
the revived version. His primary concern remained in the work
as presented, with an eye, of course, to its effect on public taste.
Granting his journalistic premise, he shows himself capable of
conventional analysis, on occasion, either to praise or to blame a
work. But his usual critical manner deliberately eschews analysis; it rests on a series of loosely related perceptions, imaginatively
developed, that create a dominant effect of salient details of the
work or of the creative or re-creative artist. His method is almost
clinically precise; the impression he captures has a vitality and a
strength that lie beyond the art of analysis. He does not always
succeed, of course. And there are works—Mozart's operas especially—to which we might wish he had given more attention. As
it is, however, he devoted more space than was customary to
criticism of these operas, and his discussion of them is far more
penetrating than that of his contemporaries.

Often Hunt introduced into his reviews the sights and sounds

of the occasion: the size of the rebuilt theatres, the effect of new
gas lighting, the taste (or lack of it) shown by new interior or
exterior decorations, various reactions on the part of the audiences, and the like, which, apart from their historical value to us,
helped bring to life for his readers the theatre-going experience
itself. Sometimes he became fully absorbed in the pursuit of an
idea, though seldom at the critical expense of the occasion that
gave rise to it. These essay-type expositions varied considerably
in tone and style, depending on the nature of the material. In
fact, Hunt avoided any set formula: he was guided by the nature
of each event and made the most of the predominant ideas they
generated. This continually shifting pattern of tone and content
produced a variety in his "Theatrical Examiners" that must have
proved gratifying fare for his weekly readers. In general, however, his reviews of new operas began with commentary on the
vehicle and the playwright, then moved to a discussion of the
songs or arias and the composer, and concluded with a critique
on the performers. They usually displayed a blend of Hunt's
responses to the occasion and an exposition of aptly relevant
ideas; the commentary served to focus on and illuminate the
central events.

To these reviews Hunt brought a quality that his son Thornton considered outstanding in the *Examiner* and its most influential contribution to English journalism—"literary finish."[86]
Drawing largely on eighteenth-century sources, Hunt created a
"voice" that had a character of its own—as unmistakable in all
the registers of its astonishing range as the indicator symbol itself. For his writing illustrates a thorough command of tone and
style, which he perfectly accommodates to his shifts in subject.
Commenting on such adventitious matters as theatre sights and
sounds, he employs an easy, relaxed manner, loose sentence structure, and diction that tends toward the colloquial but never becomes chatty. Excoriating operatic hack work, he shifts to a terse,
taut structure, a sharply incisive idiom, and a tone that often
burns with sarcasm or irony though it never becomes strident or
vituperative. Discussing the particularities of dramatic effects, he

adopts a graceful but carefully controlled medium that is asser-
tive and self-assured without being dogmatic or capricious. He
makes frequent and skillful use of analogy, employing simple
images that carry a strong visual appeal for evoking exact shades
of meaning. In more expository passages he establishes a dominant mood through rich clusters of associations drawn from all
the arts.

In general, his prose is punctuated by wit, clarity, and brilliance. His writing has finish, but not polish. He usually writes
long sentences—sometimes very long, though often broken by
semicolons—which tend to suggest formality; yet he studiously
avoids balanced periods. Indeed, his tone is paradoxical: it
creates a certain distance and objectivity while at the same time
conveying a distinct undercurrent of informality. Too carefully
modulated to be conversational, his prose often carries a colloquial flavor. Moreover, he always keeps his readers in view.
Sometimes he cultivates a deliberate confidentiality in his manner, though he is never condescending. But the reader appeal is
present even in passages charging the public with indifference to
the arts.

Above all, Hunt evokes the quality of freshness, liveliness, and
spontaniety. He tells us that prose composition took a great deal
out of him, leaving him exhausted, and that "never, after I had
taken critical pen in hand, did I pass the thoroughly delightful
evenings at the playhouse which I had done when I went only to
laugh or be moved" (*Autobiography*, pp. 136, 419–20). But he
was master of the art that conceals art. In reading his criticism
it is difficult to disagree with Blunden's impression that "it was
his faculty to be entertained; it is not a common faculty; he
seemed to be perennially going to his first play, and accordingly
his comments have a genial intentness and glittering gratitude in
them which most regular critics all too quickly exchange perforce
for a mechanical plus and minus system" (*"Examiner" Examined*,
p. 84).

Hunt brought to the *Examiner* a natural musical aptitude, a
conviviality wedded to utilitarian ideals, a broad cultural commitment, and a journalistic competence that gave him excep-

tional qualifications for the role of opera critic. His natural
attraction to the medium is suggested in "A few thoughts on
Opera"—one of his last contributions to the *News* (29 November
1807)—in which he declared that opera had the merit of combining the resources of music, painting, and poetry at the same time
and of addressing itself at once to the ear, the eye, and the imagination. If such merits were seldom to be realized on the English
musical stage during a period when the muses had all but for-
saken it, he unstintingly dedicated his critical energies to its
artistic regeneration.

3

Criticism of the English Musical Stage

"Without the fighting spirit, musical criticism would be like a smiling face without teeth."—Max Graf

LEIGH HUNT'S criticism of the English musical stage during the *Examiner* years presents a study in conflicts. Hunt loved song; yet he found good music of past generations mangled in the new productions and most contemporary composers contented with theatrical hack work. He relished good drama; yet he witnessed a gradual decline in dramatic standards that was furthered by poor opera "vehicles"—mere excuses for musical diversions. He enjoyed fine singing and acting; yet all too often he was rewarded with crude stage mannerisms and specious appeals to the gallery.

Dramas

Accordingly, much of his criticism constitutes an indictment of contemporary musical drama, that is to say, "English operas." Hunt was not generally concerned by the fact that such works were in no way genuinely operatic. In a few late reviews, to be sure, he stressed the importance of musical coherence of a more clearly operatic nature in such works. But for the most part he accepted them for what they were—plays with songs. His main objection to these works rested on the insubstantial nature of their dramatic material.

"To explore the plots of modern Operas is to dissect the

73

shadow of a post," Hunt stated early in his criticism (27 March 1808). In lieu of plays of substance, he was confronted by stock characters and trite situations. In Andrew Cherry's*[1] operatic farce *In and Out of Tune* Hunt found particularly objectionable the author's use of "stage" Negroes in a "most disgusting" manner. "Their whole speech and humour consists of the word Massa" (6 March 1808). He regarded the melodrama *The Slave* by Thomas Morton* as a potpourri "compounded out of Pizarro, Oroonoko, and Stedman's *Travels in Surinam*; and we are reminded also of Mr. [George] Colman's *Africans* [1808], and other productions relative to negroes and cockneys" (17 November 1816).[2] Stock characters ran rampant in *The Siege of St. Quintin,* a melodrama by Theodore Hook.* Worse than the historical inaccuracies of the plot was the absurdity of the dialogue. Hook's typical blundering Irishman "talks of Welshmen, Scotchmen, Irishmen, and *all other* Englishmen:—that is a specimen of *his* manner. The sentimental gentlemen tell us that freemen cannot be conquered, that ambition is a horrid vice, and that the *patriot breast* which, &c. &c. This is a specimen of *theirs.* It was like a meeting with all your old acquaintances:—How d'ye do, my boy of the bulls?—How are you, the-man-who?—Ha, Patriot Breast, are you there?" (13 November 1808).

Hunt was disgusted by the specious stage patriotism common throughout the war years. But he noted with equal distaste the vulgar manipulation of "low" characters in operatic vehicles. Of Henry Bate's* comic opera *Travellers in Switzerland*[3] he wrote: "This unavoidable propensity of the author to low characters sufficiently proves that he cannot be humourous without being vulgar: if a gentleman is attempted, he is invariably lowered to the footman standard: he cannot be lively without being pert; he cannot attempt to shew his knowledge without inevitably proving his ignorance" (27 March 1808). Hunt held no brief against "low" characters as such.[4] But he objected to the exploitation *ad nauseam* of such types in the farcical operas.

Of another Bate revival, *The Woodman,* Hunt complained that the work, "like many other pastoral operas, has a good sort of farmer in it, and a bad sort of country squire, a singing girl or two, some pretty scenery, and a very insipid lover. . . . It is just such a piece, perhaps, as Mr. Cherry would write in a happy moment of inspiration; and if this is not saying much for Mr. Bate Dudley, it is saying a good deal for Mr. Cherry" (7 February 1808). Fond of exploiting inverted hierarchies for satirical emphasis, Hunt usually assigned last place among playwrights to Andrew Cherry or James Cobb, both of whom he had earlier criticized in the *News*.

To insipidity and triteness in recent and contemporary English opera he added the charge of plagiarism. For this practice he found the influence of Isaac Bickerstaffe* much to blame. At a revival of Bickerstaffe's comic opera *Lionel and Clarissa* (1768) he wrote:

Perhaps there never was an author who stole more, or who so invariably confined his thefts to paltry little moveables, neither valuable nor worthless. His songs, which have a clear and gentle smack of the true lyric about them, are little better than centos from different authors; his characters are all old, but issue from his hands neatly clothed, and divested of their least natural peculiarities; and with regard to the whole turn of his pieces, a better idea cannot be given of his tendency to plagiarism than a complaint, which was common with him,—of his contemporaries having *anticipated* him. [8 December 1816]

Claiming a Goldoni comedy as the source for the play, Hunt concludes:[5]

Yet notwithstanding this, and notwithstanding the evidently traceable genealogy of all the characters, he is pleasant enough to go on saying, with an air as if he were taking a pinch of snuff, that he was the prouder of this favourable opinion of the town, "because, to the best of his knowledge, he had not borrowed an expression, a sentiment, or a character, from any dramatic writer extant." Here is all the nice detail of a finished falsehood.

When contemporaries such as Theodore Hook followed Bickerstaffe's example and borrowed from *him,* among others, the felony was compounded. In reviewing Hook's comic opera *Safe and Sound,* Hunt wrote: "The songs are taken by whole lines from Bickerstaff [sic] and others, who borrowed them in the same way from their predecessors; and the jests may be traced by their family faces up to the great Patriarch of modern wit, Joe Miller,[6] for there is as true a pedigree in the hacks of our dramatists as there is in the palfreys of Arabia. . . . Such, Reader, is the English Opera, formerly so much admired in the writings of Gay, Addison, and Sheridan!" (8 September 1809). It is true, of course, that "borrowings" of all kinds were almost ubiquitously indulged while England remained without sufficient copyright protection. Whether or not Hunt's fairly reliable memory holds in this instance, he pressed his attacks on this practice at every opportunity. The idea of "originality" has perhaps been too strictly identified with the Romantic movement, and yet the impulse that eventually led to respect for the imagination of the artist as a primary principle of creativity was shared by many Romantics and no doubt accounts for Hunt's repeated condemnation of artistic fabrications supplied with material from another.

Hunt particularly resented the fact that playwrights used musical and other diversions as so many tricks to conceal their inadequacies as dramatists. They "have now a habit of concealing themselves as much as possible in the very midst of their productions. They see that the public are sick of their puns and their palsied dialogue, which dances and nods about with its own weakness instead of lively intelligence, and therefore they clothe and constrict themselves with all kinds of dresses and decorations; musicians and dancers crowd round them, and the principal of the thing is concealed within the shew" (13 November 1808). But the public was not so sick of these works as Hunt suggests. The following season he remarked with some exasperation: "For pity's sake, let us hear no more of the excuses about vehicles for music: if the dramatists can make nothing but vehicles for music, why were they not bound apprentices at once to a musical carmaker?" (8 September 1809).[7]

The element of greatest musical importance in such vehicles was of course song. But the lyrics were usually disappointing. Hunt was particularly severe with William Reeve,* who often supplied the lyrics as well as the music for his numerous productions. In his operatic farce *The Fortune Teller,*

the songs were just fit to be read in that hurried undulation of drawl
and thrust at every rhyme, with which little boys are wont to repeat
their psalter. . . . For the sake of the author and my readers, I will
not quote any of the poetry. Some sick people have an aukward
knack of making you taste their physic, just to see how nauseous it is;
but though I am sick enough of the farce, I will not insist upon
exercising this abominable privilege. [2 October 1808]

More medicinal material he found in Samuel Arnold's* *Up
All Night.* "The present piece," he stated, "is a composition of
quack medicines from beginning to end, and after all not so
palatable as the usual doctor's stuff, for there is not a drop of
spirit in it: the songs are made up of the usual changes upon
flower and *bower, heart* and *impart, prove* and *love,* such as leave
the reader in doubt whether the rhymes were written first or
last" (2 July 1809).

Sometimes the very fine lyrics in original works were scrapped
in favor of inferior verses supplied by adaptors. In his review of
Frederic Reynolds's* melodrama *The Renegade,* based on Dryden's tragedy *Don Sebastian,* Hunt exclaimed:

But the songs! the songs!—Mr. Reynolds, in cutting down a fine
tragedy into a three-act melo-drame, must give us some vocal music;
and of all our other poets, Dryden unfortunately happens to have
been remarkable for the strength and beauty of his lyric pieces;
they have not the fancy of Shakspeare, or Beaumont and Fletcher,
nor the complacent courtliness of Waller, nor the idiomatic ease
and familiarity of Prior, but a stateliness and a harmony, a certain
princely condescension of power, peculiar to themselves, and quite
provocative of the musician's march and accompaniment. . . . Now
only think of this well-meaning gentleman, Mr. Reynolds, who, till
the *Examiner* taught him, did not even know how to rhyme, sitting
down to supply one of Dryden's pieces with songs of his own, in
default of having any to his hand![8] [20 December 1812]

Irish lyricism, however, had its charm for Hunt, especially in
its most popular exemplar of the time—Tom Moore.* To be

sure, these charms failed to redeem Moore's comic opera *M.P.,* *or the Blue Stocking,* which Hunt generally condemned. He made no comment on the music (see appendix one), but did find praise for Moore's lyrics (15 September 1811). Though the Irish bard never wrote another work for the stage, Hunt more fully discussed his lyric abilities in a review of the publication of the seventh number of *Irish Melodies.* The airs were less pleasing than those in the earlier numbers; however, the songs were generally fine:

The chief beauties of Mr. Moore's lyric writings consist in their being the result of evident enjoyment, in their fancy, their national character, their exquisite adaptation to the music, and in that mixture of a tendency to pleasure with a sympathy for the sufferings of others, which forms the most attractive part of the amiable. . . . With respect to the adaptation, the words are written with such a strong sense of the musical, that they almost break out into singing of their own accord.[9]

Hunt reviewed the patent theatres almost exclusively during the *Examiner* years, for he strongly supported traditional drama. The dissolution of comedy and tragedy into farce and melodrama had begun long before Hunt became drama critic, as we have seen in chapter one. But he was aware that conditions were rapidly worsening during the early years of the nineteenth century, thanks largely to the burletta and other "mongrel" forms that had developed in the illegitimate theatres and that were becoming increasingly popular in the legitimate ones.

Hunt's outspoken resistance to such changes is evident in his early critical attacks on contemporary English opera. Remarking on "these gaudy delusions called melodramas, which to the disgrace of the British stage are now taking place of the regular drama," Hunt despaired over the prospects for improvement:

Upon the whole, it does not seem that the present state of the drama will last a great while longer. Mr. Reynolds has already dropped from tragedy to comedy, from comedy to afterpiece, from afterpiece to melo-drama, and I know not at what straw he will catch in his next fall. If honest critics should produce better times, I sincerely

advise the whole dramatic corps to march off to Sadler's Wells.
Mr. Reynolds one would willingly keep for a farce or two, but Mr.
Charles Dibdin confines himself to that theatre, and I should be
glad to discover what shadow of superiority Mr. Thomas Dibdin,
Mr. Theodore Hook, or the other dramatists, possess over that
gentleman. It would be the wisest step they ever took in their lives.
Their melo-dramas would there be converted into local and
dramatic proprieties, their ignorance into good sense, their puns,
tricks, and blunders into something eminently facetious; and who
would not admire Mr. Dibdin or Mr. Hook under all these amazing
transformations! [13 November 1808]

Hunt would not banish these trifles from the stage—only from
the legitimate stage, where their influence was more pernicious
to good drama.

Hunt's attitude toward dramatic genres is further exemplified
in his review of Reynolds's *The Exile*. Its source, Sophie Cottin's
Elizabeth, or the Exiles of Siberia,[10] was a "charming novel"
which "in the hands of a man of genius might have formed a
noble play and which Mr. Reynolds himself with his own serious
powers might have rendered an excellent afterpiece, [but which]
he has injured by a mean and farcical underplot in order to
lengthen it out into a melodrama as long as a play" (13 November 1808). Hunt offers no objections to the afterpiece—a brief,
farcical diversion following the serious dramatic business of the
evening. But to lengthen its trivialities and to offer it as the
main attraction of the evening was in his view a gross transgres-
sion of dramatic propriety.

Incidentally, Hunt's allusion to Reynolds's "serious powers" is
no contradiction. In the same review he stated: "Mr. Reynolds
. . . told the public that he knew he wrote bad plays. What the
public may think of this compliment, or how his old friends may
feel at being thus contradicted, I know not, but it is nevertheless
a piece of sound self-knowledge." He once called him a writer
"too good for his task" (25 July 1819); but Reynolds had betrayed his talent, and for that reason perhaps the critic was
especially severe with him.[11]

Hunt doubted the ability of most musical playwrights to con-

struct dramas of substance: "I do not suppose," he wrote, "that
the customary dramatists of opera and pantomime could produce
a better vehicle if they wished it" (10 April 1808). His remarks
were prompted by the appearance of a new piece[12] by Thomas
Dibdin*: "I am really almost ashamed to enter into any serious
criticism upon the new burlesque melo-drama, which is the most
stupid piece of impertinence that has disgraced the English stage
for some years past; but when such a writer as Mr. T. Dibdin
commences dramatic satirist, the critics must naturally be surprised enough to enquire into his pretensions to so unexpected
an office." Hunt continued with a penetrating analysis of Dibdin's lack of comprehension of the heroic, the anti-heroic, and
the burlesque—with a consequent muddling of feelings. And he
concluded his review by returning to the idea that such playwrights and such productions were pretentious interlopers:

When the modern opera writer talks of his little claims and his
little wishes, I by no means believe this modesty of claim and this
humility of wish: I have very good reasons for supposing, that the
authors of these wretched pieces regard themselves not only as
legitimate dramatists, but as ornaments of the British stage, that
they claim the honour of supporting the finest singers, and that with
a blind self-importance they refer us to the perpetual performance
of their operas as a proof of their consummate genius.

Hunt's objections to English operas on the grounds that they
violated traditional dramatic values were largely confined to his
first year of reviewing in the *Examiner*. In view of the continued
decline in the drama (which he himself had anticipated), he no
doubt felt compelled to abandon a critical stance that was being
daily undermined by the circumstances of the theatres. Although
he never relaxed his insistence on the observance of dramatic
propriety, as time went on he seemed more willing to accept and
to evaluate musical productions on their own merits, however
slim. Perhaps as a consequence, he found somewhat more to
praise in English opera during later seasons.

A significant shift is apparent when we turn from Hunt's
castigation of Dibdin in 1808 to remarks about him in 1817 and

1818. In the latter instance Hunt actually preferred Dibdin to the "horror" tragedies popularized by August von Kotzebue in the 1790's and still intermittently revived at Covent Garden:

We think it an instance of bad taste in the public that they prefer tragedy to comedy as they have done of late,—*such* tragedy at all events,—*Fazio, Bertram,* and the gratuitous and nonsensical tortures of *Isabella.*[13] It argues a coarse want of excitement; and we would willingly do our best to get them out of it, as we did to deliver them from the more humane dominations of our old friends Messrs. Dibdin, Reynolds, and Cherry. If this were to be their only charge, we should have done them a disservice. We prefer Tom Dibdin at any time to a mere solemn poacher in books, or *tragifier* of what need not be tragic at all. He has a bit of something real and genial about him, if not in the best taste. [24 May 1818]

After a decade of maudlin melodrama, Hunt is willing to accept the laughter, however empty-headed, of a Dibdin farce as a corrective; and his "dominations," in this context, were not without positive virtues. In a review the previous year of a re-vival of Dibdin's comic opera *The Cabinet* (1802) Hunt amply documented his shift in feelings:

The *Cabinet* of our old friend Tom Dibdin was cut down on this occasion, by permision, into a machine of reasonable dimensions; and whether it was in consequence of this improvement or not we cannot tell, but we certainly enjoyed it more than we have done on much more imposing occasions. . . . Many of the old absurdities remained. . . . But whether it was what we have mentioned, or that Miss [Fanny] Kelly performed the part of Madame Storace, or that the theatre has become pleasanter to us from a long interval of absence and sickness, or that sickness itself has mollified the critical part of us, or that we think less of criticism and the said *us* to boot, or that we are fond of old habits and acquaintances, or that we are become wiser or more willing to be pleased, or that we are really good-tempered fellows ourselves who are tired of appearing the contrary, or that we have lived long enough to value any thing genuine of the pleasant order, however humble it's class,—or lastly (which is most likely) whether it is from several of these causes conjoined, we cannot precisely determine; but we were certainly glad to encounter our old friend Tom again; and with all our remaining zeal in behalf of a better state of drama, could not help being a little sorry that we had ever been under the necessity of treating him so roughly, seeing that he really has some pleasantry and tact of character about him, and appears to be what he is reported, a very kindly sort of fellow. [13 July 1817]

This review is not the unexplainable *volte face* it has been taken for. Years before, he could write: "I have known some persons astonished to hear that the illustrious Mr. Thomas Dibdin could produce a decent ballad, because they have always regarded him as a miserable dramatist" (1 January 1809). Nor has Hunt abandoned his old objections to Dibdin. It is noteworthy, too, that the opera was on this occasion given "reasonable dimensions." Nevertheless, the amelioration of tone speaks for itself. No doubt, personal factors played some part in this change, as Hunt suggests, but the most compelling reason would seem to be the one he places last: In his constant attacks on the English musical stage he had been fighting a losing battle, and he recognized the wisdom of seeking more rewarding grounds for his criticism. Hunt's later reviews show a greater tendency to praise, or, where praise was not possible, to explore broad esthetic problems confronting English operas.

Hunt's remarks on John O'Keefe* parallel those on Dibdin. In *Critical Essays* Hunt had named O'Keefe, Reynolds, Cherry, and Colman,* along with Dibdin, as among the followers of Goldsmith who had subverted British sentimental comedy with farcical or melodramatic distortions; and in the *News* he had severely criticized O'Keefe's *Wild Oats*. Hunt may have had these earlier strictures in mind, for in the passage cited above on Dibdin, he mentions all these playwrights save Colman: "As to O'Keefe, that cordial redeemer of farce, he is worth all the modern tragedy writers put together,—except one,[14] who shews he has got a heart in him" (24 May 1818). Later that year, in a review of a revival of O'Keefe's operatic farce *Rival Soldiers* (1797), Hunt suggests that the aging playwright possessed both virtues and sentiment. The production, he wrote, is a pleasing specimen, in little, of Mr. O'Keefe's dramatic spirit, which units broad humour with amiable morals more than any other writer of the same class. He makes the coarse, selfish, and degrading vices the reverse of tempting, and yet very ludicrous; while there is a constant and happy effort to elevate the social feelings of love and friendship. . . . It is the production of a kind-hearted and chearful man, who believes in the virtues he writes about, and *who realizes them because he believes*—the great secret to be discovered by those, who are always complaining of the vices instead of the follies of mankind. [30 August 1818]

Hunt's assertion of O'Keefe's amiability and belief in the goodness of man, like his reference to Dibdin's "humane dominations," strikes a new note in his criticism. Hunt's sufferings in jail, his recurrent illness, and his oppressive debts certainly took their toll, but they also had a humanizing influence. For the mature man discovered new values in a Godwinian benevolence—values he increasingly emphasized in his later criticism.[15]

Virtues similar to O'Keefe's were noted in a much earlier writer, Allan Ramsay,* whose ballad opera *The Gentle Shepherd* was offered in a truncated version that deprived the public of many of its fine songs; but Hunt seized the occasion to hail the beauties in the original:

With the real *Gentle Shepherd* of Allan Ramsay, we earnestly advise all our poetical readers to become acquainted, if they are not so already. It is a remarkable instance of what can be done by a man of no great genius, but whose portion of genius, such as it was, was on the side of simplicity and nature, and gifted with their lasting good sense. . . . His chief talent . . . lay in a perfect feeling of his own real powers and situation; and thus he avoided every thing affected, and mistaken, and contradictory; and produced a pastoral, superior, in our opinion, and with all our love for the Italians, to the *Aminta* of Tasso. [6 July 1817]

Many years later Hunt went to some pains to defend Ramsay's work, which he perhaps rated too highly.[16] Yet simplicity of diction, directness of sentiment, and a pastoralism not too elevated above the true folk level were qualities Hunt valued highly.

Music

Apart from that aspect of Hunt's criticism dealing with specifically dramatic material, we find many references to the music and the composers of English operas. Such passages, however, are often by their nature inseparable from the dramatic context. In view of his general condemnation of trite opera vehicles, for example, it is no surprise to find Hunt lamenting the deleterious effect of such material on the music for which it was written:

As to the vehicle of music and scenery, I really do not see the right which any dramatist possesses to give a bad vehicle to good music. This is not only a dishonour to the music, but it is as much as to say to the audience, "You do not care for poetry: sound is sufficient for your ears." I am very sure that Messrs. Longman and Broderip would never send home one of their pianos on a brewer's sledge; and why should a dramatist be allowed to jolt and destroy good music by any wretched vehicle he chuses? [10 April 1808]

By "vehicle" Hunt here has in mind the lyrics, which were supplied to existing tunes after the ballad-opera manner. The passage occurs in a review of *Bonifacio*, an "entertainment" by Thomas Dibdin, who was no composer. Hunt does not identify the "good music"—no doubt traditional airs—in the piece.

A more popular work was James Cobb's* comic opera *The Siege of Belgrade* (1791)—a pasticcio based on the music of such well-known composers of the past as Thomas Arne,* Stephen Storace,*[17] and William Shield.* At one of its revivals Hunt again lamented the use of good music with "wretched verse" as a vehicle for singers (14 April 1811). Contemporary composers of much promise, Henry Bishop* and Domenico Corri,* were also doomed to a similar fate. When Arnold's comic opera *Maniac* appeared with music by Bishop, Hunt deplored the fact that the music was "lavished on the most paltry songs" (18 March 1810). And in Cherry's *In and Out of Tune*, the "neat" music of Corri, which reminded Hunt of Purcell, was "thrown away" (6 March 1808).

Hunt was especially concerned over the fate of William Shield's music, for which he had a special liking. In an early review (7 February 1808) he admired Shield's music for its "happy union of expressive melody and scientific harmony"—a balance he regarded to be as rare as it was felicitous in contemporary composition. In a late review of Frances Brooke's* *Rosina* (1783) he found Shield's music "as sweet and pastoral as can well be imagined. We could slumber with our wearied brains in the corner of a box, or of a sopha, and be content to hear nothing for half an hour together but the air of *When the rosy morn appearing*. It is every thing that is young, gentle, chearful, and innocent" (15 October 1820).

Hunt's respect for Shield's music (and for music in the theatre generally) is evident in a review of a revival of Bate's *Travellers in Switzerland* (1794).[18] The opera's sporadic existence served to indicate the fate of fine composers whose music is wedded to inept verse:

Though Mr. Shield is very deservedly admired by all the lovers of music, yet I have absolutely been sometimes asked where his music is to be found. This is a problem very easily solved, when we consider that hundreds of songs, even from the pens of Geminiani, Purcell, and Handel, are scarcely known to the unprofessional lovers of the art on account of the villainous poetry which has stifled them in the birth.[19] The best composers of the Italian operas, in which the verse consists of nothing but a perpetual interchange of rhymes about *belta* and *crudelta, amore* and *cuore,* will undoubtedly share the same fate. It was but the other day Mr. Shield composed the music of an opera by Mr. Dibdin, which is already dragging the musician down to oblivion with all the sullen precipitancy of lead.[20] Once in eight or ten years perhaps, when the lucky composer has produced a song with words fit to exist, his revived popularity produces a demand for the rest of his works, and then there comes up a miserable something in the shape of an opera, like a stage-ghost rising to soft music. The phantom, according to the invariable laws of the damned, cannot stay long upon earth, and the unhappy composer, like Orpheus looking behind after Eurydice, sees it flitting down to it's accustomed shades. . . . People are surprised to see the excellent music of Mr. Shield condemned to partial fits of existence and to ultimate death: and they cannot sufficiently lament that he who ought to have been "married to immortal verse,"

is thus linked to the destiny of a dying and ungrateful muse.
[27 March 1808]

Hunt correctly regarded Bishop as the most important composer
writing for the contemporary stage. Like Reynolds and probably
other men of promise, Bishop's creative ability seems to have
been undermined by the gross demands of the theatrical hack
work required of him. Hunt did not always make excuses for
him because of the vehicle. After seeing Reynolds's *The Renegade* he reported: "Mr. Bishop, it is clear, had no very great
inspiration in . . . [Reynolds's lyrics], but we have heard much
better music of his with nearly as bad" (20 December 1812). In
a review of Morton's *The Slave* Hunt recorded his further disappointment:

We cannot say much for Mr. Bishop's music. It is not without
knowledge, nor unpleasing; but if he continue to produce no better,
he will not have performed the promise of his youth. There is a
sort of small and cold science about his style, which consciously
or unconsciously endeavours to conceal it's real want of expression
by running to extremes; and the consequence is a fondness for coarse
contrast;—he thinks he must shew his sense of every violent and
every gentle word that comes across him by an excess of vigour and
tenderness;—which is as almost absurd in it's way as the man who
accompanied the line about
        "Through the long space of ten revolving years,"
with an action suitable, as he thought, to every word,—holding up
his fingers for "ten," and twisting them round for "revolving."
[17 November 1816]

Exaggerated musical effects, one might suppose, would provide a
suitable accompaniment to a melodrama. But here as elsewhere
Hunt rejects all musical values based on appeals to the literal.
"Science" was another matter. He occasionally praised composers
and singers who showed much science. Yet sometimes he links
the word with the "mechanical" in music, when it carries pejorative overtones of excessive formalism that he associated with the
eighteenth century.

Occasionally he failed to recognize the composer's music,

owing in part, no doubt, to Bishop's uneven production and in part to a lack of ascription in the notices. He made no mention of the music for *The Knight of Snowdoun*, nor did he know the author of the piece, which had been attributed to a number of people, especially Reynolds, and which "seems indeed about the pitch of that Gentleman" (10 February 1811). (Four months later Henry Robertson, in an Italian-opera review, roundly damned the play but gave high praise to Bishop's music.) Hunt was also unaware that Bishop had collaborated with Mazzinghi in the music for Reynolds's *The Exile*. Nevertheless, Hunt gave periodic testimony to Bishop's ability. He did not print a review of *The Circassian Bride* (Bishop's finest work according to Hogarth), owing, as he explained, to the fire at Drury Lane the night following its première, but he regarded Bishop's music as "very scientific and impassioned" and hoped it had been saved from the fire, which it was not (26 February 1809). Years later, finding the newly redecorated Covent Garden wasted on Reynolds's melodrama *Duke of Savoy*, he declared: "We hope, however, that a way will be found to preserve some of the music,—we mean for the stage as well as the shop.[21] It is better than we have had [in] a long while from Mr. Bishop, and more worthy of his first promise" (5 October 1817).

The finest work of Bishop that Hunt reviewed was an operatic adaptation of *Twelfth Night*. He did not always look favorably on such adaptations, which will be discussed in another connection in the section "Musical Nationalism." In the present instance, however, both the nature of the play and Bishop's musical skill redeemed the transmogrification.[22] The work, he wrote, "is interspersed with songs, glees, and duetts, taken from the German and English masters; and Mr. Bishop, besides adapting these to the scene with his scientific hand, has added some composition, of which though a high, it is no undeserved praise to say, that a hearer must be nicely acquainted with the varieties of musical style to distinguish it from the rest." Aside from weaving a skillful pasticcio drawn from Mozart, Winter, and others, Bishop "adapted the songs to the several characters 'with difference discreet.' *Viola's* are deep and tender; *Olivia's*, like her rank and

pride, more vehement, gorgeous, and wilful; those of the others
as wilful too, but light, festive, and seasonable" (12 November
1820). In a word, Bishop had preserved in his music the dramatic
character of the play. In a later comment Hunt spoke of Bishop
as "one of the few modern composers whose writings will sur-
vive" (1 October 1820). That they have not survived is no doubt
partly due to a lack of durable theatrical material for his considerable talent, as Hunt so often proclaimed.[23]

With respect to the lesser talents among theatre composers,
Hunt was no apologist on account of poor vehicles. He attacked
the music of these ephemeral productions on much the same
grounds as the dramas: in general it was commonplace, borrowed, and vulgar. In regard to the borrowings, the objections
raised are not directed against the simple adaptations that characterized ballad opera and its successors. Rather, Hunt is concerned with the impoverished work of English stage composers,
whose "new" music possessed neither the simple virtues of traditional melodies nor the freshness that an imaginative composer
such as Shield could bring to inherited material.

Referring to the music by Reeve and Charles E. Horn* for
James B. Burges's* comic opera *Tricks upon Travellers,* Hunt
commented: "It's melodies and harmonies were what the orchestra has been accustomed to ever since it was acquainted with
fiddles:—you heard them with that kind of anticipation, with
which a two-penny postman walks through his round of streets,
knowing every turn and every rest that is to come" (15 July 1810).
Following his caustic comments on Arnold's lyrics in *Up All
Night,* Hunt ironically observed that the music of Matthew Peter
King* (a frequent collaborator in Arnold's productions) "is well
suited to the words, not only in its expression, but in its good old
age. . . . Neither in the words nor the music of the new Opera is
there a single idea or turn of composition, that has any claim to
originality" (2 July 1809).

One of the most notorious musical borrowers of the day was
Michael Kelly,* and in an early review Hunt noted that Kelly's
music for Richard Cumberland's* *The Jew of Mogadore*[24] was
"much borrowed" though graceful (8 May 1808).[25] Some years

later, however, he qualified his accusation: "We think better of some of Mr. Kelly's compositions than many do," he wrote. "If he stole them, as it is alleged, we should like to see the originals; and then we shall maintain that he has been a very tasteful thief; but till then, we must maintain, that he has sometimes shewn himself a very tasteful composer" (17 August 1817).[26]

Of the older generation of theatrical composers, none won the esteem Hunt bestowed on Shield. James Hook* was of that generation, and Hunt retained fond recollections of his songs, as noted in chapter two. A versatile composer, Hook at one time became the object of considerable jealousy among Italian musicians resident in London; apparently his talents were corrupted by attempts to suit Vauxhall tastes. Hunt found his music for his son Theodore's *Safe and Sound* "pleasing and elegant, but deficient in novelty. The days seem quite gone by, when Mr. Hook could produce such songs as the *Hours of Love, Within a Mile of Edinburgh,* &c. His Muse has lost her substance, and become the mere echo of Vauxhall" (8 September 1809). This appraisal was repeated in a later review—a revival of *Lady of the Manor* (1778) by William Kenrick,* for which Hook, the original composer, had added new music. "The music," Hunt summarized, "like the general run of this venerable composer's writings, is in some parts very pleasing, in others very common-place. The difference seems to depend upon whether he has the Italians or Vauxhall in his mind" (26 April 1818). If in Hunt's day Vauxhall suggested a debased musical taste, so Sadler's Wells—that rustic retreat of wine and extravaganza—typified all that was corrupt in contemporary dramatics.[27] These places of casual amusement represented the lowest position in his hierarchy of musical and dramatic values.

Other second-rate composers occasionally showed redeeming features. The "pleasing mediocrity" he observed in Bickerstaffe was matched in the music for *Lionel and Clarissa* by Charles Dibdin the Elder*: "There is some very nice music in this piece by old Dibdin," Hunt remarked with a trace of irony, "who with his unsophisticated but not very powerful taste, suited his author very happily" (8 December 1816). Of William Reeve's music for

The Fortune Teller he remarked that it "was airy and pleasing, and altogether much better than Mr. Reeve has produced for some time; but it had nothing original. Mr. Reeve may wander about his gamut for ever, but he will never get beyond his old hand-organ stock" (2 October 1808). And regarding Matthew King's music for Arnold's *Up All Night* he noted: "It is not deficient in taste, and indifferent music will always be more tolerable than indifferent writing, because it appeals to the senses more than to the sense" (2 July 1809). The young critic, following Addison and others, complained of the intellectual emptiness of music vis-à-vis its literary counterpart. The more experienced critic came to modify that idea (see below, chapter four). Yet, whether to the sense or senses of Hunt, music's appeal was undeniable, and by his own evidence it seems to have sustained him through many an otherwise intolerable evening at the theatre.

There is no doubt that for Hunt good songs—especially folk songs—formed a central part of that appeal. Of Ramsey's *Gentle Shepherd* he wrote: "We found our critical objections forgotten, whenever one of the songs came round. Very few indeed were retained; and one or two of the airs were not in the original piece, but they were Scotch and beautiful" (6 July 1817). He shows an appreciation not only for the genuine folk tunes that were retained but also for the later "imitative" folk songs that were supplied.

In his criticism generally, Hunt indicates considerable interest in the identity of all songs. Uninformed as to the playwright of *Lady of the Manor* (see appendix one), he inquired whether James Hook was "the author of the Scotch air of *Down the Burn, Davy, Love?*" (26 April 1818).[28] Neither playbills nor advertisements provided identification; though names of songs might be listed, the names of composers and playwrights were apparently seldom mentioned.[29] At a revival of Kane O'Hara's* *Midas* (1764) Hunt questioned Rousseau's authorship of the air "Pray, Goody, Please to Moderate" (10 August 1817). Hoping it was an English tune, he argued that it had first appeared in *Queen Mab* (1750), well before it achieved wider popularity in Rousseau's *Le Devin du Village* (Paris, 1753).[30]

Scottish songs and airs were redeeming virtues in contemporary opera as well—they were especially welcome in the work of a playwright whom Hunt generally ranked among the worst, Isaac Pocock.* At the opening of his *Rob Roy Macgregor,* one of the many stage adaptations of Scott's novel published the same year, Hunt explained to his readers that Rob Roy is the Scottish Robin Hood, though with "an air altogether not so sylvan and romantic."[31] The melodrama, he admitted,

is not well done, as far as the manufacturer is concerned. It is ill put together, and falls off every act. Yet the workman has not only fully availed himself of the original, but compiled the vocal part out of Burns, Wordsworth, and even Mr. Lee Lewis.[32] It was curious to hear Wordsworth on the stage. It seemed a great though strange triumph for his eremitical genius. There is something very striking and self-possessed in the air of one of the verses:—

>   And while Rob Roy is free to rove
>   In summer's heat and winter's snow,
>   The eagle he is lord above,
>   And Rob is lord below.[33]

These compilations and the story itself cannot fail of giving an interest to the drama; and it is not uninteresting, nor unlikely to succeed. The songs too are set to popular Scotch airs, among which we recognised *Roy's Wife, Duncan Gray,* the *White Cockade,* the *Lass of Patie's Mill,* and the delightful one of *Auld Lang Syne*; though indeed there is hardly a Scotch air that is not beautiful.[34] [15 March 1818]

One may smile with Hunt at finding Wordsworth in a melodrama, though the adaptation seems appropriate. Hunt had been severe with the poet in the first edition of the *Feast of the Poets* but placed him after Shakespeare and Spenser in the second (1814). In 1815, Haydon introduced Wordsworth to Hunt, ill at his Hampstead house, but the poet disliked "coxcomb" Hunt, and their personal relationship remained slight.

Fine English airs and lyrics were to be found in other operas that were revived fairly frequently during the *Examiner* years. One of the oldest and most popular was John Gay's* *The Beggar's Opera* (1728). Hunt's general attitude toward the work will be taken up later in another connection, but he regarded "the never-dying charm of simplicity in its songs and music" as its most valid appeal (13 September 1812). He found strong associational values in Bickerstaffe's *Love in a Village* (1762): "The songs, such as *'Hope thou nurse of young desire,'—'My heart's my own,'* —*'There was a jolly miller once,'*—&c., bring back to them [the elderly] the days of their childhood and their courtships" (27 July 1817).[35]

Similar feelings were evoked by the music in Thomas Arne's *Artaxerxes*: "There is some fine, lasting composition in *Artaxerxes,* particularly in the more tender songs. Arne's genius lay in tenderness and grace, and was a happy follower of the *amoroso* style of the Italians, especially Sacchini's.[36] You can trace the favourite turns of the latter in several of Arne's melodies, but still without destroying their real talent." The best airs from the opera were those most expressive of tenderness: "Water Parted from the Sea" and "In Infancy Our Hopes and Fears." "[These] airs become part of the recollections of our childhood, like the daisies and green fields, and the looks of one's parents" (16 April 1820). Tenderness, grace, and melody are the qualities that Hunt most admired in songs, whether simple folk types or relatively sophisticated compositions.

With *Artaxerxes* we come to the only true opera Hunt was to review at the English theatres. His comments on the recitative, some of which was occasionally retained in current productions, is discussed in another connection later in this chapter.

Singers

Hunt's comments on singers fall into several categories: vocal qualities, vocal style, and vocal mannerisms; problems of the singing actor; and vocal and dramatic characterization.

Though female singers were not without faults and males not lacking in power, Hunt by and large preferred the former. They had better voices and fewer mannerisms, and the finest artists on the English stage were women. By contrast, male performers were either too rigid or too affected. No doubt the doughty

British resistance to the musical arts resulted in a dearth of male singing talent. Michael Kelly, an Irishman, and John Braham,* a Jew, were of course "outsiders," while Charles Incledon* succeeded by appealing to John Bull instincts.

Hunt especially admired the clarity of the "typical" English female voice as exhibited in the soprano, contralto, and mezzo ranges, respectively, of Catherine Stephens,* Ann Maria Tree,* and a Miss Greene. In Stephens, he wrote, "it was easy to recognize a natural and accomplished singer. . . . There is only one note in her voice, that seems at all harsh or reedy; the rest is clear, easy, and delicious. The notes drop from her undistorted lips, like the pearls of the little girl in the fairy tale. She is truly a nightingale,—a bird not over striking in appearance, but with a song that makes even that interesting" (17 November 1816). The following year he asserted, "We think we never heard the *power* of her under tones to such advantage as on Tuesday night. They were divinely clear, full, and quiet" (16 November 1817).

When the contralto Ann Tree joined Catherine Stephens in a duet from Reynolds's *Comedy of Errors,* he wrote:

It is seldom that two such singers come together; and seldomer that their voices so well unite, or that the under tones of the female who sings second, are deep enough without being masculine. Miss Tree's however are so. If they have any fault, it is perhaps that they are occasionally too luscious, and contrasted with her upper. But they are exquisitely true. Her ear indeed throughout is one of the finest we ever witnessed. Miss Stephens's voice we think the finer of the two. It is even, clear, and sweet; and has an exquisite vein of gentle pathos throughout it, that perpetually seems to appeal to you. You wish to re-assure it;—to "kiss it up, and ease it's pain."[37] [26 December 1819]

A voice may be both luscious and clear, but richness in the lower register cannot be admired if it produces a disturbing contrast with the higher; an equable quality throughout the vocal range is for Hunt an important asset. (He avoids, by the way, frequent references to singers' being out of tune. From their context such references in other reviewers often suggest a cliché of contemporary music criticism, though the merits of such judgments cannot of course be ascertained. Hunt's appreciation of accurate intonation is nevertheless evident.) In the role of Viola in Reynolds's *Twelfth Night* Miss Tree's vocal qualities were particularly effective: "There is a strength and fullness in the lower notes, which being unusual in a female, appeared to fall in with the character she had assumed as a male" (12 November 1820).

In still another performer Hunt showed his admiration for consistent vocal qualities:

Miss Greene's voice . . . is very good in speaking as well as in singing. It is of excellent quality, round without fatness, powerful without being harsh, clear, flowing, and equable throughout. If it may not be able to go so low as Miss Tree's, it falls into the lower tones without such a marked difference of body between those and the upper. If not so fine as Miss Stephens's, it is richer. Miss Tree's voice is like a bottle of cordial with a long neck to it; Miss Stephens's like one fine-drawn pipe of chrystal; Miss Greene's is cast like the latter, but more weighty. [24 September 1820]

Hunt's delicate similies show a keen appreciation in making the distinctions between the vocal qualities of these singers. Admiring their vocal power, opulence, and range, he also suggests polarities to be avoided: power tends toward harshness; opulence tends to lose clarity; range tends toward unevenness of vocal production. But above all he demands a *clear* voice—a quality he places foremost in describing the best features of all three singers.

Yet even clarity could be pressed too far. Of a Miss Byrne, he wrote, "Her taste is so good, that she will doubtless get over a certain hardness of outline, or over-distinctness in the enunciation of her notes; yet this was most observable in her first song, *Whither, my love*,[38] and was perhaps summoned up by her in order to hinder her timidity from going to the opposite fault of over-slurring; for she was at first much agitated" (19 October 1817). Hunt raised similar objections to the vocal quality of a Mrs. Sterling in the role of Polly. "Her mode of giving 'Oh ponder well' was extremely dry; and the want of a liquid facility in her voice, that is to say, of a proper flow where flowing is requisite, made her halt occasionally upon a note before she could make it speak, though when it came at last it was perfectly true. A painter would say, that her style had a hard outline" (13 September 1812).[39]

Among the male singers Hunt noted various vocal defects. "Mr. Braham," he admitted, "is the first living singer in England, perhaps in the world. He has a melodious and powerful voice, correctness, taste, passion." Nevertheless, "the general tone of his voice has a nasal twang, which to our ears is very offensive, and involves, like the same thing in speaking, a kind of meanness and innate vulgarity" (12 February 1815).[40] Probably no other performer in English opera displayed Braham's vocal power and skill. Charles Horn had a "voice and style" that were "delicate and tasteful, though of small power," and he "seemed to want confidence" (2 July 1809). Still other male singers did not have voices "powerful enough for these large theatres" (7 February 1819).

Certain tenors, too, lacked Braham's skill in achieving an easy transition to the falsetto. Hunt observed this difficulty in Thomas Philipps* (or Phillips). "The passage between his natural voice and falsetto, has that unpleasant gurgle to jump over, which is common enough, but which in Mr. Phillips is more than usually prominent to the ear. He has to slip over it, like a bump on the ice" (19 September 1819). Incledon and William Pearman* shared a similar problem.

[Pearman's] falsetto will remind the public of Incledon's, which
it surpasses in reach and sweetness. He plays upon it like a flute.
His transition to it however from the natural voice is not happy.
It is not indeed so violent as Incledon's, who in his leap from one
to the other slammed the larynx in his throat, like a Harlequin
jumping through a window shutter; but it is poor and unskilful;
neither does he seem to care upon what sort of words or expression
he does it, so as the note is such as he can jump up to. [13 July 1817]

No doubt the serious cultivation of the falsetto and the counter-tenor, so popular in earlier English singing, had declined by

Hunt's time.[41] (Italian opera did not use the falsetto.) In some instances Hunt's comments on falsetto may in fact be references to the transition from chest to head tones. In any event he commended a smooth tonal quality throughout the range of both male and female singers.

With respect to singing styles on the English musical stage, the *Examiner* critics held different views. As discussed in chapter one, there were only two basic styles—the simple and the ornate or "scientific." Quite aside from a question of appropriateness of style for a given number, singers tended to give audiences what they wanted; patrons in the English theatres became increasingly impressed with the bravura display that only the more "scientific" singers could provide. Reviewers tended to espouse one school and disparage the other.

Barnes was dedicated to the "scientific" style. "It is obvious," he remarked, "that, with such a people [that is, the subscribers of the King's Theatre], a scientific singer can never make a permanent impression, unless in such extraordinary cases as those of Catalani and Braham, where music condescends to lay aside its technical peculiarities to adopt the simple tones of the universal passions of nature." Even at the opera house, as Barnes would have it, the "scientific" style had to be modified before it could be appreciated. On the English stage it was only to the "select few" that a truly "scientific" singer could hope to appeal (30 January 1814).

Hazlitt was equally committed, on the other hand, to the ballad style. He praised Stephens highly at her debut as Polly (*Chronicle*, 23 October 1813); in a reappraisal for the *Examiner*, however, he found too much "science" in one of the airs: "We enter our earnest protest against the trills and quavers which she introduced into the last line of 'Cease your funning'—'Never happy in their own'" (18 June 1815). Hazlitt's objection to ornamentation extended to the role of Mandane in *Artaxerxes*. (For its difficulty of execution this role was considered the touchstone of a soprano's virtuosity.) In a review of a Miss Merry in the part, he brought more attention to the art of song than is usually found in his English-opera criticism:

She appears to possess very great taste and skill; and to have not only a fine voice, but (what many singers want) an ear for music. . . . Yet in one or two passages, we thought she added some extraneous and unnecessary ornaments, and (for a precious note or two) lost the charm of the expression by sacrificing simplicity to execution. This objection struck us most in the manner in which Miss Merry sung the beautiful air, "If o'er the cruel tyrant Love," which is an irresistible appeal to the sentiments, and seems, in its genuine simplicity, above all art. . . . If vocal music has an advantage over instrumental, it is, we imagine, in this very particular; in the immediate communication between the words and the expression they suggest, between the voice and the soul of the singer, which ought to mould every tone, whether deep or tender, according to the impulse of true passion. [21 July 1816]

Hunt took a flexible position. He saw advantages and disadvantages in both styles. In general, his love of simplicity in song and his dislike of embellishment predisposed him in favor of the ballad style. Like Hazlitt, he admired Maria Bland,* for her "style has a sort of gentle-hearted, dairy-maid simplicity with it, that would set all the people in a village listening to nothing else every summer's evening" (12 February 1815). And it was for this quality that he preferred Incledon to Braham: "Notwithstanding all [Incledon's] defects, and even his inferiority in point of talent, we have oftener perhaps heard him with satisfaction than Braham himself;—so charming is simplicity, even in its least charming undress." Like Hazlitt, too, he objected to liberties taken with "Cease Your Funning." Sterling, as Polly,

seemed to have a proper and sensible idea of the simplicity with which the ballads of this Opera should be sung, though she unaccountably deviated from it in the song of "Cease your Funning,"—a deviation, by the bye, which proved that her better taste was her most politic one, for her graces were of a very prim and deliberate description, and she ran down her notes with full as much caution as correctness. But even her simplicity wants the proper amount of feeling. [13 September 1812]

Yet simplicity alone was not adequate, even in the ballad style. In this instance the singer's lapses may have been attributable to faulty vocal production. But in the role of Macheath the singer Mr. Hunt (no relative of the critic and otherwise unidentified) was too limited in execution to satisfy the critic: "Though his good taste might well have taught him not to Brahamize in the simple and beautiful ballads of this opera, he was not inclined to make any shew where it might have been even proper;—as in the triumphant and defying passages, for instance, towards the conclusion" (7 February 1819).

Hunt's changes in opinion regarding the "science" of Maria Dickons* parallel his views on her ability as an actress. "Seen to her best advantage," he asserted, "Mrs. Dickons exhibits an increasing science as well as sweetness, that advances her every day a step beyond Mrs. [Rosomon] Mountain"* (7 February 1808). At the end of the year he affirmed, "The musical honours of the piece [The Exile] certainly belong to Mrs. Dickons, who sung an ironical bravura at the beau traveller with infinite skill, taste, and vivacity" (13 November 1808).

But Dickons's "science" apparently got the better of her in subsequent years. In a retrospective in which Hunt judged the best English singers none too good, he stated, "Mrs. Dickons is the best we have after Braham, and is perhaps as correct a one as any living: she has also considerable power, and may be called upon the whole a very useful and effective singer, a pitch above mediocrity. By many indeed she is thought to possess a good deal of taste; but this we conceive to be one of the impositions arising from the bravura and florid style" (12 February 1815). Significantly, Hunt does not attack the bravura style itself, only the "impositions arising from" it. Still later, although he praised her acting in the English Barber, "with all her sweetness and facility, [she] has not got rid of the old error of overloading an air with ornaments. The verse of the air just mentioned ['For Tenderness Formed'], which she sung in answer to Mr. Pyne's, was tricked and flounced over, till the whole melody disappeared; and we really prefer, at any time, the heart and sentiment of Paesiello to the vocal millinery of the greatest singers in Europe" (18 October

Drawn and engraved by Daniel Havell
From Edward W. Brayley, *Historical and Descriptive Accounts of the Theatres of London*

Theatre Royal, King's Theatre (1826)

Angelina Catalani (c. 1807)

Teresa Bertinotti-Radicati

Teresa Giorgi Trombetta Belloc

Joséphine Fodor-Mainvielle (c. 1818)

1818). (Hazlitt's view of the singer was unequivocal: "Mrs. Dickons never appeared to us any thing but an ordinary musical instrument, and at present, she is very much out of tune" [2 April 1815].)

"Singers in general," Hunt once remarked, "seem no more able to resist a shake when they are getting out of a song, than a dog when he gets out of the water" (10 October 1819). Yet he admired "science" in a singer provided it was kept within the bounds of good taste and provided it was suited to the role. Nor was a superior vocal quality essential to the style. Ann Maria Tree, for example, was only "one of the very first of the second-rate [singers]. . . . She cannot pour it [her voice] forth in a continued stream till it fills a large theatre, nor dart it out in that triumphant manner like lightning, as Catalani [see below, chapter four] used to do. But it is not thin and feeble in itself. If it is no great traveller, it is an excellent solid homester. . . . She seems quite at home in songs that hold a middle place between the ballad and the scientific" (19 September 1819). As Philidel in *King Arthur,* she had sufficient technique for the "complete execution of our old English airs" (31 October 1819).

Hunt was acutely observant of vocal quality and singing styles in the performers. But his critical attention was primarily absorbed with dramatic problems. English opera was most effectively dramatized through the vocal characterizations of the performers. Pleasing vocal qualities were desirable for this purpose but by no means essential.

Failures in vocal characterization he usually traced to lapses in the taste of the performer that produced unfortunate vocal mannerisms and stylistic abuses. Braham, for example, the "first" English male singer, also ranked first with Hazlitt and Hunt in an assortment of mannerisms that severely limited his effectiveness. Even Braham's songs could not be separated from the mannerisms of the singer, as Hazlitt remarked on those written for *The Unknown Guest*: "The style of Mr. Braham's songs has no other object than to pamper him in his peculiar vices, and to produce that *mannerism,* which is the destruction of all excellence

in art. There are two or three favourite passages, which seem to
dwell upon his ear, and to which he gives a striking expression;
these he combines and repeats with laborious foolery; and in fact,
sings nothing but himself over and over continually" (2 April
1815).

Hunt also expressed strong distaste for the "trite transitions"
of Braham. "There is no truer mark either of a vulgar singer or
composer than confounding feeling with literality, and shewing
us how really insensible he is to the general sentiment of a song,
by a parade of his sensitiveness to the distinction of words in it.
We mean, for instance, the laying a special and contrasted emphasis on such words as *loud* and *soft, hate* and *love, war* and
peace, despair and *fair,* &c. &c. Such a man is setting a dictionary
to music, not a sentiment" (16 November 1817). Earlier, he associated this mannerism of Braham's with an excessive and tasteless
virtuosity: "The general style of his singing [is not only] meretricious, but the ornaments with all their exuberance are frequently misplaced, and so far he wants the common taste even of
floridness. He wears bells on his toes, as well as rings on his
fingers. He will run divisions upon the most insignificant words,
and trill, quaver, and roll about at you without remorse. He
lights up, as it were, fifty wax candles to exhibit a nut shell" (12
February 1815). In addition to placing an exaggerated literalness
on some passages, Braham quite misread others. Hunt objects
less to his florid style than to his abuse of it in dramatic characterization. Like Hazlitt, he recognizes a "noble simplicity" in
the singer, who was also quite at home in the ballad style (observe
Hunt's association of "simplicity" and "the true style of singing"). Unfortunately, Braham could not resist the appeal of the
"grosser multitude":

It is generally said in his behalf, that simplicity and the true style
of singing are his real talent, and that the rest is only put on for the
sake of effect. . . . True geniuses are not so apt to accommodate
themselves to inferior ones, and if they do, it is not with a
predominance of the worse taste:—the vice is occasional, and the
virtue predominant. The appeal too which the bad taste must make
to the grosser multitude, and the kind of suspicion it involves with

regard to vulgarity of intellect and the love of money-making,[42]
go very much against the better inference in these matters. Milton
wrote for posterity; but Mr. Walter Scott writes for the booksellers.

Incledon* suffered from various mannerisms, some of which
no doubt suited his Jack Tar characterizations. In *Critical Essays*
(p. 104) Hunt praised these impersonations and declared his
voice the best then on the English stage (Braham had been singing at the King's Theatre). "But when he attempts a love-song or
any more refined part of his science, he cannot help reminding us
of the sailor: . . . after the finest tones in the world and in the
midst perhaps of very pathetic words he seems about to shirk off
into a *Right fol de ra* or some such energetic kind of ballad-
singing." In a final retrospective on the singer he further analyzed this defect:

The reader, who is fond of music, may have observed that there is a
tendency in almost all singers, private as well as public, when they
arrive at the dignity of being accompanied, to put on a sort of noisy
fierceness, and, as it were, to bully the air they are singing. It
arises perhaps in the first instance only from a sense of the goodness
of the music, and a wish to send their voices well out of their throats.
We have witnessed it often, in company with musical friends who
could afford to make merry with each other on the infirmity and
get rid of it; but it is curious to see how it will cut up all expression,
and with what a neck-stretching loftiness a singer will go through
some of the tenderest or liveliest passages. Mr. Incledon carried this
error to it's extreme. He would be as nice and delicate as he could
manage when he was in a piece of falsetto, but he appeared to seize
with triumph the first opportunity of escaping, and if the end in
particular of the song gave him the least encouragement, would dash
out into a sort of splay-footed uproariousness quite defying. [30
March 1817]

Hunt detected mannerisms in William Pearman comparable
to those of Braham's; and in the pronunciation of John Sinclair*
he found an affectation at least as annoying as Incledon's sloven-
liness:

One of the very few varieties which he [Pearman] displays, consists
in that swelling and subsiding, or opening and shutting of the voice,

which in Mr. Braham's powerful instrument is like a French-horn,
but which in Mr. Pearman's is like a drinking glass rubbed round
the edge with a wet finger. . . . In short, he is a sweet singer worth
hearing, and may become a formidable rival to another of the same
class, Mr. Sinclair, who, we must confess, grows very tiresome (to
use the phraseology of the ladies) with his miminy-piminy
affectations, and his *weeths, woines,* and *diviones* [for "divoines"?]
(with, wine, and divine). [13 July 1817]

That such mannerisms reflected something deeper than mere
lapses in technique is implicit in much of the foregoing criticism.
In an interesting analysis of a Miss Buggins[43] in the role of Mandane, Hunt attributes her failure to certain vocal deficiencies;
but these in turn suggest defects in the character of the artist.
Aside from her mechanical approach to florid passages, she was
too self-conscious in her performance. She lacked the spontaneity
and "unselfconscious" qualities necessary for complete realization
of character—qualities Hunt admired in such performers as
Lucia Vestris.* He wrote:

She is deficient in what is called *body* of voice,—that is to say,
something which clothes it as flesh does the bones; and she is deficient
in *tone,* which is the soul to this body. Without these, the best
voices in other respects are but as pipes of glass, or machines of
music, or a shower of mere crotchets, or walking sticks compared
to the green bough with the sap in it,—or any thing else that may
express clearness, or power, without what is affecting and vital. . . .
She seems to feel her art too much *as* an art;—to feel as if she had
a *song to sing,* not as if singing were her natural voice, and she
expressed thought and sentiment through the medium of it.
[6 July 1817]

Failures in vocal characterization were observed in Shakespearean songs as well as in English operas. To be sure, a Miss Boyle,
playing Rosalind in *As You Like It,* achieved a risqué success,
as reported by Hazlitt: "We must not forget her Cuckoo-song;
indeed we could not, if we would. It was quite delightful. The
tone and manner in which she repeated the word Cuckoo was as
arch and provoking as possible, and seemed to grow more saucy
every time by the repetition, but still, though it hovered very

near them, it was restrained from passing the limits of delicacy and propriety" (6 October 1816). But Hazlitt did not care much for Shakespeare *sung*. He regarded the Ariel of a Miss Matthews as "a better representative of the sylph-like form of the character than the light and portable Mrs. Bland, who used formerly to play it. She certainly does not sing the songs so well. We do not however wish to hear them sung, though never so well; no music can add any thing to their magical effect.—'The words' of Shakespear would be sweet even 'after the songs of Apollo!'" (23 July 1815).[44] And he stated that the part of Ophelia "ought not indeed to be in general given to a fine singer; for it has been well observed, that 'Ophelia does not go mad because she can sing, but sings because she has gone mad.'"[45]

Hunt, on the other hand, regarded Ophelia's song as an opportunity to heighten the characterization. For its subtle musico-dramatic analysis his commentary on one unfortunate representation deserves extensive quotation:

A dramatist should be cautious how he introduces an occasional song or two in a character not essentially operatic. The actor or singer are so seldom united, that one or the other is almost sure to predominate; and as there are more singers who can manage to act than actors who can manage to sing, the author's intention is gradually done away, and instead of a song incidental to the character, the character is made incidental to the song. When Shakspeare fancied his *Ophelia,* and represented her with that amiable mixture of reserve and frankness that constitutes the charm of female manners, when he painted her as the lady, the sister, the daughter, and the fond mistress, each with it's own charm and it's united charm, when he gave us that beautiful picture of a delicate mind disturbed not distorted into madness, that insanity full of genius and of patient anguish, in which the chords are tangled not snapped, in which the last weakness of nature has not destroyed her strength of mind nor the last suffering her thoughts of her father, he little thought that such a female and such a picture could ever degenerate into a mere singing-girl, a mere opera debutante, full of stage attitudes and a ridiculous self-possession, rational when she should be insane, and insane in nothing but her rationality. Yet such has *Ophelia* been repeatedly rendered in an age that

professes to idolize Shakspeare, such is she continually represented
in English theatres, and such was she represented last Tuesday in
the person of a new *singer,* who is said to be the wife of Mr. Corri
the composer.[46] Mrs. Corri has a sensible countenance, but it
possesses no power of expression for the supernatural and ever-
shifting genius of insanity. . . . [She is] a respectable singer, much
better I dare say in a room where she has nothing to act, than on a
stage where she can act nothing. But neither a respectable singer,
nor the best singer in the world, simply considered, is a fit person to
represent *Ophelia,* whose songs were never intended to shew the
powers of her voice but the immediate power of her feelings, and
I must protest against all such degradations of Shakspeare.
[25 September 1808]

The "incidental" songs of Shakespeare's characters often reflect
their inner nature.[47] Where they do, as in Ophelia's, the role
can be entrusted only to a singing actress capable of capturing the
musical nuances of the character. Sophia Corri, who had merely
vocal ability, was out of her element on the dramatic stage. Hunt
went on to suggest that Dorothy Jordan,* although perhaps "too
large in person" for the delicate role, would have been a far
better choice. In *Critical Essays* (p. 162) he had praised her singing of Ophelia: "Her little bewildered songs in particular, like
all her songs indeed, pierce to our feelings with the most original
simplicity."

Failures in acting ability were as common as those in vocal
characterization. On the English stage, histrionic failures were
perhaps more serious. We have noted Hunt's insistence on the
importance of acting: he would not excuse "inattention to dialogue" out of an "exclusive regard to the music." He also placed
a premium on those actors who could sing, since singers who
tried to act were rarely successful. The former could adequately
fill roles in many of the operatic vehicles that called for no more
real singing ability than, say, the Broadway musical of our day.

An occasionally effective singer, Braham was no actor at all.
Hunt considered his role in *The Siege of St. Quintin*—that of a
minstrel who animates the soldiers to battle by his songs—"a very

proper method of introducing Braham, who when he is not 'most musical' is 'most melancholy' " (13 November 1808). Three years later he was "still the same automaton in a speech, the same instant enthusiast in a song" (14 April 1811). Still later Hunt wrote, "It is curious to observe how the orchestra inspires him; and what a difference there is between the tame, indifferent, vapid creatures [*sic*] that gets rid of his words with a hasty, half-breathing imbecility when speaking, and the firm, ardent, intelligent being, that throws them hither and thither with masterly power during a song" (12 February 1815).

Other criticism of performances was related to acting problems presented by certain roles or productions. Among the latter, for example, were the English adaptations of Mozart and Rossini. In his general condemnation of Bishop's *Figaro*, Hunt did not fail to note "the unsuitableness of the actors and singers" for the roles demanded of them (21 March 1819).[48] Similar problems were presented by the English *Barber of Seville*:

The truth is, that . . . the singers do not very well feel what they are about; and there is one extremely aukward and ridiculous circumstance in the adaptation of the performance, which is this,— that in default of the lover's (Mr. Jones) being able to sing, his valet (Mr. Pyne) is obliged to sing for him. That exquisite air, for instance, to which *For tenderness formed*[49] was set, and which is so full of a graceful and affectionate earnestness, is sung by the valet. . . . Mr. Liston too, who has no voice at all, is obliged to take his part in the singing. [18 October 1818]

But traditional English roles offered problems as well. The role of Macheath, for example, held particular difficulties: it did not require a gentleman, but called for an actor who could imitate one. Hazlitt found Charles Horn a gentleman, but his qualities were somewhat too precious for the role. For Macheath must ape the genuine article, not be a token of royal sycophancy:

He sung the songs well, with a little too much ornament for the profession of the *Captain*: and his air and manner, though they did not fall into the common error of vulgarity, were rather too precise and finical.[50] *Macheath* should be a fine man and a gentleman, but he should be one of God Almighty's gentlemen, not a gentleman of the black rod. . . . The class of the character is very difficult to hit. It is something between gusto and slang, like port wine and brandy mixed. It is not the mere gentleman that should be represented, but the blackguard sublimated into the gentleman. [28 July 1816]

Hunt expressed similar views. Of the singer Hunt in the same role he declared, "Such ornaments too as he did venture upon were not in character with *Macheath,* being little occasional droppings of semitones, more suited to a less boisterous inamorato. The truth is, he is a more pleasing than powerful singer, and more gentlemanly in his manners than jovial or slang-like; and the character of *Macheath* was therefore an ill chosen one" (7 February 1819). Incledon's Macheath had no gentlemanly pretensions at all. In phrases that anticipate Hazlitt, Hunt pointed out in his review that some degree of sophistication is essential for any success in the role:

His *Macheath* altogether is very far from being the true one. He is too doleful in some parts of it, and has too little of the metropolis about his general appearance:—he looks in short like a jolly young farmer sporting a new pair of boots and buckskins on a market day; whereas *Macheath,* who affects a knowledge of the town and of the cant of fashion, should at least have a certain slang of good breeding about him,—something between the pertness of the footman and the bravado of the town buck. [13 September 1812]

The criticism reviewed thus far has indicated little "art" in the performances of the period. But aside from some good voices, there were a few fine moments in the theatre when performers rose above the trite and pedestrian to achieve an effective realization of song and character. The successes that Hunt records will be considered in terms of certain qualities he praises in English opera generally: the emphasis on dramatic characterization, the expression of vivacity and tenderness, and the appeal of sentiment and faith—in art and in people. These qualities are closely related to each other as well as to the personality of the artist; indeed, in the best performers they merge altogether.

Hazlitt assuredly demonstrated his interest in the dramatic

aspects of English opera. Yet he occasionally placed primary emphasis on singing ability. In this and other respects the performances of Fanny Kelly* provide an interesting basis for comparing his views with Hunt's (and with an aside from Lamb). Hazlitt complained, "We are sorry to include in this censure Miss Kelly, whose attempts to supply the place of *Prima Donna* of the New English Opera do great credit to her talents, industry, and good nature, but still have not given her a voice, which is indispensable to a singer, as singing is to an opera" (1 September 1816). He regarded her as something of an actress, though his criticism is mixed. She pleased enormously as Lucy in *The Beggar's Opera*: "She is a charming little vixen: has the most agreeable pout in the world, and the best-humoured smile; shews all the insolence of lively satisfaction, and when she is in her airs, the blood seems to tingle at her fingers' ends" (5 November 1815). But as Flora in *Jane Shore* her change of style irritated the critic: "It was the only time we ever saw her fail. She seemed to be playing tricks with the chambermaid. . . . We hope she does not think of growing fantastical and *operatic*" (5 January 1817).

The rich irony in Lamb's review of this lady in *The Jovial Crew* extends beyond his own "special pleading" (see appendix one) to provide an accurate portrait of this artist:

But the *Princess of Mumpers*, and *Lady Paramount*, of beggarly counterfeit accents, was *she* that played *Rachel*. Her gabbling lachrymose petitions; her tones, such as we have heard by the side of old woods, when an irresistible face has come peeping on one on a sudden; with her full black locks, and a *voice*——how shall we describe it?—a voice that was by nature meant to convey nothing but truth and goodness, but warped by circumstance into an assurance that she is telling us a lie—that catching twitch of the thievish irreproveable finger—those ballad-singers' notes, so vulgar, yet so unvulgar—that assurance, so like impudence, and yet so many countless leagues removed from it—her jeers, which we had rather stand, than be caressed with other ladies' compliments, a summer's day long—her face, with a wild out-of-doors grace upon it—— . . . "What a lass that were," said a stranger who sate beside us, speaking of Miss Kelly in *Rachel*, "to go a gipseying through the

world with." We confess we longed to drop a tester in her lap,
she begged so masterly. [4 July 1819]

Lamb is closer to Hunt than to Hazlitt in recognizing the dramatic value of her voice, and he conveys better than either critic
the flavor of her stage personality. His warmth, whimsical good
nature, and impish grace are qualities that complement the colder
objectivity of Hazlitt and Hunt.[51]

In his retrospective of 12 July 1818, Hunt was content merely
with "copying a sonnet written in [Miss Kelly's] praise by the
profoundest critic now living [Lamb]." The next year, however,
he warmly defended her ability to perform in English opera. We
have already observed his objection to the public's growing demand for singing virtuosity at the expense of vocal and dramatic
characterization. His remarks, in a review of The Duenna,
were prompted by an incident that took place during the performance. It was, Hunt assumed, because the audience had become used to the "mere art of singing" in the play, that "induced
some ill-timing person to hiss while Miss Kelly was acting a
prominent part on the stage. He might surely have chosen his
opportunity better. . . . The truth is, the character of Clara,
which Miss Kelly performed, really demands no other description
of vocal powers than those which she possesses, that is to say,
powers on the side of sentiment rather than execution; but . . .
persons who have no relish for these will be impatient for the
others." Hunt tacitly admits a lack of virtuosity in the singer in
urging her to avoid "characters which have been made vocally
prominent by more professed singers,—by the quaverers, and
balancers, and scale-ascenders, and fiery crotchet-shooters, and
other Sacchis[52] of songs." Nevertheless, she "is something much
greater. Her singing should rather come as an extempore effusion out of her acting, like a lute carelessly taken up; and then it
would be felt to be what it is, a part of her general sentiment and
cordial feeling. . . . For she is . . . decidedly the actress of the
greatest variety and genuine unsophisticated feeling now on the
stage" (20 June 1819).

Hunt's praises for Fanny Kelly extended over several years. As

Diana in *Lionel and Clarissa* she was "as usual, full of charming touches and excellent self-possession. The very dress and air of this actress have more meaning in them than half the souls on the stage. We would rather hear one of her Lords! or Pshaws!, and see her turn about and walk off with her trim waist and natural step, than witness the best performance of all Rowe's heroines put together" (8 December 1816). In *My Own Rival* she sang "three or four popular songs, in the happiest manner, and upon the principle we spoke of the other day, as suiting her fine talents so well."

Hunt and Lamb saw "self-possession" and "frankness" in Miss Kelly's performances, whereas Hazlitt complained of her excessive shyness; Hunt regarded her voice, in appropriate roles, as dramatically superior to the vocal displays demanded by the public; whereas Hazlitt supposed her voice inadequate to English opera. In general, however, both critics praised her acting and responded to the charm of her personality, which quite captivated Lamb.

Catherine Stephens had a much finer voice than Miss Kelly but lacked her stage presence and verve. She was nevertheless appealing. In a review of her Lilla in *The Siege of Belgrade,* Hunt wrote:

Her contrasts have always a saving grace of resemblance to each other, and melt together like the tones of the rainbow. The little raillying burthen which she sings to her husband, and the dancing steps with which she accompanies it, wanted something of spirit perhaps; but a woman to whose performance a more general spirit is not necessary, may want a certain kind of stage self-possession, and if not aukward, be only the more touching for it. Miss Stephens was like an affectionate wife in private, who raillied, not from excess of spirit but of a wish to please.[53] [16 November 1817]

If her dynamic range was narrow, her "saving grace" was a delicate modulation of emphasis and a personal appeal that converted weakness into strength. This appeal Hunt also found in the "pathos" of her voice, as we have seen; and the previous season he remarked on the "tenderness and admiration" evoked by her complete vocal and dramatic realization:

Indeed Miss Stevens [*sic*] . . . has a certain expression that is better
even than beautiful;—it is that of a sensitive resignation, which as
she stands before you with her dark eyes and hair, crossing her
arms over her bosom, with her head a little on one side, and her
easy warble winding about our ears, is really extremely touching.
It produces that sort of feeling of mixed tenderness and admiration,
which is the highest triumph of art, and amounts to something like
personal affection. [17 November 1816]

Lucia Vestris had no obvious defects whatever to compensate
for. Indeed, Hunt declared her too good for the English musical
stage. At her Drury Lane debut in *The Siege of Belgrade* he
commented, "This theatre is justly said to have had a great
acquisition in Madame Vestris, who sang at the Opera some time
ago. Why she has not performed there again is to us incompre-
hensible; for she is a true singer, a pleasing actress, and a handsome woman; three graces, not very frequently united in the
same person." He relished the vivacity she brought to English
opera, but he admired her tenderness even more than her animal
spirits:

If we have any preference, we think her tenderer vivacity better
than her mere humour,—no ill compliment to a woman. We like
extremely the little raillying dance to that beautiful Italian air;
and we are sure the audience did, for they seemed as if they did not
know how to leave off encoring it; but we like still better that
appearance of involuntary tenderness which she throws into the
question "No more?" when *Leopold* and she have been agreeing
never to see each other again, and they stand nearly back to back,
he pretending to huff, and she making little elbow approaches to
him, throwing down her eyes the while, and looking at her lifted
fingers. The transport with which he turns around, and dances
headlong with her into a merry chorus, was never more warranted.
[27 February 1820]

More than a superior vocalist, she had the power to communicate
pleasure in song because of her personal character. Unlike the
specious purveyors of trite wares to a gullible public, Vestris
brought such conviction to her art that she could even summon
up thought and feeling in purely ornamental passages:

She is inferior to no one in the great charm of a female singer,—a
certain mixture of cordial and voluptuous sentiment. Her voice
comes from her, riding upon it's own glad breath; and the ready
smiles play about it, on the least occasion, as if in good-natured
delight at the triumph of it's sincerity. She seems mutually to enjoy
it with it's hearers,—a great charm, when it evidently arises from
pleasure rather than from pride; as it only can do, if truly charming.
Her graces also, though truly graceful, are of no easy or cheap kind,
such as the mere succession of rapid notes, the *rouleaus* of twopenny
ornaments, with which Mr. Braham condescends to bribe the shouts
of the galleries. They are either passages worth the display for their
composition, or pure graces of feeling, revolving upon a thought
which they do not like to quit.

Hunt attested her artistic integrity in other productions. In
Giovanni in London she not only played the breeches part of the
Don "with a well-bred air of unconsciousness," but she also
"sings the airs with her usual good taste; which will become false
to please nobody, and therefore at last pleases every body" (4 June
1820).[54] (He correctly predicted the ultimate artistic success of
this performer with the public.) Because of complete dedication
to her art, she subsumed her personality to that of the role (Mandane in *Artaxerxes*), bringing to her portrayal an overwhelming
power of conviction:

She has faith in the beauty and nature of what she sings, and lets
it speak for itself through the medium of her expressive voice.
The way in which she goes through the song of *In infancy our hopes
and fears* is a happy specimen of the very reverse of Braham's
superfluities. When she varies her delivery, it is not by addition but
by intonation. The low and exquisite dropping of her voice upon
the passage *Restore him to that innocence,* as if the depth of her
tenderness would not suffer her to be louder, holds the house in a
dumb transport of attention. [16 April 1820]

Spontaneity and self-possession, vivacity and tenderness, pathos
and sentiment—these qualities, which Hunt prized in the English-
opera performer, he saw as essential expressions of the artist's
personality. When to these were added an abiding joy in art and

a faith in its beauty and nature, the performer had the power to achieve the ultimate expression of dramatic characterization.

To be sure, a Vestris was a *rara avis* on the English musical stage, and Hunt's criticism of performers, as of so much else on that stage, recounts a dozen failures for every success. But in penetrating to the essence of the performer's art, his criticism is capable of making equally vivid for us not only the absurdities of voice and action but also those few moments of dramatic excellence that held him spellbound in the theatre, a century and a half ago.

Aside from a few passing allusions, there is little mention of the orchestra in the *Examiner* criticism. Presumably the theatre orchestra of Hunt's time was pretty much taken for granted— then as now—in the performance of musical plays. The resources of the "band," as it was often called, were not inconsiderable, but they could not quite meet the demands of Mozart's music, and their playing was usually uninspired.

One of Hunt's references to the orchestra was introduced for its relevance to a William Barrymore, whose theatricalities as the Duke in *Twelfth Night* he dispraised:

His delivery of the exquisite lines that open the play,

>   If music be the food of love, play on, &c. &c.

was like that of a mouthing schoolmaster hastening to finish the passage that he might proceed to lecture upon it,—that is to say, upon what he neither feels nor understands. The orchestra were in excellent accompaniment; and when the Duke called for "that strain again," because "it had a dying fall,"—gave it with as much indifference, and with as little of the *dying* in it, as if they thought his Highness was joking. [3 March 1811]

Elsewhere Hunt noted the difficulty of Mozart for the Covent Garden instrumentalists, even though Bishop's adaptation of *Figaro* (see below) had been simplified: "Either the orchestra too was very deficient on this occasion, or the accompaniments were clipped, and deprived of their richness; so that altogether, though the exquisite powers of Mozart could not but surmount all this

ill-treatment in some measure, it was a wretched introduction of
him to the public" (21 March 1819).

Yet Hunt found considerable pleasure in the music of the
orchestra, especially in the overtures and entr'actes, to which he
makes an occasional passing reference. At *The Duenna* the
orchestra seemed "to play more *con amore* than usual. . . . It
adapted itself uncommonly well to the singers; and between the
play and the farce [*Quadrille*] . . . treated the audience . . . with
some passages out of *Don Giovanni*. This is good, and giving
good measure." He regretted having arrived too late for the
overture, "which is taken from [Peter von] Winter,—a great and
deep-hearted musician" (20 June 1819).

For a critic condemned to endure the innumerable inanities of
the English musical stage year after year, these orchestral interludes could provide a welcome solace:

The general business of a critic, in seating himself in the Theatre,
is to strengthen himself against the three approaching hours; to
indulge in the remembrance of what has been, and in the pictures
of what ought to be, in an English theatre; and to snatch, as far as
the slamming of doors and the fluttering of loungers will suffer him,
the occasional relief of the music between the acts, which, compared
with the pieces it divides, is like stripes of gold-lace upon a
threadbare drugget. To go to the theatre with these anticipations,
and be presented with a piece at once new and tolerable, is about as
agreeable and surprising as it would be to a London pedestrian to
see claret gushing from Piccadilly pump or a laurel-tree starting up
in Saint Giles's.[55] [6 January 1811]

Managers, Critics, and Public Taste

Closely related to Hunt's criticism of the performances are
his numerous comments on other matters that affected the quality of the English musical stage. In his attacks on theatre managers and fellow journalists for abdicating their responsibility to
the public, Hunt reveals himself more explicitly than elsewhere
as defender of public taste. Aware that the low state of the drama
was attributable only in part to a feeble creativity, he challenged

the men and institutions that permitted and even encouraged mediocrity, and he chided a public that tolerated it.

The theatre managers were primary targets for Hunt's criticism. He held them responsible not only for the cheap and shoddy productions they offered to the public but also for their "shops," "retainers," and "money-getting" principles, since their commercial interests took precedence over every artistic consideration. He blamed them for deluding the public with newspaper "puffs" and playbill falsifications, for tampering with the artistic property of others, and for blocking the presentation of better productions with shop-made vehicles. And since the managers were also playwrights, he criticized them as dramatists.

Hazlitt and Hunt agreed that Arnold's musical productions at the Lyceum (later renamed the English Opera House) were less offensive than the general run, though this was their only virtue. After taking note of the plot of *Up All Night,* Hunt remarked, "If these incidents are lame, it must be put to the account of their old age: Mr. Arnold has sense enough to discard the grosser pertness of his brother dramatists, with their puns and their perpetual caricature; but then he has no humour to supply its place, and his Pegasus becomes a mere jog-trotting hack, with not even a sprightly vice about him" (2 July 1809). Reviewing *The King's Proxy,* Hazlitt observed that Arnold "writes with the fewest ideas possible; his meaning is more nicely balanced between sense and nonsense, than that of any of his competitors; he succeeds from the perfect insignificance of his pretensions, and fails to offend through downright imbecility" (27 August 1815). Other scattered references to Arnold's pieces appear in the columns of the "Theatrical Examiner," but Hunt had little to say about them. Concerning some trifle at the English Opera House, he once declared, "Our readers are not to be informed, that in the present condition of the stage, one or two criticisms on comedy or farce will answer for fifty other comedies and farces, and that the drama in perpetually repeating the same things, has almost reduced criticism to its own tautology" (14 July 1811).[56]

In Arnold the manager neither Hazlitt nor Hunt saw much hope for an improvement in the state of the drama. Hazlitt op-

From Ernest B. Watson, *Sheridan to Robertson*

From *The British Stage, and Literary Cabinet,* edited by Thomas Kenrick

Lucia Elizabeth Vestris (center) in scene with two unidentified players

Giuseppe Naldi as Figaro in *Le Nozze di Figaro* (1818)

From Iconography Files, Lincoln Center Music Library

Manuel del Popolo Vicente García

From Iconography Files, Lincoln Center Music Library

Giuseppe Ambrogetti (c. 1824)

Elizabeth Billington

From "The Age of Bel Canto," Brochure,
London Record Album OSA 12457

Josephina Grassini

From "The Age of Bel Canto," Brochure,
London Record Album OSA 12457

posed his theatre from the beginning, believing that his license for summer productions would only facilitate the crumbling of artistic standards, such as they were, at the two winter houses. Further, in putting forward his own productions at the theatre, Arnold blocked the road to improvement. "We think in general," Hazlitt stated, "that the practice of making the Manager bring out his own pieces on the stage is a custom which would be 'more honoured in the breach than the observance:' it is offering a premium for the rejection of better pieces than his own" (2 April 1815). Hunt, however, thought the competition offered by Arnold could have a beneficial effect on the London stage, at least in theory, though the immediate promise was admittedly dim:

The new Opera does not promise much for Mr. Arnold's theatre: Mr. Arnold is a degree above Cherry, and Mr. King some degrees above Reeve, but much better writers and composers are necessary to reform the public taste. The engagement of Mrs. Bishop, however, leads one to hope, that her husband will be employed to exercise his scientific pen on the occasion;[57] and though the overthrow of the Italian Opera is not to be atchieved but by a change of the system of education in high life, yet much good may and ought to be done to the public taste, by the encouragement of rival theatres. [2 July 1809]

Attacks against the management at Covent Garden and Drury Lane were rare, perhaps because their committee arrangements presented few individuals who could be singled out for blame. Charles Kemble* brought down Hunt's wrath when he falsified the Covent Garden playbills for Dibdin's *Bonifacio*, which "was so completely damned on its first performance last Tuesday week, that the performer who came to announce it's second representation could not obtain a hearing amidst the universal hisses and groans, and the audience departed under a romantic persuasion that the piece would be withdrawn." The piece, however, was not withdrawn. Noting that the playbills of the next day announced this as "an exquisite production which set the audience in *universal and continued peals of laughter*," Hunt chided:

This was a miserable artifice as well as a miserable falsehood. . . . Mr. Kemble, I have understood, is the present Acting Manager of

Covent-Garden, and how that grave actor or any manager whatever
can reconcile the perpetual falshoods [sic] of these play-bills to the
gratitude which is due to the public, or even to the feelings of
honest men and gentlemen, is a problem not to be solved by the
admirers of truth. It is reckoned sufficiently gross and contemptible
in any person to tell a lie to a single man, but as these bills are
intended for the whole town, they of course tell lies to every body
in the town, and every body therefore is insulted. This is the true
quackery of theatres: they must impose upon people by the vilest
puffs, before their physic can be swallowed. [10 April 1808]

Both managers and their "retainers" showed irresponsibility—
to the public as well as to other dramatists—by their tamperings
with dramatic property, though in many instances it was impossible to name the offender. Musical productions seemed especially vulnerable to such managerial mishandling, but no dramatic property was immune. Although Hunt was highly critical
of Henry Milman's* tragedy Fazio, as previously noted, he reported that the play had been represented in Bath and London
without the concurrence of the author, who totally disclaimed
the alterations made.[58] "This is not the politest or most liberal
conduct certainly on the part of the Managers; but it is part of
the cold and grasping system that prevails now-a-days in all the
upper circles of shopkeeping" (15 February 1818).

But more important works were at stake. Hunt welcomed the
revival of an adaptation of Dryden's King Arthur (1691), though
he would have preferred the original:

Covent-Garden has made another lucky hit in the reproduction of
Dryden's altered masque of King Arthur; but it would have been
luckier, had not Garrick's dry and pantomimic abridgment [1770]
hurt the effect of the original. Managers are generally more cunning
than wise in these matters; and finding that dullness cannot do
without stage-tailoring, think that genius must be cut and squeezed
to it too. Dryden's genius never appeared in so poetical or touching
a light as in one character in this piece,—that of Philidel, the fallen
young spirit, who is working it's way back to heaven with penitence.
But his want of sentiment interfered even with this; and the whole
of the piece is strangely modern-looking and meretricious for a tale

of old chivalry and romance. Now the abridgment has kept the meretriciousness, and hurt the nature and the poetry. [31 October 1819]

Inflated afterpieces were distressing, but not so disastrous as finding genius cut down by petty adaptors. Dryden was not the only victim on this occasion: "A good deal of Purcell's fine music too, which though somewhat quaint and crude is full of genius and effect,[59] is unnecessarily missed,—as the duet for instance, of *Two daughters of this aged stream* and the wintry singing of the *Frozen Genius*. However, what remains is much better than usual; and one's national vanity is laudably gratified at hearing those fine old airs of *Britons strike home, Come if you dare,* and *Fairest isle all isles excelling*."[60] Whether or not Hunt was aware that Arne adapted Purcell's music for the Garrick version, he indicates some knowledge of the original.

Similarly, Hunt pronounced Ramsay's *The Gentle Shepherd* "cut down into a short afterpiece," though he did not know whom to blame for the butchery (see appendix one). Far worse than the cuts was the gratuitous addition of

the celebrated duet, *Together let us range the Fields,* in Dr. Boyce's *Solomon*; so that instead of the Eastern Prince and his mistress, a pair of Scotch lovers were made to talk of lying "on rosy beds," and enjoying "*vineyards!*" The next thing would be to make Solomon talk Scotch, and set him to luxuriate in a kailyard. There is something besides mere criticism, that will not allow us to stand this. If we are not to have Scotch manners and proprieties in a Scotch scene, why give us such a scene at all? If we are, we cannot help entering into the scene, and every thing about it; and in proportion as we feel what really belongs to it, we recoil from this oriental piece of impertinence. The best that can be said on such an occasion, is that the two performers come forward, as it were, to sing a concert-room duet. [6 July 1817]

Contemporary adaptations were usually no better. Shakespeare supplied apparently inexhaustible resources for dramatic revisionists. At the opening of Edmund Kean's* potpourri *Richard, Duke of York,* Hunt affirmed it was not likely

that a good compilation will ever be made from the works of a
great dramatist; for in proportion as his work is good, and co-herent,
and finely coloured, this cutting up into piece-meals must inevitably
spoil it. Imagine a selection from Rafael's pictures, put together
into one picture; or an opera made out of scenes of different operas
of Mozart, Paesiello, and Cimarosa. A true painter or musician
would laugh in your face at such a proposal. What would become
of all the harmonies and gradations of colour,—of all the suitabilities
to this or that situation or person? The absurdity is self-evident.
[28 December 1817]

Nor were operatic adaptations of the bard neglected during this
period. The *Comedy of Errors* was brought out as an opera two
years later by Reynolds (who, Genest states, was too ashamed to
place his name on it), with music supplied by Bishop. Hunt, who
cared little for the play, quite rejected its musical transforma-
tion: "The original is not an opera, where every thing, being to
be sung, is made to be sung, and the very discords become con-
cordant. It is a play of endless puzzle and confusion, with characters any thing but harmonious . . . [and a plot that has] neither
time, nor temper, nor any thing else, to be dallying with duets
and sostenutos" (26 December 1819). Hunt's attitude does not
seem to reflect any Romantic veneration for Shakespeare, but his
viewpoint is literary. There is no reason why this play, adapted
by a librettist as skillful as Boito, could not be "made to be sung"
in a thoroughly operatic manner by a Verdi, though of course no
true Shakespearean operas had then been created.

Despite Hunt's strictures, the play proved to be exceptionally
popular and was followed, the next season, by Reynolds's adaptation of *Twelfth Night* (music by Bishop):

The scenery of this piece is beautiful, particularly in the Mask
which they have introduced from the *Tempest,* and which reminded
us of the times of Inigo Jones and Ben Jonson.[61] After all, we
know not whether the managers and their musician have not
imposed on us with the help of Shakspeare; and whether we ought
not to resent these "pickings and stealings" of him on that very
account. . . . In short, with all our criticism and objections, we
have been upon the whole much pleased; and if in candour we must

mention the one, in gratitude we cannot help confessing the other. [12 November 1820]

Hunt's dislike of musical tamperings with Shakespeare is again evident, though his objections are moderated by the fact that the value of the play, as spoken drama, is not severely compromised by the addition of musical numbers.

Still other English musical adaptations stemmed from a revived interest in Italian opera following the artistically successful Ayrton season of 1817. The operas of Mozart and Rossini were ransacked for tunes and plots that would appeal to audiences generally unacquainted with the King's Theatre but eager to hear the new "hit" composers. Hunt was not in principle opposed to such adaptations, which he hoped would improve public taste by making the music of Italian operas known to a wider public. In reviewing the *Barber of Seville*, Englished by John Fawcett* and Daniel Terry,* with music of Rossini and Paesiello adapted by Bishop, Hunt did not protest the changes and additions. Indeed, he felt that "the music is well adapted by Mr. Bishop, and affords some of the best specimens of those two composers" and that "its bringing out is creditable to the Managers" (18 October 1818). His main objection was to the inability of the English singers to cope with the music, as we have noted in the preceding section.

Apparently Hunt did not think that the Rossini opera, which at first he did not like, could be greatly marred by adaptation—especially a skillful one. Mozart was another matter. When Bishop's adaptation of *The Marriage of Figaro* was offered as an English opera the following season, Hunt was highly indignant at the mishandling of Mozart's music:

But what shall we say of *Figaro here?* Never, we believe, was there a sadder metamorphosis of French vivacity and Italian singing. At the first view of the matter, great credit seems due to those who adapt Mozart's music to English words, and endeavour to forward the intimacy of the public with him. People, too, augured highly of his adapter, Mr. Bishop, some of whose earlier productions displayed a good deal of real feeling for his art. But . . . what are

we to say to an adapter of Mozart, who for some of his pieces
substitutes the airs about the street, and in others alters passages to
suit the voice of the performer? Those passages were written to suit
particular passions or emotions, not to be at the mercy of this or
that incapacity. Their beauty also, and that of the context itself,
depends upon preserving the context entire. You can no more alter
it with impunity, than you can put common-places into the songs of
Comus or the *Faithful Shepherdess.* [21 March 1819]

There is no reason to doubt Hunt's assertion that Bishop
"adapted Mozart's music to English words,"[62] and his attack on
Bishop is not surprising. *Figaro* was a particular favorite of
Hunt's. But it is interesting to note for the first time in his criticism of the English musical stage a genuine concern with "preserving the context entire" of a piece, though the work cited was
of course a true opera. The emphasis on musico-dramatic unity
that he had come to respect in Mozart as an esthetic criterion was
as yet scarcely applicable to "English opera"; and in citing English dramatic parallels in this passage, Hunt significantly mentions
only the *songs* of Milton's masque and Fletcher's pastoral.

Hunt by no means opposed experimental approaches on the
English musical stage, but resisted all adaptations that weakened
or destroyed the solid efforts of competent dramatists and composers. Unfortunately, these adaptations all too frequently represented a debasement of taste, for which he found the managers
and their retainers largely to blame.

Along with theatre managers Hunt attacked periodicals in his
English-opera reviews for their inept criticism. If managers misled the public in puffing their products, the newspapers were
equally to blame for publishing them.

In his review of *The Exile* he declared, "I must protest at all
times against this innovation on the independence of the regular
drama, and I trust the independent periodical works will take
severer notice of it than they have done." And in his review of
Theodore Hook's *The Siege of St. Quintin* of the same date, he
pointed out improvements in the taste of both the press and the

public, leaving little doubt with his readers as to the *Examiner*'s role in effecting the change:

I recollect the time, when Messrs. Reynolds, Cobb and Dibdin never wrote a play, but it was panegyrized in all the newspapers and magazines; wit and fine satire went hand in hand with their puns and caricatures, their faces smirked upon us from the *superb engravings* with a sidelong satisfaction, and all the critics shuddered when I begged leave to differ with their opinions. Now however the case is considerably altered: Punch is no longer a specimen of polite learning: some of the periodical works have changed their tone because they have changed their critics, some from conviction, and others because they will always think as the public think. [13 November 1808]

These exaggerations no doubt arose from the young critic's eagerness to press claims for the *Examiner*'s success as it approached the end of its first year of publication. (In a similar mood he later declared that the *Examiner* had taught Reynolds how to rhyme—though without perceptible improvement, it would seem.)[63] Even in this review his claims can scarcely be reconciled with the predominant tone of challenge. For, as he continues, the critical revolt is not yet complete.

There still remain a few critics, who upon the strength of saying "How d'ye do?" in the boxes, and of arguing upon the public spirited principle of cheating the town to assist their acquaintances, will do violence to their better judgment and praise a bad play, yet even these gentlemen do it with so piteous a labour, with such evident shrugs and wincings and recoilings, that they are obliged, in pity to their own conscience, to confess that the piece is *light*—that is the word:—a very pleasant piece but *light*, and exactly *"what the author intended it."* We see how unwillingly they betray themselves. This word *light* in their own heartfelt sense, does not mean a quality opposed to mere heaviness, not soul opposed to corporeality, not a fairy genius composed of spirit and full of a charming volatility, but something in direct contradiction to every thing that is full, solid, and sterling, a light scale mounting from its emptiness, or a light guinea, glittering and completely worthless.

Although Hunt's skirmishes with editors and critics continued sporadically over the years, his later attacks were on the whole less trenchant. He frequently took note of the reviews in the dailies—especially those in the *Chronicle* and the *Times,* which were published before the *Examiner*'s. Sometimes he quarreled with their comments; occasionally he pronounced himself in full agreement with their judgments. Now and then his tone is patronizing, his manner suggesting the sociability of a host among guests who need to be chided. Yet the sincerity of his praise or blame is unmistakable. Hunt's modified reactions to the press in later years may reflect a genuine improvement in their criticism, yet as late as 1817 he was still occasionally censorious.

The taste of the public was also directly challenged by *Examiner* reviewers. In this connection we should consider the English-opera criticism of Thomas Barnes, for in it he was preoccupied with the total absurdity of English opera and the hopelessly corrupt taste of the English people. This attitude is apparent, too, in a number of letters from correspondents (April to September, 1814) on the question "Are the English a musical people?" that Barnes placed in the "Theatrical Examiner"—often in lieu of any remarks of his own! Signed by "Musicus," "Tallis's Ghost," "Mark Minim,"[64] and the like, they provided a kind of running debate on the question, though the consensus was that English music had a brilliant past and a wretched present. The main question in the argument was whether the English people could recover their past glory. Most contributors were pessimistic, though none so much as Barnes, who seemed never to tire of railing at the musical stupidity of the English.

Only one column by this critic on the English musical stage has substance and style. It is not a review, for, after noting that Covent Garden could change their scheduled performances "with perfect impunity" owing to the popularity of Catherine Stephens, Barnes goes on to offer what is partly a critique on that singer but is substantially a gratuitous yet pungent commentary on his favorite subject:

The English are not a musical people: with the exception of a few national melodies, their ears seem almost incapable of receiving

pleasure from musical sound. We are aware that there is a building
in the Haymarket, where, during part of the year, a subscription
assembly go to hear bad music, though they might if they pleased
hear the best: . . . If there were any national taste for music, would
the names of Handel and Purcel [sic]—though grown old in this
country in more than a century of fame among the scientific—would
they be to the great mass of the people almost unknown? Ask a
German Gentleman about any air or harmony of Haydn or Mozart,
and he will give you some notion of it either by humming or playing.
Ask many an English Gentleman about Arne or Jackson, and he
will gaze at you with all the astonishment of ignorance, unless,
perhaps, it should occur to him that you allude to the celebrated
pugilist.[65] [30 January 1814]

Barnes's interest in the cause of good music is as undeniable as
his insistence on charging the caprices of the aristocracy for its
loss to the public. On the whole, however, his criticism is disappointing. He reviewed very few productions (often forgetting
to mention their titles), and he had little to say about the work,
the music, or even the performance. When aroused by his theme
he was capable of pungent phrases and sallies of wit, yet his
writing was often marred by triteness and a washy sentimentality
curiously at variance with his later reputation as editor of the
Times. His interests were too specialized, and his biases too over-
riding, to make him a good musical journalist.

A far better journalist, Hazlitt shared Barnes's contempt for
"English taste." In his Italian-opera criticism he, like Barnes,
frequently associated this taste with the aristocracy. But he also
condemned the musical taste of middle-class audiences at the
English theatres. For example, in his review of Pocock's *The
Libertine* he stated that Mozart's music "triumphed." "Still,"
he continued,

it had but half a triumph, for the songs were not *encored*; and when
an attempt was made by some rash over-weening enthusiasts to
encore the enchanting airs of Mozart, that heavy German composer,
"that dull Beotian [sic] genius," as he has been called by a lively
verbal critic of our times, the English, disdaining this insult offered
to our native talents, *hissed*—in the plenitude of their pampered

grossness, and "ignorant impatience" of foreign refinement and elegance, they hissed! We believe that unconscious patriotism has something to do with this as well as sheer stupidity; they think that a real taste for the Fine Arts, unless they are of British growth and manufacture, is a sign of disaffection to the Government, and that there must be "something rotten in the state of Denmark," if their ears, as well as their hearts, are not true English. [25 May 1817]

This review, incidentally, discloses still another side of Hazlitt's enigmatic personality. He was not always happy about Mozart, or Italian opera, and more often than not his reviews were based on traditional British prejudices. Nevertheless, he here recognizes the new importance of Italian opera in English cultural life and indicates a degree of enthusiasm for the opera that he seldom manifests in his King's Theatre criticism.

Thus, Barnes and Hazlitt frequently condemned public taste. Their remarks were generally acidulous and often pontifical. Hunt's attitude was more complex. With the reader kept well in the foreground, his challenges, though less vitriolic, were more immediate and direct in their effect. Moreover, for Hunt the musical taste of the public was even commendable on some occasions; and its faults were susceptible of improvement. For the improvement of public taste remained his chief concern, as we have seen in a number of reviews already considered. He was genuinely convinced, for example, that the new popularity of Italian-opera composers would be a cultural asset to audiences at the playhouses. Although he disliked the English *Figaro,* he approved the opportunity to "forward the intimacy of the public" with Mozart. In his review of the English *Barber* he observed that "the evident effect of the German and Italian compositions, with which the Opera has lately improved our national taste for music, will doubtless be further assisted by the new piece."

In other comments Hunt praised the public for its good taste. Regarding Shield's music for *The Woodman,* he wrote that he "could not help admiring the correctness of the public in matters of taste, when I heard some of those fine airs which have become popular, and which are indisputably the best in the piece" (7 February 1808). Of Arne's *Artaxerxes* he stated, "There appears to be something in a genius for tenderness, which generally leads it to repose on those whom it resembles. The public naturally learn to appreciate this kind of talent more than any other, except that of humour; and the consequence is, that the best things in *Artaxerxes* are the most popular" (16 April 1820). Even in condemning the operatic *Comedy of Errors* he explained, "We do not wonder however that people go to see a comedy which ought only to be read, now that we have heard Miss Stephens and Miss Tree sing together" (26 December 1819). Elsewhere Hunt pointed to an improvement in the public's response to English opera: "Within these two or three years, the public have certainly lost a great deal of respect for those huge farces, which they were good-natured enough to call operas and comedies." And he added, "The dramatists have perceived the progress of this sound feeling among the public" (13 November 1808). If the public had indeed lost its respect, the managers would have been the first to know it. The productions of operatic farce and melodrama had by no means diminished; but in his eagerness to improve public taste, Hunt made claims that could not be justified.

On the other hand, he pointed out instances of bad public taste. We have already noted his comment on the "coarse want of excitement" in the public's preference for bad tragedies, from which he hoped to deliver them. He also cited the public's preference for bravura displays and neglect of dramatic values. He observed that Braham was encored twice for his rendering of "Scots Wha Hae" in *Guy Mannering*—"that is to say, he sang it three times over, to the irrepressible enthusiasm of the audience, who may have seen in it 'more than meets the ear' " (10 October 1819).[66] (Perhaps Hunt had grown weary of the song, for eleven years earlier he noted that Braham sang it "with a fine fermenting enthusiasm worthy of it's author" [13 November 1808].) In contrast, Arne's aria "The Soldier Tired" was a great favorite with the public, "more for the difficulty of the execution than the merit of the composition, good as the latter is" (16 April 1820). Further, with the continuing intrusion of music on the English stage the public had come to ignore the acting in an opera, provided the singing pleased: "Unfortunately the town is so accustomed to expect little else in operas besides the mere art of singing, and the vocal parts in the *Duenna* [1775] have so often been performed by mere professors of the art, that they are not readily disposed to let Mr. Sheridan's wit and nature become more prominent than the execution of the songs" (20 June 1819).

The taste of the public had its deficiencies; nevertheless it was not to be abused. Warning new performers to eschew "the most prominent characters" and risk an inglorious failure ("a fiddler is by no means sought out for concerts because he has spoiled Handel"), Hunt cited the dangers of presupposing a gullible public. "For though the world is made up of credulities, yet there is nothing it resents so much as an attempt to impose on its discernment; and if the majority have very little discernment at all, they will for that very reason be cautious of trusting a second appeal to it, lest they should be cheated a second time without knowing it" (1 January 1809).

Hunt's animadversions on the managers, the press, and the public suggest superficial contradictions. But he was less concerned with a facile consistency than with reforming public taste. To this end his varied approaches of praise and ridicule, prodding and probing, encouragement and remonstration, provided a highly effective rhetoric. Unfortunately, the improvements he sought were beyond the powers of even a unified English press.

Closely related to the question of public taste are discussions in Hunt's opera criticism on musical nationalism and on manners and morals. These issues will be considered separately in the following sections.

Musical Nationalism

The rising popularity of Italian opera at the King's Theatre was echoed in several productions at the English theatres. Stimulated by these productions and by his regular King's Theatre reviews starting in 1817, Hunt brought into his later criticism of English opera significant commentary on the nature of English music. He was especially interested in the cultural conditions that molded English composers, both early and contemporary. And he explored the relationship between English music and English national character, to which he contrasted the musical character of Continental countries, especially Italy.

Among the male singers who appealed to patriotic and nationalistic feelings of the audiences of Hunt's time, none was more successful than Charles Incledon. As we have seen, he achieved wide popularity in Jack Tar imitations and was generally regarded as the typical English stage singer. Hazlitt was perhaps being ironical when he remarked of him: "He is a true old English singer" (18 August 1816).

Although Hunt agreed that "there is always an English something about his voice, which . . . is pleasant and invigorating to hear" (13 September 1812), he did not find him "true" English. "[Incledon] has been reckoned indeed a true specimen of an English singer," Hunt noted later, "but we confess, he does not appear so to us. He may have the force, and even the sweetness; but he wants the dignity and expressiveness, or in other words, the intelligence. He is not a fit singer, for instance, for the true English composers, such as Arne and Purcell, except where they get into their most inferior ballad-style" (12 February 1815). Still later he returned to the subject in good earnest:

We do not see how such a singer [as Incledon] is to be exclusively called national, still less what is the compliment paid by so calling him either to himself or his countrymen. He may be national, inasmuch as he may represent a certain portion of the rougher and less intelligent class of Englishmen, and such as are too apt to value themselves on those very odd advantages, and to think all people and nations a pack of shallow triflers who know better. Some of these rough and unpromising persons are very excellent men, we have no doubt; and Mr. Incledon among them; but whatever the rest of them may tell each other, and however they may be convinced, that to differ with their manners is to be so much the worse in every thing else, wiser men will see nothing in all this but a gross and ignorant egotism,—a pride arising, in fact, from unconscious deficiency,—and a ridiculous assumption of being thought well of without taking the trouble of deserving it. We have

never found in the course of our own experience, that the rudest or
sturdiest sort of people have been really the most sincere or generous.
Their manners, in fact, are a gross failure on the social side at once;
and as to their feelings, when put to the test, you may generally
then discover the real cause of their affectation of sincerity. The
greatest Englishmen, those who made England what it was, and the
surviving influence of whose example has helped to keep what
remains of it, were not such people;—the Chaucers, and Sydneys
[sic], and Hampdens, and Richard Steeles, were no such gross
pretenders; the Somerses[67] and Addisons were none such;—and the
"gentle Shakspeare" was the reverse of them, as he was of every thing
else unsocial, ungraceful, and unwise. [30 March 1817]

Hunt would not confound the true Englishman with Jack Tar or
John Bull—an identity that appealed to the grosser elements in
British life. His remarks—reminiscent of his antipathies to jingo-
istic platitudes in the "Patriot Breast"—again provide a link between politics and music.

Politics aside, Hunt saw English music generally as existing
under a pall. Among the composers on whom Bishop had drawn
for his production of *Twelfth Night* were, he said,

Morley, Ravenscroft,[68] and others, who flourished during the
golden age of our poetry. Profound in all that was then known of
science, which was chiefly occupied in church music, and yet having
a people to sing their productions who were much more eager and
competent to do so than the contemporaries of their greater
successors,[69] the style of their lyrical composition, partly formal
and partly tricksome and playful, is like a young chorister
anticipating the moment when he shall escape from his surplice,
and get out among his fields and pastimes. [12 November 1820]

The golden age of English poetry was not for Hunt the golden
age of English music. His praise for the work of these early composers is tinged with regret that their musical science was limited.
He appears to have had some knowledge of their secular works,
but for him these composers barely escaped the pall of the church.
This view was no doubt inherited from the Enlightenment,
which regarded church supremacy in music with hostility. But it
was strongly reinforced by Hunt's personal antipathies towards

organized religion. In commenting on the use of Shakespeare's songs in the musical *Comedy of Errors,* he wrote:

But fine English poetry, generally speaking, is a thing not to be reached by English music. The latter wants wing to overtake it; wants airiness, ardour, continuity of flight. It is too apt, in it's liveliest moments, to take melancholy breath; to halt, and drag back, into psalmody. If we were made to excel in any music, it is church music; and we have excelled in it. But for one true flight of gaiety and inspiration, like Arne's *Where the Bee sucks,* we have fifty happy pieces of poetry ludicrously contradicted by doleful and pompous music; especially in those solemn personages called Glees, who play into each other's hands as gravely as old ladies at whist. [26 December 1819]

The English glee was lively enough in the seventeenth century, but Hunt seems to have known only the later, serious ones which he so aptly described.

Hunt detects other forces that cast a pall over English music: English insularity to Continental influences, the British climate, and encroaching commercialism. Despite its progress with regard to science, music had become trite and crabbed; indeed, Hunt apparently reflects the inconsistency of Burney when he states that the Elizabethans were remarkably versed in the art:

Some of the music, by the late Dr. Arnold,[*] is very pretty; but music in England, like every thing in China, seems to stop at a certain middling pitch, and never get farther:—at least we have not hitherto taken the inoculation of foreign music very kindly; nor with all the example of the Italian and German schools, and the efforts of individuals here and there to emulate them or excite emulation, can we reckon ourselves such a musical people as in times when there were no great schools at all. In the days of Shakspeare, for instance, music was well understood as a science;—her Majesty's lute-book, we believe, was found absolutely appalling in point of learned difficulty;[70] and what is better, it was accounted a want of common taste and good-breeding not to be able to take a part in a song. This has been held a great mystery . . . but we believe it to be wholly attributable to the national want of animal spirits, occasionally caused by climate, but chiefly by dull modes of living and habits of money-getting.

Hunt goes on to explain that the Germans, akin to the English, have lost much of their dullness, having recently been "so much mixed with sprightlier nations and shaken up by political events," and he urges "sprightlier theories in general, and a renewal of the love of nature" on his countrymen. "In proportion as a musician cultivates these, and does not button himself up in the mere common-places about him, he will be likely to make a figure in his art" (30 August 1818).

Characteristically, Hunt associates geniality of spirits with political liberty and with artistic success. Climate was not an inevitable dampener of creativity, but he believed that it took a toll on English painting and music, though not on its poetry. He had explored the subject in a review the previous year:

We admire our native country of all others in the world for its poetry; and we are persuaded that both our painters and musicians would come nearer to it, if they seized the opportunity of studying their art, more than they do, out of doors. But as it will ever be impossible perhaps for our painters to equal the Italians as *painters,* in consequence of our chill necessities of dress, and the dull medium through which we see colours; so we have little doubt, that owing to the same dullness of medium, which is that of sound also, and to our general perhaps consequent deficiency in animal spirits, we shall ever remain inferior to them in music. Poetry is another matter. It depends less on things external; and it's deficiencies even in those appear to be overbalanced, by the very disadvantages of the climate, in the additional thoughtfulness and observation to which it provokes the natural luxury of the poetical temperament. . . . There may be an exception now and then to prove the rule; but even then, we suspect, Italy will be found to have had something to do with it. Mozart, who of all the German composers had the greatest animal spirits, went there when he was a boy:—he drank at the winy fountain, and seems to have been intoxicated ever after with love and delight. [6 July 1817]

Italy was by this time becoming for Hunt a fountainhead of clarity, light, and vivacity—the source of inspiration for artists doomed to work in benighted northern fogs. And there was the example of Mozart, then at the apex of his English reputation—a German who, thanks to Italy, possessed animal spirits.[71]

Nothing could be done about English weather, but insularity was another matter. Hunt believed that one way to remedy the "middling pitch" of English music was to render the cultural climate more amenable to foreign influences. But the treatment could prove worse than the disease if it were not administered with due respect for English temperament. Hunt welcomed a touch of Italian passion on the cold English boards; nevertheless, he saw that such infusions could prove a precarious cure. For example, one of the singers from the King's Theatre was given a part in James Kenney's* comic opera *Oh! This Love!* (music by King), performed at the Lyceum with deplorable results:[72]

The curiosity of the evening was the appearance of Miss Griglietti from the Opera.[73] The part allotted to her was sufficiently insipid to favour a want of exertion, and her manner was both indolent and timid, except when she was singing, and then she gave us all the pomp and affected emphasis of her Italian stage. Timidity in a female performer is what, I confess, I am not yet critic enough to wish altogether absent, but it is not so easy to tolerate indolence and that kind of inattention to dialogue which your fine singers are apt to indulge or to affect from their exclusive regard to the music. At the Opera Miss Griglietti's acting was of course overlooked and her powers may not have been very effective, but on a little stage like that of the Lyceum, some acting is very requisite, and the audience would be content with less powers of singing, or rather with less shew of them. The Italian gesture and expression may be very well in Italians, whose climate renders them more impassioned than ourselves, and whose want of sincerity compels them to make a greater protestation of it; but this style will always contain something very ridiculous to the judgment and feelings of Englishmen. [17 June 1810]

The present instance was no infusion at all, but an unsuccessful transplantation. It would not do. Not that acting at the King's Theatre was inferior to that of the English singers (though there were arguments on both sides). But operatic traditions that might pass muster in the context of Italian opera were singularly absurd on the English stage. To be effective, Italian vivacity would have to accommodate itself to the "realism" demanded by the English dramatic tradition so as to avoid a ludicrous clash of styles. (Of particular interest in this passage, incidentally, is Hunt's attack on Italian character and his mildly chauvinistic reference to the English. Such attacks are rare; indeed, they contradict his frequent expressions of admiration for the Italian people made in subsequent years.)[74]

Ten years later Hunt fully confronted the problem of Italian versus English styles in a review of Miss Greene as Polly in *The Beggar's Opera*. Bringing superfluity of "science" to the role, "she indulged herself now and then too long with a cadence, and treated us with chromatics when our hearis [for 'hearts'?] would have been better pleased without. The character of *Polly* is intended to let its whole gentle strength lie in simplicity, vocal as well as personal." In other roles, however, the singer might well develop her penchant for Italian vivacity—provided she felt thoroughly at home in it:

We are much mistaken if Miss Greene has not both taste and skill enough to engraft something more than usual of the passionate and breathing manner of the Italians upon our style of singing. Mozart and the Opera have lately given our native warblers a little inspiriting to this effect, and we are glad to see them inclined to it; though still we would advise all singers whatsoever to feel their way thoroughly, and find out what is most suitable to their individual natures. Any thing natural and suitable, even though inferior, is better and will produce a better effect, than a beauty evidently forced and artificial. [24 September 1820]

In concluding his review he launched into a comparison of English and Italian singing styles in relation to respective national characteristics:

It ought to be observed however, with regard to what is called this and that style of singing, that if one of them may appear artificial compared with another, it will be found not to be so in the long run, when we see how it is produced and borne out by the singer's feelings. Vivacity may be less native to the Englishman than the Italian; but it is not less true, where an Englishman feels it, than where an Italian does. Mrs. Jordan was very different from our actresses in general; yet how she charmed us with her genuine and cordial manners. The English singer is apt to give us too much the idea of a musical instrument, a pipe played with exquisite mechanism. The Italian puts, as it were, the breath of her heart into her voice, as if sympathy had thrown it open, and she could not but proclaim the triumph of her emotions.[75]

Italian vivacity, no longer tinged with insincerity, is now a desirable attribute for the English singer when it is not merely imitated. Was Hunt recalling, "in the long run," his previous objections?

During these years he had become a more perceptive critic of the English musical stage. Just as he was able to shake free from political prejudices and achieve a fuller appreciation for the poetry of Wordsworth and Coleridge, so, responding to new influences, he was able to cast off the middle-class bias against Italian opera and move toward a broader view of music. The passage just cited illustrates convincingly, I think, the critic's ability to come to terms with both the English and the Italian styles—and to reconcile them perfectly in a critical relativism that is completely germane to both traditions.

One singer there was who could encompass both the Italian and English styles and be equally at home in English opera or at the King's Theatre: Lucia Vestris, whose Italian roots and English upbringing helped to prepare her for such virtuosity. Though Hunt preferred her in Italian opera, he welcomed her acquisition by Drury Lane:

The lover of singing, who is unacquainted with the Italian opera, may have an opportunity, in hearing this lady sing, which it is still more difficult to meet with: we mean, that he may hear the true Italian style of singing on his native stage, and be able to distinguish it from the other without feeling it to be too violent a contrast. This is doubtless to be attributed in great measure to her having lived so long among us, most likely been born: for she is of the stock of the celebrated Bartolozzi, who was for so many years in this country, and there is nothing foreign in her pronunciation. Neither does she Italianize her ballads or lighter songs, unless a certain southern air of warmth and vivacity be said to throw a little more sunshine over them than usual. It is in her more elaborate songs, as the one in the last act of the *Siege of Belgrade,* that she gives specimens of the more decided Italian style,—a certain syllabical marking in the pronunciation, and breathing passion in the voice; as if the spirit were divided between the earnest cordiality of it's sensations, and the pleasure of hearing itself utter them.[76] [27 February 1820]

In addition to native ability and appropriateness of role, then, the song itself provides a further criterion for the style in which it may be delivered. A sensitive singer like Vestris knew how to keep her ballads pure as well as how to breathe some welcome southern fire over those Italianate songs of Arne, Shield, and Storace that were incorporated into Cobb's pasticcio.

In yet another way Hunt encouraged Continental infusions in English opera: the use of recitative. Arne's *Artaxerxes* was still popular in Hunt's time, as we have seen, but the general practice was to convert all or a major part of its recitative to dialogue. Partly for this reason Hunt's first review of the work treats it pretty much in the same manner as any other English "opera," though his literary viewpoint must be kept in mind. Nevertheless, he was probably correct in supposing that the "special genius" of Arne was to be found in the songs of the opera.[77] When the renewed popularity of Italian opera at the King's Theatre induced Drury Lane to bring out a production with the recitative restored,[78] Hunt gave full support to the experiment:

The performance of *Artaxerxes* here continues to draw excellent houses. It was supposed, and very naturally, by some, that the retaining of the original recitative throughout the piece, instead of the speaking dialogue common to English operas, would have injured it. But either the novelty pleases, or the public, by favour of Mozart, and of the interest taken in forwarding the musical sense by such native composers as Mr. Bishop, have lately become more susceptible of the delicacies of the art: for the audiences exhibit

no symptoms of weariness. On the contrary, their attention is awake
to the very last; and luckily, the performers are so distinct or loud
in their articulation, that all the turns of the story are quite
perceivable. But then recitative is so unnatural?—Not so unnatural,
as we may imagine. Indeed, in some respects it is more natural, in
an Opera, than common speech: for grant that beings may sing at
all, instead of speak, under the influence of passionate emotions,
and it is more natural that they should sing always, than that they
should burst out into a song occasionally. Singing becomes their
mode of speech, and the air is a less departure from it accordingly.
[16 April 1820]

The problem of recitative, frequently a critical one during the
eighteenth century, was no longer a live issue. Hunt's arguments
are not new. Significantly, he does not raise them until this late
date, no doubt a reflection of his enriching experiences at the
King's Theatre. But perhaps no English literary voice since
Addison's had been raised in behalf of the view that recitative
was "more natural" than dialogue in the operatic context.[79]

He concludes his plea for recitative with the suggestion that
speech itself is musical in nature:

Nor is such a mode of speech, or something like it, so rare as a
people accustomed to our tone of colloquy, might suppose. In Italy
especially, where recitative had it's origin (if it did not rather come
from the fountain of all beauty, the Greeks), the speech of the
inhabitants of some districts is perhaps as nearly allied to recitative
as to ordinary talking. . . . There are some Italian words the
intonation of which are decidedly musical, or what is called *cantabile*.
Such are most of the last syllables but one, and especially before a
double consonant, where a very marked suspension takes place,
as if the speaker were lingering over the beauty of it. When it
closes a period, particularly at the end of a stanza, it has a great
resemblance to the favourite cadence of recitative. . . . A doubt
might even be started, how far the inflexions of the human voice in
common use are not themselves the result of an injudicious and
artificial habit. When children are learning to read, they generally
render themselves liable to be called to account for what is called
singing. This tendency seems partly to arise from the natural music

of the human voice, and partly from a sense of the importance of what they are about.

To be sure, musicality is especially evident in the Italian language, but the Englishman would naturally bring more music to his speech if he were not conditioned by society to repress it.

Manners and Morals

Also closely related to Hunt's role as challenger of public taste are the moral judgments that abound in his opera criticism of the works, playwrights, composers, and performers. Implicit in some of the criticism already encountered, Hunt's attitude deserves further analysis.

Both Hunt and Hazlitt employed identical epithets of moral opprobrium in much the same way. "Vulgar," "coarse," and "gross" occur most frequently (in various forms), though the expressions "low," "mean," "trite," and "commonplace" are also closely associated with them. It is difficult to perceive any clear semantic distinction between the terms, which are often employed interchangeably by both authors. Their usage reflects this definition of *coarse*: "wanting in refinement or delicacy; rude and vulgar; indecent" (although only Hunt brought the meaning of "indecent," that is, licentious, into his criticism) as well as this definition of *vulgar*: "having a common and offensively mean character; coarsely commonplace" (O.E.D.). In his extended definition, "On Vulgarity and Affectation" (*Works*, VIII, 156–68), Hazlitt associates vulgarity with affectation or pose. Frequently involving social distinctions, its essence "consists in taking manners, actions, words, opinions on trust from others, without examining one's own feelings or weighing the merits of the case. It is coarseness or shallowness of taste arising from want of individual refinement." Vulgarity is related to the emptiness of the cliché as well as to an affectation of manners. For both critics a perverseness of taste and feeling lies at the core of "vulgarity."

The critics use these terms in many different contexts, yet the distinctions tend to overlap and merge, so as to suggest that, with one significant exception to be amplified below, their idea of vulgarity reflects lapses not only in taste but inevitably in manners and morals as well. Vulgarity in the sense of triteness and the commonplace in the vehicles and music of English opera has already been instanced in their criticism. Hazlitt found the songs of Michael Kelly "familiar, even to vulgarity." In John Tobin's* *Your's or Mine?* he cited the playwright's "caricatures of coarseness," where triteness seems to merge with the idea of social affectations (29 September 1816). Hunt also condemned affectations in pointing to Bate's vulgar use of "low" characters and to the "pretentiousness" in the writings of Dibdin, Hook, and others. A lack of delicacy was noted by Hunt in the "loud-soft" passages in Bishop, and by both critics in the "loud-soft" style of Braham's singing. Hunt also found a "coarse want of excitement" in the public—a need that some performers were all too willing to supply.

Both critics regretted a general lack of refinement in the performers. They found Incledon's stage manners gross and his pronunciation vulgar. "Mr. [Thomas] Bellamy[*] has the most gentlemanly appearance of any singer on the stage," Hunt declared. "I mention this quality because it is unluckily rare in the profession of the stage" (27 March 1808). And the following season he complained, "It is one of the mysteries of musical taste, that it seems to have no influence, like a taste for the other arts, in refining the manners" (1 January 1809).

Hunt paid particular attention to the stage ladies. As he observed in the review just cited with respect to the appearance of one singer: "It is not romantic to speak of ladies' wigs; but a grave stage critic has no business with romance and a good deal with mere outside." Occasionally, the decorum of the female performers was unexceptionable. Such an instance was the gracious collaboration of Ann Maria Tree and Catherine Stephens in a duet. Hunt remarked,

It is pleasant to see them performing together with an appearance of cordiality. The public have been so used to expect jealousies between performers, and performers have been in such a hurry to

answer their expectations, that we are persuaded any two eminent
ones who should really make common cause with one another, would
each get more popularity individually, than if he or she had
flourished alone. It is a vulgar mistake among stage people to
imagine that their interests and reputation are advanced by a
contrary behaviour. The greater an age, and the greater the geniuses
that have adorned it, it will always be found that the finest of them
have had a regard for each other. [26 December 1819]

(Hunt's case for the compatibility of geniuses may not be histori-
cally sound. Perhaps only Shelley would have shared his sentiment, though it is significant that the English Romantic writers,
individualistic though they were, produced a large number of
works in collaboration.)

Some female performers, however, Hunt found particularly
offensive, and their vulgarity seems to have increased with their
age. Nancy Storace,* the composer's sister and Mozart's first
Suzanna at the Vienna première of *Figaro*, reached the end of
her long career during the first year of the *Examiner* (she had
last sung at the King's Theatre in 1805). "She always sings with
taste and feeling," Hunt admitted in reviewing her performance
in *The Cabinet*, but

who can refrain from disgust, when he sees an unwieldy matron
attempting all the personal giddiness and tricksome levity of a
skittish girl. . . . [Storace] shakes her whole frame with huge
enjoyment. . . . The galleries always applaud with proportionate
vehemence, for they are pleased with their own likeness; but I am
very well convinced, that it was a painful sight to the politer part
of the audience. Whence is it that one feels an absolute personal
kind of shame at such exhibitions? Is it from a mingled sensation
of pity and contempt for our countrymen who are pleased at them,
or are we afraid that the persons around us will imagine we are
pleased ourselves? [31 January 1808]

Hunt was not amused. No doubt his disgust prompted an aston-
ishingly harsh reference to her in Isaac Brandon's *Kais*, where she
was cast in the role of "a Circassian beauty": "I did not think the
Managers possessed such powers of irony" (14 February 1808).
On the occasion of her farewell to the stage, he paid tribute to

her "real talent," which was "once admired." "But whether a mere habit of vivacity gradually strengthened into boisterousness, or whether she thought it necessary to be more animated when she felt the approach of age, it is certain that of late years her endeavours to charm us have been excessively noisy and vulgar" (5 June 1808). Hunt's distaste for the buffa manner, already noted, may be reflected in these views, which were shared by that ardent Italian-opera enthusiast Mount-Edgcumbe, who found "a coarseness in her voice, and a vulgarity of manner, that totally unfitted her for the serious opera [that is, opera seria], which she never attempted."

Maria Dickons appears to have undergone like vicissitude. In an early review Hunt wrote that she and Rosomon Mountain "have considerably the advantage over all the other female singers in gentility of appearance" (27 March 1808). Later that season, however, he warned of "an occasional vehemence in [Dickons's] attitudes and trippings somewhat too nearly approaching a copy of Signora Storace. An imitation of that vivacious actress would be well enough, but for the sake of the admirers of female delicacy, let us have no decided copy" (13 November 1808). Still later Hunt observed, "There is a coarse, flaunting air in her [Dickons's] very best manner; and on no account should she ever undertake to be fascinating" (12 February 1815). Dickons was apparently growing more flirtatious with advancing years. Hunt presumably had no objections to flirting: what he found offensive was the failure of *attempts* to be flirtatious; her "trippings" were pretentious and therefore vulgar. The objection to Storace's boisterousness is reflected in Dickons's "vehemence." Hunt admires vivacity but he dislikes vehemence; the former is a natural emanation of animal spirits, the latter a crude assault on the sensibilities.

The performance of "breeches" parts was generally distressful to Hunt. In *Critical Essays* (p. 45) he declared, "It is at all times unpleasant to see a woman performing in the dress of a man even without his character." Even when the roles were justified by tradition, such as those in Italian opera formerly assigned to castrati, he found the practice objectionable. One such role was

Viola in *Twelfth Night*. When Dorothy Jordan (whom Genest called "tops" in breeches parts) performed in that role, Hunt wrote:

She appeared in thin white breeches and stockings that fitted her like her own skin. . . . I shall not be exact in my description, lest I should appear to be writing upon anatomy, but if ever woman was ingenious enough to be effectively though not actually naked, such a woman was Mrs. Jordan on Tuesday. Every delicate female in the house must have felt wretched. The display was as absurd as it was immoral. . . . [The role is a modest one]; therefore *Viola* should have been really *disguised,* not undressed as a woman under *pretence* of being dressed as a man. Besides, Mrs. Jordan has daughters, and I am told that these daughters sometimes witness her performances. For shame! For shame! [5 June 1808]

Apart from their injury to the drama, Hunt seems to have regarded such roles as devices for perpetrating a sly pruriency among the vulgar. Whether or not the females in the audience did indeed share his wretchedness, there is no doubt that his reproofs concerning indecency on the English stage are directly related to his attitude towards women. This attitude is further illustrated by the unequivocal objections he voiced in an early "Theatrical Examiner" to licentiousness in the "old plays": "I have often expressed my regret, that in the revival of old plays the managers should preserve all the indecencies of the old writers. This practice deserves a reprehension more vehement than even the faults of Messrs. Dibdin and Reynolds, and other modern dramatists, who in general are merely foolish." In particular Hunt regretted that "the young and the unsuspicious part of the audience, who are told of the excellence of the play, learn to confound the proper effect of its humour, with the effect of its gay indecencies. No modest woman, in fact, ought to visit the theatre to see such revivals. It is a strange inconsistency, that parents who would snatch the works of Congreve[80] from the hands of their daughters, should suffer them to be present at the representation of his plays, when every coarse jest is explained to their imagination by the universal roar of the house." Where such exposure is inescapable, "a calm and chaste silence, both in word and look, is the only refuge of a modest woman from the contagion of wanton discourse" (21 February 1808).

Now, as Maurice Quinlan has shown in *Victorian Prelude* (p. 68), the late-eighteenth-century revival of puritanism, exemplified by the Evangelical Methodists, merged with the conservative reaction to the French Revolution and "penetrated the whole social fabric of the country." One result was an increased absorption on the part of the public in the censorship of books and plays. John Larpent, Examiner of Plays, was a Methodist and a severe censor. But the change in moral climate was sufficient in itself to restrain playwrights and managers; the theatre, moreover, was a special target of the Evangelicals. The restraints were not altogether effective, however. According to Nicoll (IV, 7–15 passim), audiences at the larger theatres were licentious, and much of the morality was specious, for "sly interests" were exhibited in the Restoration dramatists.

That Hunt responded to this moral climate is obvious in his criticism of stage decorum and unpruned "old plays." Even musical vehicles, old and new, did not escape his censure. Although in 1809 Arnold had discarded "the grosser pertness of his brother critics," Hunt later criticized him for giving houseroom to a new comic opera, *Jealous on All Sides,* by Samuel Beazley, Jr.,* which the critic found offensive:

We may here observe, that we have noticed a tendency of late in the compositions of this theatre to a certain coarseness, which deals in the most vulgar associations. We are no prudes, and can allow some latitude of allusion to love-matters, because they contain in them a principle of grace and kindliness; but the least approach to coarseness like Swift's we abominate; and if it come in contact with women, execrate. Its alleged harmlessness, upon which ground it has sometimes been defended, is ridiculous. We are persuaded it is the most pernicious, as well as most disgusting, of all coarseness; for it tends to degrade human nature itself; and Swift felt as much, when in his bitter grinning he indulged in it. [23 August 1818]

Two years later Hunt took exception to a new comedy at the Haymarket, *Exchange No Robbery,* by "our old theatrical ac-

quaintance, Mr. [Theodore] Hook." The acquaintanceship produced no kind words from the critic; the present offering was "a
play to please coarse tastes, shallow thinkers, and old gentlemen
who have no business with their wives" (20 August 1820). In
these examples, as elsewhere, obscenity apparently presents no
problem; rather the vulgarity lies primarily in the implications
of language or situation—smirks and innuendoes that suggest a
derogatory attitude towards women.

Similar objections applied to the older English operas. Hunt
refers to the hypocrisy of both man and work in his review of
Bate's *The Woodman*: "One might have dispensed with some
allusions and speeches not very edifying to chaste ears. Perhaps
our *ryghte merrie and jolie clerke,* after the example of his venerable predecessors, Theodore Beza and Walter de Mapes,[81]
thinks a man may be a very good churchman, notwithstanding
the little literary freedoms of his youth" (7 February 1808). With
respect to Bate, Hunt seems to hold an animus against the artistic
frivolities of a social climber, especially a vindictive Tory journalist who avidly acquired titles and religious benefices to further
his rise. (Hazlitt accused him of having "puffed" into success
first Garrick and later the Prince of Wales [16 March 1828]!)
One can hardly imagine a character more representative of all
that Hunt detested.

"Borrowings" aside, Hunt held mixed views toward Bickerstaffe. *Lionel and Clarissa* showed a "pleasing mediocrity"; and
he approved *Love in a Village* for its "proof how much is to be
done by a mere taste for nature and simplicity, unaccompanied
by any other portion of genius." But he also found coarseness in
one of the characters: *"Hodge,* who when he quarrels with a
woman instantly has recourse to his fist, and who leaves one girl
to follow a prettier, just as a cur drops one bone out of his mouth
for another, is on these occasions a rather disgusting sort of person, even on the stage; but the character was perhaps necessary in
the candid picture of rusticity, and shews that libertinism is
never so brutal and licentious as when accompanied with mere
ignorance" (1 October 1820; 27 July 1817).

Although *The Beggar's Opera* was largely redeemed by its

songs, Hunt had strong reservations about Gay's work.[82] At a Covent Garden revival he took note of old liberties that could still escape the censor as well as of duplicity in a public that would still enjoy them:

It is easy to see, that the *Beggar's Opera* would long ago have lost its attractions, had it not been for the never-dying charm of simplicity in its songs and music, and for one or two gross scenes, which the audience are glad enough to enjoy in an old piece, though they would never tolerate them in a new one. . . . The habit of appealing however to common life, though it assisted the temporary views of the school in which Gay was formed, was a most serious injury to it upon the whole. If it abounded, as it certainly did to exuberance, in wit, the exuberance was of a most rank description: and there grew up a vulgarity about their habits of mind, originating perhaps with Swift, the contamination of which even the purity of Arbuthnot could not escape, and which not only polluted the language of Pope, but appears to have materially kept down and depraved his imagination. [13 September 1812]

Hunt's analysis of the appeal of Gay's satire is delicate and precise —as far as it goes. He may have been unaware of its thrusts at Italian opera, but he well understood its political implications. In his *Autobiography* (pp. 210–11) he noted that Castlereagh "has been seen applauding" Gay's satire "from a stage box" (like Walpole, however, Castlereagh may have been much less enthusiastic in private). Although Hunt cannot praise the opera, he does not subscribe to the traditional objections to the work—that it was subversive of law and order.[83] Rather, he protests "one or two gross scenes" (especially, no doubt, the scene with Macheath and his doxies [II, iv]) and the appeal to "common life." Undoubtedly, he was disturbed by the many derogatory allusions ("rank description") to women throughout the work. That his attitude toward women lay behind his attack is further confirmed by his reference to the "school" of Swift and Pope.[84]

Hazlitt took quite a different view of this opera in the "Theatrical Examiner" three years later:

We have begun this article on a very coarse sheet of damaged foolscap, and we find that we are going to write it, whether for the

sake of contrast, or from having a very fine pen, in a remarkably
nice hand. Something of a similar process seems to have taken
place in Gay's mind, when he composed his *Beggar's Opera*. He
chose a very unpromising ground to work upon, and he has prided
himself in adorning it with all the graces, the precision and
brilliancy of style. It is a vulgar error to call this a vulgar play. So
far from it, that we do not scruple to declare our opinion that it is
one of the most refined productions in the language. The elegance
of the composition is in exact proportion to the coarseness of the
materials: by "happy alchemy of mind," the author has extracted
an essence of refinement from the dregs of human life, and turns
its very dross into gold. The scenes, characters, and incidents, are in
themselves of the lowest and most disgusting kind: but, by the
sentiments and reflections which are put into the mouths of
highwaymen, turnkeys, their mistresses, wives, or daughters, he has
converted this motley group into a set of fine gentlemen and ladies,
satirists and philosophers. [18 June 1815]

(It scarcely needs pointing out that Hazlitt here uses *coarse* in
the physical sense, with a play on its broader meaning.) "We
have said all this somewhere before," he declared in summary.
He was referring to his review of the opera for the *Chronicle* of
23 October 1813, of which the above is basically a rewrite. In
both reviews, then, Hazlitt attacked the prevailing view that
Gay's opera was vulgar, for, he adds, "Gay has turned the tables
on the critics: and by the assumed license of the mock-heroic
style, has enabled himself to do *justice to nature,* that is, to give
all the force, truth, and locality of real feeling, to the thoughts
and expressions, without being called to the bar of false taste and
affected delicacy."

Finding the work especially notable for its "gusto" (26 May
1816), Hazlitt once more returned to the attack in his last
"Round Table" (No. 48) for the *Examiner,* where he leaned toward a defense of the theatre in general and *The Beggar's Opera*
in particular as a civilizing influence. "To shew how little we
agree with the common declamations against the immoral tendency of the stage on this score, we would hazard a conjecture,
that the acting of the *Beggar's Opera* a certain number of nights

every year since it was brought out has done more towards putting down the practice of highway robbery than all the gibbets that ever were erected" (5 January 1817).

Hazlitt's powerful attack was as original as it was influential. After the play's success, the Reverend Herring's sermon denouncing the immorality of *The Beggar's Opera,* while failing to diminish its popularity, established an attitude that was held for nearly a century. Thomas Noon Talfourd declared, "[Hazlitt] restored the *Beggar's Opera,* which had been long treated as a burlesque appendage to the 'Newgate Calendar,' to its proper station, showing how the depth of the design, and the brilliancy of the workmanship, had been overlooked in the coarseness of its materials; and tracing instances of pathos and germs of morality amidst scenes which the world had agreed to censure and to enjoy as vulgar and immoral."[85] Although Talfourd somewhat exaggerated the degree of structural analysis in Hazlitt's reviews, he correctly estimated the strength of his late friend's attack on the shallow and thoughtless duplicity that had become traditional with the play's detractors. Since Hazlitt's time the morality of the opera has seldom been challenged by serious critics of the stage.[86]

Hunt himself welcomed Hazlitt's views and quoted them extensively when he again reviewed Gay's opera four years later. "We are happy to find that the audience on this occasion relished the dialogue, as well as the singing," he wrote. "This is owing in good measure perhaps to a writer, whose criticisms have occasionally invigorated these columns" (7 February 1819).[87] His immediate purpose in introducing Hazlitt in this criticism may have been to praise Hazlitt's style at the expense of his detractors, to which Hunt's final paragraph refers. In any event Hunt apparently owed to Hazlitt some modification in his views of the opera, for in later criticism he never called its vulgarity into question.[88]

Lamb did not review the play but mentioned it at the conclusion of his criticism of *The Jovial Crew, or the Merry Beggars*: "By the way, this is the true *Beggar's Opera.* The other should have been called the *Mirror for Highwaymen.* We wonder the

Societies for the Suppression of Mendicity (and other good things) do not club for the putting down of this infamous protest in favour of air, and clear liberty, and honest license, and blameless assertion of man's original blest charter of blue skies, and vagrancy, and nothing-to-do" (4 July 1819). The Society for the Suppression of Vice, which Lamb here satirizes, was reaching the apex of its power. His proposed title for "the other" ironically characterizes the traditional view of Gay's work; he seems to have been celebrating a whimsical joke at the expense of the whole serious controversy.

Don Giovanni, in the various English- and Italian-opera representations, brings out interesting comparisons between the *Examiner* critics. The attitudes of Hazlitt and Hunt toward the work cannot be fully explored until we reach their Italian criticism, which must be anticipated here. Hazlitt's only reference to the Don on the English stage appears in his review of the revised production of Shadwell's *The Libertine,* where he emphasizes "the untractable, fiery spirit, the unreclaimable licentiousness" of the character, which was not caught by Charles Kemble's acting (25 May 1817). In his reviews of the Mozart opera at the King's Theatre, however, he was careful to point out that the *fire* of the character must be tempered with grace, for the Don is an intriguer "in love." He believed that the Italian buffo Ambrogetti brought sufficient grace to the role, thus mitigating "the violent effect of [the Don's] action" (see below, chapter four). Hazlitt does not specifically reject the aggressive sexuality of the Don; nor is this surprising in view of Hazlitt's belief in the inferiority of women.

Although Lamb apparently knew the Mozart opera, he never reviewed the King's Theatre. But his attitude towards the character may be examined in a review of the "burlesque fantasy" *Don Giovanni, or a Spectre on Horseback,* by Thomas Dibdin, at the Olympic (first performed at the Royal Circus in 1817). The part of the Don, Lamb wrote,

as it is played at the Great House in the Haymarket (Shade of Mozart, and ye living admirers of Ambrogetti, pardon the barbarity)

had always something repulsive and distasteful to us.—We cannot
sympathize with *Leporello's* brutal display of the *list,* and were
shocked (no strait-laced moralists either) with the applauses, with
the *endurance* we ought rather to say, which fashion and beauty
bestowed upon that disgustful insult to feminine unhappiness.
[22 November 1818]

Unlike Hazlitt, Lamb objected to Ambrogetti's playing of the
role; he apparently felt that the actor's appeal to realism destroyed the "stage illusion" necessary for the enjoyment of black-
guards in the theatre.[89] But Lamb finds the character and the
drama at fault, too, as he begs to differ with the shade of Mozart
and cites "the brutal display of the *list.*" His reference to "feminine unhappiness" places him closer to Hunt than to Hazlitt.
(Lamb, as he himself claimed, was surely no moralist; nevertheless, he maintained a "deafening silence" towards Hazlitt on the
publication of the latter's *Liber Amoris.*) More pertinent to
Lamb's objections is his concept of the comic genre. For actors
could achieve "stage illusion" only in genuine comedy—specifically, in the comedy of manners. Such illusion is not possible
in the modern "common-life" play, "where the moral point is
every thing" and where "my virtuous indignation shall rise
against the profligate wretch."[90] It would appear, then, that
Lamb regarded the Mozart—da Ponte production (and the hero)
as in the debased genre of sentimental morality rather than in
the tradition of true (morally uncommitted) comedy. The English burlesque removed all necessity for moral judgments. With a
sop to the Machiavellian tradition in England, Lamb concluded:

The *Leporello* of the Olympic Theatre is not of the most refined
order, but we can bear with an English blackguard better than with
the hard Italian. But *Giovanni*—free, fine, frank-spirited, single-
hearted creature, turning all the mischief into fun as harmless as
toys, or children's *make-believe,* what praise can we repay to you,
adequate to the pleasure which you have given us?[91] We had
better be silent, for you have no name, and our mention will but be
thought fantastical. You have taken out the sting from the evil thing,
by what magic we know not, for there are actresses of greater mark
and attribute than you. With you and your *Giovanni* our spirits

will hold communion, whenever sorrow or suffering shall be our lot.
We have seen you triumph over the infernal powers; and pain, and
Erebus, and the powers of darkness, are henceforth "shapes of a
dream."

Hunt, of course, despised the Don for his profligate behavior.
His attitude is revealed more fully in his Italian-opera criticism.
But his position is also explicit in a review of still another English adaptation two years later—an "operatic extravaganza" entitled *Giovanni in London* by the up-and-coming young playwright William Moncrieff.* Produced at the Olympic in 1817
for the sole purpose of returning Vestris to the English stage, this
proved to be the most popular of all the adaptations. When
Hunt went to see the piece at long last, he was amply rewarded.
He not only followed Lamb to the Olympic (this appears to be
his first review of that theatre), but the reviews are surprisingly
similar. Note for example the first sentence of each, but note
also that to Hunt the Don at the opera is a scoundrel *despite* the
acting of Ambrogetti:

We do not like the scoundrel at the opera, notwithstanding
Ambrogetti's acting, or Mozart's divine music. It cannot make him
a decent gentleman or goodnatured. Even the very remonstrating
lady who haunts him so, cannot reconcile us to his heartless rakery;
nor do we put up with him, till he gets into the greater inhumanity
and absurdity of hell, which is to give him endless tortures for the
finite ones he has inflicted. But that pleasant mitigated rogue,
Giovanni in London, who begins with making hell itself merry, and
seduces the very Furies into good-humour,—how can we help liking
him? He is a contradiction to all continuities of pain—a vindication
of the eternally renovated youth and fair play of nature. The piece
opens with a view of him in the infernal regions, where he makes
love to the Furies, and forces Pluto to complain that hell cannot
bear him. He is accordingly, to his great delight, ejected; and
being denied a passage by Charon for want of money, contrives,
while the ferryman is talking with Mercury, to jump into his boat,
and carry back three English women who had just arrived from the
upper world. The party enter London, and find the three husbands
of the ladies, coming reeling out of a house, and singing a jolly

glee of "We be three sure Widowers."[92] The result may be
guessed. *Giovanni* finds his valet *Leporello* in the company, and
goes with him through another set of adventures, more various
and good-humoured than in the Opera. [4 June 1820]

The piece appears to lie somewhere between da Ponte and Shaw.
Nevertheless, Hunt had no objections to light-hearted burlesques
on the opera when they were cleverly handled and when they did
not misuse, and thus debase, Mozart's music. Hoping for another
good specimen from the author, he pointed out that "there are a
number of airs, which we were glad to find were not parodied
from Mozart, but well-known English ones, all very pleasantly
adapted to parodies on common song."

Hunt's repeated charges of indecency against the English musical stage and his emphatic support of strict censorship of plays
reveal an overprotectionistic attitude towards women that had
much in common with the moralistic fervor of the Evangelical
Methodists. On the basis of such evidence Hunt has been labeled
a prude. Other aspects of his criticism, however, suggest a contradictory view of the critic.

For he not only emphatically rejected the Evangelicals' dictum
that the theatre was an immoral institution, but he attacked them
bitterly on numerous occasions for their hypocritical pretensions.
He even expressed radical views concerning the relationship between the sexes. Since it was a favorite topic in his conversation,
he sometimes shocked his listeners with his frankness. He did
not feel that marriage should bind together those who no longer
loved, and he defended the conduct of Byron and Shelley to an
outraged England. Similarly, he justified the conduct of Francesca in *The Story of Rimini* (1816). He boldly painted the pleasures of love in such poems as "Hero and Leander" and "The
Panther" (1819). And in "Choice" (1823) he hesitated to use the
word "wife" to describe the ideal mate in whom feelings of sex-
ual jealousy were banished: "A wife,—or whatever better word /
The times grown wiser, might by law afford / To the chief friend
and partner of my board" (*Poetical Works,* p. 344). Hunt even

wrote one poem, still unpublished, that perhaps borders on the licentious (Landré, II, 300).

In an England growing exceedingly self-conscious about public allusions to sex, Hunt's transgressions did not pass unnoticed by his political enemies. We have already cited in chapter two the series of attacks on *Rimini* conducted by *Blackwood's Edinburgh Magazine.* It accused the poet of moral depravity, asserting that he welcomed seduction, adultery, and even incest. Hunt's protestation and defense only brought repeated attacks, which continued intermittently for the next five years and in which Keats, Shelley, Hazlitt, and other friends of Hunt's were also implicated.[93] Politics motivated the attacks, but Hunt's enemies shrewdly traded on the increasing moral conservatism of the public to denigrate the man and dissipate whatever aura of martyrdom still clung to him from the years in Horsemonger Lane.

The *Blackwood's* attack was anticipated as early as 1815 in the case of Whitaker *vs.* Hime, in which Hunt's old acquaintance brought suit against a Dublin publisher for violation of musical copyright. The principal evidence in the case was three of the Hunt songs set by John Whitaker* and published by Button and Whitaker in 1809 and 1810. The Dublin jury found for the plaintiff, and Hime was fined £ 50 damages in violation of the statute that protected authors from piracy for twenty-eight years. Considering the history of widespread violation of the statute where books were at issue, this verdict in behalf of printed music was unusual, as the prosecutor noted. Hunt had an interest in the case both in his own right and for its connection with Whitaker. But more personal reasons compelled him to make extensive comments on the case in the *Examiner* (11 June 1815).

For one thing, the defense attorney, Mr. Joy, sought during the trial to deprecate the nature of the material allegedly pirated and thereby to undermine the seriousness of the plaintiff's case. Sir John Stevenson* appeared for Whitaker and testified as to the value of the songs and the "great celebrity"[94] of the composer, though he lacked some warmth in defending Hunt. He was cross-examined by the defense attorney:

Q. Be so good, Sir John as to read these lines, (the last verse of the song called "Silent Kisses")[95]—Don't you conceive that a little tawdry?—A. Perhaps, therefore, you gave it me to read. *(a laugh)* I own it a little *warm*.

Q. That is a new name for tawdry.—Don't you think it *hot,* Sir John?—A. That depends on the constitution of the person reading it.

Q. Are not these words warmer than the "Irish Melodies?"—A. Perhaps so—they are indeed pretty hot as you call it.

In his summation for the defense Mr. Joy declared that "a musical air, accompanied by obscene words, was never within the contemplation of the legislature, when this statute was enacted."[96]

But a more immediate cause of Hunt's *Examiner* commentary was an attack on him by the editor of the Dublin *Hibernian Journal,* who, reporting the trial in full, cited the "immorality" of Hunt's "poetic effusions" and called attention to the sentence Hunt had just served for his censure of the Prince Regent "for not being at least as pure, as amiable, and moral, as the patriotic poet himself." Touched to the quick, Hunt made a brilliant rebuttal. Concerning his own songs he stated, "The verses were written when the author was a youth, and are, it must be confessed, worth little or nothing, whatever beauty the composer breathed into them with his music. They are also, it is allowed, as warm in their ideas as is warranted by amatory songs in general." But he continued, "Had we written in our youth three songs really immoral, yet if we had totally altered the tone of our compositions ever since, we should still have had full right . . . to say what we did of his Royal Highness's example." If verses of such description were to be found obscene, "the same spirit of vicious search" would carry the charge to nearly every English author, including Spenser, Cowley, Sidney, Milton, and Thomson.

Hunt was of course no more a libertine than a prude. His early infatuations were innocent enough, and if he ever regretted his choice of Marianne over her sister, there is no evidence that he was an unfaithful husband. Moreover, his writings on free love discreetly celebrate the uninhibited happiness of family life.

They reflect Hunt's gay, sociable nature and his love of the sympathy of women; they also represent his unorthodox attitude toward British mores. But, most important, Hunt's moral liberalism, closely related to his political and religious liberalism, was based on his doctrine of love and sympathy between people—a form of "universal benevolence" that owed much to Godwin, though other sources were available (Landré, II, 44). Mary Wollstonecraft provided him with a model of the "free" woman—not masculinized, as Hannah More thought, but indeed all the more feminine because liberated from a male subjugation that would turn her sexuality into a concealed weapon (Quinlan, pp. 140–43). This view is implicit in Hunt's criticism: Women deserve the same respect as men; anything that tends to compromise that respect is inimical, whether it be a direct attack, as in the "old plays" and in the "school" of Pope, or (more often the case) in a sly allusion, a coarse gesture, a flaunting of breeches or "trippings," and situations that played upon factitious relationships.

Much of the apparent dualism in Hunt's criticism with respect to women is reconcilable. Nevertheless, the paradox remains that Hunt's excessively protectionistic attitude toward women runs counter to his insistence on regarding them as liberated from the inhibitions imposed by society. Curiously enough, other political liberals of the time held similarly paradoxical views. Richard Carlile, for example, though jailed for his "skeptical writings" largely through the efforts of the Society for the Suppression of Vice, nevertheless approved the work of the Society so far as its suppression of "indecent" literature was concerned (Quinlan, pp. 215–21). Undoubtedly, the responsibility that Hunt felt toward the public made him unduly sensitive to mounting social pressures for protecting the sanctity of womanhood. Perhaps, too, the young critic found certain aspects of puritanism congenial.

In any event, from 1815 on, Hunt's moral conservatism gradually diminished.[97] The Whitaker-Hime affair may have signaled the change, for in his commentary on it Hunt observed that when he wrote the songs in question, he "was yet to learn how far people's imaginations could carry them, and what were the pure

and complimentary notions of those persons, who whenever lips
or kisses were mentioned, attach to them all sorts of ruinous
notions, and think or affect to think that every lady within hearing is to be lost." Though Dorothy Jordan offended his taste, he
had no wish to conceal the female form in furbelows. In fact, he
spoke of feminine beauty with a freedom that irritated his most
eminent scholar (Landré, II, 43). Hunt bestowed a good deal of
attention on Ann Maria Tree's leg in reviewing her performance
of Viola:

And (as such subjects are eminently critical), we must be allowed
to say that her leg is the very prettiest leg we ever saw on the stage.
It is not at all like the leg which is vulgarly praised even in a man,
and which is doubly misplaced under a lady,—a bit of a balustrade
turned upside down; a large calf, and an ancle only small in
proportion. It is a right feminine leg, delicate in foot, trim in ancle,
and with a calf at once soft and well-cut, distinguished and
unobtrusive. We are not so intolerant,—we should rather say
ungrateful and inhuman on the subject of legs, as many of our sex;
who without the light of a good ancle can see nothing else good in a
figure. We have a tender respect for them all, provided they are
gentle. But it is impossible not to be struck, as an Irishman would
say, with a leg like this. It is fit for a statue; still fitter for where
it is. [12 November 1820]

How far Hunt's attitude had changed in later years is evident
in passages from his *Autobiography,* where he observed that although Jordan was no lady or *"comme il faut* whatsoever, . . .
[she was] so full of spirits, so healthily constituted in mind and
body, had such a shapely leg withal . . . that she appeared . . . to
hold a patent from nature herself for our delight and good opinion." Noting that "she made even the Methodists love her," he
interposed these comments (pp. 133–34):

(*Serious Reviewer, interrupting.* But, my good sir, suppose some
of your female readers should take it into their heads to be Mrs.
Jordan?

Author. Oh, my good sir, don't be alarmed. My female readers are
not persons to be so much afraid for, as you seem to think yours are.

The stage itself has taught them large measures both of charity and discernment. They have not been so locked up in restraint, as to burst out of bounds the moment they see a door open for consideration.)

Referring elsewhere to the song he sang in childhood, "Dans votre lit," he explained (p. 46) that it was "somewhat gallant, but very decorous"; but the "songs that were sung at that time by the most fastidious might be thought a shade freer than would suit the like kind of society at present. Whether we are more innocent in having become more ashamed, I shall not judge." Hunt was less a Victorian in 1850 than during his *Examiner* years!

The most significant feature of Hunt's criticism of the English musical stage is the persistence of his attacks on its artistic shoddiness. To be sure, he discovered "stripes of gold-lace upon a threadbare drugget"; but such experiences were rare. For the most part his weekly reviews dealt with usurping theatre hacks, trite vehicles, commonplace music, and inept performances.

That the period was indeed a dreary one has the unanimous support of modern historians. Yet none of this dreariness is reflected in his criticism; he never seems to have written a review out of a sense of mere obligation to his subscribers. Hunt brought to his reviews an astonishing variety of tone and analogy, vigor of expression, and range of ideas, which give them a perennial freshness of approach. And in his scrutiny of the details—the particulars—of each occasion, he substituted a richness of insight and a sensitiveness of critical response for the summary dismissal and stock responses that characterized the scant music criticism of the period.

Hunt's persistence in such an unrewarding endeavor could have been motivated only by his indefatigable zeal to improve the taste of the English musical stage and all that that implied. This goal, implicit in much of his criticism, is explicit in his attacks on the press and the managers, in the approach to his readers, in his complex attitude toward the public, and in his exaggerated claims for the *Examiner*. No doubt his zeal led him astray on some occasions; no doubt it further complicated his curious but by no means unique preoccupation with the problems of vulgarity; and no doubt it trapped him at times into making excessively caustic judgments. But it provided the energy needed by a reformer in England during the nineteenth century.

Both Hunt's zeal and his exaggerations are more characteristic of his early years with the *Examiner*; after 1815 there was less acerbity but also less brilliance in his writing. This increased mellowness was not accompanied by any diminution of concern with the musical stage. Stimulated by the repercussions of Italian opera in the English theatres and by some outstanding new performers, he brought greater depth and subtlety to his criticism. He considered historical problems in English music and musical taste, and he drew apt comparisons with the vitality of Continental music. Yet in exploring possibilities for improvement, he warned against changes that would destroy the validity of English dramatic and operatic conventions. Similarly, he admonished performers to avoid extremes of style and encouraged in them a greater artistic integrity, which could provide the only sound basis for effective musico-dramatic characterizations.

If contemporary reverberations on the English stage or in the press can be traced to percussions in the "Theatrical Examiners," Hunt was bound to fail in the hopeless task of reconstituting either the public taste or the theatre of his day—musical or otherwise. The true comic and tragic spirit of the past lived but fitfully in the first quarter of the nineteenth century; there was more life in some of the musical farces, burlesques, and melodramas—trifling as they were—than in the debased comedy and tragedy that Hunt was quick to reject. In time he came to see some value in these musical experiments. Yet he was surely right in protesting the abuse of music by managers, playwrights, and composers in the contrivance of cheap theatrical output, and he was right in deploring the lack of originality in contemporary musicals as well as the destructive adaptations of the better productions of the eighteenth century and of Italian operas. When he began his criticism of the King's Theatre in 1817, Hunt entered a richness of musical experience well beyond anything the English stage could provide.

4
Criticism of Italian Opera

Part then alone we hear, as part we see;
And in this music, lovely things of air
May find a sympathy of heart or tongue,
Which shook perhaps the master, when he wrote,
With what he knew not,—meanings exquisite.
—Leigh Hunt (from "A Thought on Music," 1815)

Leigh Hunt's Examiner *Critics*

ALTHOUGH HUNT did not review the King's Theatre until 1817, as coeditor of the *Examiner* he provided his readers with responsible criticism of Italian opera from the paper's inception. As we have seen in chapter two, that criticism was written exclusively by Henry Robertson from 1808 to 1812; it appeared in the form of an "Opera Letter" and was identified with the initials "H.R." Obviously, the "Theatrical Examiner" was intended at first to cover the English stage, lyrical or otherwise. Although Italian opera was not among the subjects specified in the paper's *Prospectus,* the appearance of regular reviews by Robertson, starting with the second issue, suggests that this feature was planned from the start.

In his Preface (1809) to the first volume of the *Examiner,* Hunt expressed his gratitude to Robertson "for an Operatical Review, which in the present times has been the first criticism of the kind worthy the attention of sound readers." Hunt did not exaggerate. In many ways Robertson's Italian-opera criticism for the *Examiner* represents a pioneering endeavor in English periodicals. For their portrayal of conditions at the King's Theatre from

1808 to 1812, for their relevance to the later criticisms of Hunt, and for their contribution to the status of the *Examiner* in the musical journalism of the day, Robertson's reviews are worth our attention.

Henry Robertson

Robertson's initial "Opera Letter" reflected the new spirit of journalism heralded in the *Prospectus*. After noting the criticisms on the English theatre in the *News* and *Examiner*, Robertson ventured to offer a few observations on Italian opera, "which, as the principal public amusement of the higher classes, should not be passed unnoticed by those who profess a general review of the times." He complained of "incorrect reports" on the opera that were appearing in the dailies, "evidently written by persons not present at the performances. If I claim no other merit," he stated, "I shall have that of accuracy, unbiassed by prejudice." Robertson indeed displays a remarkable freedom from traditional English prejudices towards Italian opera in his first review. Speaking of the King's Theatre, he continued:

This building, sacred to *Apollo*, has always suffered under the
imputation of the unmusical and illiberal, who, preferring the jingle
of Reeve . . . to the divine strains of Mozart or Cimarosa, have
incessantly exclaimed against the encouragement of foreigners, and
the ridiculous inconsistencies of the Italian Operas. With relation
to the former there cannot surely be any blame in rewarding great
talents, though from a foreign country. . . . The improprieties and
absurdities of the representations cannot so well be vindicated,
but even these have been exaggerated. The folly of dying in
chromatics and sorrowing in semibreves does not appear so great,
when it is considered that the action of the drama is merely intended
as an ornament to the music, not the music as a natural
accompaniment to the action. [17 January 1808][1]

Robertson's initial critique shows an astonishing critical independence. Apparently for the first time an English journalist deplored the banal "reviews" of Italian opera that appeared in the contemporary press, rejected the traditional British hostility toward an "exotic entertainment," regarded opera and opera criticism as subjects worthy of middle-class interest, and boldly accepted (though not without some qualification) those conventions of Italian opera that English writers had been making the object of satire for over a century. Even Hunt at this early date was not disposed to sympathize to this extent with Italian mannerisms and operatic conventions.

Robertson's launching of the "Opera Letter" coincided with the advent of Angelina Catalani,* whose domination at the King's Theatre had already become established. Joining the company in 1807, she was to reign there for several seasons. But the season of 1808 was, according to an anonymous chronicler of the King's Theatre, "the year of CATALANI," when she sang all but four nights out of the sixty![2] This presented a neophyte reviewer of Italian opera with a genuine challenge. Yet, amid the general panegyrics of the time, Robertson's criticism of the prima donna is remarkably balanced. Aware of her unusual vocal ability, he never indulged in unthinking praise. Often critical of her acting, he nevertheless praised her highly in certain roles where her artistry was revealed. But he strongly condemned her frequent lapses of taste as well as her tyrannical attitude towards music, musicians, and managers.

In his first criticism of the singer he felt she was better suited for Giovanni Paesiello's* comic roles than for the heroines of opera seria, which she preferred because of their potential for vocal display:

Playfulness and vivacity appear congenial to her natural disposition. . . . [8] In the light music of [Paesiello's] *La Frascatana*, Catalani is divested of that profusion of ornament, with which she disguised the music of the operas produced last season, and which rendered it very immaterial to the hearer whether she sung the lofty strains of Cimarosa, or the dry insipidity of Portogallo.* [17 January 1808]

Noting her absence from a performance of Paesiello's *Il Barbiere di Siviglia* owing to an indisposition, Robertson asserted that the want of ability in the company was "fully exposed, and the value of Catalani's powers more duly estimated by the experience of their loss" (20 March 1808).

Yet two weeks earlier he had found that although Catalani
acted her role well, "as a singer she did not succeed so well as
usual. She was resolved to prevent the other performers from being
heard, and exerted her Stentorian voice with all the force of
which it is capable. This is unmerciful. . . . The principal art
in singing in parts is the accommodation of the strong voices to
the weak, that the whole may be heard distinctly; . . . and the
want of it constitutes the principal defect of amateurs, who generally seem to strive who can sing loudest" (6 March 1808).[4] The
following month Robertson took her to task for execrable singing
in a Domenico Cimarosa* opera and condemned her tyranny over
the management, which was forced to permit her brother to take
the place of the best oboist in London, although he had no command over the instrument (10 April 1808).[5]

Catalani occasionally indulged a penchant for histrionic absurdities. She presented herself in something "called 'une lecon
de grace,'" apparently an afterpiece for a new opera by Sarti (see
below), in which she attempted "some attitudes with a shawl"
but succeeded only in a burlesque of her ability (3 July 1808).[6]
Catalani also had a new opera composed by Sebastiano Nasolini*
for the express purpose of her appearing in male attire. "This is
a species of indelicacy to which the actresses on the English stage
have not arrived," Robertson declared (1 May 1808)—an exaggeration, as Hunt could have told him. (The appearance of
women in male attire at the King's Theatre was at least justified
in the mounting of the older operas having roles formerly sung
by castrati.) In his final review of the year, Robertson deplored
the poverty of the season and expressed the hope that in 1809
Catalani's singing could be matched with Grassini's acting (7
August 1808; see below). But after meeting Catalani's demands,
the company could afford no other outstanding singers, and the
same old round was destined to continue.

In later seasons Catalani proved capable of performing well in
Mozart, although she avoided that composer as much as possible
because of the limitations which his style imposed on her bravura.[7] When she sang Susanna in Figaro in 1812, Robertson reported that her vivacity, "so misplaced in her serious perform-

ances, comes into full play in the character of the chambermaid *Susannah,* and there is something very pleasing in the archness of her manner, and the eager interest with which she enters into all the schemes that are to extricate her mistress and herself" (12 July 1812). She also performed well in Mayr's* popular bravura pasticcio, *Il Fanatico per la Musica* (11 March 1810).

Robertson had little to say for the other singers during Catalani's reign.[8] She was jealous of talent in others, and in 1812 her tyranny was so great that she drove off most of the performers to form their own company and produce summer Italian opera at the Pantheon (Mount-Edgcumbe, *Reminiscences,* p. 105). Robertson, describing the orchestra at the Pantheon as wretched, doubted that the competition would be good for opera in London (8 March 1812). In any event, licensing regulations required the group to perform there in English, with which the Italian singers could ill cope, and the venture quickly collapsed.

John Braham, who had delivered notable performances at the King's Theatre from 1804 to 1806, departed for the English stage on Catalani's arrival. But he did appear, during one of her absences, for the première of Paesiello's *La Didone,* when Robertson found him the only singer currently fit to perform the principal characters at that theatre (31 January 1808).[9] Another exception was Tramezzani,* who made his English debut in *Sidagero* by Pietro Guglielmi *le fils** ("*le fils,*" as the British somewhat strangely appended, since his father was P. A. Guglielmi). Robertson wrote: "His figure is manly, his action dignified, and his voice possesses a rich mellowness and strength of tone, rarely to be met with, and superior to that of any Italian singer now in the country; nor is he deficient in talent as an actor,—his general conception of character is just, and will be much improved when he restrains the violence of action so prevalent among foreign performers" (2 July 1809). Robertson often had kind words for Tramezzani, who remained at the opera until the end of the 1814 season, but never again gave him the high praise of this promising beginning.

Perhaps the most serious blow to opera resulting from the domination of Catalani and inept theatrical management was the employment of hack composers, who would turn out anything to suit the peculiar operatic whims of the prima donna. During the 1809 season, Robertson declared, there was not one good opera performed, "owing to the impolitic engagement of Composers before their talents have been ascertained, who, as they must be paid, are employed whether good or bad, to the exclusion of more celebrated masters" (13 August 1809). At best such composers produce "tolerable imitations" of better works, which, compared to Mozart, Winter, or Cimarosa, are insignificant. The appointment of P. C. Guglielmi as music director of the theatre in 1810 resulted in the performance of his own operas to the exclusion of those of "his better masters," as Robertson accurately predicted (17 December 1809). On one occasion the critic noted that the composer had found a suitable librettist in Buonaiuti[10] for his new opera, *Romeo e Giulietta*, which Robertson called "in perfect union" with the author's "contemptible language" (25 February 1810).

Among other "servile composers" that Catalani needed for her ostentatious taste (19 May 1811), Robertson included Valentino Fioravanti,* whose operas were "inferior" or "uninteresting"; Giuseppe Farinelli,* whose *Teresa e Claudio* was excessively sentimental; and "Portogallo" (Marcos Portugal), whose *Semiramide* failed to impress the critic at its revival (7 August 1808).[11] (These composers were still popular, however, at least in England; possibly Robertson's attitude toward them was colored by the dominating influence of Catalani.)

There were a few exceptions. Among the better composers he placed Giuseppe Sarti,* whose *Gli Amanti Consolati* was in good taste (3 July 1808). Although the story of *Le Feste d'Iside,* concocted for Catalani, was sentimental and absurd, he found extraordinary beauty, elegance, and refinement in Nasolini's* music, and the overture was "a very noble composition, consisting of a grand adagio and an allegro maestoso of great spirit and fancy" (1 May 1808).[12] But Paesiello and Cimarosa were particular favorites. At the première of *La Frascatana* Robertson noted that "the music of Paesiello is remarkable for its extreme elegance, the great beauty of the melodies, and that degree of science

which tends to enrich the composition without fatiguing the ear"
(17 January 1808). By "science" he refers to the texture of the
orchestral parts in Italian opera, which became more symphonic
under the influence of the "German" (more precisely, Austro-
Bohemian) school. The view that such musical texture could
become a burden to the ear was all too common at the time and
reflected the fears with which Europe was greeting the newer
trends in music. But Robertson was moderate in his objections
to these changes; in fact, he welcomed a Germanic infusion of
taste provided it did not become subversive. At the première of
Cimarosa's *Il Capriccio Dramatico* he stated, "Cimarosa, I think,
may be placed above every other Italian composer; his music
seems to be the link that forms connection between the styles of
Germany and Italy. With the sportive fancy and elegance for
which the Italian music is remarkable, he combines the solidity
and grandeur of the German school" (10 April 1808).[13] Indeed,
Robertson's avant-garde taste prompted him to reject a fine old
favorite: at a revival of Niccolà Piccinni's* *La Buona Figliuola*,
he declared that the opera would go back on the shelf, because
the days of Piccini, Mozart, Haydn, Winter, and Cimarosa had
advanced music, making the old style dry and uninteresting (8
July 1810). Robertson's placement of Haydn in this setting is
surprising. Although the composer wrote some eighteen operas,
it is most doubtful if Robertson ever saw one.[14] Perhaps he had
in mind the oratorios, or, more likely, the general influence of
Haydn's symphonic development.

Only occasionally does Robertson fail to comment on the
music or composer—usually as a result of poor performances.
Such was the situation with Paesiello's *Barbiere di Siviglia*, for
which the company was inadequate (20 March 1808), and with
the première of his *La Didone (*31 January 1808). At a revival of
Cimarosa's *Gl'Orazj e Curiazj* after Josephina Grassini's* return
to England, he informs us that she alone tried to do justice to the
composer's ideas, but he does not discuss them (5 June 1814).[15]

In his first "Opera Letter" Robertson asserted the supremacy
of music over the libretto in Italian opera. But in his subsequent
comments on librettists he revealed a strong current of tradi-

tional British "realism." Reviewing the première of a work by
Giacomo Ferrari,* he took the unidentified librettist to task:

So completely has sound established its domination over sense in the
Italian operas, that the name of the author has become a matter of
perfect indifference, and we naturally look only to the composer
for that pleasure which should be the result of their combination. . . .
The writer of the new opera called *L'Eroina di Raab,* has, with a
prudent modesty unknown to his contemporary rhymers, concealed
his name, but in other respects he bears a compleat affinity to them,
and has furnished his work according to the old established receipt,
seasoned as usual with a due proportion of chains and dungeons,
and served up in a course of very melancholy proceedings.
[25 April 1813]

These echoes of eighteenth-century attitudes were amplified in
an earlier review of the première of Vincenzo Pucitta's* *La Caccia
d'Enrico IV,* which

is as usual the production of Signor Buonaiuti, and brought out
under circumstances that render it difficult to decide what portion of
praise is due to him. It is not an original production, it is not a
compilation, a translation, or an imitation, but to use his own words,
it is "totally altered and re-written," from a French Comedy by
Monsieur Collé; I should therefore conceive, that it bears no greater
affinity to the French comedy than *Mother Goose* does to the
Tragedy of *Macbeth.* Signor Buonaiuti seems to be aware that his
expression is rather indefinite, and has consequently given the
following explanation, by way of Preface:—"The necessity of
arranging the Comedy to the rules of the Italian stage for an Opera,
has obliged us to make a new first act; as in the French Comedy
the plot is too dry, and inadequate to the musical situation and
musical colours inevitably required for an Italian Opera."
[19 March 1809]

Robertson professes ignorance of the meaning of this last statement; yet all French productions had to be "adapted" to an
Italian style that would suit the taste of English opera-goers, as
he was aware. A year earlier he had found the music of the
King's Theatre ballet composer, Venua, "heavy and dry"—too
much in the French style, "which has never succeeded in this

country, nor indeed in any other" (14 February 1808).[16] What Robertson failed to realize (a failure that lies at the heart of the English attitude towards opera) is the distinction between the drama and the libretto. The latter represents a mere scaffold for the drama; it is successful to the extent that it permits the composer to suffuse it with musico-dramatic significance. The effective librettist creates a dramatic potential, but he may not fully realize the drama, thereby preempting the composer's functions. Words and situations are worked out with primary attention to their value as vehicles for musical expressiveness. Strong literary qualities render the libretto less "workable"; instead of *poesia per musica* it becomes full-fledged drama, and the power of the music to convey expressiveness and carry the dramatic "meaning" is accordingly diminished. This is of course what Buonaiuti had in mind in his preface, from which Robertson continued to quote:

"It is the Poet's task to find out situations, expressions, and words, to call forth an imitative melody, even frequently at the expense of reason and sense." This assertion of the Signor is certainly unwarrantable. Although the words of Operas must necessarily be absurd where he is employed to write them, he should remember that they would not be tolerated for a moment, were it not for the music that accompanies them and in some degree conceals their absurdity.

In a footnote to Robertson's review, Hunt provided his only extended comment before 1817 on Italian opera; he declared that Signor Buonaiuti—the "logical musician"—"contradicts the opinions of all the finest composers . . . who have invariably sought after the best poets." The ignorance of such hacks "compels them to write nonsense, and then their insolent vanity insists that they *ought* to have written nonsense" (19 March 1809). Later, Hunt admitted that the best musicians do not always select the best poets.[17] But for him, as for Coleridge and other Romantics, there was an inevitable affinity between the great artists in all the arts —just as the arts themselves were integrally related in their highest expression.

Indeed composers often had to be satisfied with hack librettists, since the true dramatic poets wrote for the spoken stage and few understood the requirements of the libretto. A casual approach to librettos was a common ailment in moribund Neapolitan opera. The battles fought by Gluck (with the powerful aid of Calzabigi) were slow to bear fruit. Opera was in need of good librettists; likely Buonaiuti was not one. Both Robertson and Hunt sensed that a problem existed, but they were too closely oriented to the English tradition of dramatic "realism" to see the issues clearly.

After a steady diet of Catalani and Taylor's management, Robertson did not suppose that the season of 1811 would offer any improvements. It is true that the opening opera, Chevalier Federici's* *Zaira,* although appearing to disadvantage with the music of Peter von Winter's* *Zaira* "still fresh in recollection" (last presented in 1806), was at least different in style from those of the last two years. Robertson reported that Teresa Bertinotti,* who selected the opera for her English debut, had a very fine voice, but he found her too plump and without any pretence of acting. In any event the theatre was to go on, he noted glumly, under the usual bad management (30 December 1810). Nor had things improved by May, when Robertson complained that the chorus was weak and out of time, while Catalani and a Signor De Giovanni were out of tune. "Bad as the musical taste is at present," he stated, "such discordant sounds as are now to be heard at the Opera-house would not be tolerated throughout one song on an English stage" (5 May 1811).

This overstatement was the result, no doubt, of an exhausted patience, though sometimes Robertson shared with Barnes and Hazlitt an inclination to make invidious comparisons at the expense of whatever production was under review. Two weeks later, however, a startling change came over the Italian opera with the London première of *Così Fan Tutte*—the first Mozart opera performed at the King's Theatre since 1806. Robertson wrote:

To convey by words an idea of the electrical effect this music produces is impracticable, and to recommend any particular compositions to the notice of those unacquainted with the opera, would be useless, where the whole is one collected mass of excellence. It is only by hearing such music that an adequate conception can be formed of the exquisite beauty and variety of the airs, the uncommon richness of the harmony, or the genius displayed in the accompaniments, which sport through all the mazes of the science; at one time flowing with a calm solemnity, and at another bursting forth in modulations as unexpected as inspiring.

Extremely difficult as Mozart's compositions are to execute with effect, the performers were generally, and I must say contrary to my expectation, fully adequate to them. Nothing like the singing of Madam Bertinotti has been heard at the opera for some years, as it left nothing to be wished for. It was, as it has not always been lately, perfectly in tune, and given with feeling that evinced a proper estimation of Mozart's merit. No meretricious ornaments were added, but every grace was introduced in it's proper situation.[18] [19 May 1811]

Somewhat overwhelmed by the richness of the work, Robertson seems unaware of Cosi's exceptional operatic structure, for it has more ensembles than arias. No wonder he had difficulty picking out individual numbers, though Hunt was to identify several in a later review.

Robertson feared this change in fortune might not last. At the end of his review he tells us: "Owing to some inharmonious disputes between the performers and the manager, the repetition of the opera has hitherto been prevented; but it is hoped that the public will not . . . be turned back to their old insignificant acquaintance, rendered doubly tedious by the contrast." But the difficulties were settled. Cosi proved highly successful and was performed six times in less than one month.

The significance of this to Robertson was that the public taste was not so debased as the theatre managers assumed. In his next review he turned the occasion against the English stage and Sheridan in particular for "putting on cheap popular dishes" in competition with Covent Garden: "It is remarkable that those men who are foremost in speaking ill of the public taste are frequently those who tend most to destroy it." Such men think it necessary to conform to

the perverted wishes of the public. This doctrine has been disseminated by the composers of the opera, who, whatever they may profess, write badly only because they cannot write well. The fallacy of this libel, as far as it is applied to the musical world, has been proved by Madame Bertinotti, who, prompted by good taste, has ventured to free herself from the trammels of these gentlemen, in reviving *Cosi fan tutte,* the success of which must satisfy every one that there is no want of admirers when there is any thing to admire. [16 June 1811]

Probably Robertson, like Hunt, was partial to Drury Lane, as well as being distressed with Sheridan's politics; hence his indignation is all the sharper. And he shared with Hunt a confidence in the ability of the opera-going public to respond to good productions, though he was aware that public taste was susceptible to corruption by pandering managers and their hacks. Bertinotti had not always wished to escape from the trammels of "these gentlemen," among whom her husband, Radicati, must be numbered, nor is it clear how this production was made possible.[19] What was clear to Robertson, however, was the domination of third-rate Italian composers at the King's Theatre.

This outburst against the English stage prefaced his review of the London premiere of *Il Flauto Magico,* which the baritone, Giuseppe Naldi,* brought out for his "benefit."[20] Robertson expressed his delight with the overture in language that recalls Hunt's ability to describe musical effects:

Influenced by its [*Cosi's*] attraction, Signor Naldi has brought out the opera of *Die Zauber Flöte,—The Magic Flute,—*another work of Mozart's of great celebrity. Unfortunately, the state of the company, deficient in number as well as excellence, prevented this noble work from being executed as it deserved. Many of the best pieces were unavoidably allotted to Signor De Giovanni, who sings in a whisper just audible enough to shew that he is out of tune; or to Signor Beridino, whose "big voice" has no medium, but is always either growling with an undefined rumbling like distant thunder, or bellowing forth with most dissonant and ear-rending

harshness. . . . [Only Mmes. Bertinotti, who sang Pamina, and
Collini performed well.] The greatest treat the opera afforded was
the overture, which is one of the greatest efforts of musical genius,
if not altogether unrivalled. Nothing can surpass the solemnity
of the opening movement, or the animation with which it afterwards
takes its flight through all the labyrinths of science, till it at last
finds a resting place, where it is relieved by a few magnificent bursts
from the wind instruments, when it again sets forward, its
wanderings becoming more involved and intricate as it proceeds,
till it arrives at the highest pitch of grandeur to which music is
capable of soaring. [16 June 1811]

When it came to the plot, however, Robertson joined the host of
commentators on Mozart who have seen in it nothing but
absurdity:[21]

The pleasure that the wonderful music of this opera gives,
receives a serious drawback from the almost unprecedented absurdity
of its plot and language, which are so incoherent, that they can
scarcely be imagined the work of intellect above that of an ideot;
and it does not reflect a little discredit on the taste of the Germans,
that this opera, sublime as its music is, should not only be tolerated,
but even enthusiastically admired by them. Our stage has not yet
arrived at such a state of literary degradation, as to disregard
altogether the language of our operas, for we have lately seen in
Mr. Morton's contemptible drama, the *Knight of Snowdoun*, that
the admirable compositions of Mr. Bishop, many of which would
have done honour to Mozart, have not been able to protract its
existence beyond a very limited period.

And he closed with a typical Huntian caution to composers to
select carefully "the poetry on which they bestow their pains,
without which their music can never become a lasting favourite."
Like most of his contemporaries, Robertson would have been
astonished to know that *The Magic Flute* has survived, while the
enormous output of Bishop gathers dust.

The season of 1812 was equally notable for the revival of
Mozart's *La Clemenza di Tito* and the première of *Figaro*.[22]
Robertson praised the music of *Tito*, especially where it was
inspired by the libretto. He thought, however, that Mozart was

not fortunate in selecting the subject, "which is of too mild and equable a nature to call forth that variety of musical expression which more violent exertions would excite" (22 March 1812). (Presumably neither Robertson nor Hunt, who raised similar objections in a later review, knew of the adverse circumstances under which Mozart was compelled to compose this opera seria for the Emperor's coronation.) Only one scene, that in which Vitellia joins with Sextus against Titus, has excitement; here Mozart's music "like the mind of *Sextus* is all agitation, alternately melting into tenderness, and bursting with distraction." (Robertson's insight into the psychology of Mozart's music anticipates Hunt's.) The occasion also afforded "one of those fortunate and rare productions that completely assuage the critic's sorrows, [and] disarm his resentment." Catalani and Tramezzani "did much for the composer";[23] and the orchestra was "perfection itself; the spirit and refined taste of Mr. [Charles] Weichsel, the leader, infuse themselves into every individual, and the wonderful accompaniments gave the principal performers ample scope to display their talents; for the whole orchestra is constantly in motion, no vacancy is to be found, and every interstice is filled up by the delicious touches of Mozart's fancy" (22 March 1812). Opera was still so much regarded as the singer's prerogative that it took a Mozart production to elicit some attention for the orchestra.

In reviewing *Figaro,* Robertson emphasizes at the outset that the management could take little credit for the recent opportunities to hear Mozart's operas:[24]

The works of Mozart, which have long lain dormant, and enjoyed the repose due to so many of our living manufacturers of music, have at length shone forth from the obscurity in which jealousy and bad taste [i.e., of Catalani] had involved them. Till the last two or three years, this great genius has been known chiefly as an instrumental writer, and might have still have [sic] remained so, had not a society of amateurs, who were capable of perceiving where true merit was to be found, laudably exerted themselves to diffuse the delight his vocal works had given themselves. With this view, and aided by some tasteful professors, they brought forward the Opera of *Don Giovanni,* and followed it up, successively, with performances of two of his other productions, which required only to be heard, to ensure them a high reputation. Till they had gained this, none of the Opera Performers thought of reviving them, and of the four which have been performed at the King's Theatre, only one has been produced by the Manager,—so little have the Public to thank Mr. Taylor for his endeavours in their behalf. [12 July 1812]

We cannot tell whether the management produced *Tito* or *Figaro.* Catalani sang in both, and since the company was not large enough, it was necessary to bring Mrs. Dickons out of retirement for the production of *Figaro.* But Robertson's contention is clear—the continued moribund condition of the opera management and the indebtedness of the public to the influential activities of the "society of amateurs" in bringing Mozart to the King's Theatre.[25]

Concerning the opera itself he wrote:

The last which has been produced, *Le Nozze di Figaro,* is perhaps, altogether, the finest of his works. The subject is taken, with little alteration, from Beaumarchais' celebrated comedy of *"La Folle Journée,"*[26] and, in its quick succession of incident, gives full scope to the fancy, which teemed with delightful combinations of sound, and sprung from subject to subject, with inexhaustible freshness, vigour, and originality. Every air, and almost every close, has strong character of novelty, and seems carefully to shun resemblance to other authors; for even when the passages seem to lead to something we have heard before, a dexterous turn or an unexpected change redeems them from all charge of plagiarism. This attempt at constant novelty would be dangerous in unskilful hands, and might repress merit, or draw it into passages only original for their extravagance. Here, Beethoven, with all his gigantic powers, his wonderful harmony, and splendid effects, seems to have failed; and, without possessing the charms of melody that play so perpetually through the works of Mozart, he sacrifices our pleasure to our astonishment; gaining in novelty what he loses in feeling, and speaking to the ear rather than to the heart. [12 July 1812]

For Robertson, Mozart's music successfully threads a delicate course between the conventional and the novel. To a world tired of the thin stereotypes of the old style, the richness and surprise of Mozart are beginning to please. Robertson's praise of Beethoven is unusual in view of the "astonishment" that produced a negative response in most contemporary listeners. Robertson's mention of this composer again suggests an unusual context, for although his instrumental work was becoming known by 1812, London did not see *Fidelio* until 1832. An occasional blurring of musical genres is characteristic of the comparisons made by Robertson and his fellow *Examiner* critics, a confusion that may result from their more literary than musical orientation.

The performance of *Figaro* went well; both Catalani and Dickons were praised.[27] But Joseph Fischer,* who played Almaviva, proved that "unless he could get rid of his voice, his figure, and his rough German accent, he cannot reasonably hope to become a favourite. The soft flow of the Italian language he converts into most rugged and guttural sounds, and his voice is accompanied with a strong breathing, that, overwhelming the notes he would utter, produces a tone more like the bellows of an organ than that instrument itself."[28] German singers were rare at the King's Theatre and seem to have been liked no better by the public than by *Examiner* critics (see Hunt's comments below).

Had Robertson always been stimulated by opera performances, his criticism would have more importance. As it is, his general level of achievement stands higher than that of his contemporary journalists during the early years of the century. Consider, for example, the report by the *Morning Post* of the London première of Mozart's *Tito*: "Last night this elegant theatre was crowded to an overflow, a just tribute to the great talents of Mrs. Billington.[*] It must have been highly pleasing to this lady, on her benefit night, to see the whole of the boxes and the pit occupied by persons of the first distinction" (16 March 1806).[29] Such "news item" reviews were the rule rather than the exception. Although *Così* was very successful, the press apparently ignored the Mozart performances in 1811. In lieu of a report of *The Magic Flute,* the *Times* reviewed one of Astley's horse-extravaganzas! The following year, however, the *Times* did review *Tito*: ·

Our taste is still so far native, as to make us regret that this music . . . [was] employed upon a subject so bare, that nothing like the interest of a plot could be felt through it. . . . And yet it was this,—such was the taste of the stage in countries where the decay of political freedom spread through all the departments of intellectual effort the same spirit of tameness, weakness, and monotony,—that Metastasio selected for the subject of a drama to be set by Mozart[!] The fame of the composer is now almost beyond criticism; and want of delight at his works will probably be attributed in the critic to want of taste: but his composition, if it has all that can be given by science, probably bears the exclusive impression of science too strongly and too unremittingly for the general ear; and the pleasure with which the few scattered airs that occasionally relieved the ponderous and laboured character of the composition were received, might have persuaded the admirers of the unmitigated German School, that taste, nature, and simplicity might in some instances, at least, be advantageously substituted for chromatics and cadences, the crashing of disjointed harmonies, and the array of scientific discordance. [5 March 1812]

The reviewer expresses in rather ponderous prose the typical attitude of the day towards Mozart's music. Of interest, however, is the political note, which Hunt was to amplify in a much later review.

On the performance of *Figaro* that year the *Sun* said, "Mozart's standard [*sic*] opera of Figaro was performed last night with a strength of musical talent which has seldom been displayed. . . . The surprise which this new display of [Dickons's] powers excited drew down thunders of applause at the close of almost every cadence" (19 June 1812). The *Courier,* observing that it had little space for theatrical reviews due to the health of George III, took brief note of the performance: "Catalani! Anything we can say in praise of her is but the repetition of a tale a hundred times told"—then went on to give a long account of the ballet that accompanied the opera. As "Chronicles of the Italian Opera in England" (p. 72) derisively stated, Catalani even "enchained the choicest critics" by her energy;[30] the author apparently had not read the *Examiner*.

So much for the other reviewers.

After 1812 Robertson's "Opera Letter" all but disappeared from the *Examiner*. He did reappear once more in 1820, to write a review of a Rossini première for the "Theatrical Examiner," no doubt as a favor to the ailing editor; but it would seem best to take up that review later, in its proper setting.

Robertson's achievement is significant when we consider that for five years, when productions at the King's Theatre were generally deplorable, he regularly produced serious opera criticism for the *Examiner*, which in extent of coverage and critical content appears to have been much superior to contemporary musical journalism. If his reviews too often reflect the dullness of the performance, if his musical appreciations generally lack vigor and depth, he wrote better than his fellow reviewers on the other newspapers, avoiding much of their triteness and overemphasis on the prima donna, and seeking instead to render intelligent (though sometimes misguided) critiques on the composers and librettists as well as on the performances. Less sensitive and penetrating than Hunt, he brought to Italian-opera criticism many ideas that Hunt would later develop. He remained free from the social and esthetic prejudices toward Italian opera that eroded much of the criticism of Barnes and Hazlitt. He recognized the importance of the musico-dramatic elements in opera and seems to have been the first in the British press to make substantive commentary on Mozart's operas. He served the *Examiner* well in its attempt to raise the standards of public taste, paving the way during some artistically lean years for the more brilliant performances, and reviews, that lay ahead.

Thomas Barnes

When Barnes began to write for the *Examiner* early in 1813, he probably had the responsibility for reviewing Italian opera. Barnes's comments on proceedings at the King's Theatre appeared, unsigned, in the "Theatrical Examiner," along with re-

views of the English theatres. (This practice was followed by
Hazlitt and Hunt.) But if Barnes had that responsibility, it was
not in his nature to fulfill it conscientiously, for the reviews of
Italian opera during the next two years were not only rare but
often irrelevant to the opera at hand.

To be sure, conditions at the opera house during 1813 and
1814 deteriorated under a divided management. It is doubtful,
however, whether Barnes's reviewing would have been better if
written under other circumstances, for his strong biases, already
noted in his reports on the English stage, were carried into the
King's Theatre. Filled with strange inconsistencies, his criticism
often has an undercurrent of bitterness and disgust, breaking
forth now and then in tirades against English taste.

One of his more interesting "Theatrical Examiners" was, characteristically, not a review of an opera but a report on the "state
and conduct of the Italian stage." Barnes's remarks were
prompted by a riot at the theatre on the night of 1 May 1813,
which resulted in £ 5,000 damages. He linked the riot to the
practice, recently stopped on order of the Lord Chamberlain, of
persons going behind the scenes:

The chief inconvenience . . . was, that it interrupted the dancers
in their preluding for the stage, while at the same time it broke
the delusion of the scene, by shewing the naked deformity of the
decorations, and the gaunt badly-painted features of the Nymphs and
Hamadryads, who look so beautiful to the uninstructed eyes in the
back rows of the pit. The young men of fashion, warm with
champaign [sic] and the careless insolence of ignorance, will not
now be able to insinuate their pretty nothings into the ears of . . .
[the dancers and singers].[31] [9 May 1813]

Barnes's attitude toward Italian opera seems motivated both by
a pique against aristocratic privilege and by grumpiness against
English taste altogether. In remarks that echo the "Are the English a musical people?" debates, he continues:

The King's Theatre is almost exclusively visited by the highest rank
and fashion of the nation, and yet these superb aristocrats are
delighted with a style of performance which would disgust the lowest

orders. What is the reason of this? It is simply, that the highest
orders of society, with very few exceptions, are worse educated than
the inferior ranks of the middle portion of the community: that
with respect to intellect and mental cultivation and every thing but
manners, they are semi-barbarians, the consequence of which is the
utter absence of that best characteristic of a gentleman, a well-
instructed taste. . . . And yet these are the people who have the
direction of the national school of music, for so the Opera may very
properly be called. What wonder that to persons who know nothing
of poetry but its verse . . . Buonaiuti should seem as good a poet as
Metastasio, and Pucitta more delightful than Mozart? . . . If the
English ever become a musical nation, it must be from the public-
spirited exertions of the middle orders: they, and they alone, have
the knowledge, the taste, and the enterprize fit to introduce a fine
musical taste into the nation. If the King's Theatre, instead of
being a subscription assembly, were entirely public, we might then
have some hope . . . that the works of Handel, Haydn, Mozart, and
Beethoven, would consign to perpetual silence the Pucittas and the
Ferraris, who, instead of degrading the stage, would then be content
to ravish the private coteries of the fashionable and the great.

Barnes's implied praise for the taste of the lowest orders of society
is of course ridiculous; and his proposal for eliminating subscriptions at the opera house is not practical: no house operating
without state subsidy could afford, then or now, to abandon sub-
scribing patrons for the whims of an uncommitted public.
Barnes does emphasize, however, the importance of the middle
classes in the cultivation of taste. He follows Robertson, too, in
condemning hack composers and librettists as well as in bringing
the names of Handel, Haydn, and Beethoven into a discussion of
opera performances.

Regarding the performers Barnes averred, "It will scarcely be
believed by persons unacquainted with this theatre, that the performers, with two or three exceptions, would disgrace the boards
of Sadler's Wells, or the Olympic Pavilion: . . . they sing with
less taste and less in tune than the lowest order of chorus-singers
at Drury-Lane or Covent-Garden." The exceptions were Tramezzani, who is "a good actor, and sings with exquisite taste and
sweetness . . . [but whose] face is vulgar and incapable of any

expression"; Naldi, who "has some skill in music and some humour: but they are both egregiously over-rated"; and finally Catalani:

Her extatic warblings overwhelm reason with delight: criticism is content to wonder without referring to its rules of analysis: and her mistakes, if she makes any, are perceptible only to the musical pedant who thinks a deviation from a scientific canon ill compensated by the most fanciful beauties of execution. Such a man would accuse Thucydides of false grammar on account of his atticisms, or Homer of incorrect quantity for the occasional artful protraction of a short syllable. [9 May 1813]

But the powers of the siren seem to have "enchained" Barnes's reasoning: Although a Catalani merely warbles her woodnotes wild, the serious listener must study to achieve good taste. "It cannot well be otherwise," Barnes asserts after noting that the boxes are emptier at Mozart performances than at those of lesser composers: "A taste for the sublimer excellencies, and the more delicate refinements of music, is not to be attained without long study and strict attention: and how are these laborious qualifications compatible with the bustle and emptiness and perpetually-shifting flutter of fashionable life."

Barnes's praise of Metastasio, cited earlier, may have owed something to fond boyhood recollections. In a review the following year Barnes qualified his judgment:

[Metastasio's] poetry is generally of a mediocre kind, displaying tolerably smooth versification, tolerably pretty sentiment, and tolerably elegant diction; in short, every thing which might be expected from an accomplished Gentleman-Usher at an Imperial Court. . . . We do not mean to say that he never rises into dignity, because we have not forgot La Clemenza di Tito: but even there we cannot agree with Voltaire that he is sublime. . . . Compare him however with the usual composers of dramatic pieces, and he is Apollo himself. [10 July 1814]

The opera of this review was the London première of Ferdinando Paër's* La Didone Abbandonata—"altered from Metastasio," as Barnes cryptically explained. He declared that the music, "for

sweetness, variety, and the unlimited profusion of the most deli-
cate graces, is scarcely surpassed by the best compositions of
Mozart," and he went on to render trite praise to Grassini and
Tramezzani for their performances.

Only once—in a review of an unnamed opera[32]—does Barnes
offer a comment of more than superficial interest about music in
his Italian-opera criticism, showing that he was not incapable of
insights into music and opera, despite the inapposite nature of
most of his reviewing:

The music in many parts has all the beautiful fluency of the Italian
school, together with that variety which so proudly distinguishes it
from our own. An English air is like that silly species of French
verse, called a rondeau. The beginning betrays the secret of the
end, and when it is finished one feels satisfied that the composer's
fancy has been exhausted. In Italian music (we speak of the best)
there is an unlimited range, boundless as the fancies of Italian
poetry. . . . It has in short that character which should be expected
from the country of it's origin . . . diversified with all the freaks and
tricksy conceptions of the most uncontrouled imagination. [4 July
1813]

Barnes's reviews show an undeniable interest in Italian opera
(he knew some Italian) and in music generally. But if he ever
found sublimity at the opera house, he conveyed none of it to his
readers. His style has a certain power and pungency, but it is also
marred by florid patches and a general lack of coherence. The
fact is, he was ill at ease in his role as arbiter of operatic taste.
His previous journalistic experience apparently was limited to
writing on politics and literature. He was a man of decided convictions who would make his way in the world, as Talfourd noted.
But his contribution to the Hunts has been overestimated.[33]
Measured in terms of his operatic criticism, he certainly did little
to retain the respect of the readers for the critical standards that
had been established in the "Theatrical Examiner."

William Hazlitt

Hazlitt's wit and bite brought distinction to Italian-opera criticism. Yet in some respects it is as disappointing as Barnes's—and

for much the same reasons. His reviews of the King's Theatre are
relatively infrequent: although he wrote many critiques of the
English stage during his stay with the *Examiner,* he wrote no
Italian-opera criticism at all in 1815 and only one review in 1816;
in the important season of 1817 he produced only three reviews,
two on different performances of the same opera.[34] Moreover, he
devoted a large part of his column—sometimes all of it—to a discussion not of the opera or composer but of the opera-goer, the
taste of the English, the absurdity of opera, or the peccadillos of
the aristocracy.

Hazlitt may indeed have thought "that opera had no meaning-
ful relation to life, and he was too earnest to enjoy it for its style
alone," as Baker states; but Hazlitt's attitude toward opera is
more complex than Baker suggests.[35] Much of Hazlitt's animus
derives, like Barnes's, from his acceptance of the middle-class assumption that the aristocracy is effete; Italian opera has always
been a plaything of the aristocracy, therefore Italian opera is
effete. In a review for the *Champion*—one of his earliest on
Italian opera—he wrote, "The opera from its constant and powerful appeals to the senses, by imagery, by sound, and motion, is
well calculated to amuse or stimulate the intellectual languor of
those classes of society, on whose support it immediately depends.
This is its highest aim, and its appropriate use. . . . The Opera
Muse is . . . a tawdry courtesan, who, when her paint and patches,
her rings and jewels are stripped off, can excite only disgust and
ridicule."[36] He was referring to the impoverished performances
resulting from the continuing Taylor-Waters struggles for control of the opera house.

Yet Hazlitt was not impervious to the blandishments of this
courtesan, especially when her trimmings glittered. In his first
opera review for the *Examiner* he was pleased to note the return
of opulence to the King's Theatre: "Though the Opera is not
among the ordinary resources of the lovers of the drama, it is a
splendid object in the *vista* of a winter's evening, and we should
be sorry to see it mouldering into decay, its graceful columns and
Corinthian capitals fallen, and its glory buried in Chancery. We
rejoice when the Muses escape out of the fangs of the law, nor do

we like to see the Graces arrested—in a *pas de trois*" (19 January 1817). But Hazlitt's emphasis on "vista" does not suggest a desire for intimacy, and in his criticism he often reflects the traditional British attitude toward the boxholders at the opera house.

During the successful run of *Don Giovanni* in 1817, he repeated Barnes's observation that the opera house was crowded and enthusiastic on Saturday nights but thin and indifferent on Tuesday nights. It was fashionable, he concluded, for the English public to be musical only on Saturday nights. And it was also fashionable, both in England and on the Continent, to admire Mozart—now that he was safely dead (20 April 1817).[37] In a review of *Così* he compared the boxes to "sick wards of luxury and idleness, where people of a certain class are condemned to perform the quarantine of fashion for the evening"; and he concluded that the satisfaction they feel at the opera is "very much *against the grain.*" By contrast, he noted a visiting Frenchman who could not contain his excitement, exclaiming, " *'Ah, c'est charmant, c'est charmant!'* Now this, being ourselves English, we confess, gave us more pleasure than the opera or the ballet" (4 August 1816). It is hardly surprising that Hazlitt's ensuing comments on the opera are perfunctory—though he discusses the ballet enthusiastically and in some detail.

In *The Yellow Dwarf* for 23 May 1818 (*Works,* XX, 92–96), Hazlitt published an essay "On the Opera," presenting four arguments against that art form: it encompasses too much for the senses to assimilate; it is unnatural; it stifles words and therefore feelings; and it is effeminate and subverts the moral fibers of the English. With the exception of the first argument, which is closely related to the problem of "perspective" in Hazlitt's esthetics, these views are entirely traditional.[38]

Attacking opera on psychological grounds, Hazlitt's first argument reveals his uncertainty about the medium. As a critic his sensibilities apparently required a high degree of selectivity—a relatively simple group of impressions that could be fully grasped and subjected to critical intensity. At the opera too much was going on simultaneously and his senses were overwhelmed. In trying to seize onto one impression, he missed others and felt inadequate for his task as a critic. Such phrases as "leaves us at last in a state of listlessness"; "we are at some loss to distinguish an excess of irritation from the height of enjoyment"; "art . . . again eludes us"; and "the heart . . . is ashamed of its want of resources" suggest Hazlitt's frustration and perhaps resentment at an inability to come to critical terms with a medium to which he was nevertheless attracted.

Furthermore, opera was not, for Hazlitt, a "natural" art. In a passage reminiscent of Wordsworth he describes how the thrush "sings because it is happy: it pours the thrilling sounds from its throat, to relieve the overflowings of its own heart—the liquid notes come from, and go to the heart, dropping balm into it." But at the opera the French prima donna Joséphine Fodor-Mainvielle* sings

because she was hired to sing . . . she sings to please the audience, not herself. . . . [She] sings, as a musical instrument may be made to play a tune, and perhaps with no more real delight: but it is not so with the linnet or the thrush, that sings because God pleases, and pours out its little soul in pleasure. This is the reason why its singing is (so far) so much better than melody or harmony, than bass or treble, than the Italian or the German school, than quavers or crotchets . . . or any thing in the world but truth and nature!

Confirmed in his opinion that ennui pervaded the King's Theatre, Hazlitt does not suppose that others could find pleasure there. To be sure, the critic equivocates on the pleasure of Fodor's singing, both for herself and for the audience. But the point is essential to his argument, for what is pleasing must belong to nature and to truth. (In a similarly ingenuous mood, it will be recalled, Hazlitt would consign the folk song to the English countryside.) These inconsistencies are not characteristic of Hazlitt's criticism generally, though they can hardly be regarded as superficial.

Turning to the subject of meaning in opera, he continues:

The ear is cloyed and glutted with warbled ecstacies or agonies; while every avenue to terror or pity is carefully stopped up and guarded by song and recitative. Music is not made the vehicle of poetry, but poetry of music: the very meaning of the words is lost or refined away in the effeminacy of a foreign language. A grand serious Opera is a tragedy wrapped up in soothing airs, to suit the tender feelings of the nurselings of fortune—where tortured victims swoon on beds of roses, and the pangs of despair sink in tremulous accents into downy repose. . . . [Accordingly] there is hardly a vice for which the mind is not thus gradually prepared, no virtue of which it is not rendered incapable!

The opera vehicle Hazlitt here describes, typical enough of the mixed genres of buffa and seria, was of course not "grand," "serious," or "tragic." Similar melodramatic trifles on the English stage he had occasionally found agreeable enough and not at all immoral. At the King's Theatre he raised egregious comparisons to condemn opera for the same pretentiousness he noted in the boxes.

Hazlitt insists on the paramountcy of the word—the English word—which becomes associated with meaning, truth, poetry, tragedy, and morality, and which is subverted not only by the music but by a foreign idiom. His attitude toward foreign language and the effeminacy of Italian culture is typical of the doughty English middle-class tradition. Herschel Baker (p. 123) tells us that Hazlitt did not know Italian or German and had studied only schoolboy's French. Some of Hazlitt's remarks, however, suggest that he knew, or pretended to know, more Italian than he has been given credit for; for example, "[Signor Crivelli's*] tones in singing are full, clear, and so articulate, that any one at all imbued with the Italian language can follow the words with ease" (19 January 1817). "A new translation accompanies the Opera House Edition of *Don Giovanni*. It is very well executed. But as it is not in verse, it might have been more literal, without being less elegant" (20 April 1817).

Hazlitt's ideas on Italian opera do not suggest that he would bring serious musical criticism to his reviews. Yet several passages give evidence that he both understood and enjoyed a good deal of Italian opera, especially Mozart. Note, for example, his comments on the interpretation of Mozart in his review of *Così*: "Mr. Braham, we are told, sings Mozart with a peculiar greatness of gusto. But this greatness of gusto does not appear to us the real excellence of Mozart. . . . Mme. Fodor's voice does not harmonize with the music of this composer. It is hard, metallic, and jars like the reverberation of a tight string. Mozart's music should seem to come from the air, and return to it" (4 August 1816).

Hunt apparently challenged Hazlitt's somewhat superficial views on Mozart in an article for "The Round Table" that appeared the following month.[39] Arguing a close relationship between gusto and particularity in writing and painting, Hunt declared: "It is the same with music"; and he cited parts of *Tito, Così, Don Giovanni,* and the overture to *The Magic Flute* as examples (15 September 1816, p. 587). (These and other references indicate that Hunt was attending the opera house in 1815–1816, though leaving the reviews to Hazlitt.) When Hazlitt returned to *Don Giovanni* the next season, he reaffirmed a lack of gusto in Mozart's music, which he nonetheless found delightful. But he had changed his mind about the quality of Fodor's voice (see his comment in the preceding chapter) and its ability to harmonize with the music:

The personal character of the composer's mind, a light, airy, voluptuous spirit, is infused into every line of it [the opera]; the intoxication of pleasure, the sunshine of hope, the dancing of the animal spirits, the bustle of action, the sinkings of tenderness and pity, are there, but nothing else. It is a kind of scented music; the ear imbibes an aromatic flavour from the sounds. . . . To shew at once our taste or the want of it, the song of "La ci darem" gives us, we confess, both in itself, and from the manner in which it is sung by Madame Fodor, more pleasure than all the rest of the opera put together. . . . Madam Fodor's execution of her part of this duet was excellent. There is a clear, firm, silvery tone in her voice, like the reverberation of a tight-strung instrument, which by its contrast gives a peculiar effect to the more melting and subdued expression of particular passages, and which accords admirably with the idea of high health and spirits in the rustic character of *Zerlina.*
[20 April 1817]

Hazlitt made other interesting observations on this opera and its performance that will be examined below for a closer comparison with Hunt's views. His numerous references to Mozart outside his opera criticism certainly indicate a strong interest in the composer. Hazlitt does not penetrate much beneath the surface of the music, yet he shows a genuine response to song. When he turned his attention from the boxes to the opera, he could enjoy Mozart as well as a thrush.

Finally, we should note Hazlitt's high opinion of Giuditta Pasta* in her debut in Cimarosa's *Penelope*: "We received most pleasure from Madame Pasta's *Telemachus*. There is a natural eloquence about her singing which we feel, and therefore understand. Her dress and figure also answered to the classical idea we have of the youthful *Telemachus*. Her voice is good, her action is good; she has a handsome face, and *very* handsome legs" (19 January 1817). Pasta was then unknown and not too well received. Neither Hunt nor Stendhal, who heard her three years later, yet recognized her quality.[40] By 1822, however, she had achieved phenomenal success all over Europe.

It is unfortunate that Hazlitt, who was not without ability as an opera critic, brought so little of it to bear on Italian opera. As a prose stylist he easily surpassed his predecessors, though much of his rhetoric was misapplied. His reviews, like Barnes's, are more like essays than criticisms, though he had better performances to write about, not to mention a broader theatrical experience. When he turned his attention to the music, he could be a sensitive and intelligent listener; yet all too frequently he chose to dilute his criticisms with ill-considered remarks on the inadequate nature of opera and opera audiences.[41]

Leigh Hunt's Opera Criticism

There are reasons to suppose that Hunt might bring to his Italian-opera criticism much of the acerbity that marked his reviews of the English musical stage. His experiences there did little to foster a love of the operatic medium. In addition to the criticism of librettists that he appended to Robertson's review, his comments on Italian opera in his English-opera criticism were

scarcely sympathetic, as we have noted. He complained of the
hackneyed rhymes of the librettists; he found Italian-opera mannerisms most distressful; and he anticipated Barnes in declaring
that "the overthrow of the Italian opera is not to be atchieved
but by a change of the system of education in high life."

But by 1817 conditions at the King's Theatre had improved
markedly, and Hunt, who had enlarged his taste for Italian culture, began his reviews there with the air of a man bent on
enjoying himself.[42] Unlike Barnes and Hazlitt, he brought with
him none of the antipathy for the aristocratic milieu and no persistent complaints about the taste of the English. He continued
to attack the aristocracy, to be sure, but confined his attacks to
the "Political Examiners." At the opera house he directed his
interests toward the discovery and rediscovery of Mozart and
Rossini. Even those readers who might not attend the King's
Theatre would be curious about the sudden popularity of *Don
Giovanni,* which was exploited by the playhouses. But an increasing segment of the middle class was also finding its way into
the pit and gallery of the opera house.

Hunt enjoyed the attractions of the audience, the size and glit-
ter of the house, the opulence of the entertainment. Rather than
complain about fashionable Saturday performances, he suggests
the superiority of the Tuesday gatherings, which

has its advantages, especially for those who like as much silence
and room as possible; and this house, to our minds, is always
delightful. The very best part of the upper classes,—those who have
the most sympathy with their species,—come there to look at their
gracefullest, and to feel at their sociallest; and there is a general
sense about you of ease, elegance, and kindliness,—a sort of
under-toned music of the passions, in harmony with the livelier
business of the stage. [19 April 1818]

He could, on occasion, chastise the behavior of the audience,
though he was ready to blame its restlessness on a poor performance. *La Clemenza di Tito,* he asserted, was not well performed:
"The thin benches, and the chattering non-attention in which
the coxcombs among the audience think themselves warranted in

indulging, are additional proofs of it" (27 July 1817). But on the whole he, like Shelley and Peacock, relished the well-bred, cosmopolitan atmosphere of the opera. "We are heartily glad to see this Theatre fill so well," he wrote in his initial King's Theatre review, "for we like Italian, and music, and dancing, and beautiful mythologies, and the sight of spectators from various countries amicably mingling together" (23 March 1817).

Nor was the size of the house a disadvantage insofar as the music and singing were concerned (Hazlitt, from the rear of the theatre, complained about the loss of facial expressions, however). Hunt declared that "the insurmountable objection to the English winter theatres,—their enormous size,—does not apply to a large musical house; because singing is naturally of a louder and more distinct utterance than talking; . . . and if an objection remains as to countenances, an equal variety of distinctness of expression is not demanded of them, nor even wanted, the vocal expression being clear and just, and supplying the feeling to the spectator" (30 May 1819). In fact, the opera offered positive qualities in entertainment that were not available elsewhere: "This house is the only theatre now, at which you are sure of hearing something both modern and masterly."

The opulence offered by the King's Theatre productions, at least during the Ayrton seasons, was another important feature— adventitious for Hazlitt, essential for Hunt:

It is understood, that they [Ayrton and Ebers] set out upon liberal principles; and the re-appearance of the former in the concern is an earnest of its being conducted upon principles of good taste. Nothing else will do in an establishment of this nature. The same notions of economy, which are the only true things in some instances, become equally false ones in others. A concern which is to be saved by mere saving, is a very different thing from a concern which is to be saved by pleasing. You may build your private house up again by pinches and atoms, as a swallow builds its nest. You may rise in the world, after a fashion, by mere cunning. . . . But if the very groundwork of your pretensions is pleasure and good-taste, you must do nothing but gratify. A man or a family who go to an extreme economy . . . have only themselves to answer to; but the hundreds and thousands of people who constitute audiences, will not blink the question as to what you lay before them, for the sake of you and your establishment. Their ears will not drink sing-song for nothing. They will not patronize your ragged curtain. They will not sit down, contented, to your ill-done leg of dancer. If you will not or cannot get good fare, farewell to your bad. [18 March 1821]

When the proprietors economized in 1818, after Ayrton's departure, which resulted from a dispute with them and the singers over his artistic direction, Hunt observed that the subscribers "are enquiring into the falling off of the entertainments this year; and we leave the manager for the present to settle the matter with them. . . . Does he not make the fatal mistake of supposing, that the audience in reality care little about the goodness of the entertainment, and come there only to see and be seen? We think it likely, . . . and a manager, who finds economy a desirable thing, is likely on many accounts to fall into it" (7 June 1818).

Opulence meant not only good productions but also good operas. Hunt praised the managers in 1817 for bringing to the house important revivals of Mozart, Cimarosa, and Paesiello. But Ayrton's seasons were not the only ones praised; he regarded the 1819 season as a credit to the manager. He also offered his own suggestions for performances: Paesiello's *Nina* and Mozart's *Idomeneo* (23 March 1817), Mozart's *Abduction from the Seraglio,* and operas by Gluck, Cimarosa, and Winter: "What would we not give to have Winter's *Ratto di Proserpina* again, with all its voluptuous pathos and Greek beauty,—

'A Sicilian fruitfulness' " (22 August 1819).[43]

Though Hunt was to be disappointed in his particular requests, he met with some of the best seasons of Italian opera since Catalani's arrival in 1807. And if Hunt's deficiency in economics could provide no suggestions for placing opulence on a paying basis, he recognized what opera audiences have usually insisted on—a certain quality of festivity (consecrational or otherwise) in the performances.[44]

In his first review of the King's Theatre—a revival of Paesiello's

La Molinara—Hunt mingled valid musical insights with several incidental observations that reveal his limitations as an opera critic. He begins:

The music of *La Molinara* is very pleasing, and in some respects very original. Paesiello has not the untired strength and superabundance of Mozart; but at times he equals him in expression, that is to say, the air is quite suitable to the sentiment intended to be conveyed, and would be injured by adapting it to a different one. This perhaps is the highest character that can be given to music in any one particular point, though of course the author's merit is in proportion to the precise nature of the sentiment itself, and to its greater or less degree of difficulty and dignity. [23 March 1817]

Comparisons with Mozart were inevitable, and Hunt delicately weighs the merits of the composers. The importance of a close relationship between sentiment in words and music, to which he called attention in his criticism of English opera, is here given greater depth and significance. (The use of the term "author" for "composer" was common at the time.)

In exploring the problem of "expression" in music, however, Hunt tends to muddle the musical issues with national and literary biases:

But expression,[45] in all it's degrees, we take to be the particular feature of the Italian school of music, to which we doubt whether sufficient honour is done now-a-days. We are not for disputing the pre-eminence of Mozart, who (as far at least as any other human being can be so called, and in an art much inferior,) may be called the Shakspeare of Music; but Paesiello,[46] though a modern, is of an older school; and it is *that* school which set the example of invention and sentiment to the Germans, and brought them genius to render vital and beautiful the crude mass of their learning. Mozart was in Italy while a boy, and at that early period perhaps caught the fine spark from the southern sunshine, which (to our apprehensions at least, and they pretend to judge of music only from the feeling of a sister art) animates, to any very great extent, *his* works exclusively. We do not except even the placid mastery of Haydn, nor the fanciful passion of Beethoven, though the latter sometimes reminds us of Ariosto, and sometimes of Dante himself.

Hunt protests the "German" influence, but he does not show where it exists in opera or just why it should be considered objectionable. He only notes those German composers then known primarily for their instrumental works—a peculiarity observed in other *Examiner* reviewers. He shows a growing appreciation of Beethoven, who was becoming popular in London about this time. Much earlier, as we have seen, he recognized Haydn's exuberance as well as his placidity. But his knowledge of their orchestral music was limited almost entirely to selections presented at the oratorios, or to the piano transcriptions played at various musical evenings.

Extramusical considerations are evident in Hunt's attitude toward Germans and German art. He was too much a son of the Enlightenment to praise the Gothic, though against it he posits not French but Italian taste. He did not know German and was repelled by what he considered the somberness and obscurity of German art. And, as we have seen, he reacted strongly against the *Sturm und Drang* melodrama so popular before the end of the eighteenth century. For Hunt and the second generation Romantic writers, anti-German feelings may have been strengthened by antipathy to Coleridge and his metaphysics. Finally, there were political considerations, instanced by his allusion to the "court fashion" for the German school (22 March 1818). No doubt Hunt shared the distaste among liberals for the Hanoverians in Buckingham Palace; in a rash attack he had discredited the Prince Regent for appointing a foreigner as his Historical Painter. Furthermore, Castlereagh was known to be unsympathetic to Italian independence, while the Congress of Vienna, which the *Examiner* attacked repeatedly in 1815, established the domination of Austria over what was to Metternich only a "geographical expression." In time Hunt would modify his attitude toward the German nation (see *Table Talk*, preface and "Goethe," pp. 165–70). Meanwhile, for Hunt the internationalism of eighteenth-century music was over; a country could not be separated from the character of the music it created.[47]

Returning to the review, we find Hunt concluding with commentary on *La Molinara* that was more specifically musical:

The recitative in particular, is not so bald as it is apt to be in almost every composer but Mozart; and there is a fine easy vein running throughout, of what we believe is called the *parlante* or conversational style. But the author's wing is not strong enough to carry him equally through the whole piece; and indeed we may here remark what has often appeared to us,—that musicians, not having so obvious a necessity to generate thought after thought as writers, are too apt to content themselves with one or two inventions,—a circumstance particularly observable in the first parts of songs, as compared with the second; and also in the fondness for what are called *subjects,* which are nothing more than a solitary fancy or so, upon which the composer afterwards spins out his paper by running changes. [23 March 1817]

Hunt's attitude toward the composer's art, here as earlier, shows a strong literary bias. Not only is that art "much inferior" but it requires little thought—traditional views, as discussed in chapter one. In the example cited, he was thinking of the strophic song common to English opera; he did not realize what inventiveness is needed for a through-composed piece or even the da capo aria. In *Feast of the Poets* and elsewhere Hunt had plenty to say about poetasters; his failure to make similar distinctions between composers shows that he still clung obstinately to the primacy of poetry.

In referring to the recitative, moreover, Hunt does not distinguish between the *secco* and the *accompagnato.* All eighteenth-century composers of Italian opera, including Mozart, used *secco* extensively. But in the *accompagnato* and the arias Mozart employed more complex harmonies and a symphonic texture that brought greater musico-dramatic values to Italian opera. Paesiello, who learned from Mozart, imitated these qualities, although, as Hunt suggests, his style lacks Mozart's richness and imagination. But these developments of Mozart's were linked, as Hunt also suggests, to the "German" school. The dichotomy in Hunt is evident: he praises the "Italian school" for its melodic expressiveness, which permits greater musical articulation of the sentiment, and he resents the encroachment of the "German school" in Italian opera, distrusting German art altogether. At the same time, he admires the richness that Mozart has brought to Italian opera and begins to sense a baldness and lack of invention in the older school of composers.

It is evident that his increased exposure to Mozart's music made him more critical of other opera composers. In a review of Paesiello's early opera *La Modista Raggiratrice* he observed that "the accompaniments are more than usually light, and there is a want of abundance in it altogether amounting to the bald. The finale in particular is dismissed with singular haste and indifference;—all which has a double effect of poverty after the exuberant harmonies of the German school, and the lavish gaieties of Rossini" (21 February 1819). He did praise one air, "Di piacer mi balza il cor"; but in his next review (21 March 1819), he candidly confessed that this was found to be an interpolated air by Rossini![48] Even the oft-revived *Il Matrimonio Segreto* of his beloved Cimarosa was beginning to pall:[49]

We dislike to find fault with an Italian composer, because we think the music of his country unrivalled in one great respect, which is sentiment,—and because it appears to us much undervalued at present, owing to the tempting riches of German harmony. But we missed in the Opera before us what in an Italian composer of celebrity we had a right to look for,—sentiment in general, and beautiful melodies in particular. . . . The most admired air in the piece, *Pria che spunti in ciel l'Aurora,* is to us, we must confess, a great deal too literal as well as important. We cannot hear of post-coaches being got ready so pompously and horses galloping to such very illustrative notes, with any of the grave admiration desired of us. Yet this opera, they say, is a favourite with the Italians. Not very lately, we hope,—since their tastes have been shaken up in common with the rest of the world; and *till* very lately, we know that their tastes were remarkable for nothing but their exceeding kindness and toleration, taking Pompeo Battoni for a

great painter, Bettinelli for a fine poet,[50] and Metastasio for an
absolute perriwigged Apollo. [7 June 1818]

Hunt's predicament is again evident in his failure to find, in
"an Italian composer," operatic virtues that should rightfully be
his, while that German enchantress, harmony, threatens to
undermine traditional values. And again he fails to identify German composers of Italian opera as culpable; indeed, he could
not, for such composers as Handel, Johann Christian Bach, and
Mozart were as thoroughly Italianate in their outlook as born
Neapolitans.

More important in this passage is his vigorous rejection of the
imitative and pretentious in music, which he here associates with
Italian Neoclassicism. For all his love of Italian grace and spirit,
he is as emphatic in rejecting the emptiness of its eighteenth-
century art as he is certain of the change in taste brought about
by the revolt that we call Romantic. But he found imitative
qualities in German composers as well. In his oratorio criticism,
for instance, he observed, of *The Creation,* that when Haydn's
"instruments undertake to be particularly vocal or dramatic, he
is apt to become too literal in his taste, . . . turning his sounds
into pictures . . . instead of expressions of feeling. . . . But when
he avoids the temptation, he can put forth noble and touching
melodies. Such is his vernal invocation, *Come Gentle Spring.* . . .
This is the true thing; and not attempting to make the grass
grow, or to personify daffodils by crotchets" (12 March 1820).[51]
The persistence of such attacks suggests that a distaste for literal
representation is the most characteristic feature in Hunt's musical criticism. Together with the many passages touching on the
imaginative resources of music, this feature confirms Hunt's essentially Romantic viewpoint.

Inevitably, Hunt criticized Italian-opera librettos and librettists. Yet his attacks are far less frequent than might be supposed
after a review of his English-opera criticism. Hunt's debt to
dramatic realism is everywhere apparent, of course; but his careful emphasis on the effect of bad librettos on composers and per-

formers suggests a growing awareness of the distinction between a musical play and a libretto.

Il Matrimonio Segreto he found to be "a washy abridgment of our play of the *Clandestine Marriage* [by George Colman], openly taking the materials, and yet melting them down into shapelessness and want of character like stolen plate. Thus the best thing in the original, the tottering old lover and fine gentleman, is turned into a middle-aged non-entity, neither tottering, nor fine, nor any thing else. The music seems to have been subdued to the quality of the dialogue. It is marked with nothing at all." Therefore, he adds, the whole performance suffered, "—one of the natural consequences of having bad elements to work upon" (7 June 1818). The dialogue of Paesiello's *La Molinara,* "as in most instances of the Italian opera," he had earlier observed, "is a poor business,—a circumstance which we do not mean to pass over in future productions of that kind, not being at all alive to the pleas in behalf of the union of bad poetry with good music. *The Maid of the Mill* is a good old theatrical material, and so is a set of lovers; and yet, such a deteriorating faculty have these compilers of operas, that they can make nothing of it" (23 March 1817).

But his greatest indictment of a librettist occurs in his review of Mozart's *Tito.* His opening remarks on Metastasio (from whose libretto Caterino Mazzolà made the adaptation for Mozart's opera) may owe something to Barnes's review of 10 July 1814. Hunt began:

In the first place, we do not much admire the piece itself as a drama, nor, to confess the truth, with all our love of Italian Literature, are we admirers of the author, Metastasio. He is, it is true, at the head of Opera writers hitherto; that is to say, all other Opera writers hitherto have been very poor ones; but he is no more to be instanced as a specimen of Italian genius, as many have instanced him, than Addison's *Cato* or Smith's *Phaedra and Hippolytus*[52] are to be brought forward as specimens of English. Tasso would have scorned his pretensions, and Ariosto laughed at them. Poor Dr. Burney was taken in, as the phrase is, by his smirking manners, his cheap sentimental common-places, and above all, by the additional reputation he gave to operas and opera music,—

which is unquestionable. But this was an easy task for a man who had any poetry in him at all; and from the Doctor's own elaborate and eulogistic account of him, as well as from his dramas and letters themselves, he seems to us to have been a very middling poet, and a cold, servile, over-prudential man.[53] [27 July 1817]

These qualities, so antithetical to Hunt's own nature, commonly mark artists that he condemns. But Burney, whose views on music Hunt often reflects, was not entirely "taken in" by Metastasio, for he noted that the poet seemed by prudence, urbanity, "and a politeness which bordered upon flattery to avoid literary quarrels such as those that plagued Dryden, Boileau, Pope and Voltaire." In fact, the summary of Metastasio that follows in the review is based almost entirely on Burney's *Memoirs of the Life and Writings of Abate Metastasio,* though Hunt alters the case a good deal by dropping not only the "eulogy" but some of the facts that tend to favor the poet. He finds particularly reprehensible Metastasio's action in "turning his back on country and countrymen" to settle for life in "the metropolis of the Goths": "Metastasio's total desertion of his native soil seems to have been revenged upon him by the fogs and stoves of Germany, which Ariosto held in such horror" (compare Burney, *Métastasio,* II, 151–52). Hunt was of course unjust, misled mainly by his own German prejudices. For Vienna, like other Continental centers, was thoroughly Italian in its operatic outlook.

Probably Hunt's repugnance for religious pretentiousness motivated this attack, for he quoted a letter that Metastasio had written to his mistress, the celebrated actress Romania:

"I would not have any dry and severe critic say to me, 'What! don't you fear hell? don't you hope in God?' . . . It is true, in answer I might say, Most sagacious Sir! I have known from my infancy, as well as you, that God and *hell* are *indisputable truths*; and *if this was not my belief, I should not have recommended myself to God, at the close, in the manner I have done*" [Hunt's italics].—Here is true Laureat religion;—the getting on at one court, as people get on at another;—the old degrading notion of the Deity as a dispenser of favours upon application, and a threatener of interminable horrors. Now true virtue and religion we conceive to be as different from all this, as equity and humanity are. [Compare Burney, *Métastasio*, I, 86]

The especially bitter tone of Hunt's attack is understandable in view of his two years in Horsemonger Lane, unavoidable only because he refused to compromise his perhaps too uncompromising principles. But beyond the personal element his attitude suggests that the artist is inseparable from the man and is distinguished from the artisan by adherence to political and religious independence. The second generation Romantics in particular rejected all forms of patronage as a taint on art: the time-serving artist was especially reprehensible. Hunt saw in Metastasio an opportunist who had betrayed his calling. Against him he set a younger contemporary and countryman of Metastasio's: "Alfieri, who went to the opposite extreme of savage independence, intended to be introduced to him, when in Germany; but was so disgusted at seeing him one day paying servile court to the Empress in the Garden at Schoenbrunn (the place rendered famous by Bonaparte's residence), that he threw up the design in a fit of contempt."[54]

Returning to the libretto of *Tito*, Hunt does not damn it altogether. Metastasio, he declares, even has

a certain taste for nature and simplicity singularly spread over a great deal of common-place. We cannot compare him better, generally speaking, than with the upper class of mediocrity in sculpture. There is the same feeble elegance, the same small air of classical propriety, the same sort of decency, suavity, and cold material. . . . His passion was soon checked by his want of enthusiasm; and his simplicity was rather a knowledge of the defects on the other side, than a feeling for the beautiful and elemental. He had no poetry whatsoever, particularly so called; that is to say, he saw nothing in nature beyond common eyesight. . . .

Now this sort of poet is as ill calculated as possible for a musician like Mozart, who was a much greater and more inspired person,— albeit, as still greater lovers of poetry than music, we say it with a grudge. But Metastasio was a pretty musician in poetry; and Mozart was a fine poet in music. The particular difference of their natures was unfortunate for a conjunction. . . . Mozart's tendency

was to feel all that he said, to be conscious of every idea in the shape
and touch of a positive pleasure. He is therefore always at his best
in direct enjoyment. . . . He could not feel mediocrity, which is
the Leaden Mean; and the stone-coloured classicalities of *La
Clemenza di Tito* must have put him out, almost as much as the
dreary decencies of an English tea-party did Madame de Stael,[55]
or as a quaker would have neutralized Titian.

Metastasio represented the dead hand of Neoclassicism—that
wasteland of mediocrity to which the Romantics consigned most
of the eighteenth century—while Mozart represented for Hunt a
kindred spirit who had compromised his genius in this unholy
alliance.[56] Accordingly, he placed *Tito* well below the other
Mozart operas he knew, in contrast to most of his fellow critics
and to the public, with which the opera was long a favorite.[57]
That the performance of the opera suffered he blames squarely
on the lack of inspiration in the libretto.

Hunt took notice, nevertheless, of the popularity of some of its
music beyond the walls of the opera house: "The lovers of music,
small as well as great, have instinctively selected one or two of the
airs . . . and harped upon them in forgetfulness of all the rest,
particularly the two duets of *Deh prendi* and *Ah, perdona*."
Later he observed the wide popularity of "O cara armonia"
from *The Magic Flute*: "We were going to say that the public
are intimate with this air, under the name of *Away with Melancholy*; but we should rather say they are on speaking terms with
it. The original, with its accompaniments, and with its appendix
of another air, is a great deal finer" (30 May 1819). In this instance the non-opera-going public missed much of the musical
effectiveness of the original setting. Elsewhere, Hunt noted that
some of the airs from *La Molinara* "have been long known and
admired in England," but he pointed up the loss of dramatic
effectiveness in the mangled English words that had been adapted
to the airs. "This suitableness of expression is of course lost in
'Whither my love,' and thus it is, that some of the finest Italian
airs, whatever they may retain, lose the chief part of their beauty,
when ignorantly put to other words. It is the same with *Nel cor
piu* [più] *non mi sento,* which is not the sentiment of 'Hope told

a flattering tale,' though somewhat more reconcileable with it, but an expression of passionate restlessness and pungency. The English hearer ought to be aware of all this, that he may do justice to the composer" (23 March 1817).

Hunt also instructed his readers on the inadequacies of a poorly translated libretto, as he continued:

In the very translations which are sold in the house on the night of performance . . . the version itself is sometimes almost as wide of the mark. This we hold not only to be an over frolicksome vindication of a translator's license . . . but by no means politic on the part of the managers. . . . We will just give the reader a specimen, to shew him how deplorably it is managed. The following is the original of the song last mentioned:—

> Nel cor più non mi sento
> Brillar la gioventù
> Cagion del mio tormento,
> Amor, sei colpa tù. . . .

Which may be thus translated:—

> No more I feel within me
> My youth and it's sunshine;
> A torment has got in me,
> And, Love, the fault is thine! . . .

This little piece of restless remonstrance, pretty enough, is sublimated by our Opera Bard into the following solemn version:—

> Ah! where are fled the joys of youth
> Which danc'd within this breast?
> Ah! where are fled the halcyon days,
> And nights of peaceful rest?—. . .

This is casting Mercury in lead, and giving his features a huge twist by the way!

Whether or not his strictures were responsible for some improvements in these translations, Hunt later remarked: "We have again to quarrel with the translation of the Operas, which we are very loth to do, as they have been much better since the beginning of the last season" (12 April 1818).

The musical and dramatic losses encountered in English adaptations and translations; the effect of poor librettists on composers and performers; the influence of politics, religion, and nationalism on the artist; literalism in music; the old style of opera and the new—these show the many facets of Hunt's operatic interests. But his criticism was also concerned with the evaluation of individual operas, composers, and performances. And it was Mozart who produced some of his most interesting critical responses. When he reviewed *Don Giovanni,* which "has already been criticised in this journal by a great writer" (Hazlitt), he found the opera more than made up for a lack of merit in *Tito,* for

here the notes are struck up to love, and gaiety, and coquetry, and all the intensities of pleasure; and Mozart is himself again. When he gets into this vein, he turns criticism into mere admiration and transport. One has nothing to do but to reckon the songs in succession, and panegyrize them as they go by, like a dance of beauties. What can be more jocund and full of anticipation than the *Giovinette, che fate all 'amore* [all'amore], with it's undulating commencement and it's jump in the fourth bar? What more genteel on the one side, and hesitating and tremulous on the other, than the duet, *La ci daram* [Là ci darem] *la mano,* with it's ardent close and delicious symphonies? What more airy, thoughtless, and triumphant than *Fin ch' han dal vino?* What a prettier little irresistible piece of penitence than *Batti, batti, o bel Masetto,* with it's humble beginning, and the tearful and heaving repetitions on the words *Staro qui?* What more suggestive of beautiful turns and movements,—more elegantly self-possessed, than the minuet, when the maskers enter? . . . What more expressive than the half-grumbling half-whining commencement of *Notte e giorno faticar,* with it's ascent on the climax, and then the prodigious *politesse* of the sequel, *Voglio far il gentiluomo?* [3 August 1817]

The effect Hunt produces is that criticism has been disarmed. Elsewhere he declared, Mozart "reduces us, as usual, to nothing but smiling surprises and exclamations" (25 January 1818). But Hunt does much more than panegyrize; his "exclamations" show acute perception of each aria and precision in capturing its essence. These little phrases, strung together like the arias them-

selves, quickly but deftly characterize the dominant musico-
dramatic impression of each piece.

Yet *Don Giovanni* was not without its faults. Hunt's objections to the title role have been anticipated in the last chapter.
Before examining these views more closely in his Italian-opera
criticism, we will return to Hazlitt's comments on the acting in
the opera. Hazlitt did not care for Naldi's Leporello: "His
humour is coarse and boisterous, and is more that of a buffoon
than of a comic actor. . . . The gross familiarity of his behaviour
to *Donna Elvira,* in the song where he makes out the list of his
master's mistresses, was certainly not in character; nor is there
any thing in the words or the music to justify it." And at first he
was not happy with Ambrogetti* as the Don. The singer did not
give the serenade, *"Deh vieni alla finestra,* any thing like the
spirit of fluttering apprehension and tenderness which character-
ises the original music. Signor Ambrogetti's manner of acting in
this scene was that of the successful and significant intriguer, but
not of an intriguer—in love. Sensibility should be the ground
work of the expression: the cunning and address are only acces-
sories" (20 April 1817). Seeing the opera a month later from a
seat closer to the stage, Hazlitt observed no improvement in
Naldi; but Ambrogetti appeared to much better advantage:
"There is a softness approaching to effeminacy in the expression
of his face, which accords well with the character, and an insinuat-
ing archness in his eye, which takes off from the violent effect of
his action" (18 May 1817).

Hazlitt's selection of the word "effeminacy" here carries no
pejorative connotations. On closer inspection Ambrogetti
brought the right degree of modulated sensibility for mitigating
the behavior of an unprincipled rascal. This was not an attempt
to make the role palatable to an audience; for Hazlitt, Mozart's
Don was an intriguer "in love" and should be so played. (On the
other hand Naldi violated the character of Leporello by an un-
justified coarseness of behavior.) Hazlitt was untroubled by the
Don's moral character, either as conceived by Mozart or as projected by Ambrogetti.

Hunt agreed with Hazlitt's reconsidered views of the performance of Ambrogetti—he was both "gentlemanly and vehement." But significant differences arose as Hunt probed into Ambrogetti's characterization:

In *Don Giovanni* he contrives to be at once gentlemanly and vehement, and makes us lose sight of the redundancy of his size in the youthful fire of his vivacity. He is always ready and energetic; and perhaps, considering he is so active, makes even his robustness contribute to a certain air of the imposing, defying, and sensual.[58] We do not think he succeeds in the serenade, *Del* [Deh] *vieni alla finestra,* but then he succeeds as much perhaps as *Don Giovanni* should: for Mozart in this instance has outrun his character, as Shakspeare was accustomed to do; and made his profligate hero say more than he intended. The song is too sincerely amorous, and would suit *Romeo* better than a rake. Signor Ambrogetti is very happy in his mixture of acting with singing. He completed, by this means, the effect of *La ci darem,* turning away, in all the self-will of mere debauchery, with an impatient movement at *Zerlina's* mention of *Masetto.* His *Fin ch'han dal vino is* also a complete thing, full of animal ardour and a sort of remorseless enjoyment. [3 August 1817]

Ambrogetti's Don is a superb creation, even in the "amorous" serenade, "Deh vieni"; for here it was Mozart who violated the Don's character. Unlike Hazlitt, Hunt regards the Don as a reprehensible, even vicious cad, and Mozart had no business making him sing like Petrarch.[59] The characterization requires the gentlemanly touches Ambrogetti provides, to be sure; but it is the Don's sensuality and "remorseless enjoyment" that Hunt deplores. Ambrogetti's energies perfectly capture these qualities, nor would Hunt wish the role played otherwise.

But Hunt finds the Don disagreeable despite Ambrogetti's impersonation. It is of course the Don's unmitigated licentiousness that disgusts him:

To say the truth, the better the character of *Don Giovanni* is performed, the more disgusting at times he becomes; for there is nothing whatever to excuse his villainy,—no jealousy, no resentment, no ill treatment, no scorning or being scorned,—nothing that makes a shadow of excuse for his contempt of others' comfort. He cannot even muster up for himself the common rake's excuse, of conferring pleasure in spite of pretences; for he is visited by an eternal reminding of his hard-heartedness from those he has seduced; and one's impatience sometimes arises at seeing a fellow ranging in this manner among women as if they were unreflecting cattle, till the catastrophe comes.

Hunt's attitude toward women undoubtedly lies behind his expressions of contempt. The Don's behavior displays the opposite of what Hunt sought in a free relation between the sexes based on sentiment, mutual respect, and an absence of jealousy. As a result, Hunt failed to see any humor in the Don's intrigues and utterly rejected him on moral grounds. Hunt of course tended to view the role (and the opera) as essentially more serious in nature than did Hazlitt. Despite their differences neither critic found in the Don anything of the "Romantic" nature with which at least one Continental critic had already identified him.[60]

But Hunt held one further objection to the opera—Mozart's treatment of the "marble ghost" in the last act. His attitude toward the Don has some bearing here, but deeper critical issues are raised. Before examining them we should again turn to Hazlitt's earlier remarks on this part of the opera. In a passage that demonstrates Hazlitt's strength as a critic of Italian opera, he wrote:

We hear of nothing but the sublimity and Shakespearian character of *Don Juan*. Now, we confess that, with the single exception of the Ghost scene, we not only do not feel any such general character of grand or strongly-contrasted expression pervading the composition, but we do not see any opportunity for it. Except the few words put into the mouth of the great Commander, *(Don Pedro)* either as the horseman ghost, or the spectre-guest of *Don Juan*,—which break upon the ear with a sort of awful murmur, like the sound of the last trumpet ringing in the hollow chambers of the dead, but which yet are so managed, that "airs from heaven" seem mingled with "blasts from hell,"—the rest of the opera is scarcely any thing but gaiety, tenderness, and sweetness, from the first line to the last. To be sure, the part of the great Commander is a striking and lofty catastrophe to the piece; he does in some sort assume a voice of stern authority, which puts an end to the mirth, the dancing, the love and feasting, and drowns the sounds of the pipe, the lute, and the guitar, in a burst of rattling thunder;—but even this thunder falls and is caught among its own echoes, that soften while they redouble the sound, and by its distant and varied accompaniments, soothes as much as it startles the ear. This short episode . . . is the only part of the opera which aims at the tragic: this part is not of a pure or unmixed species, but is very properly harmonized with the rest of the composition, by middle and reflected tones. . . . Except, then, where the author reluctantly gives place to the Ghost-statue, or rather compromises matters with him, this opera is Mozart all over; it is no more like Shakespear, than Claude Lorraine is like Rubens or Michael Angelo. It is idle to make the comparison.[61] [20 April 1817]

Hunt's claims to the contrary notwithstanding, he held little in common with Hazlitt in his criticism of this part of the opera. Hunt wrote:

Then as to the Statue,—we must confess, however unwillingly, and with whatever mixture of humility in our opinion, that we not only, in common with the friend who formerly criticized this piece for us, regard it as inferior to the other parts of the opera, but as a total failure and mistake. There is certainly some good music in the part, and the dreary undulating accompaniment in one passage has a fine effect; but the whole is too loud and crashing, and of too vulgar a description of the terrible. We know not that an apparition of stone has any particular claims to be noisy and bullying. The terror of spectral visitations consists in ghastliness, obscurity, and sepulchral hollowness, like the Ghost in *Hamlet*,— in short, in the quietest possible exhibition of power, which is always awful in proportion to it's ease, and to it's contempt of human vehemence. [3 August 1817]

These remarks must have created a stir, for in the "Theatrical Examiner" two weeks later he refers to some misunderstandings and takes up most of the article with a full explication of his objections to the ghost. First of all he emphasizes that he has nothing but praise for the cemetery scene:

The cemetery by moonlight, the gleaming in it . . . of the statue on horseback, the air of deathlike repose, the solemn and mute inclination of the statue's head, . . . and then the terrible words it utters—

Di rider finirai pria dell' aurora—

Thou shalt have done with laughter before morning—

in which every word is syllabled out with so awful a monotony, till there comes a drop on the *o* in *aurora*—present a combination, than which nothing can be more grand or fearful; but then nothing at the same time can be more quiet, and full of a conscious power.[62] [17 August 1817]

But he emphatically protests the last scene, where the statue of the Commendatore summons Don Giovanni to hell and everlasting damnation. "It is the *noise,* and the noise only, of the music in which the Ghost is concerned, that we find fault with, not the chords, or the rest of the feeling. But to the noise we have very strong objections, and we think they are founded in reason, and in the practice of Mozart's brethren, the poets." As Hunt explains:

There is no necessity for the Ghost to make a noise. He is not a pretender, and therefore he need not resort to the arts of human ones; and all power is great, and commanding, and awful, in proportion to it's ease. The loudness, the crashing, the slamming thumps, are all comparatively vulgar. We rouse ourselves instinctively against them:—we seem to say—"Oh, is that your mode of proceeding?—Well, I can be as noisy as you." There is a feeling of equality in it, as well as a reference to common human terrors, extremely hurtful to the ideas of the supernatural and the potent.

He concludes his discussion with a number of analogies drawn from Greek mythology, the Old Testament, Milton, and Shakespeare, to show how the best poets achieved great effect in describing supernatural power by emphasizing its quiet strength.

Now Hunt surely misconstrued Hazlitt in claiming that the latter had regarded the last Statue scene as inferior. On this scene they agree only that it is exceptional.[63] True, Hazlitt does not find this part "pure": it introduces tragic elements. Yet even this tragic intrusion with which Mozart "compromised" was satisfactorily resolved; he lessened the shock of thunder by weaving it into the harmonic texture of the music (by which I take "middle and reflected tones" to suggest). So far from being inferior, it is the only part of the opera where Hazlitt can see any justification for attributing Shakespearean sublimity to the composer. Although Hunt agrees with Hazlitt that the undulating accompaniment has a fine effect, the scene is a complete failure for Hunt. So far from being tragic, it has degenerated into farce.

In evaluating Hunt's objections, we cannot ignore problems presented by contemporary interpretations.[64] As noted earlier, Mozart's operas were for years mangled beyond belief. Hunt's repeated references to "crashing" and "slamming thumps" suggests the presence of melodramatic effects quite out of keeping with Mozart's intentions.[65] If the Statue was indeed burlesqued, Hunt would regard him as only a bigger bully than the Don, and the musical power of Mozart's *fortissimo* would be transformed into a crude appeal to literal force.

Aside from problems of interpretation, which continue to this day,[66] the sharpness of Hunt's reaction to melodramatic violence in *Don Giovanni* is echoed in his other writings. Referring to "Monk" Lewis's *The Castle Spectre* (1798) as "a play of the very worst taste," he stated: "To the credit of the present century, I think the play would now, as a new production, be hooted from the stage. . . . We are now on our guard to laugh at every thing that is meant to frighten us" (19 June 1808). The instances, which could be multiplied,[67] no doubt had complex roots in Hunt's childhood—the "Mantichora" about which his older brothers had terrified him, his hatred of school bullies, and the "particularly aweful" effect that thunder and lightning had on him while at Christ's Hospital.[68] They are also apparent in Hunt's "Romanticism."

Referring to the review just considered (17 August 1817), the Houtchenses have pointed out that "Hunt's Romanticism is apparent in his conception of the supernatural."[69] That there were different Romantic conceptions of the supernatural, however, is suggested by comparing the views of Hazlitt and Hunt. Hazlitt's more subjective review is somewhat lacking in clarity. Unlike Hunt, he makes no distinction between the supernatural elements of the scenes in which the "Ghost" appears; that is, he specifically considers the two scenes together as "the single exception" to the tone and style of "the rest of the composition." The dramatic qualities Hazlitt associates with the supernatural, however, are all of a piece. They are "strongly-contrasted," "grand," and "Shakespearian"; they contain "blasts from hell," they aim at the "tragic," and they have "sublimity." The supernaturalism of Hazlitt, then, reflects something of Gothic terror, the grandeur and sublimity of Burke, and the spine-tingling excitement that most critics have found in the scene.[70]

Hunt's reaction to the "cemetery" scene contrasts sharply to his reaction to the final appearance of the ghost. In the latter scene he remained unimpressed by the physical sublime (as emphasized in the tradition of Edmund Burke's influential *Philosophical Enquiry into the Origin of Our Ideas of the Sublime and Beautiful* [1757]), while emphatically rejecting the Romanticism of terror: it aroused his indignation; he found in it only a shocking sensationalism. The powers of the Spirit could not speak to the imagination in the simulacra of angry men. By contrast, the "cemetery" scene had a grand impressiveness for its evocation of awe and fear because of a *quiet* and *conscious* power.

Yet neither here nor elsewhere does Hunt associate the fearful or the supernatural with the tragic. He, too, cites Shakespeare among the "preceptors" of Mozart (the Ghost in *Hamlet* moves slowly, speaks slowly, "and when it goes away, it *fades*"). (The association of Shakespeare and Mozart by these and other contemporaries implied, of course, no influence, literary or otherwise. The Bardology erected by Coleridge provided these literary critics with a *ne plus ultra,* to which only the genius of Mozart, in the musical world, could be compared.) But most of the citations are from Classical literature and Milton, and none of them is tragic in implication. Rather, they are visitations of Fate—and Fate lies beyond tragedy. To be sure, its power is unequivocal. Yet that power can become manifest only through the cooperation of man's imagination—a "willing suspension of disbelief." In his emphasis on its quiet strength, Hunt's Romanticism of the supernatural is closer to Coleridge's than to Hazlitt's. "Enemy of that which had too much rigor in a narrow Classicism," Landré wrote of Hunt (II, 131; author's translation), "he reacted no less strongly against that which he thought to have too much violence in a wild Romanticism."

Hunt reviewed two other Mozart operas in 1818. For the first of these, *Le Nozze di Figaro,* he had nothing but praise:

It is perhaps the most delightful work of a most delightful author. *Don Giovanni* disputes the palm with it; but the best things in *Don Giovanni* are of the same nature as those of which *Figaro* entirely consists. Mozart here gave himself up to the intoxication of his animal spirits, not in their noisiest, but in their most graceful and enjoying moments; and we listen . . . with our senses crowned with roses. All is a smoothing interchange of enjoyments,—a series of sprightly turns or lapping pleasures. [25 January 1818]

His running commentary on the arias again contains acute perceptions of their musico-dramatic effect:

What can be more airy and yet sufficing than *Se a caso Madamo* [Madama]? What more pettishly ironical, and then indignant, than *Via resti servita, Madama brillante*? What more hurried, mysterious, and occupying, with a leaning to the pleasurable, and with those little fretful notes at intervals, than *Non so piu* [più] *cosa son,* or than *Voi che sapete*? What more elegantly raillying, and then strutting off into a military air . . . than *Non piu* [più] *andrai*? What more sweet-voiced and feeling, what more consuming, what a more delicate and melodious utterance of passion, a more intense mixture of feebleness and strength, than *Porgi, amor*? . . . What more perfect in skill, taste, smartness, sweetness, courtship, and triumph, than the duet of *Crudel perchè finora,* which is perhaps the very finest effusion of this great master of transport? The three chords in the symphony alone announce an inspired hand.

A complete delight, the opera remained Hunt's favorite.

Così was also revived later the same season. Hunt found it "altogether taken up with those subjects and feelings, which Mozart played to in so happy a manner,—gallantry, arch humour, gracefulness, laughing enjoyment, voluptuousness, and an occasional pathos which is rather the suspension of pleasure than the sufferance of pain." The plot has "the advantage of being simpler and more obvious in its incidents,—of telling its own story better, than any we have ever witnessed"; accordingly, he found it "perhaps the most completely performed opera on the stage." He had no prudish objections to the plot,[71] though he suggested that the young ladies "ought, if not to have kicked them [their lovers] into atoms, at least to have let them suffer on as much as they pleased. . . . But unfortunately, they were made of too pitiful stuff. . . . *Cosi fan tutte,* says the play; 'It's the way of them all;' and so we must think the worst of it, and then make the best. O wise we!"

But the music was the best part of the drama:

What an inexhaustible succession of beautiful airs and harmonies is there in Mozart! One combination after another does not start out with a more sparkling facility in the far-famed Kaleidoscope. . . . [After the first aria] comes, like a gentler note . . . the other of *E la fede delle femmine,* the sounds of which absolutely talk and gesticulate; then . . . the invocation for gentle winds on the voyage, *Soave sia,* with those delicious risings of the voice, like a siren's from the water; the exquisite laughing trio, *E voi ridete,* with its slippery rhymes, its uncontroullable and increasing breathlessness, and the grave descending notes of the pitying old gentleman in the base. . . . What do we not owe to an art and a master like this, who as it were spoke music as others speak words; and who left his magic imprinted for ever in books, for the hand and the voice to call forth, whenever we want solace in trouble, or perfection in enjoyment! [2 August 1818]

The following year Hunt reviewed the last and, in some ways for him, the greatest of Mozart's operas, *Il Flauto Magico*—"better known and long admired in private circles under its German name of the *Zauber Flöte.*" The performance in this revival also left a good deal to be desired. The cast had to be filled out with new and younger performers, who, however, "are to be treated with tenderness; the most promising young singers may reasonably be allowed to be deficient in giving such compositions their proper effect." There was trouble with the stage effects: "There is surely . . . no necessity for the extreme vivacity of the two whirling globes in the scene where the Queen of Night comes

down from her throne. They emulated her singing and the orchestra with a noise, of which none but tin heads could have
been capable."

But the main objection was that "the opera then, as performed
on Tuesday, is justly accused of being a third too long"; Hunt
suggests that "the remedy of this however is obvious, and we
suppose was put in practice on the second night."[72] It is not the
dialogue that Hunt wants cut, but the music—not because it is
poor but, on the contrary, because it is so good and there is so
much of it:

Now the music is, throughout, excellent; but setting aside other
considerations, the most excellent music in the world will not bear a
theatrical performance so continued. It's very excellence, unmingled
with intervals of other enjoyment as in private society, would tend
to overstretch and exhaust attention, just as it strains the faculties
to look for hours together at a variety of fine pictures. . . . On
Tuesday evening for the first time in our lives, and not without
some shame, we found ourselves dropping and shutting our eyes in
the company of Mozart, not in order to listen with the greater
luxury, but to catch a willing unwilling slumber. [30 May 1819]

For the connoisseur there can be too much of a good thing![73] Despite the dilettantism suggested by Hunt's reference to the more
diluted entertainments in private circles, his reaction more likely
reflects both the intensity with which he entered into all experiences of art and the demands made on him as a listener by this
music, which was more difficult than anything hitherto presented
at the opera house. Nor should it be forgotten that the opera was
not intended to be presented with long ballets between the acts,
extending the performance considerably. Incidentally, it is odd
that we hear nothing from the critics of this translated singspeil
opera about the *dialogue,* which was surely rare enough at the
King's Theatre to cause comment. In view of the many liberties
taken with opera scores at the time, it is not inconceivable that
the Italian dialogue was set to recitative accompaniment by the
house composer, though what effect this would have on the
listener could not be calculated. Italian dialogue was illegal at

the King's Theatre under their license restrictions, which had already compelled them, on at least one occasion, to suspend production of an opera (Mount-Edgcumbe, *Reminiscences,* p. 110).

These objections aside, Hunt has nothing but praise for *The Magic Flute.* Contrary to most critics, he does not find the libretto a stumbling block:

We do not participate in the objection made to the nature of the story, which because it is a fairy tale is thought frivolous. Alas, how frivolous are most of the grave realities of life![74] We own we have a special liking for a fairy tale; and if we are not greatly mistaken, Mozart himself was of our opinion, and got his wife to read one to him before he sat down to write that divine overture to *Don Giovanni.*[75] Thus his pleasurable and fanciful mind made a fairy tale even a medium of inspiration. And it has a right to be so. It is full of some of the pleasantest associations of one's life. It has "eyes of youth." It is even more; it anticipates for us something of the good, which the human mind, as long as it is worth any thing, is so anxious to realize,—some thing of a brighter and more innocent world, in which the good-natured and flowery will is gratified; and the evil spirit, only furnishing a few more anxieties and occupations by the way, is always felt to be the weaker of the two, and sure to be found so at last.

Accepting the story as a fantasy drawn from Egyptian mythology and Freemasonry, Hunt does not look for a complex symbolism that Mozart probably never intended. Nor does the opera suggest to him a kind of Fraternity of Man, which later critics saw as an anticipation of Beethoven's choral symphony.

Yet the fairy tale held "grave realities," and as Hunt turns to the music of this, the "most romantic and passionate" of Mozart's operas, he glimpses the darker aspects of the composer's genius:

There is, first of all, the finest Overture in the world; then there is bird-like hilarity of *Gente e qui l'uccellatore;* . . . the abundant pomp and solemnity of all the grand melodies and harmonies connected with the Priests and their worship;—the placid depth and dignity of *Sarestro's* [sic] description of his earthly paradise,—*Qui sdegno non s'accende;* and then again, the delicate and tricksome stepping of the return of the Genii, *Gia fan ritorno,* with a quick and dimpled smilingness running throughout it. But the whole opera is one continued and deep river of music, breaking into every possible turn of course and variety of surface, and exhibiting every aspect of the heavens that lie above it. Mozart's genius is here in it's most romantic and passionate character, undoubtedly. We can hardly say it is in his best, for nothing can be better than *Figaro*; neither do we conceive it will be so popular as that opera and *Don Giovanni.* It is, we suspect, too poetical to be so;—too much referring to indefinable sentiments and sensations out of the pale of common experience. . . . It is to Mozart's other works what the *Tempest* is to the most popular of Shakspeare's comedies. We are not sure, for our own parts, that we do not admire it more than any of his operas, if we could candidly rid ourselves of a preconceived notion that Mozart's powers were chiefly confined to the gayer part of enjoyment,—a misconception to which all men of various genius seem to have been liable, in return for their bestowing gladness.

The Magic Flute, a deep and unified work, flows like a river (reminding us of the Arve in Shelley's "Mont Blanc") that reflects both the light and the darkness of an inner reality. For Hunt, it is here rather than in *Don Giovanni* that he finds Mozart the Romantic, though his poetry may be too evanescent for popularity.[76] It is in the poetry of Romantic comedy (yet a comic spirit tinged with tragic overtones) that Hunt finds the perfect analogy between the highest reaches of the two arts. (He may have been the first to make the oft-repeated comparison with *The Tempest.)* And it is a Romanticism of serious passion to which Hunt would give the palm, as he remains poised in uncertainty as to whether he grasps the real Mozart in his somber moods.[77] Hunt's self-questioning shows the strength of his criticism, which was capable of dealing with its own delusions. Sensitivity and self-knowledge provide a clue to his successes in accommodating a far wider range of experience than any other critic of the period.

The mood of farce, meanwhile, reasserted itself at the King's Theatre. Starting in 1818, several Rossini premières provided

Hunt with a startling and disconcerting contrast with the older composers. It did not take Rossini thirty years to reach a London production: *Il Barbiere di Siviglia* was produced there just two years after its Rome première. The Rossini fever overtook London quickly and lasted some ten years before it showed signs of abating. Hunt was caught up in this flurry of excitement, and his critical faculties were put to their sharpest test.

Like many of his fellow critics, Hunt's initial approach was strongly colored by his indignation at the composer's baldly taking over a favorite opera of the popular and still-living Paesiello.[78] At the King's Theatre première of the *Barber* he wrote, "We were among those who thought, that the author's having taken up an opera to set to music, which had been already composed by so fine a master as Paesiello, was not a piece of ambition in the best taste, or a very promising symptom of excellence. We expected that we should find little genius exhibited, at least on the score of sentiment; and we conceive that we were not disappointed" (22 March 1818). Finding absent from this opera all the vaunted excellences of the Italian school, he declared, "We should be loth to speak so decidedly, after only one hearing; but what renders an Opera most delightful, and makes one recur to it over and over again and grow fonder on acquaintance, is a succession of beautiful airs; and of these the new *Barbiere di Siviglia* appears to us to be destitute. We do not recollect one." If this is the most egregious blunder in Hunt's operatic criticism, it can be partly explained by his strong antipathy to the artistic disrespect he supposed Rossini to be guilty of. Moreover, he qualified his comments by recognizing that a single hearing is perhaps not sufficient ground for a conclusive opinion—a reservation he endorsed on subsequent hearings of Rossini.

In the balance of the review Hunt recovered his better judgment. He noted the tendency in Rossini towards the musical cliché—"You might always know the comment which the fiddlebow was going to make." Yet he also recognized both the enigmatic nature of the composer and the characteristic verve of his work:

The piece is not destitute of merit, or even, considering the author's
youth, of great promise, though not on the higher sides of genius.
Its good qualities are a sort of sprightly vehemence, and a talent
for expressing oddities of character. . . . Some of them [the
passages] fairly beat it into us. . . . We never met with a composer
who gave us such an harmonious sense of discord,—who set to music
with such vivacity what is vulgarly called a *row*. . . . The general
effect is raw and inconsistent. Sometimes, for instance, there is
hardly any accompaniment, sometimes a numerous one; sometimes
the stage is all in a bustle, and sometimes unaccountably quiet. . . .
The young author in a sort of conscious despair of a proper quantity
of ideas, dashes his crotchets about, as it were, at random: and
among a number of grotesque effects, gives now and then a fine hit.
He resembles, in the latter respect, the ancient painter, who in a
fit of impatience at not being able to express foam at the mouth
of a hound, dashed his spunge against the animal's jaws, and
produced the very thing he despaired of.

When Hunt came to the same opera a year later, much was
forgiven. Recalling his earlier charge of plagiarizing Paesiello,
he now declared he "ought to have remembered that something
like this was an old Italian custom, at least in books. . . . Perhaps,
from passages which we have seen of Paesiello's *Barbiere*," Rossini's music is an improvement, as in the *Pace e Gioia* passage
which is "altogether finer in Rossini." Repeated hearings improved his opinion:

The more we hear this opera, the more highly we think of it. All
works of genius require, as it were, to be *read* with attention,—
painting and music as well as poetry. At the first hearing of a fine
opera, one misses nine out of twenty parts of it, from the mere hurry
of it's passage. It is like dashing in a post-chaise through a fine
landscape. We must hear it again and again; and then we get
acquainted with all those varieties of expression, those intentions,
and overflowing meanings, with which a man of genius abounds.
[25 April 1819]

These remarks suggest that Hunt's artistic hierarchies were being
further revised; at least some music now demanded as much attention as painting and even poetry![79] (By 1832, incidentally,

Hunt thought this the best of Rossini's operas, though he still preferred Paesiello's *Barber*.)[80]

Even if Rossini now revealed flashes of genius and melody, Hunt by no means abandoned some of his reservations about the composer: "We still think of Rossini as we did, that is to say, as to the *quality* of his music. He has a greater *quantity* of beautiful things than we supposed at first,—of melodies as well as accompaniments. But upon the whole, he strikes us as having less originality than animal spirit." Yet Hunt was ready to excuse these faults in the composer; he observed the adverse conditions under which Rossini was forced to compose, citing the evidence of "Count Stendhal."[81]

Earlier in 1819 Hunt attended the English première of a second Rossini opera, *L'Italiana in Algeri,* which he found "of a piece" with the *Barber*: "that is to say, there is more animal spirit than intellectual, and good compilation than novelty." But he preferred it to the *Barber* despite his fellow critics' views and an admitted falling-off in the last act:

The author seems to delight in expressing a precipitate and multitudinous mirth; and sometimes works up and ferments a passage, and pours in instrument upon instrument, till orchestra and singers all appear drunk with uproariousness, and ready to die on the spot. He carries this feeling, we think, to a pitch of genius, and even to something exclusive, and peculiar to himself. . . . He is like a wit fond of punning and intoxicated with social enjoyment. Old jokes and new, his neighbours, and his own, all run merrily through his hands. His good things exalt the occasion; and the occasion, in return, does as much for his bad.[82] [31 January 1819]

Hunt also spoke well of his serious passages, which showed a gift for melody. But the libretto left much to be desired.

Still another London première at the end of the season showed the growing popularity of Rossini. This was his *L'Inganno Felice* —an early Rossini, as Hunt remarks, that will not bear comparison with his *Barber,* though noteworthy in some ways and worth going to hear. Introducing a technical note, Hunt writes, "We were struck in particular with one or two of those wind-like risings of the instruments, in which the notes gather and pour in upon each other by quick and fervent degrees, till at last they burst into a triumphant change of the key" (1 August 1819). In his review of *L'Italiana* Hunt noted that the "*pizzicato* opening of the overture [is] very striking." This is about as close as Hunt ever comes to the use of the technical language of music.

Hunt was apparently too ill to attend the King's Theatre in 1820.[83] Only one opera was reviewed that year in the "Theatrical Examiner." The occasion was the London première of Rossini's *La Cenerentola,* and the reviewer, introduced by Hunt as "an old critical acquaintance of the reader's," was Henry Robertson. Disappointed with the plot of the opera, Robertson found the music charming: "It runs on in his usual pleasant strain with all sorts of quips, crancks, and quaintnesses, flippant divisions, and rapid utterance, but it breathes at the same time the air of Italy, seems tinged with its sunshine, and overflows with sparkling and buoyant hilarity" (16 January 1820). Apparently he felt the Italian school was again in need of support, for he continued, "That great genius [Mozart] is taken as the standard of perfection, and lesser men are measured by it. Now, there is certainly no reason why we should destroy our delight by these uncomfortable modes of criticism. . . . Let us enjoy what is before us, and Mozart and Rossini will either of them furnish a delightful meal, by no means the less to be enjoyed for the various taste of the caterers." Robertson had made plenty of comparisons himself without finding this mode of criticism uncomfortable. Was he afraid that the cult that was developing around Mozart was keeping other composers off the boards? If so, Rossini was hardly a sufferer, at least with the public, although many professionals remained obdurate against him.[84]

In 1821 Hunt reviewed still another Rossini première, *La Gazza Ladra.* Whereas he had thought Rossini occasionally thin in his accompaniments, he now is apprehensive about the growing complexity of Rossini's music.[85]

La Gazza Ladra is the story of the *Maid and the Magpye*. It is said to be the most admired of Rossini's operas in Italy. Hearing this

report, and that the opera was extremely choral, and having met
with his *Othello*,[86] which is still more so and a favourite, we began
to fear that the principle of instrumental music was at last
encroaching too much in Italy upon the genius for melody. We
were afraid that Rossini, accustomed as he is to write in a hurry,
under various other disadvantages, found original airs too great a
demand upon his spirit, and so took refuge in an imposing multitude
of voices. But *La Gazza Ladra* undeceived us,—delighted us. There
is indeed a great deal of the choral in it, nor is it easy for any one
who is not scientific in music to enter into the relishes of this at a
first or even second hearing; but we can see that it at least has a
meaning as it rolls and revels along. Such niceties as we are capable
of appreciating, we must get at when the storm of a first hearing
is over. But the airs and duetts, &c. we can enjoy at once; and
here are beautiful ones. [18 March 1821]

Hunt still shows concern about the effect of German music on
opera. He is alert to the fact that Rossini was bringing something of the northern symphonic complexity into a vocal form
acceptable to Italian opera-goers. Ever on guard against encroachments on lyricism, he notes that a multitude of voices,
serving as so many instruments, could effectively conceal a want
of melody, which to him was like concealing the poverty of
thought. Yet he appears less presumptive here than in his earlier
remarks. Experience had taught him not to make rash judgments
with respect to Rossini. And though he does not easily find meaning in the new music, he acknowledges a need to become better
acquainted with it—to apprehend those pleasures that lie beyond
an immediate appeal of an accessible melody. He maintained a
qualified admiration for Rossini in later years, Vincent Novello's
"loathing" for the composer to the contrary notwithstanding (*A
Mozart Pilgrimage*, p. 263).

This was Hunt's only opera criticism in 1821 and his last at
the King's Theatre before leaving for Italy. No doubt the deterioration of his health was the primary reason for this lessening
of his activity. The inordinate length of the opera-plus-ballet
(especially on the Tuesday nights that Hunt usually attended)
was a deterrent. The critic did not remain for the whole of *La*

Gazza Ladra, as he tells his readers, "not being quite stout enough for the critical hours of twelve and one." Hunt found a welcome relief from the demands on his energies when he sailed, three months later, for his beloved Italy, happily unaware of the disasters he would encounter there.

Singers

As in his criticism of performers on the English musical stage, Hunt is ever alert to mannerisms that betray a lapse in musico-dramatic taste. He never indulges in the kind of mass denunciation that delighted Barnes, and his evaluations are less capricious than Hazlitt's. There are few singers at the King's Theatre that Hunt does not occasionally reprimand, and few that he will not sometimes praise. His critiques are usually made with the singer's role in mind, and sometimes they are relevant to the entire drama, as we have seen. For comparative purposes, however, his remarks on the singers may best be evaluated by considering them together at this point.

Looking back on this period in 1850, Hunt observed that the male singers were not very remarkable.[87] As for tenors, he was at the King's Theatre too late to review Braham there, though he heard him in the oratorios, where his opinion differs little from his verdict on Braham's English-opera performances. In his few *Examiner* references to Tramezzani, Hunt found the tenor too elegant.[88] Only Manuel García* received much notice from the critic, who regarded him as a good actor, especially in the broader roles. But in his first critique of him, Hunt felt that García's musical power was apt to slip over the line of good taste and run into "flowery extravagance" (12 April 1818). On second hearing, Hunt found him "running about in vain with his gratuitous notes, like a dog that scampers about ten miles to his master's one; and in this respect indeed, it must be allowed that we heard Cimarosa [*Il Matrimonio Segreto*] to disadvantage; for the progress of the melody was rendered scarcely perceivable through the dust of Signor García's gambols" (7 June 1818). Finally, Hunt had to spell out his objections: reviewing *L'Italiana in*

Algeri, he pointed to the beautiful melody "Languir per una bella," but

Signor García, with his superbundant flourishes, would not let it take place. . . . We wish some friend of his would . . . [show him] the absurdity of this extravagance, which, carried to such a pitch, is really like nothing better than so much stammering set to music;— La-a-a-a-a-a-a-a-a-an—gui-i-i-i-i-i-i-i-ir—per u-u-u-u-u-u-u-u-una be-e-e-e-e-e-e-ella. It is as ridiculous as if a Gentleman, in asking a Lady how she did, were to say *How*—and then take a scamper round about the pavement,—*do,* and then another scamper—*you* (scamper again);—and so on, to the astonishment of the gathering spectators. [31 January 1819]

Perhaps some friend translated the criticism for García; when Hunt heard the singer as Tamino in *The Magic Flute* some months later, he noted that García, "since he has clipped his exuberance, continues to be equally full of power, judgment, and taste" (30 May 1819).

The basses and baritones fared somewhat better. At first Hunt, like Hazlitt, did not care for Naldi: "We either do not understand the style of humourous Italian acting, or in his hands it is somewhat too manual and pantomimical for us" (23 March 1817). But he, too, may have been corrigible, for the following season Hunt noted that "Naldi, whom it is a pleasure to hear pronounce Italian, appears to have got rid, at least in this character [probably as Count Almaviva], of the extremes to which we ventured to object last year. . . . [He] does not fling himself so much about the stage" (25 January 1818).

Hunt found Carlo Angrisani* a fine, versatile actor with a noble bass voice. As a substitute for Naldi in *Figaro,* "he attends in a lively manner to the business of the scene; sings the basser parts in an admirable manner with that deep metallic voice of his, which sometimes seems to issue from a cauldron; and if his reported age [about fifty-nine] be true, is altogether a wonderful performer, both in voice, spirit, and looks." Angrisani lacked Naldi's humor and self-possession, and his "upper notes sometimes fail him; so much so, that he occasionally avoids them out of a consciousness to that effect. His voice is decidedly and exclusively a bass,—the noblest we ever heard" (21 March 1819). His Sarastro was, of course, excellent.

The best of the group, and a great favorite, was Ambrogetti. His acting was better than his singing, but Hunt occasionally found too much coarseness in his acting style.[89] Of his performance as the Governor in *La Molinara* Hunt wrote, "Signor Ambrogetti is a clever singer with a good voice; but his humour is a great deal more unaccountable to us than Naldi's; and so the audience seemed to think it, till he put himself into such uncouth postures, and made signs of such mysterious insinuation, that they felt themselves obliged either to laugh or to hiss, and like well-bred spectators preferred the former" (23 March 1817).

Ambrogetti was much improved in the role of Don Giovanni. He also excelled as Figaro, a character that "enables him to expatiate, like *Don Giovanni,* instead of his being tempted to deviate into those unaccountable gestures and elaborate pointings to the moon, which he baffled us with in *La Molinara*" (25 January 1818). No doubt his size made him look ridiculous in certain roles. As Papageno in the *Flute* he was disappointing; Hunt quipped, "He looks too beef-eating for a bird-catcher" (30 May 1819). And as Count Robinson in *Il Matrimonio Segreto* he "looked more like an excessive footman than any thing else, an effervescent suit of clothes, a sort of wardrobe personified, a full-dressed surfeit, an absolute plethora of haberdashery" (7 June 1818). But in a bravura piece like Mayr's *Fanatico per la Musica,* where he had room to expatiate in the farcical commedia dell'arte style, he could be enormously appealing:

Never in our lives did we see a performer enter his character with such hearty and indefatigable zeal. . . . The orchestra is of course ready made for him by the one in the theatre; and up and down this he ranges, like a cat watching fish in a river. . . . Now he gives his sign to the bassoons, now to the violins, now to the flutes; and of every separate instrument he evinces the most intense and overwhelming conception, as if he were ready to groan off in transport with the bassoons; or smooth, skip, and tremble with the violins; or flutter, and trill, and be like a bird with the flutes. . . .

Were not the exhibitor so stout, we should almost have expected him
really to drop down, like the sick organist whom Dr. Burney got to
play for him, on one of those awful Dutch instruments, which seem
to have required a regular training on the part of the assailant;—a
course of beef, we suppose, for the sharps, and mutton for a psalm
in D. minor.[90] [1 August 1819]

A rather different case for diet was presented by Hunt in reviewing a "Signor" Albert, who sang Figaro at the opening of
the 1819 season:

This gentleman, we presume, by his name as well as his appearance,
is a German; and it may tend to soften the objections we are compelled
to make against him, to observe, that the Germans, however great as
a musical people, certainly do not excel in the vocal part of music.
. . . Figaro, as well as being lively and rattling, has a great substratum
in him, of cunning and plotting. . . . Now Signor Albert is as
unlike all this as a German can be. He is short, thick, and
somewhat corpulent; with a face as innocent of intrigue as a
dumpling. . . . [In short] for a rogue of a Spanish servant, quick,
sly, sidelong-eyed, and of a race which takes a long time to get the
look of hunger out of it, he will certainly bear no comparison with
any singer that has lately appeared in this character. [26 December
1819]

Hunt did not find corpulence in other singers a handicap, however. Ambrogetti was far from bird-like, yet he had made one of
the best of Figaros. What he had that Albert had not was vivacity—"animal spirits"; and it was this quality, rather than any
traces of hunger, that distinguished the performers. Albert was
not well received by the English public, whose taste had been
conditioned by a century of Italian singers.[91] Robertson and
Hunt apparently shared this taste. In any event Hunt's anti-
German bias is again evident, for there is an element of seriousness in his suggestions that beef and mutton provide energy while
sauerkraut and dumplings generate plethora![92]

The women singers during this period were neither so sensational as Catalani nor so great as their immediate successors
would prove to be. Yet at least three were fine singing-actresses—

the sopranos Fodor and Bellochi* and the contralto Vestris*, who
returned to the King's Theatre for the last time in 1821. (Vestris
filled a department neglected at the opera since the departure of
Grassini in 1806 and gained popularity for the contralto voice—
long overshadowed by the sopranos.)

Violante Camporese,* who made her stage debut at the King's
Theatre in 1817, had a fine voice but was no actress. Though she
made a good Sesto in *Tito*—"considering the awkwardness of a
female's acting a male"—Hunt was not satisfied with her acting
(27 July 1817). As Susanna she was "rather a correct and powerful than delightful singer" (25 January 1818).[93]

At this performance Hunt took note of Pasta, finding more
pleasure in the duet that she sang with the tenor Begrez* ("Ah!
Perdona") than anything else in the opera. But "she threw away
all her love upon the spectators, and suffered her hand to be
pressed to no purpose by her innamorato, who seemed in vain to
try and recall her wandering affections." Nor did Hunt find her
a very effective Cherubino in *Figaro* (25 January 1818).[94]

Frances Corri-Paltoni,* who filled the place left by Camporese's departure, made her debut at the *Figaro* performance;
but Hunt was reluctant to criticize her acting on account of her
nervousness. There was more need for acting in an opera like
Figaro than "in most," Hunt declared. "The better performers
they are at any time, the better effect it gives to their singing."
He thought her voice showed promise, as a worthy pupil of Catalani, but noted a deficiency "in the intellectual part of her art,—
in propriety of expression. She throws her lights and shades too
indiscriminately" (25 January 1818). A year later she had been
given a fair trial: though Hunt admitted that she produced some
nice coloratura flourishes as Queen of the Night in *The Magic
Flute*, "We cannot say we are ever moved by this inexorably
frigid performer" (30 May 1819).

By Fodor, however, Hunt was always moved—sometimes to
anger, usually to delight.[95] He said of her in *La Molinara*:

Madame Fodor wants the lighter figure and air of Catalani in
such characters as *Rachelina*; but she performs the part on the whole

with sufficient vivacity, and sings with great mellowness and spirit. After the proofs she had given us however of her feelings and understanding in *Figaro,* we were not a little surprised to hear her, without giving us the *subject* first, overwhelm the . . . air, *Nel cor,* in such a load of variation as absolutely to do away all features of it. It was no longer a pretty little complaint, but a piece of flowery giddiness. [23 March 1817]

She overloaded Mozart with ornament, too, in *Tito*; nor was her costume allowed to pass without comment: "Madame Fodor dresses herself very ill in this part [Vitellia], making the stoutness of her person too conspicuous, and pulling her hair close and tight at the back of her head like a drummer-boy's without it's queue, till she seems all face. This is very inelegant. If our excellent singer studies Roman costume, . . . she may find that it is possible to know . . . a little better than to select the worst kind of head-dress" (27 July 1817). The trend toward historical accuracy in the theatre and the current fashion for Classical simplicity in dress and decor were factors singers needed to be aware of (prima donnas still dressed about as they wished—a department the stage manager did not yet dare tamper with).

But if Hunt was "desperately rude"[96] to the singer on that occasion, it was because Fodor, in defiance of Ayrton, had taken it upon herself to transfer an aria from the last act to act two.[97] The *Chronicle,* which had challenged her authority, published her rebuttal, in which she justified the change on grounds of dramatic logic. Hunt printed both sides of the controversy, the details of which need not detain us; but whereas the *Chronicle* based its opposition on the authority of Metastasio, da Ponte, and Mozart himself, Hunt attacked the singer's argument on her own grounds, stating that the original position of the aria most nearly reveals the character of Vitellia.[98]

Less than a week later, however, Hunt saw a quite different Fodor in *Don Giovanni*: "Madame Fodor in *Zerlina* retrieves all the reputation she lost in *La Clemenza di Tito,* singing with the truest taste and simplicity. . . . She sang all charmingly, particularly *Giovinette che fate all' amore,* with a face full of glee, and *Batti, batti, o bel Masetto,* with quite a reverse aspect and in a

most submissive and patient tone of appeal" (3 August 1817).
Hunt praised her "animal spirits" as Susanna the following sea-
son (25 January 1818) and took note of the absence of her talent
when her place was taken in 1819 by Mme. Bellochi (Teresa
Belloc). Of the latter's performance as Zerlina in *Don Giovanni*
Hunt wrote:

Zerlina is a creature of impulse, to an excess. Her faculties are
borne away by the sudden addresses of the splendid *Don Giovanni*;
and she has to intreat her husband's pardon in a song beginning
with exquisite pathos and simplicity—*Batti, batti, bel Masetto.* Now
in these matters we do not think Madame Bellochi so much at home
as in sheer vivacity. There she revels and enjoys herself at will. . . .
But when she is grave, she is undone; and when she would be
pathetic,—she tumbles to pieces. There is something strangely sour
in her gravity; an apalling [*sic*] intensity of frown,—a kind of
thickset sulky maliciousness. . . . In *Zerlina,* we have no hesitation
in giving the palm, every way, to Madame Fodor. How charming
were her cordial tones, that used to come forth with all the strength
imaginable, and yet as if her heart, as the phrase is, was in her
mouth! It was the triumph of the most triumphant thing in the
world,—a woman's voice. [4 April 1819]

Hunt had noted Bellochi's mannerisms at her debut earlier
that season in *L'Italiana in Algeri.*[99] Yet she was a capable
singer and gave promise as an actress: "She seems, in her favourite
passages, to nod and look her own relish of them at the audience,
and in a manner to become one of themselves. . . . Under an
appearance of thinking of herself, it shews that she thinks of her
art still more" (31 January 1819).

Bellochi was admirable in *La Modista Raggiratrice* (21 February 1819), but her best role seems to have been that of Susanna
in *Figaro*:

In her *Susanna,* it is true, we miss something of a certain cordial
tone of voice which used to breathe forth in Madame Fodor. . . .
Still however, the "linked sweetness" of Madame Bellochi's notes,
all beautifully strung together, yet all separate, . . . render her an
excellent representative of this brilliant queen of ladies' maids,
"Adroite et rieuse." A brother-critic in the *Morning Chronicle*

thinks that she overdoes the part, is too boisterous,—in short, not
well-bred enough for the original as drawn in the comedy of
Beaumarchais. But we doubt whether he does not reason too much
from English premises on this occasion. Beaumarchais undoubtedly
says . . . that with all her adroit and tricksome nature she is not
to have "the gaiety bordering on effrontery too common to the
ladies' maids of these degenerate times;" but after the cold tea
of the ordinary English character, the winy vivacity of a French
soubrette, may appear somewhat extravagant, even in it's most
reasonable state of fermentation. . . . [Our brother-critic] protests
against "the rude slap of the face given to *Figaro,* before many
persons, when she suspects his fidelity." Yet this is expressly
enjoined by the French author: *"Suzanne lui donne un soufflet;"*—a
plain, unsophisticated box on the ear.[100] [21 March 1819]

Here is another instance in which Hunt remarks on the unsuitableness of "well-bred" performers in certain operatic roles—
English or Continental. With respect to situations that did not
involve a compromising attitude toward women, Hunt shows
that he is more liberal than his "brother-critics." No cosmopolitan, he nevertheless condemns insular smugness and reasserts his
interest in national traits. His critical relativism is alert to the
subtle changes wrought on a temporal art when transplanted in
another culture. And again he shows critical astuteness in his
evaluation of the singer in terms of the concept of the role created
by Mozart.

Finally, in his last review, Hunt had a chance to praise Vestris
in Italian opera. (He had not reviewed her 1815–1816 performances, though references in his English-opera criticism indicate
that he had seen her then.) "We rejoice," Hunt wrote in his
review of *La Gazza Ladra,* "to see Madame Vestris on her own
ground. She suits it as a rose does her native tree, or a bird the
company of birds. She has the part of a village-youth in this
opera, and looks and sings it delightfully. It is worth while going
to the opera, to hear the sweetness with which she utters the
single word *tenera* in the air ['Di piacer']" (18 March 1821). As
we have observed, this singer, who had already shown the promise
of a remarkable career on the English stage, pleased Hunt even

more in Italian opera. But this was to be her final season at the King's Theatre.[101]

In his reviews of the King's Theatre, Hunt reveals superb skill in criticizing the performers, where they were more rewarding vocally if not histrionically than those on the English musical stage. Nothing seems to have escaped his attention. Stage appearance, dress, decorum, personality—to say nothing of the singing and acting—all were brought to life in his criticisms. The spontaneity and vitality of an occasion leap from the page.

But Hunt's achievement went far beyond generating facsimile vignettes of his experiences at the opera house. For, as in his English-opera criticism, he was primarily concerned with dramatic characterization. He explored the relation between personality and performance and between performance and role. Sometimes he even explored the concept of the role itself in attempting accurately to evaluate the artistry of a performer. He persistently decried mannerisms in singing or acting that distorted or destroyed musico-dramatic values. (His strictures may have been effective, too, in some cases, though he no longer made such claims for the *Examiner*.) The mark of coldness in a performer, however correct a technician, was unforgivable; in a singer who projected warmth and vivacity many shortcomings could be overlooked. Simplicity and sentiment Hunt praised especially; a singer who could combine these qualities, and at the same time give to the words their proper dramatic value, received his highest acclaim. This required artistic intelligence—sensitivity to the role and the dramatic situation as well as to the music. For these qualities alone make possible the singer's expression. And expression was, for Hunt, the key to opera—the heart of the drama in the music, and the meaning in the drama. Only performers who were also artists could give it voice.

Avoiding the dreary accounts of opera plots that were typical in the concurrent reviews of such sober journals as the *British Stage* and the *Quarterly Musical Review*, Hunt nevertheless gave particular attention to the libretto and its effect on the composer, the performers, and the audience. He emphasized the need of

good verses for good music, and he pointed up the lapses in translations of librettos and adaptations of songs. As a veteran drama
critic, he analyzed the function of the roles and the dramatic
situations in the operas, yet he willingly accepted nonrealistic
conventions of the genre.[102]

Although his viewpoint was admittedly literary, he was able to
shed a great many of the traditional English attitudes on opera—
far more than most of his contemporaries—in his Italian-opera
criticism. There he never seriously questioned the importance of
the music. He demonstrated the dramatic power and unity to be
found in the music of Mozart, perceptively characterizing those
elements in the songs and arias. And he effectively communicated his own abundant pleasure in the music at the King's
Theatre. His tastes were conditioned by the melodic resources
and simple harmonies of the Italian school, and he was apprehensive of the symphonic infusion from Germany, partly on
extramusical grounds. Yet his tastes appear to be ahead of his
English contemporaries. He rejected the cold stylism of Metastasian opera; he welcomed repeated hearings of the newer
music; and he grew in appreciation of the richer harmonies.
Moreover, as a Romantic, Hunt strongly supported the independence of the serious artist from the whimsical dictates of
patron and manager, public and press.

He brought to his assessment of composers the same sureness
of taste that marked his criticism of poetry. His preliminary
judgments (in both fields) were sometimes mistaken, but in subsequent reappraisals his critical power displayed a remarkable
capacity to recover its equilibrium and to dispel its own delusions. His praise of Paesiello and Cimarosa seems just, though
changes in taste have unfortunately all but eliminated these
composers from modern repertories. His appraisals of Mozart
and Rossini are outstanding. Despite some stormy first hearings
of Rossini, he quickly put his finger on both the strength and
the weakness of that composer. Though he found that the best
in Mozart exactly suited his taste, he never idolized him. His sensitive and penetrating discussions surely advanced the under-

standing of that composer in England and still stand up well against the vagaries of time.

Finally, as an editor as well as a writer, Hunt brought to his readers a new awareness of an art that had traditionally been regarded as an aristocratic prerogative. For under his editorship the *Examiner,* though known in its day as in ours primarily as a political, literary, and theatrical organ, carried reviews of Italian opera which, for extent of coverage, seriousness of approach, and skill in execution, appear to stand well in advance of the musical journalism in England during the early nineteenth century.

Reprise

"Tout son être semblait vibrer
au contact du génie."—Landré

LEIGH HUNT brought special aptitudes and experience to his *Examiner* opera criticism. Endowed with an ear for music as well as language, he found encouragement at home for his musical and literary interests. Through early friendships he greatly expanded his musical experiences, bringing an engaging manner and a fine singing voice to these relationships. Gifted with an eye that drank in every dramatic nuance at the theatre, he soon became an apprentice critic and a budding journalist. From his brother John he acquired his first taste of the power of independent criticism, John providing the stability of temperament that was essential to the success of the *Examiner*.

As a weekly, the *Examiner* reflected the radical spectrum of the periodical press of 1808, challenging the quasi-official organs of reactionary Tories and desiccated Whigs alike. Leigh Hunt's animadversions in the "Political Examiners" drew the journal into disastrous conflicts with the Establishment. But the paper's critical independence was more accurately determined by its insistence on considering the arts—even Italian opera—as subjects of legitimate interest to its readers, worthy of serious and sustained criticism. For the other radical weeklies quite ignored the arts, while the dailies or monthlies paid them scant heed.

Not that opera in early-nineteenth-century England could often provide a very rewarding experience. As an integral part of the British stage, what passed for "English opera" inevitably suffered from the decline that had plagued the drama since the days of Goldsmith and Sheridan. Changes in the size and character of the playgoing audience and a proliferation of dramatic genres succeeded in creating an uncertainty of direction. Leading per-

227

formers gained complete ascendancy over their stage "vehicles."
Handicapped by rising costs and by violent public resistance to
increased prices, managers economized by resorting to cheap
musical adaptations, if not outright vaudeville extravaganzas, for
a theatrical appeal popular enough to sustain their precarious
enterprises.

Italian opera, supported by the aristocracy, was less vulnerable.
Nevertheless, during the *Examiner* years the King's Theatre suffered financial and artistic losses due to prolonged proprietary
squabbles and the demands of Catalani. Thanks to William Ayrton and others, certain seasons testified to the stirring of a new
spirit; London could finally hear Mozart's operas, and Rossini
was quickly discovered. But the artistic successes could not be
sustained, and the King's Theatre continued to depend on the
capricious taste of its boxholders.

Hunt recognized that both aristocratic and middle-class values
exhibited corrupting influences on the arts. But he was thoroughly committed to the idea that the prevailing cultural lethargy could be redeemed only by appealing to the middle classes.
In an independent press, Hunt thought, lay the power for awak-
ening at least the "better part" of that class to a need for reform
in taste. "Taste," for Hunt, represented no mere appreciation of
the arts; it involved political and moral considerations as well.
In the *Examiner* he found a perfect resource for the broad exercise of his "independent criticism." Largely because of the presumed influence of the theatre on public taste, theatrical criticism
presented a most important medium for Hunt's critical talents.
Through his criticism of the English musical stage and Italian
opera, he challenged his middle-class readers to a vision of life
more enriching than commercial aggrandizement or artistic titil-
lation.

This challenge was carried forward in varying degrees by other
critics in the *Examiner*. As Hunt accurately observed, Robertson
wrote the "first criticism" at that time "worthy the attention of
sound readers." For five artistically lean seasons at the King's
Theatre he produced generally balanced appraisals of performers and operas. He was apparently the first English journalist to

bring sound and consistent judgment to the criticism of Mozart's operas. He shared with Hunt a remarkable freedom from middle-class prejudices against Italian opera, and he was able to recognize, well before Hunt did, the necessity for musical supremacy in opera if it was to achieve its true character and power as an art form. In other respects his views correspond closely with Hunt's, though his criticism is less penetrating. While it avoids the exceeding triteness displayed by critics in other periodicals, Robertson's prose suffers considerably by comparison with his more literary successors in the *Examiner*. Yet his criticism deserves a significant place in the history of English musical journalism.

Thomas Barnes brought wit and pungency to his *Examiner* opera criticism, together with a strong desire to purge the King's Theatre of its inanities. He was not insensible to the charms of English songs, and he seems to have had no strong objections to Italian opera per se. But he hardly ever reviewed actual performances, and he fulminated at length and without much logic about conditions at the King's Theatre. He assisted the Hunts in a time of need, but he did little to advance the criticism of opera.

William Hazlitt shared some of Barnes's characteristics, especially in Italian-opera criticism, where he often indulged in generalities instead of reviewing performances. But on the whole he wrote with greater coherence and far greater brilliance. His antipathies included the "form" of Italian opera as well as the habitués of the King's Theatre. But when he was not on the defensive, he could communicate a palpable enjoyment of Italian-opera performances. As an opera critic he was neither "dutiful" nor "dull":[1] he was far less prompt than either Robertson or Hunt in reporting on the King's Theatre, but when he wrote on opera, whether to review performances or to theorize about them, he was lively indeed.

In their English-opera criticism both Hazlitt and Hunt lashed out at the cultural depravations of theatre managers, the triteness of musical vehicles, the vulgarity of singers. Both men saw very similar merits and deficiencies in the performers, though Hunt's criticism usually avoided the stinging barbs that Hazlitt enjoyed. Hazlitt consistently upheld the ballad style of singing. (Barnes could admire only the "scientific.") Hunt, who leaned toward the "simple" style, was more flexible in his views, recognizing that style must be dictated by the nature of the song and the related dramatic situation. In his "crotchety" moods, Hazlitt wanted his music in meadows rather than in the theatres; otherwise, he insisted on fine vocalists for leading roles in English opera. Hunt saw dramatic rather than purely vocal ability as the most desirable quality in performers. With his largely amoral attitude toward women, Hazlitt saw no vulgarity in breeches parts, in Don Giovanni's lustiness, or in Gay's *The Beggar's Opera*. At first blush Hunt's sensibilities were scandalized by all three.

In their Italian-opera criticism they often agreed on details about the performers; otherwise there is little basis for comparison, for Hazlitt did not say much about the operas themselves. Although Hazlitt tended to regard Mozart as a "pretty" composer, he found him capable of "sublimity" on at least one occasion. For Hunt, who saw more of his dramatic power, Mozart usually expressed gaiety, though his greatest passages were touched with a deep solemnity.

In comparing the dramatic criticism of Hazlitt and Hunt, some critics have praised the power and strength of the former, which they have often associated with his superiority in "theory"—a quality they find conspicuous for its absence in the latter.[2] Now it is true that Hunt avoided theorizing; he was, in fact, deliberately set against an abstract mode of criticism. But Hazlitt also rejected critical abstractions, though he developed theories for rejecting them. (Indeed, his theories accurately describe Hunt's practice!) Both men depended strongly on sense-oriented responses, but were interested in the intellectual appeal of ideas stemming from those responses rather than in any superficial impressionism.[3]

Both men occasionally indulged in generalizations, however, though they were least reliable in such passages. Hazlitt of course went further than Hunt in introducing theoretical observations in his criticism: a certain restlessness often propelled him toward formulations more immediately satisfying to the intellect —a process that generated a greater vigor and argumentative edge in his prose. But he often attained "gusto" and coherence at the expense of remoteness from the actuality of the performance. In keeping his critical senses more closely attuned to the evening's proceedings, Hunt proved not merely a "better recorder" than Hazlitt but a more effective dramatic critic as well. To be sure, there is a certain inconclusiveness—an elusive and tenuous insubstantiality—that characterizes Hunt's criticism and gives his prose a *"pâle et diffus"* quality, as Landré observes, in contrast with Hazlitt's. But Hunt provides greater relevancy to the occasion, more penetrating insights into the works and performances, and sounder, more accurate judgments and evaluations.

The nature of Hunt's criticism makes final assessments difficult. The very profusion of his ideas, interests, and responses offers a wealth of evidence for adducing conflicting conclusions about the man and his work. His distaste for systems and theories, his occasional ambivalence, and his hesitation in rendering final opinions present obstacles to a balanced appraisal. Perhaps this is why, in recounting his contributions, "something of the essence of Hunt seems to get left out."[4] Nevertheless, several general tendencies or forces—traditional and personal—are observable in that criticism. They are not mutually exclusive. They have both positive and negative effects on its ultimate value. But they account for many of its features and suggest a certain dimension by which its achievements can be estimated.

Hunt's Romanticism is a strong force in most of his criticism. In a broad sense it lies behind his commitment to a "politics of sentiment," his challenge to the mediocrity of public taste, and his literary "fusion" into all subjects—a kind of prose synesthesia.

Romantic impulses are evident in Hunt's emphasis on nationalism: in his admiration for "folk" airs; in the "cold English" responses toward opera; in the "obscurity and dullness" of German art; in the dry pertness of the French; and in the "extravagance" and "fire" of the Italians. Typical, too, was Hunt's attraction to the Italian language and poetry. Mozart, a German in speech only, was in Hunt's view preserved from the dangers of "German" art by virtue of an early baptism in Italian sunshine. Hunt's Romantic nationalism also finds expression in the musical antithesis he stresses between "German" harmony and "Italian" melody.

With its revolt against eighteenth-century values, Romanticism placed a greater emphasis on new, individual modes of creativity. Hence Hunt's frequent appeals for originality and his denunciations of "borrowings" by composers and playwrights. Sometimes his complaints stem from ignorance of the tradition of the libretto as an adaptation—an error he cheerfully admitted with respect to Rossini's *Barbiere*. But the producers of English opera, who went to inordinate lengths in their operatic spoliations, deserved the rebukes administered by Hunt and other *Examiner* critics.

Romantic forces are apparent in Hunt's attacks on literalism, formalism, the "mechanical"—qualities he associates with Neoclassic coldness and failure of the imagination. For Hunt these characteristics are observable in both eighteenth-century and contemporary works; they account for most of the mannerisms in opera performers. To the contrary Romantic qualities—imagination, spontaneity, vivacity, warmth, and sincerity—he gives abundant praise.

The quality of sincerity—a seminal one in Hunt's Romanticism[5]—is closely related to his emphasis on artistic independence. He believed that valid art could be created, or re-created, only by artists who had complete faith in art and in their own artistic powers. He regarded subservience to the interests of politics, patronage, or commerce as inimical to genuine creativity; and he praised the artistic integrity of those who cast off the shackles of sycophancy.

Literary influences are also manifest in Hunt's opera criticism. He was passionately fond of both music and literature. But he emphasized the superiority of poetry over music, which he felt held less intellectual appeal. The persistence of this view during the *Examiner* years, despite the occasional modifications of his hierarchy, reveals the tenacity of his literary bias, which he inherited from Addison and other eighteenth-century writers.

(From Dr. Burney, who had avant-garde leanings, he also derived some peculiarly contradictory attitudes towards Purcell and early English music.)

The literary tradition that upheld the "realism" of the spoken drama is especially evident in Hunt's belief that English operas should be banished from the "legitimate" theatres. Their influence was considered pernicious to serious drama, already severely corrupted by farce and melodrama, with which so much contemporary English opera was identified. That tradition is also evident in his violent rejection of Italian operatic decorum on the English stage and in his corrosive indictment of "meaningless" plots and "absurd" dialogue in English-opera vehicles. (These views are of course more typical of his earlier criticism.)

Hunt's special interest in songs illustrates a personal literary influence as well. He singled out the songs of Dryden, Ramsay, Gay, and Burns for their excellence. He condemned the "vile" poetry in most contemporary operas. He paid particular attention to the relationship between words and music in songs and arias. His praise for music was in direct proportion to its identification with, and expression of, the sentiment of the verse. And he criticized English translations of Italian arias that did violence to musical meaning. But until he had to provide translations that were singable for "Musical Evenings," it is not clear that he fully confronted the problems of reconciling—even subordinating—the literary quality of songs to the vocal demands of music. Perhaps the fact that he had written verses that were found to be eminently suitable for musical settings strengthened his early conviction that songwriters for the stage were under a greater service to literature than to music.

In a different sense the literary tradition is implicit in Hunt's style. It is of course not a "literary" style, being in the journalistic vein of Addison and Goldsmith, but closer to the modern "plain" idiom. It was marvelously fluent and controlled. In describing theatrical effects, for example, his prose found just the right balance between spontaneity and precision, the perfect tone and metaphor, turning sounds into pictures and bringing the *mise en scène* to life. But the range of his effects is considerable.

On the whole his style suggests a certain "distance" and objectivity, even when his passions are aroused. The "cold mirror" of his prose may have less immediate attractions for some readers than the "gusto" of Hazlitt or "warmth" of Lamb, but it is a quality that reflects Hunt's approach to the critical function itself.[6] He does not escape the mawkish passages that crop up occasionally in all the reviewers for the *Examiner*. But Hunt's attention to style brings more "finish" to his opera criticism than that of any other journalist of his time.

Personal as well as traditional forces are explicit in his views about women and about the Church. By no means unique to Hunt, and not without some historical justification, his protectionistic attitude towards women led to certain distortions in his judgments on *The Beggar's Opera, Don Giovanni,* and other works, and to questionable observations on some performers. It is difficult to say whether Burney's influence or his own distaste for organized Christianity was more responsible for his views concerning the supposed harmful effect of the Church on early English composers. Certainly he was correct, however, in deploring the religiosity that made the Lenten oratorios a dull and gloomy business.

The power of the living theatre probably represents the strongest personal force in Hunt's opera reviews. He was drawn to theatrical criticism initially by a curiosity about the "strange superiority of the mimetic" attributes of the stage; the particular appeal of the performers and their art continued to play a vital role in his opera criticism. But his penetrating analyses went far beyond the superficial accomplishments or deficiencies of the singers. His energies were absorbed by *revealed* drama—to such an extent at times, it would seem, that he could not "tell the dancer from the dance." He strove to capture the performance in the very process of its dramatic realization. This aspect of his criticism tended to supplant discussion of opera vehicles themselves. For he focused on the dramatic substance itself—the episodes and situations that breathed life into the theatrical experience. In this respect his criticism often goes to the heart of opera, revealing that special quality of the art form wherein vocal nuances blend with melodic expressiveness, capturing and projecting the essence of dramatic characterization.

Two complementary forces at work in Hunt's character—his self-assurance and his self-doubt—find expression in his opera criticism. The former quality underlies the confidence and assertiveness, curiosity and challenge, that distinguish his reviews. Under stress, however, Hunt becomes overconfident, tending to make provocative attacks, rash assumptions, mistaken generalizations. The quality of self-doubt is evident in his questioning attitude, his need to reexamine, his openness of mind and freedom from dogmatism. At times, a distrust of his own opinions leads to a certain hesitance, ambivalence, and inconclusiveness in his reviews.

The shifts noted in Hunt's attitudes on opera owe much to an interplay between these forces, the one quality serving as a corrective to the other. Thus he gained the capacity to seek new experiences and to learn from them. For the overall trend of these shifts is toward a greater catholicity of taste and toward sounder, more realistic judgments. During the *Examiner* years, for example, he learned to discount his optimism regarding attempts to improve the taste of playwrights and the public, and to stimulate improved criticism in the press. He relaxed his hold on feminine morality and gave belated appreciation to Gay and Bickerstaffe. He grew more lenient toward English operas as a threat to the "legitimate" stage and even welcomed some of their experimental approaches. He became more understanding of Italian-opera styles, recognized the value of Continental influences on English opera, and made a strong appeal for the restoration of recitative. He accommodated himself to a thickening of harmonic textures in the music of Italian operas, corrected his mistaken impressions of Rossini, and reached a deeper understanding of Mozart. From Mozart, too, he acquired a new respect for composers and saw that music could achieve heights he had thought reserved only to poetry.

On the other hand, many of Hunt's initial views needed no further qualification; they reflect the sureness of his own good taste. His appraisals of performers, operas, librettists, and composers, often remarkably consistent, generally agree with the more responsible opinion of his time and with the consensus of modern historians. They show a perceptiveness unparalleled, so far as we can ascertain, in his contemporaries. Responsive to the vocal beauty and technical command of the singers, he nevertheless protested their tendency to subordinate dramatic values in opera to "vocal millinery." In English and especially in Italian opera he explored the relationship between melodic resources and dramatic power. Dismayed by the English operas flooding the stage, he did not merely dismiss them as the inconsiderable trifles they were, but went to some pains to expose their musical and dramatic pretensions. He recognized the merit of Shield and the potential of Bishop. He effectively communicated the lyrical delights in earlier works, badly mangled though they were by various adaptors. Undisturbed by the presence of the "upper orders" at the King's Theatre, he gave its productions his full and sympathetic attention. Although he was cautious about the encroachments of harmony, his taste went well beyond an appreciation for music that was *"assez simple"* (Landré, II, 137). He accurately assessed the powers of melodic expression in Cimarosa and Paesiello. If they began to sound somewhat "thin" after hearing Mozart and Rossini, his newly acquired taste no doubt placed him in the avant-garde of his time. But the genius of Mozart touched him most deeply. Hunt relished his melodic resources, freshness, and spontaneity. Above all, he appreciated his musical power in capturing subtle dramatic characterizations. He found coarseness and lack of subtlety in Rossini, yet he relished his verve and vitality.

For the quality and quantity of Hunt's opera reviews, for the range and power of his musical ideas, for his expert judgments, vivid re-creations, and subtle probings into musico-dramatic character, Hunt stands foremost among the musical journalists of the early nineteenth century. Indeed there are passages that for their musical insight and power of expression might well be the envy of music critics of any period. An eminent musicologist of our own time, Percy Young, has declared that there are "few

more competent critics" in musical journalism.[7] Hunt himself
found England in need of a music critic, not considering himself
to be one, presumably because of his commitment to literature
and his lack of adequate musical training. But in his opera criticism he pursued what he considered the primary concerns of the
music critic: to "extend enjoyment," "to show the links of art
and nature . . . in as universal a spirit as possible," and to address
a general rather than a special audience.

For Hunt these aims applied to all valid criticism of art. They
were related to the ideals of "independent criticism" and the
"politics of sentiment" that motivated the founding and development of the *Examiner*. They were indispensable to a reformer
of public taste. Through his opera criticism Hunt challenged
that taste mainly by bringing to the operatic works of that period
(the darkest in England's musical history) an honest and coura-
geous responsiveness of mind and spirit. Through his passionate
devotion to artistic truth, his sympathetic readers undoubtedly
became more absorbed in the cultural life of the times and
shared his concern for its regeneration.

We have, of course, no evidence of Hunt's influence as an
opera critic during the *Examiner* years, though his importance
in journalism is clear enough. With respect to any improvement
in public taste, Hunt was less optimistic as time went on. But
even before launching the *Examiner,* he suggested a pervasively
subtle and tenuous basis for critical influence generally. Referring to the "perishable subject" of criticisms of the contemporary stage, Hunt wrote in the preface to *Critical Essays*:

Succeeding ages very often acquire an unconscious tone from the
most trifling exertions. Like the child who was awakened every
morning by his father's flute,[8] they arise in the calm possession of
their powers, unconscious of the favourable impulse that has been
given them.

Appendix I
The English Musical Stage

Reviewers, Reviews, and Performances

The reviewers cited are: LH—Leigh Hunt; TB—Thomas Barnes; WH—William Hazlitt; and CL—Charles Lamb.

Theatres cited are: DL—Drury Lane; CG—Covent Garden; KY—the King's Theatre; HY—the Haymarket; OLY—the Olympic; and LY—the Lyceum, later names for which are NEO—New English Opera House—and EOH—English Opera House.

Unless an earlier performance is cited, the first listing of a work indicates a review approximately at the time of its London première.

Usually the titles, "genres," and attributions ["N"] follow Nicoll: B—Burlesque; BO—Ballad Opera; C—Comedy; CO—Comic Opera; D—Drama; E—Extravaganza; F—Farce; M—Melodrama; O—Opera; OE—Operatic Extravaganza; OF—Operatic Farce; OR—Operatic Romance.

Aside from Nicoll, the more important sources for this appendix include *Grove's Dictionary, Annals,* Genest, Baker's *Biographica Dramatica,* Hogarth, Mount-Edgcumbe, Walker, and the D.N.B. (see the bibliography for complete citations).

Reviewer	Theatre	Date of Review	Work
LH	DL	31 Jan. 1808	*The Cabinet* (CO, 1802), T. Dibdin. Music by Reeve, Moorehead, Davy,* Corri, and Braham.
LH	CG	7 Feb. 1808	*The Woodman* (CO, 1791), Bate. Music by Shield.
LH	DL	14 Feb. 1808	*Kais; or, Love in the Desert* (O), Isaac Brandon. Music by Reeve; songs by Braham.
LH	DL	6 Mar. 1808	*In and Out of Tune* (OF), Cherry. Hunt says that it was plagiarized from Dennis Lawler; cf. *Biographia Dramatica*, II, 321. Music by Corri.

239

Reviewer	Theatre	Date of Review	Work
LH	CG	27 Mar. 1808	*Travellers in Switzerland* (CO, 1794), Bate. Music by Shield.
LH	CG	10 Apr. 1808	*Bonifacio and Brigetina; or, The Knight of the Hermitage; or, The Windmill Turrett; or, The Spectre of the North-East Gallery* (E), T. Dibdin. ["Songs"-N.]
LH	DL	8 May 1808	*The Jew of Mogadore* (CO), Cumberland. Music by Kelly.
LH	DL	25 Sept. 1808	*Love in a Village* (CO, 1762), Bickerstaffe. Hunt (by implication) and Nicoll give Charles Dibdin the Elder credit for the music. Other authorities ascribe the music to Arne and sixteen other composers. Dibdin, then aged seventeen, was probably only a later adaptor.
LH	CG/KT	2 Oct. 1808	*The Fortune Teller* (OF), author unknown. Music by Reeve.
LH	DL	13 Nov. 1808	*The Siege of St. Quintin; or, Spanish Heroism* (M), T. Hook, Music by J. Hook.
LH	CG/KT	13 Nov. 1808	*The Exile; or, The Desert(s) of Siberia* (O), Reynolds. Music by Mazzinghi and Bishop.
LH	LY	2 July 1809	*Up All Night; or, The Smuggler's Cave* (CO), Arnold. Music by King [no ref.-N.].
LH	LY	30 July 1809	*The Russian Impostor; or, The Siege of Smolensko* (O), Siddons, with alterations by Arnold. Music by Addison [no ref.-N.].
LH	LY	8 Sept. 1809	*Safe and Sound* (CO), T. Hook. Music by J. Hook.
LH	LY	18 Mar. 1810	*The Maniac; or, The Swiss Bandetti* (CO), Arnold. Music by Bishop.
LH	LY	17 June 1810	*Oh! This Love!; or, The Masqueraders* (CO), Kenney. Music by King.
LH	LY	15 July 1810	*Tricks upon Travellers* (CO), Burges. Music by Reeve and Horn.
LH	CG	10 Feb. 1811	*The Knight of Snowdoun* (M), Morton (based on Scott's *Lady of the Lake*). Music by Bishop.
LH	DL/LY	14 Apr. 1811	*The Siege of Belgrade* (CO, 1791), Cobb. The music was a pasticcio drawn from Arne, Shield, and Storace, among others (much was taken

Reviewer	Theatre	Date of Review	Work
			from Martín y Solar's *Une Cosa Rara*, 1786). Storace probably adapted the music; two years earlier he had used similar borrowings in the music for Cobb's *The Haunted Tower*.
LH	LY	15 Sept. 1811	*M. P.; or, The Blue Stocking* (CO), Moore. Nicoll credits Moore with the music; *Grove's* states that Horn provided both the overture and orchestration. The *New College Encyclopedia of Music* states that Moore was joined in the composition by Horn. Moore, a self-taught musician, composed the music for many of his songs.
LH	LY	10 May 1812	*The Devil's Bridge; or, The Piedmontese Alps* (OR), Arnold. Music by Horn and Braham.
LH	CG	13 Sept. 1812	*The Beggar's Opera* (BO, 1728), Gay. Overture composed and airs arranged by Pepusch.
LH	CG	20 Dec. 1812	*The Renegade* (D), Reynolds (based on Dryden's *Don Sebastian*, 1689). Music by Bishop.
TB	CG	17 Oct. 1813	*Artaxerxes* (O, 1762), Arne. Lib. based on Metastasio's *Artaserse*.
LH	—	12 Feb. 1815	"Sketches of Singers"
WH	DL	2 Apr. 1815	*The Unknown Guest* (M), Arnold. Songs by Kelley and Braham [no ref.-N.].
WH	CG	18 June 1815	*The Beggar's Opera*
WH	DL	5 Nov. 1815	*The Beggar's Opera*
WH	NEO	21 July 1816	*Artaxerxes*
WH	NEO	28 July 1816	*The Beggar's Opera*
WH	NEO	18 Aug. 1816	*Love in a Village*
WH	NEO	1 Sept. 1816	*The Castle of Andalusia* (CO). [No ref.-N.] Hazlitt's comments indicate that this is a new adaptation—probably of O'Keefe's opera of that name (1782) and probably with much of Dr. Arnold's music retained.
WH	CG	29 Sept. 1816	*Your's or Mine?* (OF), Tobin. Music [no ref.-N.] probably by Shield (based on Hazlitt's comments).
LH	CG	17 Nov. 1816	*The Slave* (M), Morton. Music by Bishop.

Reviewer	Theatre	Date of Review	Work
LH	DL	8 Dec. 1816	*Lionel and Clarissa* (CO, 1768), Bickerstaffe. Music by Dibdin the Elder.
LH	DL	22 Dec. 1816	*Ramah Droog* (or *Ramagh Droogh*; M, 1798), Storace. Music by Reeve and Mazzinghi.
WH	CG	25 May 1817	*The Libertine* (M), Pocock (based largely on Shadwell's *Libertine,* 1676). Songs introduced from Mozart's *Don Giovanni.*
LH	LY	6 July 1817	*Artaxerxes*
LH	CG	6 July 1817	*The Gentle Shepherd,* Ramsay. He wrote the words to genuine Scottish tunes collected by his friend William Thomson, a singer, who published them in his *Orpheus Caledonius* (1725). In the same year Ramsay published his pastoral drama, *The Gentle Shepherd,* which included only four of the songs. Subsequent to the success of *The Beggar's Opera,* it was published as a ballad opera in 1728 but was not performed publicly until 1758. Meanwhile, Colley Cibber's son Theophilous adapted it into a one-act opera, *Pattie and Peggy* (1730), changing the Scots dialect. Four other adaptations followed by as many playwrights, the best probably being Richard Ticknell's, for which Linley provided musical adaptations. In 1811 A. Maclaren brought out still another version. The piece Hunt saw, probably based on Ticknell and retaining part of Linley's music, was a new revision by G. Bethune, to which Bishop contributed still further musical alterations. Hunt's reference to William Boyce provides further curiosities, since he never worked directly with the Ramsay story. The selection instanced came from Boyce's cantata *Solomon* (1743); presumably Bishop included it, since Hunt was familiar with another version.
LH	LY	13 July 1817	*The Cabinet*
LH	LY	27 July 1817	*Love in a Village*

Reviewer	Theatre	Date of Review	Work
LH	CG	5 Oct. 1817	*Duke of Savoy; or, Wife and Mistress* (M), Reynolds (adapted from *Les deux petites Savoyards*, Paris, 1789). Music by Bishop.
LH	DL	19 Oct. 1817	*The Haunted Tower* (CO, 1789), Cobb. Music (pasticcio) by Storace.
LH	CG	16 Nov. 1817	*The Siege of Belgrade*
LH	DL	16 Nov. 1817	*Love in a Village*
LH	CG	15 Mar. 1818	*Rob Roy Macgregor; or, Auld Lang Syne!* (M), Pocock (adapted from Scott's novel *Rob Roy*). Music by J. Davy.
LH	DL	26 Apr. 1818	*The Lady of the Manor* (CO, 1778), Kenrick (based on *The Country Lasses*, 1715, by Charles Johnson). Music by J. Hook, with "additions" for this production.
LH	EOH	12 July 1818	"Season Preview"
LH	EOH	23 Aug. 1818	*Jealous on All Sides; or, The Landlord in Jeopardy!* (CO), Beazley. Music by Jolly.
LH	HY	30 Aug. 1818	*The Rival Soldiers* (OF, 1797), O'Keefe (based on his *Sprigs of Laurel*, 1793). Music by Dr. Arnold.
LH	CG	18 Oct. 1818	*Barber of Seville* (CO), John Fawcett in collaboration with D. Terry (based on Beaumarchais). Music by Bishop, including adaptations from Paesiello and Rossini.
CL	OLY	22 Nov. 1818	*Don Giovanni; or, A Spectre on Horseback* (B). Possibly the same work listed by Nicoll as T. Dibdin's with performances at Royal Circus, 1817; CG, 1819; and LY, 1820; but not at OLY.
LH	CG	7 Feb. 1819	*The Beggar's Opera*
LH	CG	21 Mar. 1819	*The Marriage of Figaro* (CO), adapted by Holcroft from his play *Follies of the Day* (1784), copied from Beaumarchais's *Le Mariage de Figaro* (Paris, 1784). Holcroft memorized the lines at the theatre with a friend; each later wrote out what he remembered, checking the copies for discrepancies, then returned to another performance for verification. Still, the

Reviewer	Theatre	Date of Review	Work
			production was adapted to "English taste." See Hazlitt's "Life of Thomas Holcroft," *Works*, III, 112–13. Bishop, who provided his own overture, did more than "merely arrange" Mozart's music [N.]; see above, chapter three and notes.
LH	LY	20 June 1819	*The Duenna* (CO, 1775), Sheridan. Linley, who is often credited with the music, disapproved his son-in-law's procedure but did adapt the tunes, which Sheridan himself selected from folk and other sources. See *The Plays and Poems of Richard Brinsley Sheridan*, ed. R. Crompton Rhodes (New York: Russell & Russell, 1962), I, 248–54.
CL	EOH	4 July 1819	*The Jovial Crew; or, The Merry Beggars*. The prototype was Richard Brome's play of the same title, first acted 1641. It was converted into a ballad opera by Roome, Concanen, and Sir William Yonge (six eds., 1731–1767). Probably other versions followed. Lamb states that this piece was revived after seven years [no ref.-N.].
LH	EOH	25 July 1819	*My Own Rival; or, Sophy, Lucy, and Lucy, Sophy* (OF), author unknown. Music by Hart.*
CL	EOH	1 Aug. 1819	*The Hypocrite*. An operatic adaptation by Arnold of Bickerstaffe's comedy (1768), which was based mainly on Cibber's *The Non-Juror*. [N.-first performance 11 July 1818, "author unknown."]
CL	EOH	8 Aug. 1819	*Belles without Beaux* (Operetta), adapted from a French work. Music by G. Ware.*
LH	EOH	22 Aug. 1819	*The Brown Man* (O), author unknown. Music by Reeve.
LH	CG	19 Sept. 1819	"Season Preview"
LH	DL	10 Oct. 1819	*Guy Mannering* (M), Terry, in collaboration with Scott. Music by Bishop. Nicoll lists its première CG 12 Mar. 1816, and shows no DL production. Genest says the play was never

Reviewer	Theatre	Date of Review	Work
			acted at DL. In his review Hunt calls the piece new but states that if he had not known the house he was in, he would have mistaken the work for the one at CG.
LH	CG	31 Oct. 1819	*King Arthur; or, The British Worthy* (Dramatic Opera, 1691), Dryden. Music by Purcell. Revised by Garrick (1770) with musical revisions and additions by Arne.
LH	CG	26 Dec. 1819	*Comedy of Errors* (CO), Reynolds. Music by Bishop with adaptations from Arne, Stevenson, and others.
LH	DL	27 Feb. 1820	*The Siege of Belgrade*
LH	DL	16 Apr. 1820	*Artaxerxes*
LH	OLY	4 June 1820	*Giovanni in London; or, The Libertine Reclaimed* (OE, 1817), Moncrieff. No credits for music.
LH	CG	24 Sept. 1820	*The Beggar's Opera*
LH	CG	1 Oct. 1820	*Love in a Village*
LH	HY	15 Oct. 1820	*Rosina* (CO, 1782), Frances Brooke. Music selected and composed by Shield.
LH	CG	12 Nov. 1820	*Twelfth Night* (CO), Reynolds. Music by Bishop, with adaptations from Mozart, Winter, Stevenson, Morley, Ravenscroft, and others.

Playwrights, Composers, and Performers

Addison, John (c. 1766–1844), composer and instrumentalist. He rose from "humble beginnings" to share in some of Kelly's enterprises and is credited by Nicoll with about ten compositions for the stage.

Arne, Thomas Augustine (1710–1778), the leading composer of his day, wrote songs (including "Rule Britannia"), masques, oratorios, operas, and keyboard music. His first opera was a setting of Addison's *Rosamond* (1733). For *Artaxerxes* (1762), his most important opera, he wrote his own libretto based on Metastasio. Among his many works for the stage is his comic opera *Thomas and Sally* (1760), which has been successfully revived in the present century.

Arnold, Dr. Samuel (1740–1802), organist at Westminster Abbey after 1793.

He composed some forty operas and other musical pieces for the stage, Vauxhall, etc., including several oratorios.

Arnold, Samuel James (1774–1852), son of the composer. He wrote several successful musical plays before obtaining a license to present English opera at the Lyceum in 1809. With Elliston and others he managed DL after its bankruptcy, until 1814. He acquired control of LY (extensively rebuilt by Beazley) in 1816, renaming it the English Opera House, and managed it successfully for many years when most theatres were losing money.

Bannister, John (1760–1836), actor. He early discovered an aptitude for imitations of well-known actors, making his DL debut in 1778. Although he achieved some success in tragedy, his outstanding roles were comic (Hunt called him the "first low comedian on the stage") and for many years he remained a leading London player.

Bate [Dudley], The Reverend (later Sir) Henry (1743–1809). Though he took orders and succeeded to his father's rectory, he lived as a man of pleasure in London. During his years as editor he had numerous quarrels and duels (partly in defense of purchased benefices) and once was jailed for libel. He later assumed the additional name of Dudley, willed to him by a relative of that name. He was at one time a close friend of Garrick's and began writing for the stage about 1774. Dr. Johnson would allow him no merit as an author, only courage (D.N.B.).

Beazley, Samuel (1786–1851), occasional playwright but better known as an architect of theatres. Besides LY he reconstructed DL and St. James's.

Bellamy, Thomas L. (1770–1843), bass. He sang at CG, 1807–1812; DL, 1812–1817.

Bickerstaffe, Isaac (1735?–1812?), playwright. He relied heavily on Charles Dibdin the Elder for selecting the music for his works. *Lionel and Clarissa* was his most popular, though later audiences seemed to prefer *Love in a Village*. His *Maid of the Mill,* founded on Richardson's *Pamela,* was also a great success.

Bishop, Henry Rowley (1786–1855), wrote a large number of works for the stage, especially CG, which company he joined in 1811. He composed the music for *Maid Marian* (1822), based on Peacock's novel. Also a noted conductor (Philharmonic and Ancient Concerts), he was knighted in 1842. He is now remembered for a few songs, e.g., "Home, Sweet Home" (from *Clari*) and "Lo, Hear the Gentle Lark."

Bland (née Romanzini), Maria Theresa (1769–1838), a very popular singer early in the century. (She was in the first play Hazlitt ever saw.)

Braham, John (1777–1856). Of Jewish parentage (early reviewers called him Abram or Abraham), he was early orphaned and taken under tutelage by his uncle, Michael Leoni (Myer Lyon), whose voice was said to have been superior to his nephew's and who composed music for Jewish rituals. The young singer made appearances as a boy soprano at CG, 1787–1788. After his voice had changed he made his debut as tenor at DL, 1796. He studied abroad before appearing at CG in 1801 and soon began his custom of composing all the music for his own parts in English operas. From 1804 to 1806, and again in 1816, he sang at KT, but his greatest success was on the English stage and in oratorios. In 1816 he married a Miss Bolton of Ardwick, by whom he had six children. By Nancy Storace he had a natural son (c. 1802), who took Anglican orders.

Brooke, Mrs. Frances (1724–1789), wrote essays, novels, poems, and plays, several of which were successfully produced at CG. Her *Rosina* was the most popular.

Burges, Sir James Bland (1752–1824), politician and playwright. As M.P., he supported Pitt and Wilberforce. Retiring from politics in 1795 with a baronetcy, he devoted his remaining years to letters. He wrote eight plays, only two of which were produced.

Cherry, Andrew (1762–1812), like many of his theatrical brethren, was an actor turned playwright.

Cobb, James (1756–1818). Once a clerk in India House, he produced mostly trivial farcical opera between 1779 and 1809.

Colman, George, the Younger (1762–1836), active in HY after 1777, he assumed management on the retirement of his father in 1789. He was successful there as manager and writer of farces until 1820, after which he was appointed Examiner of Plays.

Cooke, Thomas Potter (1786–1864), went to sea in his early years. Appointed stage manager at the Surrey in 1809, he acquired experience as singer and actor, making his DL debut in 1816. Later (1827) he was regarded as the best "sailor" on the stage.

Corri, Domenico (Rome, 1746–London, 1825), a singing master and music publisher as well as theatrical composer. He was in London after 1790.

Cumberland, Richard (1732–1811), dramatist, was educated at Trinity College, Cambridge. After government service, he began writing plays; his first was a musical, produced in 1765. *The Brothers,* a comedy, was a success at CG in 1769. *The West Indian* (1771) is regarded as his best play. Again in government service in the 1770's, he produced many plays in the sentimental vein after 1782. He also wrote two novels and a memoir.

Davy, John (1763–1824), composer.

Dibdin, Charles, the Elder (1745–1814), largely a self-taught composer, wrote the words for many of his songs, of which his nautical ones were especially popular. Although Dibdin wrote strongly against naval whippings in his *Musical Tour of Mr. Dibdin* (1788), Pitt gave him an annual pension of £ 200 (probably between 1794 and 1801) to write songs that would encourage volunteers for the Napoleonic wars. Dibdin ceased writing for the stage about 1806, though *The Waterman* and *The Quaker* had later revivals.

Dibdin, Thomas John (1771–1841), illegitimate son of Charles and half-brother of Charles Dibdin the Younger (1768–1833; manager and producer of musicals at Sadler's Wells until 1819). Thomas produced many musical "vehicles" for the patent theatres, some with music of his own, but most composed by others. In 1801 he received £ 2600 as playwright-in-ordinary to CG, in addition to £ 293 from other sources, and in 1804 he earned £ 1515 from his stage productions. After 1814 he confined his activities to the Royal Circus, where he was manager until 1819. He then became manager of the Surrey.

Dickons (née Poole), Maria (1770–1833), soprano at Vauxhall and other concert halls from 1787. She first appeared at CG, 1793; DL, 1811; and KT, 1812.

Dryden, John (1631–1700), poet, dramatist, critic. Although his comedies enjoyed considerable popularity, his dramatic fame rests on his tragedies, of which the best known is *All for Love* (1677). Many of his poems were composed for musical setting, and the comedies and masques for musical intermezzi. Attracted by Purcell's music for Betterton's *Dioclesian,* he worked with the composer on *King Arthur* (1691), in which the musical numbers, though more numerous than in *Dioclesian,* were still not dramatically integrated.

Edwin, Elizabeth Rebecca (1771?–1854), actress. At age eight she appeared in Dublin in an O'Keefe farce. She was at CG briefly in 1789, but was not at London regularly until 1809 (DL), after which she made a success in comic roles. She retired about 1822.

Fawcett, John (1768–1837), actor and playwright. Son of an actor and a pupil of Dr. Arne, he played low comedy roles. He came to CG in 1791, played later at HY, and retired from the stage in 1830. He was the original Bartholo to the Figaro of John Liston in the English *Barber.* He wrote a few pantomimes and melodramas, some with T. Dibdin.

Gay, John (1685–1732), poet, playwright, and friend of Pope, Swift, and other important figures of his time. *The Beggar's Opera* (1728) was

his only stage triumph. *Polly,* a sequel (1728), was suppressed by Sir
Robert Walpole and was not performed until 1777.

Hart, Joseph Binns (1794–1844), organist and compiler of dance music,
which he began adapting for private balls in 1815. From 1818 to
1821 he was associated with LY, where he wrote songs for farces
and melodramas.

Hook, The Reverend Dr. James (1746–1827), wrote many songs for Marylebone Gardens and Vauxhall and composed two stage works of his
own as well as those of his son Theodore. He also composed overtures, oratorios, and other works. His songs were in the English
tradition: "Within a Mile" was often mistaken for a folk tune.

Hook, Theodore (1788–1841), son of James Hook, composer. While very
young, he wrote lyrics for songs in his father's operas, and in his
early twenties produced several farces and melodramas. Gay and
sociable, he loved practical jokes and became a favorite of the
Prince of Wales. Appointed Accountant-General and Treasurer at
Mauritius in 1813, he was charged in 1817 with the loss of $62,000
—a responsibility he never discharged. He was nevertheless given
editorship of *John Bull,* an organ designed by the Administration
to counteract popular enthusiasm for Queen Caroline. In later
years he wrote many novels.

Horn, Charles Edward (1786–1849), was both singer and composer. Though
Hunt had little to say for his songs in the *Examiner,* he later remembered with pleasure Horn's most famous song, "Cherry Ripe."

Incledon, Charles (1763–1826), countertenor. He first sang in London in
1790 and was in the CG première of Haydn's *Creation* (1800). He
long remained an exceedingly popular character performer in English operas.

Johnstone, John Henry (1749–1828), actor. He first appeared in Dublin as
Lionel in *Lionel and Clarissa* about 1773. He appeared at CG
from 1783 to 1803 and thereafter at DL. He became known as
"Irish Johnstone" for his superiority in Irish roles.

Jordan, Dorothy (1762–1816), a singer and actress with strong personal appeal. For twenty years she was the mistress of the Duke of Clarence
(William IV), by whom she had ten children.

Kean, Edmund (1787?–1833), actor. He first appeared at DL (1814) as
Shylock, the success of his performance assuring his future as one
of the greatest tragic actors of his age. He was outstanding in
Shakespearean roles. Touring the U.S. in 1820–1821 and again in
1825, his career was broken by ill health in 1826.

Kelly, Frances ("Fanny") Maria (1790–1882), singer, had many ardent followers. One rejected admirer shot at her from the pit but fortunately missed. As Barry Proctor states, she was present at Lamb's Wednesday gatherings in 1817. Lamb's infatuation with Fanny, fifteen years his junior, culminated in a proposal by letter (20 July 1819). (Cf. his review of *The Jovial Crew;* in another review, of 1 Aug. 1819, he roguishly announced: "We have not the pleasure of being acquainted with her.") Fanny rejected with grace, and Lamb acknowledged his defeat with equal grace, suggesting that they nevertheless remain friends and hoping she would not deny him the "bones" upon request (the tessera used to fill "orders" or passes). They remained good friends for the rest of Lamb's life; she died, still unwed, at ninety-two.

Kelly, Michael (1762–1826), Irish tenor, actor, composer, stage manager, theatre director, music publisher, and (like his father) wine importer. On the Dublin stage before 1779, he studied in Italy, became a friend of Mozart's while in Vienna, and sang in his operas. He performed at DL from 1787 to 1800. For some years after 1793 he was also stage manager for KT. Bankrupt with Sheridan in 1811, he gave his last appearance that year in a Dublin benefit. By his own count he wrote sixty-two stage pieces between 1797 and 1821. Regarding his "borrowings" he claimed: "The professional, would-be theatrical composers, the music-sellers and their friends, gave out that the music [for *The Blue Beard*] was not mine. . . . But I laughed them to scorn; conscious that I never even selected a piece from any composer to which, when I printed it, I did not affix his name" (*Reminiscences,* p. 132). But London was more impressed with Sheridan's epithet for him: "Importer of music and composer of wines."

Kemble, Charles (1775–1854), came from a large family of actors. (His brother John was one of the great Hamlets of the age; he also managed DL from 1803 to 1808.) Charles first appeared as Malcolm in *Macbeth* in 1794 but achieved greatest fame in comic roles. Made acting manager of CG as early as 1808, he did not assume full management until 1822; nor was he successful financially until his daughter Fanny appeared there in 1829. Together they were a popular attraction; they toured the U.S. in 1832–1834. Kemble retired in 1840.

Kemble (née De Camp), Maria Theresa (1774–1838), appeared at age six as a cupid in a KT ballet. Her first success was in the role of Macheath (HY, 1792)! She married Charles Kemble in 1806 and often appeared at CG under his management.

Kenney, James (1780–1849), dramatist. His first play, *Raising the Wind,* a farce, was produced at CG in 1803 and was frequently revived. This was followed by several comic operas, all very successful, though he also wrote straight comedy as well as two tragedies. A prolific writer for most of his life, he produced plays at all the theatres, his most popular being *Sweethearts and Wives* (1823).

Kenrick, William (1724?–1779), hack writer of diverse talents. His works for the stage were supported by Garrick, until they quarreled. Later George Colman the Elder supported him at CG until he quarreled with Colman. Few of his plays were successful.

King, Matthew Peter (1733–1823), composer and student of C. E. Horn. He was briefly associated with LY productions.

Mathews, Charles (1776–1835), son of a bookseller and preacher. He gained success in comic roles in the circuit theatres. He appeared at DL in 1804 and later at HY, with great success. Lameness resulting from an injury led, after 1814, to his giving "imitations," in which he toured the U.S. and the Continent.

Milman, Henry Hart (1791–1868), cleric, later Dean of St. Paul's. He wrote mainly poetry and history; of his few plays only *Fazio* had moderate success.

Moncrieff, William (1794–1857). Law clerk, journalist, and songwriter in his early years, he became an outstanding actor, manager, and playwright.

Moore, Thomas (1779–1852), Irish poet. He is best known for *Irish Melodies,* issued between 1808 and 1824 and set to music by Sir John Stevenson and others. Mainly a lyricist, writing many of his songs to folk airs, he did occasionally compose some of his own music. *M.P.* was his only work for the lyric stage. *Lalla Rookh* (1817), an Oriental romance in verse, was his most popular work.

Moorehead, John (d. 1804), Irish violinist and composer. He was brought to London by T. Dibdin as house composer at Sadler's Wells. Later (1798) he moved to CG, where he collaborated on the music for many of their stage productions.

Morton, Thomas (1764?–1838), dramatist. He was first drawn to the stage as an actor. His first play, *Columbus,* was successfully produced at CG in 1792. He thereafter produced an enormous number of successful comedies, farces, and operas, of which *Speed the Plough* and *The Way to Get Married* were the most popular.

Mountain (née Wilkinson), Sara (1768?–1841), called "Rosomon" after the name of the proprietor at Sadler's Wells where her parents were circus performers. Trained by Dibdin at the Royal Circus, she appeared at CG, 1786–1798; HY, 1800; and thereafter at DL (until 1815). She never reached front rank.

O'Hara, Kane (1714?–1782), writer of burlesques. He took his B.A. and M.A. at Trinity College, Dublin. He resided in Dublin many years and assisted in founding a music school there. Becoming interested in the new Italian burletta, he composed *Midas* in 1759, his most successful production. He wrote other musicals of this type as well as Irish songs.

O'Keefe, John (1747–1833), actor and playwright. Author of the well-known song "I Am a Friar of Orders Grey," he was a prominent actor until 1797, when he became blind. *Wild Oats* (1797) was the most popular of his many plays and operas.

Pearman, William (fl. 1810–1824), began as a singer of Dibdin's nautical songs at Sadler's Wells. He made his debut at EOH as Orlando in the *Cabinet* in 1817 and leaped into favor. He was regarded as the best Macheath on the stage. He was at DL and CG briefly, but his voice was unsuited to large houses. He sang in *Der Freischütz* in 1824 at EOH.

Philipps (Phillips), Thomas (1774–1841), singer. He first appeared in London in 1796.

Pocock, Isaac (1782–1834), a painter in his earlier years. Though his first play was produced at HY in 1808, he did not become successful until 1818, when he began to turn the Waverly novels into operas. From then on, he became a prolific playwright, producing many farces and melodramas at all the theatres.

Purcell, Henry (1659–1695), organist and composer. He was active in almost every field of music. His theatre music includes six operas, but only *Dido and Aeneas* (1689) is set to continuous music. He wrote incidental music for some forty stage productions, of which the most important are *Dioclesian* (1690), *King Arthur* (1691), *The Fairy Queen* (1692), *The Indian Queen* (1695), and *The Tempest* (1695).

Ramsay, Allan (1686–1758), lived much of his life at Edinburgh, where he produced volumes of Scottish songs (*Tea-table Miscellany*, 1724), some of which he "improved." He was also a capable Horatian lyrist. After 1730 he continued to write but ceased to publish, fearing to damage his good reputation. He built an octagonal house to which he retired, describing himself at seventy as "prudent" and "successful" (D.N.B.).

Reeve, William (1757–1815), uncle of the comedian John Reeve. He acted in various theatres in earlier years. By 1783 he was composing music for Astley's Circus. Following Shield's differences with CG over *Oscar and Malvina,* left unfinished, Reeve was appointed composer-in-ordinary there and completed the opera. In 1792 he adapted Gluck's *Orpheus.* For several years he collaborated in many productions with Mazzinghi (who wrote the more serious parts) and others. In 1802 he acquired part ownership of Sadler's Wells, where he was stage composer until his death.

Reynolds, Frederic (1764–1841), abandoned law for playwriting. His first play was given at Bath in 1785, his second at CG in 1786. Turning from tragedy to comedy, he achieved wide popularity in the *Dramatist* (CG, 1789). He wrote nearly one hundred plays, many of which were printed. From 1814 to 1822 he was theatrical adviser for CG, a function he later served for DL.

Sheridan, Richard Brinsley (1751–1816), actor, playwright, manager, and later proprietor of DL following Garrick's retirement (1776). Rebuilt in 1794, DL slowly began to fail, Sheridan defraying the large expenses out of his own pocket. He became bankrupt following the fire that destroyed the theatre. A close friend of the Prince (c. 1802), he moved away from his earlier liberal views as a Whig M.P. in the 1780's. He alienated supporters from 1806 on, finally losing his seat over the Catholic Emancipation issue. No longer immune, he was arrested for debt in 1813. Following a misunderstanding with the Prince Regent, whose aid he spurned, he died in debt. In later years he drank heavily.

Shield, William (1748–1829), composed about thirty dramatic pieces. His first (*Flitch of Bacon,* by Bate, 1788) was so successful he was engaged as theatre composer for CG until 1791.

Siddons, Sarah (1755–1831), actress. A daughter of Roger Kemble, she was born into a family of actors. After juvenile experience, she was brought to DL in 1775 by Garrick, but her performances there were unsuccessful. She went on to brilliant successes at Manchester, Liverpool, and Bath, playing many roles though her strength was in tragic ones. In 1782 she returned to DL and was an immediate success. She left DL in 1806 for CG, from which she retired in 1812. "She was probably the greatest actress this country has known" (D.N.B.).

Sinclair, John (1791–1857), tenor. He appeared at HY in 1810 in Shield's *Lock and Key.* At CG for seven years, he sang tenor roles in several Bishop productions. In 1819 he pursued vocal studies in Paris, and in 1821 sang for Rossini at Naples; the composer wrote the part of Idreno in *Semiramide* for him. He appeared in opera throughout Italy and also toured the U.S.

Stephens, Catherine (1794–1882), pupil of Thomas Welsh. She appeared anonymously at CG, 23 September 1813, as Mandane; after her success she repeated the role as "Miss Stevens" and, still later, under her own name (hence the variant spellings). She was a leading singer on the English stage for many years and was permanently engaged by the Ancient Concerts in 1814. She retired from the stage in 1835.

Stevenson, Sir John Andrew (1761–1833), Irish composer. He wrote much for the Irish stage and was knighted in 1803. He also wrote songs, glees, and oratorios, but is best known for his settings for Moore's *Irish Melodies.*

Storace, Ann Selina ("Nancy"; 1766–1817), sister of the composer. A versatile soprano, she sang in opera buffa (under Mozart and later at KT) and in English opera.

Storace, Stephen (1763–1796), composer-in-residence at DL under the Linley-Sheridan management. He was a child prodigy, performing on the violin. Later he traveled to Italy and to Vienna, where he benefited from his association with Mozart. Engaged by Kelly to superintend productions at KT, he soon became disgusted with the petty rivalries there. His most successful English opera was the *Haunted Tower,* which ran fifty nights in one season. He borrowed heavily from Continental and English music and was the first to introduce concerted finales in English operas.

Terry, Daniel (1780?–1829), actor and playwright. First training in the circuits, he appeared at HY in 1812. He created some original characters in unimportant plays at CG from 1813 to 1822; later he acted there in minor roles. He idolized Scott, whose *Guy Mannering* he turned into a musical in 1816. He also collaborated in a number of other plays.

Tobin, John (1770–1804), playwright. His dramas were "gifted with a sense for poetry" (Nicoll, IV, 164); Hunt admired his poetic style and regretted his turning to farce in later productions.

Tree, Ann Maria (1801–1862), later Mrs. James Bradshaw, an older sister of Ellen Tree (a famous comedienne, wife of Charles Kean). Ann Maria was a pupil of Thomas Simpson Cooke (1782–1848), who first sang at LY, 1813, where he was a leading tenor for twenty years. Ellen was the heroine of Hunt's *The Legend of Florence*—a performance she regarded as the best of her career.

Vestris (née Bartolozzi), Lucia Elizabeth (1797–1856), descendent of Gaetano Stefano (1757–1821) and Francesco (1727–1815). Her grandfather Francesco was a clever Florentine goldworker; he invented the "red-chalk" manner of engraving, which for a time drove out line engravings. Lucia married Armand Vestris, dancing master at KT, in 1813.

Trained under Corri, she first appeared there in Winter's *Proserpina* (20 July 1815). Shortly afterwards the couple left for Paris, where Vestris's family was prominent in ballet (Armand's father perfected the pirouette and other movements). There the couple separated; Lucia, adopting "Mme. Vestris" as her stage name, returned to London and KT with improved abilities. She first appeared at the playhouses in 1820. She managed the Olympic in 1831 in partnership with Maria Foote (who soon withdrew). Her popular extravaganzas there were considered models of good taste. She married the actor Charles James Mathews, son of the comedian, in 1838, and together they appeared on the stage and also managed the Olympic and, later, CG theatres.

Whitaker, John (c. 1776–1847), composer. He was a friend of T. Dibdin's as early as 1808, when Whitaker was organist at St. Clement, Eastcheap. He composed seven stage works between 1811 and 1817, two in 1822–1823, and one in 1829. He collaborated in most of these with Reeve and other composers (including Bishop in 1817). Upon Reeve's death in 1815 he was appointed theatre composer at Sadler's Wells.

Appendix II
Italian Opera

Reviewers, Reviews, and Performances

The reviewers cited are: HR—Henry Robertson; TB—Thomas Barnes; WH—William Hazlitt; and LH—Leigh Hunt.

Unless an earlier performance is cited, the first listing of a work indicates a review approximately at the time of its London première.

To the important sources for this appendix, which are cited under appendix one, should be added "Chronicles of the Italian Opera in England" and *Enciclopedia dello Spettacolo*.

Reviewer	Date of Review	Opera
HR	17 Jan. 1808	*La Frascatana Nobile* (Venice, 1774; London, 1776), Paesiello; lib. by F. Livigni, with alterations.
HR	31 Jan. 1808	[*La*] *Didone* (Naples, 1797), Paesiello; lib. by Metastasio.
HR	6 Mar. 1808	*Il Furbo contro il Furbo* (Venice, 1796), Fioravanti.
HR	20 Mar. 1808	*Il Barbiere di Siviglia* (St. Petersburg, 1782; London, 1789), Paesiello; lib. by Giuseppe Petrosellini, based on Beaumarchais's *Le Barbier de Séville*.
HR	10 Apr. 1808	*Il Capriccio Dramatico* (London, 1794), Cimarosa. Nicoll states: "adapted by L. da Ponte from G. M. Diodati, *L'Impresario in Angustie*; translation by G. Mazzinghi." *Grove's*, *Spettacolo*, and *Annals* do not list *Il Capriccio Dramatico* as a work of Cimarosa's, but all agree that Diodati wrote the libretto for his *L'Impresario* (Naples, 1786); *Annals* lists no English performance, though there were numerous Continental ones. *Il Capriccio*, which must have been substantially modified for KT production, enjoyed considerable popularity there until about 1812, according to "Chronicles."

Reviewer	Date of Review	Opera
HR	1 May 1808	*Le Feste d'Iside* (or *La Festa d'Iside*), Nasolini.
HR	3 July 1808	*Gli Amanti Consolati* (Turin, 1779), Sarti.
HR	7 Aug. 1808	*Le Semiramide* (London, 1806), Portugal—apparently a pasticcio composed for Catalani.
HR	15 Jan. 1809	*La Capricciosa Pentita* (Milan, 1802), Fioravanti; lib. by L. Romanelli.
HR	5 Feb. 1809	*I Villeggiatori Bizzarri* (*I Viaggiatori Bizzarri*), Pucitta.
HR	19 Mar. 1809	*La Caccia* [*di*] *d'Enrico IV*, Pucitta; lib. by Buonauti based on Charles Collé's *La Partie de chasse de Henry IV* (c. 1764).
HR	31 Apr. 1809	*Teresa e Claudio* (or *Teriza e Claudio*; Venice, 1801), Farinelli; lib. by G. M. Foppa.
HR	21 May 1809	*La Serva Raggiratrice*, Guglielmi *le fils* (c. 1803).
HR	2 July 1809	*Sidagero*, Guglielmi *le fils*.
HR	25 Feb. 1810	*Romeo e Giulietta*, Guglielmi *le fils;* lib. by Buonaiuti.
HR	11 Mar. 1810	*Il Fanatico per la Musica* (Venice, 1798; London, 1806), Mayr. Billington and Naldi displayed their virtuosity in this work by playing the piano and the cello, respectively, while singing (Mount-Edgcumbe, *Reminiscences,* p. 114). The pasticcio allowed singers every opportunity to introduce their favorite numbers.
HR	8 July 1810	*La Buona Figliuola* (Rome, 1760; London, 1766), Piccin[n]i; lib. adapted from Goldoni's play of the same name, based in turn on Richardson's *Pamela* (1740). The playwright William Dimond added some touches to this performance.
HR	30 Dec. 1810	*Zaira* (Milan, 1803), Federici.
HR	19 May 1811	*Così Fan Tutte; ossia, La Scuola degli Amanti* (Vienna, 1790), Mozart; lib. by da Ponte.
HR	16 June 1811	*Il Flauto Magico,* Mozart. Lib. by G. de Gamerra: Italian trans. of lib. by E. Schikaneder for *Die Zauberflöte* (Vienna, 1791; London, 1829).
HR	22 Mar. 1812	*La Clemenza di Tito* (Prague, 1791; London, 1806), Mozart. Lib. by Metastasio (first set by Antonio Caldara in 1734) was altered for Mozart by Caterino Mazzolà. Further alterations were made by Serafino

Reviewer	Date of Review	Opera

Buonaiuti for the 1806 production and probably retained in the 1812 revival (Arundell, *Critic*, p. 284). *Tito* was first produced at KT at the suggestion of the Prince of Wales, who gave a copy of the score to Billington (who was rumored to have been his mistress) for her "benefit." "Chronicles" asserts (p. 71) that Mozart was at that time "the delight of every amateur circle"; however, the singers at KT did not like the composer since one of his finales "required more study and trouble than a whole opera of the good olden times." At the première the accompaniments were changed; a harp (later a viola) was substituted for Vitellia's aria "Non più di fiori," and not until a City of London Amateur Concert long afterward were the genuine accompaniments heard. According to Hogarth (*Memoirs*, II, 368) "the audiences of that day were [no] more enlightened than those of the performers." (The opera was presented six times that season, then dropped from the repertory.) Thus Einstein errs in stating (*Mozart*, p. 408) that *Tito* was the only opera of Mozart's "that did not have to suffer the mutilations to which the others, until very recent times, continued to be subjected" in London performances.

HR	12 July 1812	*Le Nozze di Figaro* (Vienna, 1786), Mozart; lib. by da Ponte based on Beaumarchais's *Le Mariage de Figaro* (1778).
HR	25 Apr. 1813	*L'Eroina di Raab,* Ferrari; "author unknown."
HR	5 June 1814	*Gl'Orazj e Curiazj* (or *Gli Orazi ed i Curiazi;* Venice, 1796; London, 1805), Cimarosa; lib. by A. Sografi.
TB	10 July 1814	*[La] Didone Abbandonata,* Paër; lib. "altered" from Metastasio (1724). There were many settings by various hands. Nicoll lists the present performance but assigns no credit. Among the five settings in *Annals* none is by Paër, nor is the work cited in *Grove's*. *Spettacolo* and "Chronicles" list this production (c. 1810) as Paër's.
WH	4 Aug. 1816	*Così Fan Tutte*

Reviewer	Date of Review	Opera
WH	19 Jan. 1817	*Penelope* (Naples, 1794), Cimarosa; lib. by G. M. Diodati.
LH	23 Mar. 1817	*La Molinara,* first known as *L'Amore Contrastato; ossia, La Molinarella* (Naples, 1788; London, 1794), Paesiello. Lib. by G. Palomba based on Bickerstaffe's *Maid of the Mill* (1765), which in turn was based on *Pamela.*
WH	20 Apr. 1817	*Don Giovanni* (Prague, 1787), Mozart; lib. by da Ponte.
WH	18 May 1817	*Don Giovanni*
?	9 June 1817	*Agnese di Fitz-Henry* (Parma, 1809), Paër; lib. by L. Buonavoglia, based on the "realistic" novel *The Father and Daughter* (1801) by Amelia A. Opie (1769–1853).
LH	27 July 1817	*La Clemenza di Tito*
LH	3 Aug. 1817	*Don Giovanni*
LH	17 Aug. 1817	*Don Giovanni*
LH	25 Jan. 1818	*Le Nozze di Figaro*
LH	22 Mar. 1818	*Il Barbiere di Siviglia* (Rome, 1816), Rossini; lib. by Cesare Sterbini based on Beaumarchais's *Le Barbier de Séville.*
LH	12 Apr. 1818	*Il Barbiere* (Rossini)
LH	7 June 1818	*Il Matrimonio Segreto* (Vienna, 1792; London, 1794), Cimarosa; lib. by G. Bertati, based on G. Mazzinghi's translation of *The Clandestine Marriage* (1766) by Colman (and possibly Garrick).
LH	2 Aug. 1818	*Così Fan Tutte*
LH	31 Jan. 1819	*L'Italiana in Algeri* (Venice, 1813), Rossini; lib. by Angelo Anelli.
LH	21 Feb. 1819	*La Modista Raggiratrice* (Naples, 1788; London, 1796), Paesiello; lib. by G. B. Lorenzi. Nicoll lists the revival of this work under its earlier title, *La Scuffiara; ossia, La Modista Raggiratrice,* but its revival (16 Feb. 1819) is incorrectly listed as 16 Dec. 1819.
LH	21 Mar. 1819	*Le Nozze di Figaro*
LH	4 Apr. 1819	*Don Giovanni*
LH	25 Apr. 1819	*Il Barbiere* (Rossini)
LH	30 May 1819	*Il Flauto Magico*

Reviewer	Date of Review	Opera
LH	1 Aug. 1819	*L'Inganno Felice* (Venice, 1812), Rossini; lib. by G. M. Foppa. Written for Bellochi, this opera was Rossini's first great success.
LH	26 Dec. 1819	*Le Nozze di Figaro*
HR	16 Jan. 1820	*La Cenerentola; ossia, La Bontà in Trionfo* (Rome, 1817), Rossini; lib. by J. Ferretti.
LH	18 Mar. 1821	*La Gazza Ladra* (Milan, 1817; London, 1821), Rossini; lib. by Giovanni Gherardini, based on *La Pie Voleuse* by d'Aubigney and Caigniez.

Composers, Librettists, and Performers

Ambrogetti, Giuseppe (1780– ?), Italian bass-baritone. He was apparently brought to KT by Ayrton, remaining there from 1817 through 1822 and perhaps later. Of his performance of the mad father in Paër's *Agnese,* "Chronicles" stated (p. 247) that: "The *vraisemblance* was too harrowing: Ambrogetti had studied the last degrading woe of humanity in the hospitals, where all its afflicting varieties were exemplified, and had studied it too well. Females turned their backs to the stage to avoid the sight; but a change of posture could not shut their ears to the dreadful scream of partial recognition with which the first entrance of his daughter was marked." After a few nights, the work was withdrawn.

Angrisani, Carlo (c. 1760– ?), Italian bass. He sang in the original cast of *Die Zauberflöte.* Brought to KT in 1817, probably by Ayrton, he remained there at least through 1822. A dignified singer, he was widely praised by contemporary critics.

Begrez, Pierre Ignace (1787–1863?), French tenor.

Belloc (Bellochi), Teresa Giorgi Trombetta (1784–1855), French mezzo-soprano. She was derided by some English critics for Italianizing her name for professional purposes, though the practice was not uncommon (cf. Portugal) owing to the favoritism toward Italian musicians shown by the "upper orders."

Bertinotti (Radicati), Teresa (1776–1854), Italian soprano, was at KT for the 1811 season only. During that year "her company," managed by Kelly, performed in Dublin. She interpolated arias written for her by her husband, Felice Radicati, and also appeared that season in her husband's opera *Phaedra.*

Billington (née Weichsel), Elizabeth (1768–1818), a coloratura. She appeared at CG in 1786 and studied later under Sacchini in Paris. She gained popularity in Italy and returned to KT in 1801, where she was admired for her great vocal range, although her dramatic ability was slight. After retiring from KT in 1806, she made many "special" appearances at CG and DL until 1811.

Camporese, Violante (1785–1839), Italian soprano. She had no stage experience before her London debut, having previously given concerts only at Paris. "Chronicles" reports that she was a woman "of birth and education" with "a true Roman profile of considerable beauty" and that she was better in serious roles.

Catalani, Angelina (or Angelica; 1780–1849), made her first appearance at Venice in 1797. She was engaged by KT in 1806, where she remained until 1813 and where she obtained the highest fees of any singer in Europe. When the terms for her second season in London were submitted to the manager, he protested that he could afford to offer the town no other talent. Her husband, M. Valebrèque, is reported to have replied: "Et, qu'est-ce que c'est que vous vouliez? Un opera? Ma femme et quatre ou cinq poupets—voilà tout ce qu'il faut." By 1811 her vogue was diminishing and the management obtained her on its own terms. After leaving London, she sang throughout Europe; for a time she managed the Théâtre Italien in Paris. Described as simple and warm-hearted in her personal life, she contributed liberally to charitable causes.

Cimarosa, Domenico (1749–1801), composer. Although he was for some time in Russia and in Vienna, he was mainly active at Rome and Naples, where he helped to welcome the French republican army in 1799. On the return of the Bourbon monarchy, he was imprisoned for a short time before his death. Often called the "Italian Mozart," he brought lightness and grace to his many opere buffe.

Corri-Paltoni, Francesca (1795– ?), daughter of Natale Corri, music publisher, and niece of the composer Domenico Corri. She studied under Catalani in 1815–1816. "Chronicles" states that she had a good voice and "deserved more popularity than she obtained." She remained with KT for three seasons.

Crivelli, Gaetano (1768–1836), Italian singer.

Farinelli, Giuseppe (1769–1836), studied at Venice and wrote some fifty operas from 1792 to 1817, of which *Teresa* was the most successful. Rossini drove him and Nasolini from the stage, though he had enjoyed an enormous vogue from 1800 to 1810.

Federici, Francesco. Little is known of this composer, who was active in Genoa. According to *Grove's* and *Annals*, his opera *Zaira* received its Milan première under the name of another composer—one Vincenzo Federici (1764–1826), who often produced this opera in Europe under his own name! *Spettacolo*, however, states the opera *is* Vincenzo's. Vincenzo was in London between 1790 and 1800 as conductor, composer, and manager of KT, where he became involved with the "intrigues" of the house. It is presumably Vincenzo to whom Robertson refers as "Chevalier," though what species of knighthood his intrigues may have acquired remains undetermined.

Ferrari, Giacomo Gotifredo (1763–1842), came to London in 1792. He wrote *L'Eroina di Raab* especially for Catalini.

Fioravanti, Valentino (1764–1837), produced over seventy-five operas, mainly from 1789 to 1819. "In many of his operas there is a genuine vein of comedy, a freshness and an ease in the part-writing, which made them very popular in their day" *(Grove's)*. His *Le Cantatrici Villane* (Naples, 1799) was revived in Germany in 1931 and has been recorded on LP.

Fischer, Joseph (1780–1860 or 1862), was more an impressario than a singer. He was a son of Ludwig Fischer, friend and ally of Mozart and the first Osmin in *Entführung*.

Fodor-Mainvielle, Joséphine (1789–1870), French soprano, joined KT in 1816. Though she rebelled against Ayrton's firm hand in 1817, she had her way in 1818; it is not clear why she left the company at the end of that season. Hogarth's statement *(Memoirs,* II, 381) that Ayrton brought her to England is not supported by "Chronicles" or others. Later, in Paris, her voice was subject to recurrent hoarseness; she ceased her active singing career in 1825.

García, Manuel del Pópolo Vicente (1775–1832), Spanish composer, singer, and father of the famous singer Malibran. He first appeared in Paris (1808) and later went to Italy, where Rossini wrote the part of Almaviva in *Il Barbiere* for him. He joined KT in 1818, when "Chronicles" thought his voice was already "half worn out." After one more season there, he left the company. He established a singing school at London and later traveled to the U.S. and Mexico.

Grassini, Josephina (1773–1850), studied and sang in Italy and Paris before arriving at KT in 1804. Until her appearance there, the female alto voice was little appreciated. In 1807 she went to Paris. Upon her return to London during the Peace of Paris, she sang at KT as a soprano; "Chronicles" and Mount-Edgcumbe agreed that she had ruined her voice.

Guglielmi, Pietro Carlo, *le fils* (c. 1763–1817), was in London from 1808 to 1810. His influence there appears to have been undistinguished,

although his father (1728–1804), who had also visited London, was
very popular at KT (he wrote over one hundred operas).

Mayr, Simone (Johann Simon; 1763–1845), Italian composer of German
origin. Largely self-taught, he composed sixty-one operas; most
were produced at Venice. His popularity did not decline until the
advent of Rossini. In 1802 he became maestro di cappella of the
church of Santa Maria Maggiore at Bergamo.

Naldi, Giuseppe (1770–1821), Italian baritone. He succeeded Morelli in
KT company in 1806 and remained an extremely popular buffo
there until 1819, when he went to Paris. Two years later he was
killed while demonstrating a steam-cooking apparatus to a friend.

Nasolini, Sebastiano (c. 1768–c. 1806), studied at Venice. He wrote thirty
known operas, of which some enjoyed a vogue early in the century,
thanks to Mara, Grassini, and Billington.

Paër, Ferdinando (1771–1839), composed forty-three operas in various cities
in Europe; he was also an opera conductor in Paris for several
years.

Paesiello (Paisiello), Giovanni (1740–1816), was active primarily at Naples.
At Paris in later years, he was appointed director of music under
Napoleon, who admired his music. He composed over one hundred
opere buffe as well as much other music.

Pasta, Giuditta (1797 or 1798–1865), singer. She first appeared on the stage
in Italy and was at Paris in 1815. There she and her husband were
engaged by Ayrton at £ 400 (each) for the 1817 London season. She
was not successful at London and later carefully restudied her roles.
She appeared at Venice in 1819 with great success, which reached
its peak at Paris in 1822. Although her voice never lost its rough-
ness and was always somewhat difficult to handle, she was a great
singing-actress, and the individuality of her impersonations was
remarkable.

Piccin[n]i, Nic[c]olò (1728–1800), produced many operas, both comic and
serious, in Rome and Paris. In Paris he became the center of the
faction opposed to Gluck and his opera reforms.

Ponte, Lorenzo da (Emmanuele Conegliano; 1749–New York, 1838), poet
and librettist. He became a priest in 1773, but by the following
year was court poet at Vienna, where he met Mozart. Later he
taught Italian in London and elsewhere. In 1805 he fled from his
creditors to New York, where he taught at Columbia College.

Portugal (Portogallo), Marcos Antonio (1762–1830), Lisbon composer. In
1792 he went to Naples, where he wrote many successful operas.
In London for a short period about 1800, he also created a vogue

(1796–1812) for his operas there, some of which he wrote for KT production.

Puc[c]itta, Vincenzo (1778–1861), Italian composer. He wrote over thirty operas and was for a time in great demand.

Sarti, Giuseppe (1729–1802), was active as conductor, teacher, and composer in Italy, Denmark, and Russia, composing operas to texts in all three languages. Mozart used some of his music in *Don Giovanni* and elsewhere. Distrusting the German musical influence, he was one of the last of the Metastasian composers (Grout, *Short History*, p. 221).

Tram[m]ezzani. I have been unable to further identify this Italian tenor, who sang leading roles at KT from 1808 to 1815.

Weichsel[l], Charles (c. 1765– ?), son of the oboist Carl Weichsell. He was a prominent violinist and in his early years gave joint recitals with his sister, Mrs. Billington. For many years "leader" of the band at KT, he was also leader at CG when his sister appeared there, commanding as much as £ 500 for those performances.

Winter, Peter von (1754–1825), was active at Mannheim, Munich, and elsewhere. He composed three operas during a visit to England (c. 1800–1805). The most famous of his more than thirty operas was *Das unterbrochene Opferfest* (Vienna, 1796). "Chronicles" perhaps somewhat unfairly accused him of composing *Zaira, Proserpina,* and other works out of "the portfolio with which their author quitted Germany."

Notes

Abbreviations of theatre names used in notes:
CG—Covent Garden
DL—Drury Lane
EOH—English Opera House
HY—the Haymarket
KY—the King's Theatre
LY—the Lyceum
NEO—New English Opera House
OLY—the Olympic

PREFACE

1. Edmund C. Blunden, *Leigh Hunt's "Examiner" Examined* (London: Cobden-Sanderson, Ltd., 1928) and *Leigh Hunt, A Biography* (London: Cobden-Sanderson, Ltd., 1930).

2. See, respectively, Percy M. Young, "Leigh Hunt—Music Critic," *Music and Letters,* XXV (1944), 86–94; Edward D. Mackerness, "Leigh Hunt's Musical Journalism," *The Monthly Musical Record,* LXXXVI (1956), 212–22; David L. Jones, "Hazlitt and Leigh Hunt at the Opera House," *Symposium,* XVI (Spring, 1962), 5–16. David R. Cheney, through his edition of Hunt's manuscript of *Musical Evenings, or Selections Vocal and Instrumental* (Columbia, Mo.: University of Missouri Press, 1964), has further documented the extent of Hunt's musical interests.

3. In *"Examiner" Examined* (p. 3) Blunden remarked on the neglect of Robertson "by literary historians."

4. The chronological listing of reviews provides a full cross reference for *Examiner* quotations in the text. Titles of Italian operas follow the English form. Where discrepancies occur between *Examiner* and other references, the listings in the reference have usually been added parenthetically in the appendixes. An asterisk following the first appearance of a person's name in the text directs attention to the fact that it is listed in the appendixes.

5. J. C. Trewin, "Leigh Hunt as Drama Critic," *Keats-Shelley Memorial Bulletin,* X (1959), 17.

6. A few opera reviews by Hunt appear in *Leigh Hunt's Dramatic Criticism 1808–1831,* Lawrence H. and Carolyn W. Houtchens, eds. (New York: Columbia University Press, 1949).

7. Hazlitt, whose *Complete Works* have been edited by P. P. Howe (Lon-

267

don and Toronto: J. M. Dent and Sons, Ltd., 1930–1934), is quoted far less copiously. Hazlitt made numerous changes in the *Examiner* reviews that he later reprinted; Howe's text for these is based on the later versions.

CHAPTER 1

1. Donald Jay Grout, *A Short History of Opera* (New York: Columbia University Press, 1947), pp. 4–5.

2. As Paul Henry Lang writes in *George Frideric Handel* (New York: W. W. Norton and Co., Inc., 1966, pp. 177–78): "Since Handel was a German and a former court musician to an unpopular Hanoverian king [George I], the Tories immediately espoused Bononcini's cause as a form of indirect affront to the dynasty and to its chief political agent, Prime Minister Walpole. This being the case, the Whigs came to Handel's defense—and the war was on. The Prince of Wales, though well-disposed toward Handel, joined the Bononcini camp out of hatred for his father, a move that surely created a curious alliance, since the Tories' real target was the royal family."

3. Quoted by Dennis Arundell in *The Critic at the Opera* (London: Ernest Benn Ltd., 1957), pp. 158, 165–67.

4. A singer named Roselli had been the last castrato to appear in England (1800).

5. The drama was sung throughout, but this was merely an attempt to circumvent Puritan restrictions on the theatre. See Edward J. Dent, *Foundations of English Opera* (Cambridge: The University Press, 1928), p. 65.

6. Eric Walter White, *The Rise of English Opera* (New York: Philosophical Library, 1951), p. 44.

7. Cf. Grout, *Short History,* p. 332, and Ernest Walker, *A History of Music in England* (2nd ed.; London: Oxford University Press, 1924), p. 262. (J. A. Westrup revised and enlarged Walker's book [3rd ed.; Oxford: Clarendon Press, 1952], but the passages cited in this and following chapters are identical in both editions.)

8. Lang, *Handel,* p. 259; Dent, *Foundations,* p. 3. In the Preface to *King Arthur* (1691), John Dryden* complained of changes requested by Purcell in the songs: "I have been obliged to cramp my verses, and make them rugged to the Reader, that they may be harmonious to the Hearer."

9. The first of these was *Arsinoe, Queen of Cyprus* (1705), by Charles Dieupart and Thomas Clayton, libretto by Nicola Haym. The same year saw the first opera sung wholly in Italian—*The Loves of Ergasto* by Johann Greber.

10. In the same number of the *Spectator* (21 Mar. 1711) he added: "If it [music] would take the entire Possession of our Ears, if it would make us incapable of hearing Sense, . . . I would allow it no better Quarter than *Plato* has done, who banishes it out of his Commonwealth." See Joseph Addison and Richard Steele, *The Spectator,* Donald F. Bond, ed. (5 vols.;

London: Oxford University Press, 1965), I, 78–82. See other numbers of the *Spectator,* especially 5, 13, 29, and 278.

11. An all-sung opera. The setting by Thomas Clayton apparently did little for the work (Walker, *History of Music,* p. 187). Later settings were by Thomas Arne (1733) and Samuel Arnold (1767).

12. E.g., see Benedetto Marcello's "Il teatro alla modo" (c. 1720), in *Source Readings in Music History,* William Oliver Strunk, ed. (New York: W. W. Norton and Co., 1950), pp. 518–21.

13. Allan Ramsay's *The Gentle Shepherd* (1725) did not reach the public until 1758 (see appendix one). *The Beggar's Opera* is still revived with some frequency, as in the adaptation by Benjamin Britten, though its twentieth-century successor, the Brecht-Weill *Threepenny Opera* (*Die Dreigroschenoper,* 1928), is better known.

14. Lang (*Handel,* p. 704) says, "Handel's imitators tried to follow him for a century and a half, but in their worshipful hands the biblical heroes became provincial church elders."

15. Richard, Earl of Mount-Edgcumbe, whose *Musical Reminiscences, containing an account of Italian opera in England, from 1773* (4th ed.; London: John Andrews, 1834) offers valuable observations on the period, disliked the change, in which the basses, "now called *basso cantante* (which by the bye is a kind of apology, and an acknowledgment that they ought not to sing)" are "thrust up into the first characters, even in serious operas"; he could not understand why Mozart wrote leading roles for that voice (pp. 122–23).

16. Pietro Metastasio (Trapassi), 1698–1780, was the most popular librettist of opera seria. He tightened its dramatic structure, dominated the operatic world from about 1725 to 1760, and was seriously compared by his Italian contemporaries to Sophocles.

17. For details on these and other Italian-opera composers and their works, see above, chapter four and appendix two.

18. Charles Coffey's ballad opera *The Devil to Pay* (1731) was translated into German in 1743; the English tunes were probably retained in German productions (Grout, *Short History,* p. 264).

19. *Le Devin du Village* (1752) by Jean Jacques Rousseau (1712–1778) employed *vaudeville* with recitative. In his *Lettre sur la musique française* (1753) he argued for the greater melodic expressiveness of Italian opera (see Strunk, *Source Readings,* pp. 636–54), thus becoming an Italian partisan in the "Querelle des Bouffons" that raged after the introduction of opera buffa in France. But the controversy lacked point since it compared French *serious* with Italian *comic* opera.

20. David E. Baker's *Biographia Dramatica* (4 vols.; London: Longman, Hurst, Rees, Orme and Brown, 1812) observed, with regard to Miles Peter

Andrew's *The Election* (1774): "What nauseous potions will not music wash down the throat of the public."

21. *La Governante* (1779), translated by C. F. Badini and set by Bertoni.

22. George Hogarth, whose judgments on the period in *Memoirs of the Musical Drama* (2 vols.; London: Richard Bentley, 1838) are usually sound, appears to be excessive in his praise of Storace's ability "to write pure Italian melody to the prosody and accent of English poetry with a felicity which has never been excelled by any other composer" (II, 445).

23. See Walker, *History of Music,* pp. 229–32, 249.

24. Ibid., pp. 232–33, 249–52. See also above, chapter three and appendix one, for further details on composers and works and for comments on the playwrights.

25. Watson Nicholson, *The Struggle for a Free Stage* (London: Archibald Constable and Co., Ltd., 1906), p. 247.

26. As early as 1776 this exchange occurs in *New Brooms!* by Colman:
    Phelim.—What will the stage do then?
    Crotchet.—Do!—Musical pieces, to be sure—Operas, Sir—our only dependence now.—We have nothing for it now but wind, wire, rosin and catgut.

27. Mrs. Clive's *The Rehearsal; or, Bays in Petticoats.*

28. Ernest Bradlee Watson, *Sheridan to Robertson: A Study of the Nineteenth Century London Stage* (Cambridge, Mass.: Harvard University Press, 1926), p. 35. See also Nicoll, IV, 138–39.

29. Grout, *Short History,* p. 266. Rousseau's *Pygmalion* (1770) helped to make the type popular.

30. Sedaine's libretto was based on the "escape" plot, which became highly popular following the Revolution and appeared as late as *Fidelio* (1805). The music was adapted by Linley. French music was not admired by the English. Mount-Edgcumbe remarked (*Reminiscences,* p. 88): "Of French music, the less that is said the better; . . . that human ears can bear it is marvelous."

31. After fire gutted both theatres in 1808 and 1809, they were rebuilt to comparable dimensions: the new Covent Garden held 3,000; Drury Lane, 3,110. The King's Theatre (rebuilt in 1790) held 3,280. (Cf. New York's Metropolitan Opera House, 3,619; Carnegie Hall, 2,710; Martin Beck, 1,280.) The Lyceum and Haymarket held about 2,000 each; both were enlarged despite riots over the inability to hear performers. See Edward Wedlake Brayley, *Historical and Descriptive Accounts of the Theatres of London* (London: J. Taylor, 1826).

32. At the Olympic, for example, the extravaganza *Giovanni in London* called for a cast of twenty-three principals and a large supporting company.

33. Nicoll, IV, 120. Hunt was not the only critic to complain of long hours at the theatre; see Watson, *Sheridan to Robertson,* p. 100.

34. George W. Stone, Jr., ed., *The London Stage: 1660–1800. Part 4: 1747–1776* (3 vols.; Carbondale, Ill.: Southern Illinois University Press, 1962), I, cxxxii ff. The orchestra at DL consisted of five first violins (two doubled on clarinets); four second violins (two doubled on clarinets); first and second violas (a third doubled on trumpet); first and second hautboy; first and second faggots (bassoons); first and second cornu (French horn); four cellos (two doubled on double bass); and one who played bass bassoon, tabor, and pipe. They also had a large harpsichord and an organ. This survey, based on the theatre's account books, probably reflects an accountant's approximation; as Lang points out, it is a peculiar ensemble since it had practically no strings when the fiddlers blew!

Charles B. Hogan, in the same work, *Part 5: 1777–1800*, III, 2211, shows that in the 1799–1800 season DL had forty-six musicians, though this included the oratorio season, when the regular players would presumably be augmented.

35. With a good house, a play that had a run of only nine days was considered a success. J. R. Planché, *The Recollections and Reflections of J. R. Planché* (2 vols.; London: Tinsley Brothers, 1872), II, 39.

36. As Watson claims, *Sheridan to Robertson*, p. 12; cf. Hunt's *Autobiography*, p. 136. But the King's Theatre was not without occasional violence; see above, chapter four.

37. See Walker, *History of Music*, pp. 184–85; Grout, *Short History*, p. 261; and J. A. Fuller-Maitland, *English Music in the XIXth Century* (New York: E. P. Dutton & Co., 1902), pp. 38–39. House lights remained on throughout performances (candles and lamps were replaced by garish gas jets c. 1816).

38. John Ebers, *Seven Years of the King's Theatre* (London, 1828), p. 29.

39. Hogarth (1783–1870), Edinburgh amateur cellist and composer. According to D.N.B. he did not come to London until 1830, but his *Memoirs* demonstrate that his presence in London dates from a much earlier period. He contributed articles to *Harmonicon* and joined the staff of the *Morning Chronicle*. In 1846 he became music critic of the new *Daily News*, edited by Charles Dickens, who had married Hogarth's daughter in 1836.

40. A friend of the impresario Johann Peter Salomon, Ayrton (1777–1858) assisted him at the second (1794–1795) Haydn festival, for which he was decorated by George III (C. F. Pohl, *Mozart und Haydn in London* [2 vols.; Vienna: Druck und Verlag von Carl Gerold's Sohn, 1867], II, 84, 147). Ayrton held the post of "Master of the Children" at the Chapel Royal until resigning in 1805. Aside from his King's Theatre activities, he was for many years a musical writer and editor (see above, chapter two). He was a promoter and member of the London Philharmonic at its founding (1812) and later became a director. Herschel Baker surely errs in including him

among those "of no particular mark or likelihood"—*William Hazlitt* (Cambridge, Mass.: Belknap Press of Harvard University Press, 1962), p. 154.

41. Hogarth, *Memoirs,* II, 380–81.

42. *The British Stage and Literary Cabinet,* Thomas Kenrick, ed. (3 vols.; London: J. Chappell, 1817–1819), I (1817), 102 f., 176.

43. Arundell, *Critic,* p. 302. Some operas were accorded a full month of rehearsals. Even normal operating expenses were high. In 1828, for example, Ebers listed eleven principal singers; a chorus of twenty-eight; twelve principal dancers; a corps de ballet of thirty-two. Among the "ludicrous prerogatives" to be maintained were separate dressing rooms for the first and second lady (the prima donna got a sofa and six wax candles; the seconda, no sofa and only two wax candles).

One may question Reginald Nettel's assertion in *The Orchestra in England* (London: J. Cape, 1946), p. 104, that the opera-house band was "efficient only for the flimsy accompaniments usually required in Italian opera." It was surely superior to those at the playhouses. In 1826 Brayley (*Historical Accounts,* p. 30) called it "very large," "upwards of sixty persons," and "unquestionably the first in England." In 1834 Hogarth (*Memoirs,* II, 33) held that Handel's accompaniments would appear thin and poor "amidst the richness and variety of the modern orchestra," though he doesn't specify which orchestra. Perhaps Thomas Rowlandson's caricature "John Bull at the Opera" has been taken too seriously!

44. See Arundell, *Critic,* pp. 268–72, on the management problems stemming from those committees.

45. If, as Carl R. Woodring estimates in *Prose of the Romantic Period* (Boston: Houghton Mifflin, 1961), p. 380, a whole day's wage of a "lower clerk or a skilled laborer" approximated the price of a ticket to the pit (3 *s.* at the majors), few of the lower middle classes could afford the 10-*s.* price for the pit at the King's Theatre, or even the 5-*s.* gallery. (There was a small upper gallery where admission was 3 *s.*, the only part of the house where full dress was not required.)

46. Glee composers of importance in the early nineteenth century were Samuel Webbe (1740–1816), whose grandson was a close friend of Hunt's; John Wall Callcott (1766–1821); and R. J. S. Stevens (1757–1837).

47. Fuller-Maitland, *English Music,* pp. 127–29.

48. Hogarth, *Memoirs,* II, 461–64.

CHAPTER 2

1. The main sources for the first section of this chapter are the *Autobiography,* supplemented and corrected by *Leigh Hunt's Autobiography: The Earliest Sketches,* Stephen F. Fogle, ed. (Gainesville, Fla.: University of Florida Press, 1959); by Landré; and by Edmund C. Blunden's *Leigh Hunt, A Biography* (London: Cobden-Sanderson, Ltd., 1930). The *Correspondence*

has been supplemented by letters, including those edited by Hunter P. McCartney *(Letters of Leigh Hunt in the Luther A. Brewer Collection: 1816–1825* [microfilmed Ph.D. dissertation; University of Pennsylvania, 1958]), and other documents in the Luther A. Brewer Collection at the University of Iowa, as well as other sources cited below. A list of manuscripts in the Novello collection at the University of Leeds (England) has also been consulted for reference to the Hunt circle.

2. Chandos (1731–1789) had no sons and the title died with him. In his *Autobiography* Hunt expressed strong admiration for the Duke, the nephew (1765–1823), and the nephew's son, the later Lord Leigh (1791–1850).

3. The daughter of "an eminent chymist," she was a friend of the Hunt family, with whom young Leigh became quite infatuated; see Fogle, *Earliest Sketches,* pp. 13–14.

4. John Frederick Lampe (1703–1751), a native of Saxony, was active in London after 1725 as bassoonist in the opera orchestra and later as composer of English operas and Wesleyan hymns. Other composers are identified elsewhere herein. By "genuine compositions" Hunt was thinking of songs; likely he knew nothing of Boyce's symphonies, for example. This paragraph is based on chapter two of Hunt's *Autobiography*; see, especially, pp. 41–46.

5. On the Italian-opera composers, see chapter four and appendix two of this volume.

6. Hunt always spoke of Vauxhall in derogatory terms. See chapter three.

7. Hunt recommended to his *Examiner* readers Callcott's forthcoming concert, calling his glees "so truly English of their kind, so roaming at will through all the manly harmonies of the science" (14 Feb. 1813).

8. In an article entitled "Proserpina"—vignettes on Hunt's circle written by Thornton Hunt and first published by Blunden *(Leigh Hunt,* pp. 358–67)—John Robertson is described as the "agreeable bass singer who is too nervous to be more than a chorus singer on his native stage." Thornton further states that John entered the Novello circle "by right of music, and with him his brother"—Henry. The account is almost enigmatically cryptic, appears to suffer from misleading punctuation, is second-hand, and in other respects appears to be inaccurate. Nevertheless, Thornton clearly links John Robertson with the Novellos before the renewal of hostilities with France in 1803 and implies that he brought not only Henry but Leigh into that circle far earlier than any other evidence indicates.

9. François Hippolyte Barthélemon (Bordeaux, 1741–London, 1808), violinist and composer. Long active in England, he was leader of the band at the King's Theatre and at Marylebone Gardens, was associated with Haydn during his two London visits, and composed music for the stage and for solo violin.

10. Undoubtedly Henry Thompson, last of a long line of music publishers and instrument makers who maintained an establishment at St. Paul's

Churchyard. In 1805 Thompson sold his business to Button and C. H. Purday; the latter retired in 1808 and his place was taken by Whitaker. The partnership built up a large business by 1814. From 1819 to 1824 Whitaker was the main proprietor.

11. *Shelley and his Circle,* Kenneth Neill Cameron, ed. (Cambridge, Mass.: Harvard University Press, 1961), II, 694–95. On the same day Hunt wrote Marianne from Cambridge: "Take care of my Handel" and "regards to Button." He did not purchase the music there, as Percy M. Young states in "Leigh Hunt—Music Critic," *Music and Letters,* XXV (April, 1944), 88.

12. *Correspondence,* I, 82. Others were interested in setting Hunt's songs. In 1809 William Horsley requested permission to set "Throw the Gaudy Roses from Thee" (*Correspondence,* I, 46). About 1887–1888 Arthur Hoote published his setting of "If You Become a Nun, Dear" (Hunt's weekly *Indicator,* 3 Jan. 1821), previously composed by Novello. As late as 1902 Henry Gadsby set an adaptation by O. D. Bartoleyns excerpted from Hunt's translation of Tasso's *Amyntas* (1820).

13. Landré's "Leigh Hunt: His Contribution to English Romanticism," *Keats-Shelley Journal,* VIII, pt. 2 (1959), 138–39. Hereafter cited as "Contribution."

14. Novello (London, 1781–Nice, 1861), organist, choirmaster, composer. All musical London attended his recitals in the Portuguese Chapel. One of the founders of the Philharmonic, he also established other musical societies. He was delegated by London subscribers to convey £ 60 to the aging and impoverished sister of Mozart in Vienna in 1829. A composer of many sacred and secular pieces, he also edited and published masses by Haydn and Mozart at his own expense after failing to find a publisher. While editing Purcell's sacred music (1828) he established a music-publishing business with his son Alfred. In many of Novello's editions the original scores were badly mutilated through changes in harmonies and other tamperings (e.g., he added wind parts to Handel's *Judas Maccabaeus*). But he rescued four of Purcell's anthems, having transcribed the manuscripts shortly before they were destroyed by fire. His primary aim was to produce cheap editions, for the general public, of music that could be played by amateurs in piano transcriptions.

15. See Rosemary Hughes's introduction to her edition of *A Mozart Pilgrimage, Being the Travel Diaries of Vincent and Mary Novello in the year 1829,* trans. and comp. by Nerina Medici di Marignano (London: Novello and Co., Ltd., 1955), pp. xxxiv ff. The *Quarterly Musical,* pp. 216–18, reported that Novello was exonerated from charges brought by a group of Catholic laymen that he had adapted "frivolous" opera airs to music for sacred services.

16. Mary Cowden Clarke, *The Life and Labours of Vincent Novello* (London: Novello and Co., [1864]), pp. 1, 40, 60.

17. Hunt was less tolerant of Quakers and especially Methodists owing mainly to their puritanical attitude toward the arts. In *Critical Essays,* p. 100, he wrote: "Mr. Liston [in Thomas Dibdin's *Five Miles Off*] made his *Quaker* like something natural in spite of the farcical speeches put into his mouth, which a Quaker would call profane, and the farcical love-song, which a Quaker, whose sect never sings, would shudder to hear." (Hazlitt, too, protested that the Quakers "heard no music"—Herschel Baker, *William Hazlitt* [Cambridge, Mass.: Belknap Press of Harvard University Press, 1962], p. 153.) They did, however, sing "party-rhymes" at their meetings. Hunt praised the Quakers vis-à-vis the Methodists ("Examiner," 12 June 1808), but he was disturbed by the radical and bigoted activities of the Evangelicals (Landré, II, 22). Reginald Nettel's assertion in *Sing a Song of England: A Social History of Traditional Song* (London: Phoenix House, 1954), p. 167, that singing was as important to the Methodists as preaching does not apply to the Evangelicals. Hannah More, for instance, denounced even sacred music (see also chapter three above). The Wesleyans of course remained fervent singers.

18. Cf. *The Liberal: Verse and Prose from the South* (2 vols.; London, 1822–1823), II, 47–65, where Hunt blames the "chicanery" and other deterioration in the modern Italian character on the "Court of Rome." See also Landré, II, 27, 58; and George Dumas Stout, "Political History of Leigh Hunt's *Examiner*," *Washington U. Studies* (New Series: Language and Literature, No. 19, 1949), p. 17.

19. Possibly the piece to which Keats refers in a letter to Clarke (25 Mar. 1817), in which he looked forward to an evening at Novello's where "we shall have a Hymn of Mr H's composing 4 Voices—go it!" See *The Letters of John Keats, 1814–1822,* Hyder Edward Rollins, ed. (2 vols.; Cambridge, Mass.: Harvard University Press, 1958), I, 126–27, and Hunt, *Poetical Works,* p. 728.

20. Leigh Hunt, *Musical Evenings, or Selections Vocal and Instrumental,* David R. Cheney, ed. (Columbia, Mo.: University of Missouri Press, 1964). There may have been other collaborations. Percy M. Young in *Grove's* ("Novello") credits both Hunt and Novello with "Music for the Open Air." Mary Clarke (*Novello,* p. 36) links the work only to her father; but Blunden (*Leigh Hunt,* p. 286) states that Novello sought out Hunt's assistance on this work in 1840. Novello wrote some of the incidental music for Hunt's play, *A Legend of Florence.*

21. Hunt could not decide quite what tone to adopt for a work that contained such disparate appeals as an overt popularization, a scholarly exegesis of divers musical and literary matters, and a loose essay on Italian song types. Whatever the publisher James Power had in mind for the work (see Hunt's preface, p. 15) certainly added to the complications. This explains the many long footnotes (uncharacteristic of Hunt) and the many notes to

be supplied. As it stands, incomplete, the work does not achieve a "popular" approach, and if the publisher rejected it for that reason, Mary Clarke's explanation is still more sound than the editor's attempts to discount it (see pp. 3–4).

22. From Mozart's *La Clemenza di Tito*. The other songs have not been identified.

23. Hunt may have met the playwright James Kenney, the actor John Liston, and the actress Fanny Kelly, who were occasional visitors there. See E. V. Lucas, *The Life of Charles Lamb* (3rd ed.; 2 vols.; New York: P. Putnam's Sons, 1907), I, 511 ff.

24. See *The Complete Works and Letters of Charles Lamb* (New York: The Modern Library, 1935), pp. 35–38.

25. The character of Will Honeycomb undergoes subtle changes, but Hazlitt presumably had in mind the somewhat empty-headed man-of-the-world type sketched in Addison's *Spectator*, No. 2 (2 Mar. 1711), for example.

26. Crabb Robinson records meeting Alsager (1779–1846) at Lamb's early in 1815, noting that he was a musical and financial writer of the *Times*. Perhaps it was from this hint that Lucas stated that Alsager "controlled" the music criticism of that paper for years (*The Letters of Charles Lamb and Mary Lamb*, E. V. Lucas, ed. [3 vols.; New Haven, Conn.: Yale University Press, 1935], II, 171n). *Grove's* and the *Concise Oxford Dictionary of Music* state that the *Times* is "supposed" to have been the first London daily to have a "regular music critic," the *Oxford* crediting Alsager with creating this post. *The History of "The Times"* (New York: The Macmillan Co., 1935), Vol. I: *The Thunderer in the Making, 1785–1841,* 415, merely asserts that he joined the paper in 1817 as city correspondent and by 1821 was an expert on the money market. His primary function during Barnes's editorship was that of business manager.

27. Another more famous daughter was Clara Anastasia Novello, later Countess Gigliucci, soprano, who became famous throughout Europe. She formed a lifelong friendship with Rossini and was soloist at the première of his *Stabat Mater*, Bologna, 1842.

28. Aileen Ward, *John Keats* (New York: The Viking Press, 1963), pp. 36–37.

29. Richard A. Altick, *The Cowden Clarkes* (London: Oxford University Press, 1948), p. 31. According to Keats's letter to Clarke of 25 Mar. 1817, however, Clarke was still on a formal basis with the Novellos, whose invitations to him were extended through Hunt.

30. Walter Jackson Bate, *John Keats* (Cambridge, Mass.: Harvard University Press, 1963), p. 19; see Keats's verse epistle (Sept., 1816) "To Cowden Clarke," ll. 109–14.

31. Charles Clarke and Mary Cowden Clarke, *Recollections of Writers* (London: Sampson, Low, Marston, Searle and Rivington, 1878), pp. 192–93.

32. Clarke, *Novello,* p. 15; in *My Long Life* (New York: Dodd, Mead and Co., 1896), p. 26, she called him a "sterling musician." These remarks are difficult to reconcile with her assertion in *Recollections* (p. 142) that Holmes ought to have been an "educated" musician for "the passion was in him." Hunt thought that Holmes was "supra-educated."

33. Max Graf, *Composer and Critic: Two Hundred Years of Musical Criticism* (New York: W. W. Norton and Co., Inc., 1946), p. 178.

34. Holmes and Hunt were good friends of Egerton Webbe (1810?–1840); Holmes married Webbe's sister during the 1830's. Webbe, grandson of the great glee composer Samuel, wrote glees and other musical works. Some of his music was used in *A Legend of Florence.* He also wrote farces and contributed to *Leigh Hunt's London Journal.*

35. Willard B. Pope, "Leigh Hunt & His Companions," *Keats-Shelley Journal,* VIII, pt. 2 (Autumn, 1959), 90n3.

36. Thornton Hunt's second-hand evidence from "Proserpina" that Shelley had no ear for music appears unfounded. In the *Autobiography* Leigh declared that music affected Shelley deeply.

37. Based on evidence supplied by Olwen W. Campbell, *Thomas Love Peacock* (London: Arthur Barker, Ltd., 1953), p. 77; *The Letters of Percy Bysshe Shelley,* F. L. Jones, ed. (2 vols.; London: Oxford University Press, 1964), *passim*; Newman Ivey White, *Shelley* (2 vols.; New York: Alfred A. Knopf, 1940), I, 520, 555; and Peacock (*The Works of Thomas Love Peacock,* H. F. Brett-Smith and C. E. Jones, eds. [10 vols.; London: Constable and Co., Ltd., 1924–1934], I [1934], 406, and VIII [1934], 81, 114), Shelley and Peacock saw *Don Giovanni* on 23 May 1817 and again on 10 Feb. 1818; *Figaro* between 10 Jan. and 7 Feb. 1818 (probably on 21 Jan., the performance Hunt seems to have attended—his review appeared 25 Jan.); and the London première of Rossini's *Il Barbiere di Siviglia* on 10 Mar. 1818—the last time Peacock saw Shelley.

38. Some of the "cumulative effect of changing rhythms" heard in the operas may have had their echo in Act IV of Shelley's *Prometheus Unbound,* as White conjectures (*Shelley,* II, 134).

39. Young ("Music Critic," p. 89) writes: "Under his [Novello's] tutelage Hunt steered a straight course for Haydn and Mozart, touched on Purcell, and learned to adore Mendelssohn." But Hunt fell under Mozart's spell before he knew Novello; his "touches" on Purcell show the direct influence of Burney; he had mixed feelings about Haydn; and he clearly disagreed with Novello's views on Rossini. To be sure, little is known about Hunt's relations with Novello before 1815, when, as we have seen, other important influences than Novello's were also available to him.

40. Thornton Hunt, in the introduction to his father's *Autobiography*

(New York and London: Smith, Elder and Co., 1891), p. vii. Hereafter cited as "Introduction." The 1891 edition is a reprint by the same publishers of the posthumous edition (1860) that first contained the introduction.

41. Edward D. Mackerness, in "Leigh Hunt's Musical Journalism," *Monthly Musical Record,* LXXXVI (1956), 216, writes: "To Hunt, evidently, the experience of music is associated with something that is spontaneous and informal; it belongs to the world of private (not to say indolent) enjoyment, and has little to do with corporate social duties. Hence, the enormous significance of opera, and the musical expression of individual passion."

42. "A Man of Letters of the Last Generation," *Cornhill Magazine* (Jan., 1860), I, 85–95. Hereafter cited as "Man of Letters." The italics in which the names of some of the *characters* appeared have been removed.

43. Edmund C. Blunden, *Leigh Hunt's "Examiner" Examined* (London: Cobden-Sanderson, Ltd., 1928), p. 61.

44. Quoted by Blunden, *Leigh Hunt,* p. 117. *Così Fan Tutte*: see chapter four above. The songs have not been identified.

45. Landré, I, 44. Except for the appendixes to *Critical Essays,* Hunt's reviews for the *News* are not generally available (1806 is missing and perhaps no longer extant). See William Archer's introduction to *Dramatic Essays of Leigh Hunt,* William Archer and Robert W. Lowe, eds. (London: W. Scott, Ltd., 1894)—essentially an edition of *Critical Essays,* together with selected reviews from the *Tatler.* (*Critical Essays,* however, is apparently no mere redaction of reviews from the *News* but, as Hunt claims, original material.)

46. Hunt praised Fawcett in *Critical Essays* (p. 89): ". . . few of them [comedians] can display his readiness of ear for harmony, and his peculiar skill in burlesque melody."

47. Francis Jeffrey had set the tone for independent criticism when he established *The Edinburgh Review and Critical Journal* in 1802, but it was limited to criticism of literature, reached a more elite audience, and was a relatively conservative Whig organ.

48. Alexander Andrews, *The History of British Journalism* . . . (2 vols.; London: Richard Bentley, 1859), II, 27; *The Life and Times of Frederick* [sic] *Reynolds, Written by Himself* (1826).

49. About 1808–1809 Hunt visited the open houses given by Thomas Hill (1760–1840), proprietor of the *Monthly Mirror,* where Hunt met journalists, actors, and playwrights. Its editor, Edward Du Bois (1774–1850), was, according to Hunt, "a lively critic of the theatres; but half the jokes in his magazine were written for his friends, and must have mystified the uninitiated" (*Autobiography,* p. 181). Earlier Hunt had made the acquaintance of John Bell (1745–1831), owner of the *Messenger,* at whose home Hunt enjoyed discussions of literature and dramatic criticism.

50. George W. Stone, Jr., ed., *The London Stage: 1660–1800. Part 4: 1747–1776* (3 vols.; Carbondale, Ill.: Southern Illinois University Press, 1962), I, cciii–cciv. See also Charles Beecher Hogan, ed., *The London Stage: 1660–1800. Part 5: 1776–1800* (2 vols.; Carbondale, Ill.: Southern Illinois University Press, 1968), I, clxxvii–clxxx.

51. Michael Winisanker, "Musico-Dramatic Criticism of English Comic Opera, 1750–1800," *Bulletin of the American Musicological Society* (13 Nov. 1948), pp. 82–83. The magazines cited are the *Monthly Magazine,* the *European Review,* and the *Analytic Review,* the latter two edited by Thomas Busby (1755–1838). Winisanker states that the best criticism in these periodicals was impartial but stressed "scientific" music, expressing horror at consecutive fifths or octaves.

52. Charles A. Gray, *Theatrical Criticism in London to 1795* (New York: Columbia University Press, 1931), pp. 20, 228, 297, 308–10. Gray states that his study concentrates on the chief serials and writers rather than on the content of the reviews.

53. Derek Hudson, in *Thomas Barnes of "The Times"* (London: Cambridge University Press, 1944), p. 26, appears premature in asserting that this appointment showed that Walter welcomed the "new wind" in English journalism created by the Hunts, a view also expressed in *The History of "The Times,"* I, 190.

54. Leigh also intended to write dramatic criticism for the evening *Statesman,* but there is no evidence that he did so. The *Statesman,* an outspoken Whig newspaper, was also prosecuted by the government. H. R. Fox Bourne, *English Newspapers: Chapters in the History of Journalism* (2 vols.; Chatto and Windus, 1887), pp. 354–68; Andrews, *British Journalism,* p. 61.

55. Baker (*Hazlitt,* p. 230) quotes Hazlitt's eloquent tribute in the dedication to the *Political Essays* (1819) but points out that John was probably instrumental in the book's publication.

56. Cf. Shaw: "Now clearly a critic should not belong to a club at all. He should not know anybody," quoted by Hesketh Pearson in *G.B.S.: A Full Length Portrait* (New York: Harper, 1950), p. 107.

57. See the introduction by Carl R. Woodring to Leigh Hunt's *Political and Occasional Essays,* Lawrence H. and Carolyn W. Houtchens, eds. (New York: Columbia University Press, 1962), pp. 3–71. Hereafter cited as *Political Essays.*

58. R. Brimley Johnson, ed., *Prefaces by Leigh Hunt* (London: T. Hollings, 1927), p. 9.

59. Estimated at about one-and-one-half million in 1780 to seven or eight million in 1830. Maurice Quinlan, *Victorian Prelude: A History of English Manners, 1700–1830* (New York: Columbia University Press, 1941), pp. 160–61. Richard D. Altick, in *The English Common Reader* (Chicago, Ill.: University of Chicago Press, 1957), pp. 41, 82–83, emphasizes the growth of the

reading public in that "amorphous stratum between the old-established middle class . . . and the working class proper."

60. London had but one weekly in 1777; by 1813 it could count eighteen dailies and sixteen weeklies (Bourne, *Newspapers*, I, 289). By 1810 the circulation of the Sunday press exceeded that of the dailies—Raymond Williams, *The Long Revolution* (London: Chatto and Windus, 1961), p. 189.

61. Cf. George Bernard Shaw's comment: "Musical criticisms, like sermons, are of low average quality simply because they are never discussed or contradicted," quoted by Graf, *Composer and Critic*, p. 323. Hunt frequently attempted to engage his "fellow critics" on other journals in a kind of public colloquy on the arts but apparently seldom succeeded.

62. Bourne (*Newspapers*, I, 331) wryly observes: "It is only charitable to suppose that Cobbett's convictions, such as they were, were undergoing a change at this time, but we may reasonably assume that they would have remained unchanged had he received from the government the encouragement that he thought he deserved."

63. Though a certain interest on the part of the public lay behind the founding of the Philharmonic in 1812, it long maintained the atmosphere of a professional club and went to great lengths to preserve the high social status of the audience. Reginald Nettel, *The Orchestra in England: A Social History* (London: Jonathan Cape, 1946), pp. 110–61; J. A. Fuller-Maitland, *English Music of the XIX Century* (New York: E. P. Dutton and Co., 1902), p. 142.

64. It is uncertain how long either Field or Barnes wrote theatrical reviews for the *Times* (see Hudson, *Barnes*, pp. 9–18, 136–37, and *The History of "The Times,"* I, 88). Barnes apparently wrote no Italian-opera criticism before joining the *Examiner*. Following his stint with the latter, he returned to the *Times*. In 1816, Walter appointed him editor, a post he held for the rest of his life, being responsible for much of the success of that paper, which outstripped its competitors by the introduction of the steam printing press in 1814. See Andrews, *British Journalism*, II, 77; Williams, *Revolution*, p. 188.

65. 5 Oct. 1813 (British Museum Add. MSS. 38108, fol. 85).

66. Mary Cowden Clarke, *Life*, p. 26. John Byng Gattie (1788–1821), of the Treasury, was described by Hazlitt as "a set of airy crotchets in the shape of a man."

67. Henry Saxe Wyndham, *The Annals of Covent Garden Theatre from 1732 to 1897* (2 vols.; London: Chatto and Windus, 1906), I, 348; II, 122–25. This was probably William James Brandon, listed by Hogan (*London Stage*, II, 2211) as "box-books and housekeeper" in the 1799–1800 season at CG.

68. *Letters*, E. V. Lucas, ed., II, 367. The next day Charles Lamb sent a copy of Robertson's note to John Howard Payne, asking for instructions.

The play is presumably a farce presented under that title at DL on 25 May 1825 (listed by Nicoll under "unknown authors") and is likely the work of Payne. Alfred Bunn in *The Stage: Both Before and Behind the Curtain* (3 vols.; London: R. Bentley, 1840), I, 83–84, stated that for three months in 1824 Robertson, no doubt at Kemble's request, issued 11,000 "orders," worth £ 3,851—a "ruinous practice" for theatre managers.

69. A perusal of obituaries in the *Times, Gentleman's Magazine,* and the *Annual Register* from 1850 to 1861 failed to turn up his name.

70. Graf states that European newspapers gave little space to music criticism until Beethoven's fame had become established (c. 1810), citing E. T. A. Hoffmann's "classic" review that year of his Fifth Symphony (*Composer and Critic,* pp. 191, 113–15).

71. Eric Walter White, in *The Rise of English Opera* (New York: Philosophical Library, 1951), pp. 77–78, calls William Gardiner (1770–1853) a "shrewd critic," a phrase used by Lydia M. Middleton in her D.N.B. article on him. But neither Gardiner's pedantic annotations to Stendhal's [i.e., Henri Beyle's] *The Lives of Haydn and Mozart* . . . (2nd ed.; London: J. Murray, 1818) nor his other writings show him to be more than an amiable hosier who found a pleasant diversion in music. Following Haydn's second London visit, Gardiner sent him six pairs of stockings with themes from Haydn's works woven into them. Later he wrote Beethoven offering him £ 100 to write an overture to a pasticcio oratorio Gardiner had put together.

72. Stout, "Political History," p. 37. Other liberal weeklies showed the same decline. Some, like the *Register,* avoided the tax by dropping all news and achieved extraordinary sales, thus beginning a split between the "pauper press" and the "respectable press"; but the economic basis of the former remained precarious. Williams, *Revolution,* pp. 186–89.

73. "Periodical and Newspaper Press, No. IX, Examiner," *London Literary Journal* (Sept., 1852), quoted by Stout, "Political History," p. 26. Altick (*Common Reader,* p. 322) states that middle-class families with an annual income of less than about £ 300 could not afford the price of the London dailies—7 *d.* after 1815.

74. For his radical writings Carlile (1790–1843) spent over nine years in prison but kept his weekly *Republican* going with the help of his wife and sister. He was associated with William Hone (1780–1842) in other radical publications.

75. Haydon's rapid disillusionment with Hunt is apparent in his entries for 23 Sept. and 25 Oct. 1816, and 20 Jan. 1817; see *The Diary of Benjamin Robert Haydon,* Willard B. Pope, ed. (2 vols.; Cambridge, Mass.: Harvard University Press, 1960), II, 46–47, 62–63, 80 ff.

76. Thomas H. Escott, *Masters of English Journalism* (London: T. Fisher Unwin, 1911), p. 149. See also William S. Ward, "Periodical Literature," *Some British Romantics: A Collection of Essays,* James V. Logan, John E.

Jordan, and Northrop Frye, eds. (Columbus, O.: Ohio State University Press, 1966), pp. 306–9; and Arthur Aspinall, "The Social Status of Journalists at the Beginning of the Nineteenth Century," *Review of English Studies,* XXI (1945), 216–32.

77. According to Graf *(Composer and Critic)* and Fuller-Maitland *(English Music),* among the more successful was the *Harmonicon* (1823–1833), edited by Ayrton. But if the samplings of its views on Beethoven as recorded by Norman Demuth in *An Anthology of Musical Criticism from the 15th to the 20th Century* (London: Eyre and Spottiswoode, 1947), pp. 152–53, are representative, little can be said for its critical acumen. Other publications cited are: the *Musical World* (1836–1891), edited for a time by Cowden Clarke; *Atlas* (founded in 1826), which according to Graf owed its importance in music to its critic, Holmes; and the *Musical Times,* founded in 1844 by Alfred Novello. Articles by Hunt appeared in the last three publications.

78. Archer and Lowe, *Dramatic Essays*; see especially pp. xv–xxx. Jeffrey A. Fleece in "Leigh Hunt's Theatrical Criticism" (unpublished Ph.D. dissertation, State University of Iowa [1952], pp. 139 ff.) makes similar observations. Dibdin (against the advice of his friend Charles Incledon, who declared it would do no good with the "damned boy") wrote to Hunt denying authorship of a play he had condemned in the *News* and ascribed to Dibdin. Hunt printed Dibdin's letter, together with a rebuttal that "a maker of bad watches in a town" shouldn't complain of being misused "if one was mistaken for his."

79. Cf. Hunt's comments on singer Charles E. Horn: "Of his compositions we would rather not speak, unless we are compelled. What an ungracious office is a critic's,—obliged to say these things of men who may be the best fellows in the world off the stage" (12 July 1818). In contrast, some of Hazlitt's scalding remarks seem to have no justification; e.g., see his comments on one Mr. Herring (28 July 1816).

80. E.g., Baker, *Hazlitt,* pp. 230–32; Ward, *Keats,* pp. 72–79. Ward concludes that Hunt was "a man who had rarely if ever doubted . . . the rightness of his convictions," passing over Thornton Hunt's assertion (p. xi) that Leigh "was never able to rest with a final confidence in his own judgment."

81. Hunt, *Musical Evenings,* pp. 20–21. Hunt is not the only English Romantic who would have been astonished at Alfred Einstein's observations in *Music in the Romantic Era* (New York: W. W. Norton and Co., Inc., 1947), p. 21, that "there was no poet of the Romantic era who did not think of his artistic medium—language—as inadequate" and that "genuine" Romantics actually regarded music as "the primal cause, the very womb from which all the arts sprang and to which they were again to return."

82. *Leigh Hunt's London Journal,* II (1835), 48. Fuller-Maitland, *English Music,* p. 32, cites the *Musical Magazine,* edited by Button's old associate

C. H. Purday, among the better musical reviews of the early nineteenth century. It was, however, unsuccessful, surviving only two years.

83. Cf. Stendhal's views on the importance of avoiding discomforts that obstruct the enjoyment of music: "One stops listening *naturally* and starts listening *academically*; one *feels it one's duty* not to miss a single note. O, what a phrase: to *feel it one's duty!* How unspeakably *English!* How anti-musical! It is as though one were to *feel it one's duty* to be thirsty!" Henri Beyle's *Life of Rossini,* trans. Richard N. Coe (New York: Criterion Books, 1957), p. 13.

84. From a musicological viewpoint Hunt clearly follows the eighteenth-century tradition of placing a "disproportionate emphasis on extra-musical values" (Winston Dean, "Criticism," in *Grove's*).

85. In literature, too, Landré has praised Hunt's "extreme catholicity" of taste: he never praised one type of literature at the expense of another. Landré ascribes this characteristic to his "gluttony" for books ("Contribution," p. 139). But since it is an attribute that permeates Hunt's thinking, an explanation must also be sought in his personality and the influences that formed it.

86. Thornton Hunt, "Man of Letters," p. 92. For the influence on Hunt's prose style of such eighteenth-century writers as Addison, Steele, Goldsmith, Johnson, and the "Nonsense Club" and their *Connoisseur* (1754–1756), see Landré, II, 102 f., and Melvin R. Watson, "The *Spectator* Tradition and the Development of the Familiar Essay," *English Literary History,* XIII (1946), 189–205.

CHAPTER 3

1. An asterisk following the name of a playwright, composer, or singer indicates that further information is provided in appendix one, which also lists the reviews chronologically.

2. *The Narrative, of five years' expedition, against the revolted Negroes of Surinam* . . . (2 vols.; London: J. Johnson, 1796), by John Gabriel Stedman (1744–1797), influenced Coleridge, among others. Several Pizarros and Oroonokos—plays exploiting the exotic background of New World conquests —were popular from the later eighteenth century. Among the former, Sheridan's (1799) was the best; the last Oroonoko, by an unknown hand, was given at Surrey Theatre in 1813. Melodramas with West Indian settings were popular as early as Colman's *Inkel and Yarico* (1787), providing vehicles for "stage Negroes" decades in advance of American melodramas of this type that invaded England in the 1830's (Walter H. Rubsamen in "The Ballad Burlesques and Extravaganzas," *Musical Quarterly,* XXXVI [1950], 554). Hunt's humanitarian interests in the Negro began with his early poem "The Negro Boy"; in many "Examiners" he was outspoken in behalf of Negroes.

3. Nicoll (III, 207) calls this the best of the playwright's "somewhat ordinary productions."

4. Note Hunt's comments on Charles Incledon later in this chapter. In *Critical Essays* (London: John Hunt, 1808), p. 119, he praised John Johnstone,* the Irish comedian: "The air of confidential repose on his audience which he assumes during his excellent Irish songs, with his occasional semitonic whining, is peculiarly original and characteristic."

5. Although Bickerstaffe's indebtedness to Goldoni for other plays is indicated, Nicoll does not show a source for this play, which he regards as the playwright's best.

6. Joseph Miller (1684–1738), English comedian at DL and erroneously known as the author of *Joe Miller's Jests,* which John Mottley published in 1739.

7. Hazlitt, too, struck out against the transparent artificialities of the musical stage. Of Samuel Arnold's melodrama *The Unknown Guest* he observed that the work "is, we suppose, to be considered as a dramatic trifle: it is one of the longest and dullest trifles we almost ever remember to have sat out. . . . The dialogue bears no proportion in quantity to the songs; and chiefly serves as a vehicle to tack together a certain number of unmeaning lines, arranged for different voices, and set in our opinion to very indifferent music" (2 Apr. 1815).

8. Cf. Peacock, who called "modern" English musical poetry "astounding and impertinent nonsense—answering no purpose, if it happens to be heard, but to distract the attention from any degree of natural feeling and expression which may belong to the music or the voice" (*The Works of Thomas Love Peacock,* H. F. B. Brett-Smith and C. E. Jones, eds. [London: Constable and Co., Ltd., 1924–1934], IX [1926], 232).

9. *Examiner,* "Literary Notices," 3 Jan. 1819, p. 11, and 17 Jan. 1819, pp. 43–44. The next year Hunt observed that Moore had found a new composer (Bishop) worthy of him in his National Airs, No. 2 ("Literary Notices," 23 Jan. 1820, p. 105).

10. The sentimental novels of Mme. Cottin (née Risteau; 1770–1807) were popular in England. Her *Elizabeth* was published in Paris in 1806.

11. Reynolds, who obtained £ 600 for *The Exile* and was highly paid for his afterpieces, which were "easy to write," "had no conscience" toward the drama and turned easily from sentimental comedy to melodrama (Nicoll, IV, 25–72 *passim*).

12. *Bonifacio* . . . —see appendix one for full title. The "burlesque melodrama" was dubbed an "extravaganza" in the printed edition. For Hunt's full dissection of the piece see Lawrence H. and Carolyn W. Houtchens, eds., *Leigh Hunt's Dramatic Criticism, 1808–1831* (New York: Columbia University Press, 1949), pp. 10–14.

13. Shelley, more susceptible than Hunt to Gothic *frissons,* liked *Fazio,*

though in general he cared little for the English stage. See Peacock, *Works,* VIII (1934) 82. On *Fazio,* see n. 58 of this chapter. *Bertram* (1816), by Charles Robert Maturin. *Isabella,* altered from Southerne by Garrick (1757) and John Kemble (1814).

14. Probably Richard Cumberland, sentimentalist writer of comedies, tragedies, and melodramas, whose earlier works Hunt praised; see also n. 24.

15. O'Keefe was praised by Hazlitt as well as by Hunt for the "redeeming" moral value of his pieces, which was absent from the farces of contemporary writers. In his *Autobiography,* p. 158, Hunt referred to O'Keefe's "conscience" as a saving grace.

16. See *Correspondence* (II, 63 ff.) and his *A Jar of Honey from Mt. Hybla* (London: Smith Elder and Co., 1848), chapter eight.

17. Hunt's references to Storace are scant though usually commendatory. The *Quarterly Musical Magazine and Review* (1818), p. 205, thought him overrated and attributed the popularity of his stage music to his songs for tenor voice. At a DL revival of his *Ramah Droog* (1798) Hunt found the work trivial and the music (by Mazzinghi and Reeve) not much better (22 Dec. 1816).

18. Hazlitt also admired Shield's music (see *The Complete Works of William Hazlitt,* P. P. Howe, ed. [London: J. M. Dent and Sons, 1930–1934], II, 286), but in his only extended comment on him in the *Examiner* he offered ambivalent praise. *Your's or Mine?,* he wrote, "has nothing to recommend it. . . . What[,] not the music of Shield? We really do not know. It is very pretty pastoral music; but we seem to have heard it before, or something very like it. The airs are Irish or Scotch, or both. It is what the milkmaids sing under the hedges, or the ploughmen in the fields . . . but we had rather hear it in the open air, amidst the fragrance of the hawthorne . . . than at either of our Theatres" (29 Sept. 1816). In his more crotchety moods, Hazlitt wanted music out of the theatre and amidst nature, or preferred nature's music altogether! Shield introduced many folk songs or adaptations into his works. William Hogarth, in *Memoirs of the Musical Drama* (2 vols.; London: Richard Bentley, 1838), II, 441, said Shield was "perfectly English" and was considered equal to Arne.

19. For Burney's reaction to Purcell's unfortunate librettos, see below, n. 59. Addison attacked Rossi for his libretto for Handel's *Rinaldo,* though Burney found it unobjectionable. The reference to Geminiani is curious since he wrote no songs.

20. I can locate no reference to a collaboration between Shield and any of the Dibdins. Hunt may have had in mind O'Keefe, for whom Shield composed *Poor Soldier* (1783), among others.

21. By "shop," Hunt here presumably refers to music publishing; sales of printed music often provided an income exceeding the fee for the stage rights.

22. John Genest, in *Some Account of the English Stage* (10 vols.; Bath: T. Rodd, 1832), IX, 99–100, was, however, outraged: "This was Shakespeare's play degraded to an Opera—it was a wretched piece of business, but as it is not printed, it is impossible to point out the quantum of its demerits—In the Devil's name, why does not Reynolds turn his own plays into Operas?—does he think them so bad, that even with such music as he has put into *Twelfth Night,* they would not prove successful?—or has he such a fatherly affection for his own offspring that he cannot find it in his heart to mangle them?"

23. Cf. *Quarterly Musical,* 1818, pp. 209–11, which blamed the lapses of this "eclectic" musician on the songs: "Throughout our entire examination of Mr. B's voluminous works, we scarcely recollect the words of half a dozen songs that could ever have attracted the voluntary notice of an educated man." Yet the airs almost never sink to a level of insipidity. Hogarth (*Memoirs,* II, 453) felt that Bishop's fame rested on his earlier works; his composing for CG debased his style and "thus lowered the character of English music." On the other hand, Alfred Bunn in *The Stage: Both Before and Behind the Curtain* (3 vols.; London: Richard Bentley, 1840), III, 7, blamed Bishop's decline on his adaptations from Italian opera: "If he were but *himself,* the stuff is still *in* Bishop; but trying first to be Rossini, and after to be Weber, knocked it all *out* of him."

24. Modeled on his popular comedy *The Jew* (1794). Of the operatic version Hunt stated that the author's "pen still outlives his genius." Of a later Cumberland production Hunt remarked that his anticipations that the playwright could no longer write genuine comedy were not disappointed. He regretted, and called a disgrace to the "Administration," the fact that a man of genius should be reduced at his age to "expedients so mortifying" (10 June 1810). Cumberland gave high praise to *Critical Essays* in his review in *London Review,* No. III (1 Aug. 1809), pp. 1–21.

25. Cf. Hazlitt on Arnold's *The Unknown Guest,* music by Braham and Kelly: "The music of this opera professes to be by Mr. Kelly and Mr. Braham, except that of one song, which is modestly said to be—selected;—a title which we apprehend might be extended to the whole. We do not recollect a single movement in the airs composed by Mr. Kelly which was not familiar, even to vulgarity" (2 Apr. 1815).

26. A judgment he confirmed in *Autobiography,* pp. 123–24. But he found Kelly a poor singer. Kelly seldom performed during the *Examiner* years, but Hunt once referred to his singing in a duet with Braham as a "knife-grinder's wheel accompanying a flute" (14 Feb. 1808). He regarded him as no actor at all (22 Sept. 1816, pp. 602–3). Both Hogarth in *Memoirs,* II, 450, and Richard, Earl of Mount-Edgcumbe, in *Musical Reminiscences, containing an account of Italian opera in England, from 1773* (4th ed.; London: John Andrews, 1834), p. 74, concur in these evaluations.

27. At the "Vittoria Fete" in honor of Wellington all the newspapers with the exception of the *Examiner* were loud in its praise, while Hunt observed that Vauxhall was "a confined and comparatively mean place: . . . only a better sort of tea-garden, and which, in spite of the rank of those who occasionally visit it, inevitably conjures up ideas of vulgarity and debauchery" ("Political Examiner," 20 July 1813). The gardens were infamous for prostitution after mid eighteenth century, though their public entertainments were at least respectable before the nineteenth. See James G. Southworth, *Vauxhall Gardens: A Chapter in the Social History of London* (New York: Columbia University Press, 1941), pp. 77–111.

When John Fawcett commissioned an opera from Charles Dibdin in 1814, he wanted the author's name kept a secret, "as it was thought that if it were known to be the work of a Sadler's Wells dramatist it would prejudice the critics against it" (*Professional and Literary Memoirs of Charles Dibdin the Younger,* George Speaight, ed. [London: The Society for Theatre Research, 1956], p. 108).

28. Sears credits Hook with the melody and Robert Crawford (see n. 30 below) with the lyrics.

29. As late as 1776 the names of authors and composers were not among the ten items that commonly appeared in playbills and advertisements (*The London Stage: 1660–1800. Part 4: 1747–1776,* George W. Stone, Jr., ed. [3 vols.; Carbondale, Ill.: Southern Illinois University Press, 1962], I, lvi, lxxii). Cf. problems encountered by Nicoll (IV, 238) and others in attribution of printed plays, even with the Larpent listings. Hogarth (*Memoirs,* II, 425) states that so little value was attached to the opera libretto that "it is seldom thought worth while" to supply the author's name.

30. *Queen Mab,* produced by Henry Woodward (1714–1777), was a pasticcio, variously attributed to James Oswald (d. 1769?), a collector of Scottish tunes, to Rousseau, and to Burney *(Grove's).* Sears credits the air "Pray, Goody, Please to Moderate the Rancour of Your Tongue" to D. Maigh, words by Robert Crawford (d. 1733), who wrote several Scottish songs, knew Ramsay, and contributed to his *Tea-table Miscellany.* Desiree Charms and Paul F. Breed, *Songs in Collection: An Index* (Detroit, Mich.: Information Service, Inc., 1966) call "Pray, Goody" an old English air.

31. In a footnote to his review Hunt wrote, "We are happy, by the way, to inform our readers, that Robin is the hero of a work which has been taken in hand by a friend of ours, quite able, both from the sylvan turn of his genius and from an amiable philosophy, to do him justice." He was referring to Keats's poem "Robin Hood—To a Friend"; the friend was J. H. Reynolds, to whom Keats sent the poem in a letter (3 Feb. 1818) in which he declared that he would "have no more of Wordsworth or Hunt in particular." Keats in his illness had blown hot and cold about Hunt since the

preceding May, yet he, Reynolds, or another acquaintance had shown a copy of the poem to the editor.

32. Unidentified, unless this was Stuart Lewis (1756–1818), Scottish poet and "vender" of songs and ballads, some having "intrinsic merit" (D.N.B.).

33. Cf. Wordsworth's "Rob Roy's Grave" (1807), ll. 57–60:

> And thus among these rocks he lived,
> Through summer heat and winter snow:
> The Eagle, he was lord above,
> And Rob was lord below.

Peacock took note of these changes in an article (*London Review*, Apr., 1836) in which he praised the old English songs as models of simplicity and dispraised the newer ones (including Moore's) for their false representations; in this respect *Rob Roy* particularly offended (*Works*, IX [1926], 234–35). With his less fastidious taste Hunt found pleasing qualities in the "old" airs.

34. "The White Cockade," however, is an English folk song. "Roy's Wife O'Aldivalloch": music credited by Sears to Niel Gow (1727–1807) but probably only collected by him; words by Mrs. E. Grant. "Duncan Gray Cam Here to Woo": words by Burns to the Scottish folk air "Duncan Gray." "Lass of Patie's Mill": a seventeenth-century Scottish air, words by Allan Ramsay. "Auld Lang Syne": words partly rewritten by Burns (1794 version); the air was a popular song (probably originally a folk song), an early version of which appears in the overture to Shield's *Rosina*.

35. "Hope . . .": air by John Weldon; words by Bickerstaffe. "There Was a Jolly Miller Once," also known as "The Miller of the Dee": a seventeenth-century air.

36. The influence, if any, was rather the other way round. Arne had produced his first important work when Sacchini (1730–1786) was only three; he had completed all of his major productions before the Italian came to London (1772–1782). Arne did, however, tend to follow the newer Italian models in preference to the Handelian tradition; thus both composers were influenced by sentimental modes in opera for which the term *"amoroso"* is not inappropriate.

37. Cf. "Kiss Me Once, and Ease My Pain"—refrain from Dryden's *Rondelay*: "Chloe Found Amyntas Lying."

38. As Hunt points out later in his review, the song is Paesiello's air "La Rachelina" from *La Molinara*, "one of the sweetest in the whole circle of melody."

39. Barron Field, in one of his few *Examiner* reviews, remarked on the same quality in Elizabeth Edwin*: "Her enunciation . . . is rather too painfully distinct. She presses her consonants harder than they will bear" (22 Oct. 1809). Hunt also noted this trait in the singer (8 Jan. 1815).

40. In his *Autobiography* (p. 126) Hunt provides a remarkable commen-

tary on this quality, "which has been observed in Jews, and which is, perhaps, quite as much, or more, a habit in which they have been brought up than a consequence of organization. The same thing has been noticed in Americans; and it might not be difficult to trace it to moral, and even to monied causes; those, to wit, that induce people to retreat inwardly upon themselves; into a sense of their shrewdness and resources; and to clap their finger in self-congratulation upon the organ through which it pleases them occasionally to intimate as much to a bystander, not choosing to trust it wholly to the mouth." (Elsewhere [p. 66] Hunt recalled his dislike, shared by the Bluecoat boys, of the nasal tone that characterized the singing of the "charity" boys.) Whatever validity Hunt's generalization may have, it did not arise out of anti-Semitism. Indeed, as a young man he was impressed with the music of the synagogues and even attracted to the Jewish religion (Landré, I, 32; II, 29–30). In *Critical Essays* and the *Examiner* he was outspoken in defense of Jews.

41. The decline may have paralleled that of the English glee, a unique feature of which was the prominent part assigned to the high countertenor—"a particular development of falsetto singing which has persisted in our cathedral choirs," according to Ernest Walker, *A History of Music in England* (2nd ed.; London: Oxford University Press, 1924), p. 248.

42. Braham commanded the highest fees of any singer in England with the exception of Catalani, but he ultimately lost much of his wealth in theatrical speculations. See appendix one.

43. Singer unidentified. Several airs were omitted from her performance in *The Beggar's Opera* on 19 June 1817, owing to her limited vocal ability (see William Schultz, *Gay's Beggar's Opera: Its Content, History and Influence* [New Haven, Conn.: Yale University Press, 1923], p. 93).

44. As reprinted in *A View of the English Stage*, the quotation marks are removed from "The words." See Hazlitt's *Works*, V, 237, 409, where Howe provides the source: *Love's Labour's Lost*, V, ii, 941.

45. Herschel Baker, in *William Hazlitt* (Cambridge, Mass.: Belknap Press of Harvard University Press, 1962), p. 297, attributes the quoted statement to Hazlitt by implication. Was Hazlitt quoting himself? It was presumably Hazlitt who berated the CG managers for imposing Tom D'Urfey's "disgusting" song on Miss Stephens in this "delicate" part; see *Works*, XVII, 444.

46. Not his wife but his daughter, Sophia Giustina Corri (born in Edinburgh, 1775; died sometime after 1828). She played the piano and harp and was a composer as well as a singer.

47. One of Coleridge's eight "Characteristics of Shakespeare's Dramas" was the "interfusion of the lyrical—that which in its very essence is poetical—not only with the dramatic . . . but also in and through the dramatic. Songs in Shakespeare are introduced as songs only, just as songs are in real life,

beautifully as some of them are characteristic of the person who has sung or called for them, as Desdemona's 'Willow,' and Ophelia's wild snatches, and the sweet carollings in As You Like It" (quoted from *Prose of the Romantic Period,* Carl R. Woodring, ed. [Boston: Houghton Mifflin Company, 1961], pp. 122–25).

In the introduction to *Shakespeare's Dramatic Songs* (1815–1816) William Linley complained of the lack of attention paid to those parts of Shakespeare's plays "where the power of music has been called in to heighten the effect of the scene." But the original music, no doubt lost, "could not, in the present day, be so shaped as to be palatable to a refined musical ear" (quoted by D. S. Hoffman in "Some Shakespearian Music, 1660–1900," *Shakespeare Survey,* XVIII [1965], 98–100, who declares that not until 1871, in Arthur Sullivan's music for *The Tempest,* was a serious attempt made "to bring music back into the structure of Shakespearian art").

48. Hogarth (*Memoirs,* II, 435) mentions this problem as a continuing impediment to the improvement of English opera. In the CG *Figaro,* a character, Fiorillo, "quite unconnected with the plot," was introduced to sing the music of the Count, who could not sing. Hunt noted the "utter nothingness" in the voice of John Liston (1776?–1846), who played the Count. When Liston played Leporello in the revised *The Libertine,* Hazlitt observed, "He played it in a mixed style between a burlesque imitation of the Italian Opera, and his own *inimitable* manner. We like him best when he is his own great original, and copies only himself" (25 May 1817).

49. "For Tenderness Formed," a popular English version of "Io sono Lindoro" from Paesiello's *Il Barbiere di Siviglia.* For Hunt's comments on the English translations of Italian arias, see chapter four above.

50. Hunt also observed the "very formal and theatrical" acting of Horn (12 July 1818).

51. Hunt greatly admired Lamb's critical abilities, once commenting on his "nine, closely-written octavo pages" of criticism making way for an account of the new pieces by "an impudent rogue of a friend, whose most daring tricks and pretences carry as good a countenance with them as virtues in any other man, and who has the face above all to be a better critic than ourselves" (8 Aug. 1819).

52. Giovanni Antonio de Sacchis (c. 1484–1539), a Venetian fresco painter who assumed the name of Pordenone, among others. His decorations for Venetian palaces were in great demand.

53. The *British Stage* (1817), p. 3, echoed *Examiner* criticism in praising her vocal qualities but found her dramatic abilities not quite first rate.

54. In a *Beggar's Opera* performance the following month at HY, she added enough "feminine touches" to make her attire less unpalatable (30 July 1820). Colman's transvestite innovation spawned many imitations, growing respectability to the contrary notwithstanding!

55. St. Giles's fountain—in the heart of London slums.

56. Percy M. Young, in "Leigh Hunt—Music Critic," *Music and Letters,* XXV (1944) 89, has perceptively pointed out that Hunt "owed his critical faculty to the rare gift of knowing when seriousness was inapt. Thus he avoided the sententiousness of the earnest."

57. The next year Bishop did follow his wife to the theatre, when he composed Arnold's *Maniac*—with what paltry results Hunt observed. Bishop's wife was the former Miss Lyon, who sang at DL in 1807 and who married the composer about 1809. She took small parts in the *Circassian Bride* and *Maniac.* Hunt mentions her again only in his "Sketches," where he noted that her singing, "to our ears at least, is sharp and glassy" (12 Feb. 1815).

58. The play had a curious history. First acted at the Royal Circus (Dec., 1816) in an adaptation by Thomas Dibdin under the title *The Italian Wife,* the play was presented as *Fazio* at Bath (6 Jan. 1818), where Genest noted Milman's objections to the alterations, though they made the play "fit for representation" and assured its success, leading to the CG performance. "The Bath manager had a reprimand from the Lord Chamberlain's Office for acting *Fazio* without a license—he conceived, as it had been acted at some theatre, that it had been licensed—Cerberus received his sop, and all was well" (*English Stage,* VIII, 670). After the CG version, the play was again acted as *The Italian Wife* at OLY (Nov., 1817) in a version altered by an unknown hand.

59. Here as elsewhere Hunt appears to follow Charles Burney, *General History of Music,* Frank Mercer, ed. (4 vols.; New York: Dover Publications, 1957; first published 1776–1789). Burney declared (II, 380–90) that Purcell wrote in a dull and uninspired period and unluckily built his fame with "perishable materials" such that "his worth and works are daily diminishing." His music for the theatre used melody and instrumental coloring, giving it an "impassioned voice." Unfortunately, "Handel's superior knowledge and use of instruments, and more polished melody . . . will always turn the public scale." He concludes: "Exclusive admirers of modern symmetry and elegance may call Purcell's taste barbarous; yet in spite of superior cultivation and refinement, in spite of all the vicissitudes of fashion, through all his rudeness and barbarism, original genius, feeling, and passion, are, and ever will be, discovered in his works." Burney did not generally share the enthusiasm of his contemporary Sir John Hawkins for the older music. Unfortunately, Hawkins's *General History of the Science and Practice of Music* (New York: Dover Publications, 1963), also originally published in 1776, never achieved the popularity of Burney's work.

60. "Britons Strike Home," an old sea chantey according to Sears, was in any event not from *King Arthur* but from *Bonduca, or the British Heroine,*

adapted from Beaumont and Fletcher and composed by Purcell in the same year.

61. Likely the masque was either by Boyce or Arne, both of whom composed masques for the productions of *The Tempest* at CG and DL, respectively, in 1746, though Arne's was more popular in later times. On Shakespearean opera see Hoffman, "Shakespearian Music," p. 97.

62. Cf. the *Times's* review: "[The piece] shows that the beauty of . . . [Mozart's] music is perfectly independent of language, and that in any form it cannot but charm and captivate"! Though some of Bishop's music "suffers not a little by comparison with Mozart," lovers of music will like the piece (from Dennis Arundell, *The Critic at the Opera* [London: Ernest Benn Ltd., 1957], p. 301). The *British Stage,* Apr., 1819, p. 119, blamed the managers for Bishop's substitution of his own overture for Mozart's; but for preferring his own overture to Rossini's in the English *Barber* the *Quarterly Musical* blamed only the composer. Even Thomas Dibdin, of all people, complained in *Reminiscences* of Bishop's "helter-skelter" adaptations (see Edward J. Dent, *Foundations of English Opera* [Cambridge: The University Press, 1928], p. 88). Hogarth (*Memoirs,* II, 452–53, 456) sums up Bishop's influence: This "English Mozart" taught the public to admire the "highly wrought choruses and concerted pieces"; yet his Mozart adaptations were mutilated beyond recognition. The public was "captivated" by the melodies, and the composer thus created a demand, "prevailing ever since," of supplying the English stage with musical materials drawn from Continental productions. As a result, English musicians had withdrawn (1838) entirely from dramatic composition. In the present piece Bishop no doubt retained the Shield number, "Ah! Well-a-Day, My Poor Heart!" from the Holcroft production (see appendix one). Bishop also "refurbished" several English operas, including Burgoyne's *Lord of the Manor* (1812); *Lionel and Clarissa* (1814); *Artaxerxes* (1814); Garrick's *Cymon* (1815); and Milton's *Comus* (based on Dalton's adaptation of 1738). See Dent, *Foundations,* p. 87, and *Grove's.*

63. Reynolds continued to produce plays steadily (mainly for CG but occasionally for DL) until 1840. Cobb's effective production had ceased by 1803, though revivals of his works were frequent for years, as we have seen. Thomas Dibdin produced twenty works for CG or DL between 1809 and 1816.

64. Presumably no relative of Dr. Johnson's small critic, Dick Minim (*Idler,* No. 60, 9 June 1759); a minim is a half-note. Thomas Tallis (c. 1505–1585), English composer.

65. John Jackson (1769–1845), known as "Gentleman Jackson." The musician was of course Jackson of Exeter (1730–1803), a versatile but second-rate composer.

66. "Scots Wha Hae": words by Burns to the Scottish folk air, "Hey Tuttie Taitie, or Now the Day Dawis."

67. Baron John Somers (1651–1716), English statesman who presided at the framing of the Declaration of Rights (1688).

68. Thomas Morley (1557–1602), whose *Madrigals to Four Voices* (1594) was the first publication devoted exclusively to madrigals. Thomas Ravenscroft (c. 1590–c. 1633) wrote many rounds and catches in his *Melismata* (1611), of which one was perhaps used in early productions of *Twelfth Night* (II, iii). Both composers wrote religious and secular music. The latter was master of music at Christ's Hospital, where his music was doubtless still played in Hunt's time and where Hunt may have been a "young chorister."

69. Edward W. Naylor, in *Shakespeare and Music* (London: J. M. Dent and Sons, Ltd., 1931), p. 19, states: "Even a *public-house song* in Elizabeth's day was a cannon in three parts, a thing which could only be managed 'first time through' nowadays by the very first rank of professional singers."

70. Burney (*History*, II, 22–24) quotes Camden's *Annales, or the History of Elizabeth, late Queen of England* (trans. R. N. Gent, 1635): "[The Queen] was able to play on the lute prettily and sweetly," to which Burney adds: "If her Majesty was able to execute any of the pieces that are preserved in a MS. which goes under the name of *Queen Elizabeth's Virginal Book*, she must have been a very great player." Her abilities on the lute were also attested by Melville in his *Memoirs* (1660), according to Naylor, "Shakespeare," p. 10.

71. Hunt's interest in climate and esthetics is evident in his prospectus to the *Reflector*, I, vi–vii, where he cited Winckelmann's theory that the English have no taste for art owing to their climate. (Winckelmann's *Geschichte der Kunst des Altertums* [1764] was widely influential in suggesting the relation between the clear skies of Greece and her preeminence in the ancient arts.) Hunt asserted, "[Winckelmann] forgot that our poets have never been surpassed . . . and that Athens is situate beneath a fickle sky." Hunt admitted that a lucid climate predisposed the mind to art and that taste will be more "diffused" among warm countries. But an "intellectual nation" is the best milieu for the development of genius: "It is government—not easy or happy government in particular, but government of a disposition to patronize, or of a nature to rouse emulation, that has the greatest influence in these matters." He reluctantly admitted that the English had no great love of the arts, although that love was growing. By 1817 Italy appears to have won, for Hunt, a clear victory in painting and music—politics to the contrary notwithstanding. English poetry, meanwhile, continued to hold its misty ground. (See also the preface to "Rimini," *Poetical Works*, xxi.)

72. Hunt may have become acquainted with Kenney through the Lambs,

though probably not as early as this; in the review Hunt stated that his hopes for Kenney were "dashed" and that even the songs were dull.

73. It was most unusual for Italian opera singers to perform on the English stage, not only because of their poor English, but specifically because it violated the 1792 Opera Agreement (Ernest B. Watson, *Sheridan to Robertson: A Study of the Nineteenth-Century London Stage* [Cambridge, Mass.: Harvard University Press, 1926], p. 15). Exceptions were made for the Lenten oratorios and for the "benefits" of privileged performers. Griglietti, not a KT regular, has not been identified.

74. Some traces of chauvinism persisted long after. Note Hunt's reference to the "fickle sky" of Athens already cited. Even after his arrival in Italy he could observe, "My northern faculties were scandalized at seeing men [at the opera] in the pit with *fans*! Effeminacy is not always incompatible with courage, but it is a very dangerous help towards it; and I wondered what Doria would have said, had he seen a captain of one of his gallies [*sic*] indulging his cheeks in this manner" (*The Liberal*, I, 284). Yet in the same volume ("Letters from Abroad—Pisa," pp. 97–120) he could write, "An Italian annoys you neither with pride like an Englishman, nor with his vanity, like a Frenchman. He is quiet and natural, self-possessed . . . and ready for cheerfulness without grimace." As Carl Woodring states in his introduction to *Leigh Hunt's Political and Occasional Essays,* Lawrence H. and Carolyn W. Houtchens, eds. (New York: Columbia University Press, 1962), pp. 46–47, "When not on guard Hunt could appear as insular as a snail."

75. With respect to the lack of development of opera in England, Dent observes (*Foundations,* p. 2): "The answer lies simply in our national attitude toward music. To the Italian music is a means of self-expression, or rather of self-intensification; to the Englishman music is a thing apart, a message from another world. The Italian singer creates the music that he utters, or at least appears to create it; the English singer is a sensitive medium through which music is made audible. Music for the Italian is the exaggeration of personality—for the Englishman its annihilation."

76. Cf. Addison's *Spectator,* No. 29 (3 Apr. 1711), where he observes that the birds of England "learn to sweeten their Voices . . . by practicing under those that come from warmer Climates. In the same manner I would allow the *Italian* Opera to lend our *English* Musick as much as may grace and soften it, but never entirely to annihilate and destroy it. Let the Infusion be strong as you please, but still let the Subject Matter of it be *English*."

77. In his *Autobiography* (p. 43) Hunt praised Arne's songs and regarded him as a "real musical genius" though not "of the very first water." In a series of exchanges with the composer John Barnett that appeared in the *Tatler,* Hunt argued against Barnett's claims for the greatness of *Artaxerxes* and scoffed at his assertion that some of Bishop's music was worthy of

Mozart. For a summary of this interesting controversy, see Edward D. Mackerness's "Leigh Hunt's Musical Journalism," *Monthly Musical Record*, LXXXVI (1956), 217. When Hazlitt called *Artaxerxes* the "most beautiful opera in the world" in the *London Magazine* (June, 1820), p. 338, he was probably echoing received opinion. Walker (*History of Music*, pp. 215–16) states that *Artaxerxes*, thought by contemporary critics to be his masterpiece, is a very great disappointment. The great bulk of it is ordinary decorously stilted work; . . . Arne practically failed altogether when attempting anything on a large scale."

78. The *Quarterly Musical*, 1820, p. 377. At another revival Hazlitt rebuked Braham for omitting "some of the most exquisite airs" in *Artaxerxes* (*Works*, XVIII, 338–39). Braham also curtailed the recitative of the opera. Scattered references in the *Examiner* indicate, however, that at least some recitative was occasionally retained.

79. Cf. *Spectator*, No. 29 (3 Apr. 1711): "But however this *Italian* method of acting in *Recitativo* might appear at first hearing, I cannot but think it much more just than that which prevailed in our *English* Opera before this Innovation: The Transition from an Air to Recitative Musick being more natural than the passing from a Song to plain and ordinary Speaking. . . . Everyone who has been long in *Italy* knows very well, that the Cadences in the *Recitativo* bear a remote affinity to the Tone of their Voices in ordinary Conversation."

80. Curiously, Hunt names no other "older dramatist" whom he would suppress. In a commentary appended to an article by Barron Field in the *Reflector*, I (1811), 451–66, entitled "Is it justifiable to reprint the Pruriencíes of our Old Poets?" in which Field twice cited the "Theatrical Examiner" just mentioned, Hunt argued strongly for censorship, though among the dramatic poets he added the names of only Dryden and Massinger. On the other hand he praised Congreve and Farquhar in the *News*, and later he brought out his own edition of *The Dramatic Works of Wycherley, Congreve, Vanbrugh and Farquhar* (London: Edward Moxon, 1840).

81. Theodore Beza (1519–1605), a French Reformer and Calvinist theologian. Publication of his Latin amatory verses (*Juvenilia*, 1548) was later an embarrassment to him. Walter Map (or Mapes), c. 1140–c. 1210, archdeacon of Oxford, received preferment under Henry II. His *De nugis curialium* shows Map as a wit and a man of the world. Hunt translated one of his drinking songs, "The Jovial Priest's Confession" (*Examiner*, 13 June 1819).

82. One cannot ascertain just which of *The Beggar's Opera*'s Hunt may have seen. Late-eighteenth-century changes in the opera, for example, began with an introduction of Arne's song, "A-Hunting We Will Go," composed for the occasion (CG, 1777). Garrick followed with his own DL version that included "alterations in the symphonies" by Linley. Not to be outdone, Colman reversed the characters, Polly being sung by a male and Macheath

by a female, making the play "so absurd it was a popular oddity" (Schultz, *Beggar's Opera,* pp. 76–94). About 1785 Julian Marshall brought out an edition "as it is performed at both theatres" with "additional alterations and new basses by Doctor Arne" *(Grove's).* A "wretchedly distorted" two-act version was introduced at CG in 1813 by Harris and Bishop, which was brought out in succeeding seasons. Genest reports the opera was acted properly at DL on 28 Sept. 1815; but Hogarth (*Memoirs,* II, 436) reported that the Linley accompaniments were still in use (1838).

No full score of the work is extant, though much of it survives: see the third edition (1729) reproduced in *The Beggar's Opera,* Louis Kronenberger and Max Goberman, eds. (Larchmont, N.Y.: Argonaut Books, 1961). Pepusch, who is often credited with the music, was apparently called in at the last moment to compose an overture and write out musical accompaniments.

83. As Schultz says of this period (*Beggar's Opera,* p. 262), "Hardly an editor or publisher of the play at this time could resist his fancied obligation to take sides, no matter how far he missed the mark, on the question that had remained one of the real dramatic issues of the day." Hogarth (*Memoirs,* II, 55) regarded both the licentiousness of the play and the beauty of its music a "draw" but felt that the former quality would soon banish it from the stage.

84. Apparently similar feelings motivated his various attacks on Voltaire, Rabelais, Defoe, and Smollett for vulgarity, though he admired Fielding (Landré, II, 18 ff.). With respect to Swift and Pope, Hunt may have been influenced by Johnson's *Lives of the Poets* (1781), which strongly impressed the young critic (Landré, I, 41). Nevertheless, "without thinking of politics," he adopted the very name of his paper from the Tory journal that Swift had edited in 1710; and a motto attributed to Swift was displayed on the masthead until amended to "Pope" (26 Mar. 1815).

85. William Hazlitt, *Literary Remains of the late William Hazlitt,* E. L. Bulwer and Sergeant N. Talfourd, eds. (2 vols.; London: Saunders and Otley, 1836), I, cxiv.

86. Wilfrid Mellers, however, in *Music and Society* (New York: Roy Publishers, 1950), p. 140, states that the opera projects a middle-class view that patronizes the lower classes, jeers at the upper, and "has no understanding of what either stood for."

87. Though he had already published in the *Examiner* two sources that were substantially the same, Hunt cited, and quoted from, Hazlitt's *Lectures on the English Poets* (London, 1818), Lecture VI—no doubt an endeavor to promote his book.

88. Hunt even wrote two brief sketches, "Scenes and Songs in the new Beggar's Opera" (15 and 22 Oct. 1820), which, though trifling, show Hunt's "Macdeath" in the true humor of the opera. He reflected ideas similar to

Hazlitt's in his "Political Examiner" of 4 Jan. 1818, in which he stated that
pleasure is or should be a virtue and that virtue and vice are not so far
apart as had been thought.

89. Cf. Lamb's essay "Stage Illusion," in *Prose of the Romantic Period,*
Carl R. Woodring, ed., pp. 243–46, and Sylvan Barnet's analysis, "Lamb's
Contribution to the Theory of Dramatic Illusion," in *PMLA,* LXIX (Dec.,
1954), 1150–59.

90. Lamb's "On the Artificial Comedy of the Last Century" in *Prose of
the Romantic Period,* pp. 246–53.

91. The transvestite Don of this play was performed by Mrs. T. Gould
(Miss Burrell). Hazlitt, finding Mme. Vestris too feminine in *Giovanni in
London,* would have preferred Mrs. Gould in the role (*Works,* XVIII, 352).
"Shapes of a dream": Coleridge's "Religious Musings," l. 398.

92. Adapted from "We Be Three Poor Mariners," a seventeenth-century
English sea song.

93. Hunt's review of Moore's *Irish Melodies* ("Literary Notices," 17 Jan.
1819, pp. 43–44) was in part a defense of Moore against a charge of licentiousness brought by the *Quarterly Review,* "who would find Nature herself
ribald!" But Hunt had earlier alluded to this reputation of Moore's as a
"dangerous" habit that he had rid himself of.

94. Stevenson composed new music for O'Keefe's farces in 1781–1782 to
make possible their performances in Dublin! The first number of *National
Airs,* composed by Stevenson, was praised by the *Quarterly Musical,* 1818,
pp. 225, 228, for both words and music; but they noted a concluding Rus-
sian air that began note for note with a glee published by W. Knyvett.
"The co-incidence . . . is too great to have been the mere effect of similarity of thought." Whitaker (see appendix one) was hardly the "great
celebrity" Sir John claimed, though he was well known for his song arrangements and stage collaborations. He was neither as prolific nor as
popular as many others of this period. Though Hunt never mentioned
Whitaker in his reviews, he directed salvos at almost all of those with whom
the composer was associated.

95. Yes, when our lips move, yet have nothing to say,
   And our eyes in each other's warm beam fade away,
   'Tis then my heart springs up, and trembles to thee,
   As the arrow still trembles when fixed in the tree.
   Oh! never let ear rob a part of our blisses,
   Oh! all for the heart be our—Silent Kisses. [*Musical Copyright,* p. 10]

96. *Musical Copyright,* pp. 14–15, 19. This thirty-one-page pamphlet,
printed by G. Richards, London, is undated, but according to Landré it
was published in 1816. It contains a reprint of the court transcript and of
Hunt's commentary that had appeared in the *Examiner* the previous year.

97. Cf. Hunt's shifting views on Andrew Marvel: he charged the poet

with grossness in 1813; repeated the charge in 1820 but added that he was a sincere patriot; admitted in 1823 that his satire, sometimes coarse, was excusable owing to the age in which he lived; and still later praised his depth of spirit and patriotism (Landré, II, 170).

CHAPTER 4

1. Unless otherwise identified, dates following quotations of Robertson's "Opera Letters" or of "Theatrical Examiner" reviews identify the *Examiner* issue in which they appeared. An asterisk following the name of a composer, librettist, or singer indicates that further information is provided in appendix two, which also lists the reviews chronologically.

2. "Chronicles of the Italian Opera in England," *Harmonicon*, 1830, p. 73. Hereafter cited as "Chronicles."

3. George Hogarth, in *Memoirs of the Musical Drama* (2 vols.; Richard Bentley, 1838), II, 164, called this one of Catalani's most charming roles.

4. According to Hogarth (*Memoirs*, II, 379) one of Catalani's tricks was to overpower "the whole brazen instruments of the orchestra . . . [in which] she was always triumphant." Dennis Arundell in *The Critic at the Opera* (London: Ernest Benn Ltd., 1957), p. 293, states that Queen Charlotte wanted to put cotton wool in her ears when Catalani sang. Hunt recalled these contests with the orchestra in his *Autobiography*, p. 124.

5. The player was Carl Weichsel,* father of the "leader," Charles Weichsel. "Chronicles" reported (p. 112) that "the best oboist in Europe" was "turned out to make room for the worst" (Griesbach). Years later in his "Diary" Novello bitterly recalled the episode. He regarded Weichsel (who was only temporarily superseded) as "a perfect master of this generally disagreeable [difficult to play?] Instrument"—*A Mozart Pilgrimage, Being the Travel Diaries of Vincent and Mary Novello in the year 1829*, trans. and comp. by Nerina Medici di Marigano and ed. by Rosemary Hughes (London: Novello and Co., Ltd., 1955), p. 265.

6. These "attitudes" were apparently customary in the ballet and pantomime interludes. "Chronicles" states (p. 198) that Vestris's "attitudes might challenge even antique statues for their elegance." Cf. Keats's "Fair attitude" in his "Ode on a Grecian Urn."

7. Richard, Earl of Mount-Edgcumbe, in *Musical Reminiscences, containing an account of Italian opera in England, from 1773* (4th ed.; London: John Andrews, 1834), pp. 97–100, remarked on the uncommon quality of her voice, which was "capable of exertions almost supernatural"; however, "her excessive love of ornament [spoiled] every simple air. . . . She detested Mozart's music, which keeps the singer too much under the controul of the orchestra, and too strictly confined to time, which she is apt to violate." And Hogarth (*Memoirs*, II, 243) observed that Mozart's music rejects tampering with by the singers. "An expressive appoggiatura—a delicate and

sparing use of the *tempo rubato*—a glide—a slight anticipation of the following note—a few graceful notes introduced in a cadence,—these are all the liberties that a singer of taste and judgment will ever think of taking with the text of these melodies: Their simple beauty rejects the aid of Italian ornament."

8. Mme. Dussek made a mockery as Aeneas in Paesiello's *La Didone* (31 Jan. 1808). Mme. Collini exhibited a rich voice on the occasion of her debut in *La Capricciosa Pentita* by Fioravanti (15 Jan. 1809), then went unnoticed until 1811. Mme. Pucitta had a sweet though weak voice at the KT première of her husband's *I Villeggiatori Bizzarri*, which Robertson found pleasing but without much novelty (5 Feb. 1809); and a Mme. Bussoni was disappointing in her debut in *La Serva Raggiratrice* by Guglielmi *le fils* (21 May 1809). None of these singers lasted more than a very few seasons.

9. After an account of the singer on the English stage, this judgment sounds strange; as Mount-Edgcumbe explains, "The fact is, that [Braham] can be two distinct singers, according to the audience before whom he performs, and that to gain applause he condescends to sing as ill at the play-house as he has done well at the opera" (*Reminiscences,* p. 95).

10. Presumably the same librettist who helped to rewrite Mozart's *Tito* for its London première; see opera listing in appendix two.

11. "Chronicles" (pp. 72–73) admired Catalani's acting in the opera in 1807 but added: "[She] astonished all ears, by running, for the first time within the memory of opera-going man, the chromatic scale up and down. This achievement sealed her reputation. . . . Rounds of applause rewarded the daring exhibition of bad taste."

12. Hogarth (*Memoirs,* II, 152) reports that Sarti was still very popular (1838), but he regarded him as much inferior to the "now forgotten" Sacchini and to Paesiello. "Chronicles" (p. 12) called Nasolini a not very good imitator of Cimarosa.

13. Hogarth (*Memoirs,* II, 165–67) regarded him as a finer composer than Paesiello, *Gl'Orazj* as the finest of his serious operas, and *Il Matrimonio Segreto* as his *chef d'oeuvre.*

14. *Annals* does not cite a single performance of a Haydn opera in England before the twentieth century, although several, particularly *Orlando Paladino* (1782), were popular on the Continent in the 1770's and 1780's. *L'Anima del Filosofo,* written for London on the composer's first visit there, was not performed; selections from his operas were presented by the newly organized "Opera Concerts" at KT on his second visit. See Rosemary Hughes, *Haydn in London* (London: J. M. Dent and Sons, Ltd., 1950), p. 92.

15. Robertson declared that the singer returned "with improved [vocal] powers"; but his lack of further comment in later reviews suggests that he may have changed his mind. See appendix two.

16. On another occasion (25 Feb. 1809) Robertson condemned Venua (otherwise unidentified) for patching up his music with borrowings from Beethoven and Haydn. With respect to French adaptations to the English stage, Michael Kelly in *Reminiscences* . . . (2nd. ed.; London: Henry Colburn, 1826), pp. 178–202, explains that though the original French music was very good, it was "not calculated for an English audience; I therefore recomposed the whole of the music for them." And he adds that Grétry's music is beautiful "although not sufficiently effective for the English taste; which, in the musical way, requires more Cayenne than that of any other nation in the world."

17. In union with words, music takes a higher place, though "inferior to poetry in the abstract," Hunt wrote in *Table Talk* (London: Smith, Elder and Co., 1882), p. 165. "For when music is singing, the finest part of our senses takes the place of the more definite intellect, and nothing surely can surpass the power of an affecting and enchanting air. . . . On this account, I can well understand a startling saying attributed to the great Mozart; that he did not care for having good words to his music. He wanted only the *names* (as it were) of the passions. His own poetry supplied the rest."

18. Mount-Edgcumbe (*Reminiscences,* p. 104) supports this view, but Hogarth (*Memoirs,* II, 324) remembers her voice as not up to the role. "Chronicles" (p. 114) tells us that the production was not the best that the house could afford and that Bertinotti omitted two airs, substituting one from *Figaro* ("Porgi amor") and another from Dorabella's part in *Così.* "The Italian influence struggled in vain to support the unmeaning prettinesses and easy nothings, with which the town had so long, perforce, been satisfied; but it was contending against the stream: Mozart had been heard; and the public demanded to hear more of him."

19. That Bertinotti was chiefly responsible for the production is supported by "Chronicles" (p. 113): Bertinotti "can hardly be blamed for patronizing her own husband's opera; but, had her musical sins been as red as scarlet, she would have atoned for all by affording the English public, at her benefit, the first opportunity of hearing a comic opera of Mozart." Alfred Einstein in *Essays on Music* (New York: W. W. Norton and Co., Inc., 1956), p. 207, mistakenly *separates* Signora Radicati from Mme. Bertinotti.

20. "Chronicles" (p. 114) states that both the glory and the faults of the production belonged to Naldi. The opera required singers that "Naldi could not command, a chorus such as had never been heard within the walls of the King's Theatre, and a judgment which he did not possess." Hogarth (*Memoirs,* II, 375) claimed that the audience seemed neither to understand nor relish the opera. It was repeated only once more that season, for the benefit of Collini. (Arundell [*Critic,* p. 286] reports that a performance of this opera, probably abbreviated, took place at the Sans Souci theatre on

18 June 1806. For a time this theatre was the home of German drama; a German company of child actors was there early in the century [Nicoll, IV].)

21. Edward J. Dent, in *Mozart's Operas: A Critical Study* (London: Chatto and Windus, 1913), p. 394, states: "It is only natural that Mozart's most completely German opera should have been less popular in other countries than its Italian predecessors. . . . 'Die Zauberflöte' pleased German audiences for the less dignified of its national characteristics, and the audiences of other countries voted it nonsense. . . . We can hardly wonder when we read the stock Italian translation, and note the horrible mutilations which it imposed upon the music."

22. See appendix two regarding the London première of *Tito* and its aftereffects.

23. "Such was now the taste for the music of Mozart," wrote Hogarth (*Memoirs*, II, 375), "that . . . Catalani herself was constrained to give way to it." She sang well in *Tito* and *Figaro*; but the tenor Tramezzani took the part of Sesto, written for a mezzo, "unquestionably to the detriment of the music." "Chronicles" (p. 115) records, however, that the tenor sang his part well and played it better, "while Catalani was, perhaps, the best Vitellia we have ever seen or heard."

24. Myles B. Foster in *History of the Philharmonic Society of London, 1813–1912* (London: John Love, 1912), p. 3, credits Ayrton for "one or two benefit performances" of *Così* and *Flauto Magico* in 1811 and 1812. The same information is given by Max Graf in *Composer and Critic: Two Hundred Years of Musical Criticism* (New York: W. W. Norton and Co., Inc., 1946) and by Edward F. Rimbault in "Ayrton" *(Grove's)*. Just how Ayrton, who then had no official connection with KT, may have assisted, is not mentioned. The author of "Chronicles," who wrote for Ayrton's publication, does not mention his connection with any of these performances.

25. "Chronicles" (p. 113) informs us that a group of amateurs performed *Don Giovanni,* followed by *Tito* and *Figaro*—all presumably before 1811. The anonymous author of "Autobiography of an Amateur Singer," *Harmonicon*, II (1831), 106–7, 135–37, who sang the Commendatore in *Don Giovanni* and whose German friend brought the score over from Germany, tells us that the operas were enacted "oratorio fashion" in a floor-cloth factory loaned by a Mr. Hayward. The group, half professional and half amateur, had no "paying only" members: each had to furnish some money as well as some service. Apparently a few years before this time Hunt heard *Figaro* played by another group—"a party of amateurs at the Crown & Anchor"—an inn with large public rooms used for concerts and the like. Stendhal took note of "certain distinguished dilettanti who, although few in number, will always manage in the end to determine public opinion in the arts" due to their sincerity and insistence on their considered verdict ([Henri Beyle], *Life of Rossini*, trans. by Richard N. Coe [New York: Cri-

terion Books, 1957], p. 36). In his *Foundations of English Opera* (Cambridge: The University Press, 1928), p. 78, Edward J. Dent declares: "English music has at all times been particularly indebted to the energy of amateurs."

26. Beaumarchais' comedy was of course *Le Mariage de Figaro*. Holcroft's copy of the play (see appendix one) was entitled *Follies of the Day* (1784), the source for Bishop's *Figaro*. None of the recent revivals of the Holcroft play shows the title after this curious French form.

27. "Chronicles" (p. 338) reports that, as the Countess, Catalani appropriated the aria "Voi che sapete" from her Page. The aria was also sung by Susanna in later performances; not until 1822 was it restored to Cherubino. Tramezzani unaccountably refused the part of Almaviva, considering it beneath his dignity to appear in a comic opera (Hogarth, *Memoirs*, II, 375); yet he had already appeared in *Così!*

28. "Chronicles" (p. 115) states that the singer was popular only with "those amateurs who forgot, in his perfect knowledge of the proper style of singing Mozart's music, a voice which, though extremely deep, was husky and hoarse-toned."

29. For these newspaper reviews I am indebted to Arundell, *Critic*, pp. 284–94.

30. Cf. the usually intelligible *Quarterly Musical Magazine and Review*, 1818, p. 170: "Mara, Billington, and Catalani, are never spoken of by persons of judgment and feeling, but in the language of veneration and enthusiasm."

31. According to other sources, the riot ensued when Catalani, her salary being in arrears, refused to appear in the advertised *L'Eroina di Raab*, and *La Caccia d'Enrico IV* was substituted. Hogarth (*Memoirs*, II, 378) reported that Catalani's audience continued to fall off, for styles had changed and "Pucitta and Portogallo would no longer do." See also Kelly, *Reminiscences*, p. 366.

32. Probably the London première of Orlandi's *La Dama Soldato*, in which Frelendis made her debut on 13 May and which was repeated several times that season, including 22, 26, and 29 June.

33. According to *The History of "The Times,"* Vol. I: *The Thunderer in the Making, 1785–1841* (New York: The Macmillan Co., 1935), I, 191, Barnes's Parliamentary criticism was better than the best of his "Theatrical Examiners." Edmund Blunden in *Leigh Hunt's "Examiner" Examined* (London: Cobden-Sanderson Ltd., 1928), pp. 36, 43, joins others in praising Barnes's "Political Sketches" but also cites his "remarkable journalism" in the "Theatrical Examiners." Perhaps Barnes was better when criticizing "straight" drama. *The History of "The Times"* (I, 191) goes on to claim that "the *Examiner* lived through the year 1813, largely by the personal loyalty of Barnes and Lamb." If Hunt had not continued to write his

columns from behind bars, his readers would have had scant fare indeed. In his prospectus at the end of 1814, Hunt apologized to them for neglect of the theatrical criticisms. Moreover, the claim made by Derek Hudson in *Thomas Barnes of "The Times"* (London: Cambridge University Press, 1944), p. 140, in behalf of Barnes's independent judgment on the basis of his contempt for most of the Italian singers and of his admiration for the "scientific" singing of Miss Stephens lacks critical relevance.

34. It should be noted that the seasons from 1813 through 1815 were remarkably dull, and Mount-Edgcumbe called 1815 an "operatic blank." Probably they were no worse than 1809 and 1810, however. Cf. "Chronicles," passim.

35. Herschel Baker, *William Hazlitt* (Cambridge, Mass.: Belknap Press of Harvard University Press, 1962), p. 297.

36. 14 Aug. 1814; see *The Complete Works of William Hazlitt*, P. P. Howe, ed. (21 vols.; London: J. M. Dent and Sons, 1930–1934), V, 196–98.

37. England, however, was somewhat behind the Continent in recognizing Mozart's genius. *Don Giovanni*, in particular, whose full score was published in 1801, gained early popularity. Nevertheless, in 1852 Hector Berlioz (*Evenings in the Orchestra*, trans. by C. R. Fortescue [Baltimore, Md.: Penguin Books, 1963], p. 129) wrote: "Ten or fifteen years . . . [after Mozart's death], the Paris Opéra felt bound to put on *Don Giovanni* and *The Magic Flute*; but it presented them mutilated, sullied, disfigured, transformed into vile pastiches by wretches whose names should be anathema." And if Vincent Novello's diary is to be trusted, Viennese performances in the 1820's were little better: Mozart's sister reportedly told him that she could not bear the poor performances, which were scarcely recognizable to her (*A Mozart Pilgrimage*, pp. 52, 102, 267, and 272).

38. These inherited attitudes are of course modified by Hazlitt's personal and Romantic adumbrations. For a concise analysis of his esthetics see Walter Jackson Bate, ed., *Criticism: The Major Texts* (New York: Harcourt, Brace and World, 1952), pp. 281–92.

39. Erich Hertzmann, in "Mozart's Creative Process," *The Creative World of Mozart*, Paul Henry Lang, ed. (New York: W. W. Norton and Co., Inc., 1963), p. 30, states: "What the majority of contemporary listeners found in Mozart, they could have found in a great many other composers. The profound depth of his music, the intensity of its emotional content, as well as its wonderful craftsmanship, had to escape an audience whose ears could not perceive anything beyond the sensuous sound, the beauty of melody and harmony."

40. Coe, trans., *Rossini*, p. 361. See also Hogarth, *Memoirs*, II, 381. "Chronicles" (p. 247) states that Pasta "made no impression then [1816–1817] on the public, though some few persons saw in her the germ of future excellence."

41. Although Talfourd was not thinking of his friend's criticism, he did point out instances when "the *personal* has prevailed over the *abstract* in the mind of the thinker; his else clear intellectual vision has been obscured by the intervention of his own recollections, loves, resentments, or fancies" (*Literary Remains of the late William Hazlitt*, E. L. Bulwer and Sergeant Talfourd, eds. (2 vols.; London: Saunders and Otley, 1836), I, cxxi–cxxii). Alvin Whitley is not the only modern critic who goes too far in declaring that the sincerity and integrity in all Hazlitt's work "cannot be questioned" ("Hazlitt and the Theatre," *Studies in English, The University of Texas,* XXXIV [1955], 71).

42. His study of Italian, begun in 1805 in company with Barnes, was intensified during his two years in jail, where he also worked on *Rimini*. He apparently attended KT with some regularity beginning in 1815; there is no positive evidence that he attended the opera before then.

43. Paesiello's *Nina* was first given in London in 1797; there were apparently no revivals until 1825. Mozart's *Idomeneo* (Munich, 1781) did not receive its London première until 1938, when it was performed in English; some of the music for the opera was adopted for M. R. Lacy's *The Casket* (DL, 1829). *Die Entführung aus dem Serail* (Vienna, 1782) was presented as *The Seraglio* (CG, 1827) in an adaptation by William Dimond with additional music by J. B. Cramer! (For an interesting account of this production see Einstein, *Essays,* chap. fifteen.) After hearing the overture and a quartet from the opera at the "oratorio," Hunt presumed that it was early Mozart, for he recognized little genius in the pieces (12 Mar. 1820). Gluck had not been performed in London since 1801 (*Alceste*); his *Orfeo* was produced in English (CG, 1792) with additional music by Handel, J. C. Bach, Sacchini, Weichsel, and Reeve! Winter, whom Hogarth (*Memoirs,* II, 361) called without a rival in Germany after the death of Mozart, was very popular in England early in the century. His *Zaira* was revived as late as 1816, and his *Proserpina,* in which Vestris made her debut, had several productions in 1815 (they were not reviewed in the *Examiner*). If Hunt had not seen the latter at that time, he was perhaps recalling its last performance in 1806.

44. But Hunt was not prepared to subsidize music. In *Leigh Hunt's London Journal* (2 vols.; London: Charles Knight, 1835), II (4 Mar. 1835), 67, he wrote: "Music is a luxury, not a necessity: at least it is so thought; it goes, at all events, upon the principle of attraction, and if it cannot attract money out of pockets, as well as a cheaper attention, we know not that a moral ground of complaint lies against the non-payers. The desideratum is to refine their tastes." This was in response to a correspondent who had cited examples of impoverished musicians living in a society that tried to obtain free concerts only to spend money on trifles.

45. Cf. Peacock's statement in *The Works of Thomas Love Peacock,* H. F. B. Brett-Smith and C. E. Jones, eds. (10 vols.; London: Constable

and Co., Ltd., 1924–1934), IX, 225, that the object of Italian opera is "above all, or rather the crown of all, expression—expression—expression: the one all-pervading and paramount quality, without which dramatic music is but as a tinkling cymbal."

46. On "Paesiello" in *Table Talk*, pp. 184–85, Hunt wrote: "They who wish to know how far a few single notes can go in reaching the depths of the heart, should hear the song of poor Nina, 'Il mio ben' in the opera of 'Nina.' . . . I admire the rich accompaniments of the Germans; but more accompaniments than the author has given the singer would be like hanging an embroidered robe on the shoulders of Ophelia." Cf. Hogarth's comments on the composer (*Memoirs*, II, 164): "His scores are now called thin, but it may well be questioned whether the change of taste, which has led this to be considered a fault, is favourable to dramatic music." Stendhal expressed similar views. In his *The lives of Haydn and Mozart, with observations on Metastasio* . . . [M. Bombet, pseud.], trans. by the Reverend C. Berry and R. Berwin (2nd ed.; London: J. Murray, 1818), pp. 126–64, he admired Paesiello's "grace" and "easy comprehension"; he believed that a fine air "should stand up even stripped of its accompaniments"; and he declared that German music generally "is spoiled by the frequency of modulation, and the richness of the chords. This nation is fond of learning in every thing, and would unquestionably have a better music . . . if its young men were less attached to science, and rather fonder of pleasure." Though Stendhal borrowed extensively for his work (1st ed., Paris, 1814), there is every reason to believe these are his views. On the borrowings, see the preface by Romain Rolland to Beyle's *Vies de Haydn, de Mozart, et de Métastase*, Daniel Muller, ed. (Paris, 1914). Rolland states that as late as May, 1820, London still did not know that Bombet was Stendhal; one of the compilers of the D.N.B. *still* did not know.

47. Cf. Stendhal: "It is my considered opinion that music can only appeal to the spirit of man by conjuring up a pattern of imaginative imagery, which in some ways corresponds to the passions by which the listener is already swayed. It will therefore be evident that music, indirectly perhaps, but none the less inevitably, will reflect the political structure of its country of origin, since the individual listener is himself determined by the political atmosphere in which he exists" (Coe, trans., *Rossini*, p. 9).

48. From *La Gazza Ladra* (London, 1821); see text above.

49. Hogarth (*Memoirs*, II, 167–68) called this opera "not to be equalled even by the productions of Mozart." It has rich and brilliant accompaniments, although the "brazen instruments" are removed from the orchestra. Hunt reconsidered his views in the *Tatler* (28 Feb. 1831), where he called it the best comic opera since Mozart. Stendhal had particular affection for the work. Donald Jay Grout in *A Short History of Opera* (New York: Colum-

bia University Press, 1947), pp. 253–54, finds the work comparable to Mozart's for its "tunefulness and spontaneity."

50. Pompeo Batoni (1708–1787), Italian painter, whose work is characterized by a cold Neoclassicism. Saverio Bettinelli (1718–1808), Italian poet and critic, aroused opposition by his attacks on the style and structure of Dante's *Divine Comedy*.

51. Cf. Hunt's *Musical Evenings*, David R. Cheney, ed. (Columbia, Mo.: University of Missouri Press, 1964), pp. 42–43.

52. Edmund Smith's only tragedy (1709), for which Addison wrote a prologue attacking Italian opera, had a reputation in the eighteenth century as a "typical failure."

53. Cf. Augustus William Schlegel, *A Course of Lectures on Dramatic Arts and Literature*, trans. John Black (London: Henry G. Bohn, 1846), p. 219: "I have heard a celebrated Italian poet assert that his countrymen were moved to tears by Metastasio. We cannot get over such a national testimony as this, except by throwing it back on the nation itself as a symptom of its own moral temperament." Metastasio, he concludes, has "an unsparing pomp of noble sentiments, but withal most strangely associated with atrocious baseness."

54. Vittorio Alfieri (1749–1803), Italian poet and author of tragedies. Stendhal (*Haydn and Mozart*, pp. 442–45) considered that Metastasio was superior to Alfieri and was one of the great masters of Italian literature because of his clarity and precision.

55. Cf. Mme. de Staël's remarks in *Considérations sur les principaux événements de la révolution française* (3rd ed.; Paris: Delaunay, 1820), pp. 274–75: "Dans aucun pays du monde, la réserve et la taciturnité n'ont, je crois, jamais été portées aussi loin que dans quelques sociétés de l'Angleterre; et, si l'on tombe dans ces cercles, on s'explique très-bien comment le dégoût de la vie peut saisir ceux qui s'y trouvent enchaînés." Cf. also Stendhal's remarks (Coe, trans., *Rossini*, p. 453): "The Englishman's most striking characteristic is his shyness. . . . It is dangerous to *expose oneself* [in English]; and this fear of ridicule, which inhibits every young Englishman, compels him to preserve the strictest silence concerning his emotions. But this very reticence, itself answering the exactions of a spirit of proper pride, lends itself to the encouragement of music; music is his only confidant; yet to music he will often entrust the secrets of his most intimate and personal feelings."

56. Hunt mentioned Mozart in a letter to Novello from Italy, slightly modified for publication as "Letters from Abroad, Letter III" in the *Liberal*, II (1823), 47–51: "But I will tell you one thing, which, albeit you are of Italian origin, will mortify you to hear; viz. that Mozart is nothing in Italy, and Rossini every thing." Mozart is hissed at Florence and his name "suppressed by agreement." Explaining the Italian distaste for "that richness of

accompaniment, with which the Germans follow up their vocal music, he states that the Italians further dislike Mozart because he was a German by birth. "The Germans in Italy, the lorders over Italian freedom and the Italian soil, trumpet his superiority over Italian composers" and not even Mozart's nonchalance toward kings could reconcile them. Footnoting this point, Hunt cites Stendhal's *Haydn and Mozart* (see pp. 388–89) and its review in the *Quarterly Review* for the episode about Emperor Joseph II, who on first hearing *The Abduction from the Seraglio* told Mozart: "This is too fine for my ears; there are too many notes." "I beg your Majesty's pardon," replied Mozart, "there are just as many as are necessary." Mozart, Hunt continues, provides an example to German "men of talent, who do not blush to fall in with all the nonsense of the Allied Sovereigns. How delightful would it be, for instance, if . . . the Emperor [Metternich) should say, . . . 'My dear Gentz, this is too free for my notions: there are too many popular provisions,' for M. Gentz to answer, 'I beg your Majesty's pardon: there are just as many as are necessary.' " Hunt's commentary is replete with irony. Friedrich Gentz, Metternich's secretary at all the congresses, was the brain of the Holy Alliance, as Hunt, who had bitterly condemned the Congress of Vienna, well knew.

Early in the century Mozart was scarcely known in Italy, partly owing to the difficulty of performing his works. As late as 1835 Peacock (*Works*, IX, 338) could write: "Mozart has never been relished in Italy, where the antinational use which factious pedantry has made of his name has caused him to be looked on as a sort of national enemy."

57. Hogarth (*Memoirs*, II, 260) called the opera "as dramatic as it is beautiful" and deplored its neglect in performance. Yet after 1811 it had a sustained popularity with the public.

58. At a performance of the opera the same season, Shelley remarked to Peacock that Ambrogetti was "the very wretch he personates" (Peacock, *Works*, VIII, 81).

59. See *Musical Evenings*, pp. 24–25, where Hunt for this reason avoided a "translation" of the song but "aspired to give something a little more approaching to the sentiment of the music." Da Ponte's* Italian is typically sparse and direct; Hunt imparts an elegance to his song that is closer to the elevated tone of Mozart's music without departing from the literal meaning. In the "Round Table" for 15 Sept. 1816, p. 587, he had commented on the serenade: "You feel that the sounds must inevitably draw his mistress to the window. Their intenseness even renders them pathetic; and his [the Don's] heart seems in earnest, because his senses are." Although Einstein in *Mozart: His Character, His Work,* trans. by Arthur Mendel and Nathan Broder (London: Oxford University Press, 1945), p. 440, has pointed to the dramatic weakness of this scene, he states that "Mozart was not afraid of . . . [these inconsistencies]. At such moments the proceedings on the stage lose

their air of reality and become mere play-acting." Referring to the trio that precedes the serenade and that he links with it, Patrick Hughes in *Famous Mozart Operas* (New York: The Citadel Press, 1958), pp. 113–14, writes: "The dramatic situation itself does not deserve music of such an absorbing and overwhelming character, for the dramatic situation, after all, is flippant, comic, and not to be taken seriously unless we wish to charge both da Ponte and Mozart with an almost unforgivable lapse of taste."

60. E. T. A. Hoffman's "A Tale of Don Juan," in *Tales of Fantasy* (1813), reprinted in *Pleasures of Music,* Jacques Barzun, ed. (New York: Viking Press, 1951), is one of the earliest exploitations of the view that the Don is a heroic, even tragic, figure. Byronism, if not *Don Juan* (unrelated to the traditional story), may have contributed to this view (see below, n. 66).

61. Two years later Hazlitt did not think it so idle. "I fancied," he wrote in "Thoughts on Taste," *Edinburgh Magazine,* Oct., 1818 (*Works,* XVII, 62), "that I had a triumph some time ago, over a critic and connoisseur of music, who thought little of the minuet in Don Giovanni; but the same person redeemed his pretensions to musical taste in my opinion by saying of some passage in Mozart, 'This is a soliloquy equal to any in Hamlet.' "

62. Dent (*Mozart's Operas,* p. 275) calls this "the one scene in the opera in which it is admissible to aim at a certain effect of mystery."

63. David L. Jones in "Hazlitt and Leigh Hunt at the Opera House," *Symposium,* XVI (1962), 5–16, makes some interesting observations, particularly with respect to the discrepancies between Hazlitt's "theory" and "practice" in his opera criticism. But he draws some erroneous conclusions regarding the criticism of *Don Giovanni* by Hunt and Hazlitt; namely, that in his amplification of 17 Aug. 1817 Hunt "modified" his review of 3 Aug. 1817; that Hazlitt took note of Mozart's lack of dramatic unity in the review cited above; and that Hunt and Hazlitt both agreed on the effect of the Commendatore in the opera.

64. We have already noted Peacock's reference to the problems of critical judgments with respect to garbled and mutilated productions. He frequently attacked the introduction of stage devils at the close of this opera, and he noted that "for the first time in memory" (1832) the opera concluded as it should, with no dance of devils (*Works,* I, 404, 432). Some of these effects probably filtered into KT from the English stage, as in the case of the revised *The Libertine,* where Hazlitt approved the Don's final consumption in "a lake of burning brimstone on a splendid car brought to receive him by the Devil, in the likeness of a great dragon, writhing round and round upon a wheel of fire—an exquisite device of the Managers, superadded to the original story, and in striking harmony with Mozart's music!" (25 May 1817). Cf. also Kelly's remarks (*Reminiscences,* p. 127) on the earlier *Castle Spectre*: "The sinking of the Ghost in a flame of fire, and the beauty of the whole scene, had a most sublime effect." Other problems were pre-

sented by different versions of the opera (see Dent, *Mozart's Operas,* pp. 193 ff.). The *Times* critic wrote (15 Apr. 1817) that the musicians and servants remained on stage all during the address by the "spectre," whereas "it is logical they should fly; these errors were corrected the second performance" (Arundell, *Critic,* pp. 296–97). Hogarth (*Memoirs,* II, 248) noted that "though, in the piece as written, [the dramatis personae] are assembled on the stage at the conclusion, yet, in performance, it is not found worth while to introduce them again," and he regretted that such lovely melodies were given to the "low buffoneries" of the stage. Dent comments in *Mozart's Operas,* pp. 258–76 passim, that the last scene, from the point where Leporello returns having seen the statue, "is a strange mixture of tragedy and farce." Leporello's description of the statue's arrival is "frankly comic"; it is important, therefore, to treat the appearance of the statue "in a fairly matter-of-fact style."

65. Hertzmann, in "Mozart's Creative Process," p. 29, states: "Throughout his life Mozart adhered to the esthetic doctrines of Rococo art. He expressed this eloquently in his well-known letter to his father of September 26, 1781: 'Passions, whether violent or not, must never be expressed in such a way as to excite disgust; and music, even in the most terrible situations, must never offend the ear, but must please the hearer, or in other words, must never cease to be music.' "

66. The serious intent behind Mozart's opera is reflected in its full title, *Il dissoluto punito; ossia Il Don Giovanni,* as well as in its original designation of "dramma giocoso"—a drama (or melodrama) with comic elements. Mozart may well have seen "Faustian" traits in the figure, though according to Oscar Mandel, ed., *The Theatre of Don Juan: A Collection of Plays and Views, 1630–1963* (Lincoln, Nebr.: University of Nebraska Press, 1963), p. 17, in the literary tradition that runs through da Ponte the Don is not primarily a rebel but a sensualist. Thus, some conflict in interpretation seems evident in the opera's conception, and da Ponte stated that Mozart wished to treat the subject seriously—"too much in the manner of *opera seria*" (Dent, *Mozart's Operas,* p. 217). The comic and tragic elements in the opera have led to conflicting interpretations that stress one aspect rather than the other and that place greater or less emphasis on the picaresque, supernatural, morality-play tradition that preceded da Ponte. In addition to Dent and Mandel, see, for example, Einstein, *Mozart,* pp. 441–42; Eric Blom, *Mozart* (rev. ed.; London: J. M. Dent and Sons, Ltd., 1952), p. 292; Joseph Kerman, *Opera As Drama* (New York: Alfred A. Knopf, 1956), p. 118.

67. Cf. Hunt's preface to *Foliage* (London: C. and J. Ollier, 1818), pp. 35–38, where he criticizes August von Schlegel for recommending that "we imitate Greek tragedy rather than their gladness. It is Aetna among the fields of Sicily." And he rejects Schlegel's idea that Shakespeare's tragic spirit comes from the Greek sense of destiny. "Shakespeare may or may not

have believed in destiny; I believe he did, just about as much as he believed
in the contrary. . . . Because there is evil mixed with good . . . [Shakespeare
would refuse to] blaspheme the obvious beauty of nature, and have chimney-
corner fears about a 'great Sphinx who will eat you up, if you do not
discover her secret.' "

68. See Thornton Hunt, "A Man of Letters of the Last Generation,"
Cornhill Magazine, I (Jan., 1860), 86; Willard B. Pope, "Leigh Hunt &
His Companions," *Keats-Shelley Journal*, VIII, pt. 2 (Autumn, 1959), 89–91.
See also Lamb's "Witches and Night Fears," *London Magazine* (Oct., 1821),
and "Letter of Elia to R---S--- [Robert Southey]," *London Magazine* (Oct.,
1823); *Works of Charles Lamb*, E. V. Lucas, ed.; Vol. I: *Miscellaneous Prose*
(New York: Macmillan and Co., 1913), p. 273 and notes; *The Letters of
Charles Lamb and Mary Lamb*, E. V. Lucas, ed. (3 vols.; New Haven, Conn.:
Yale University Press, 1935), II, 407.

69. Lawrence H. and Carolyn W. Houtchens, *Leigh Hunt's Dramatic
Criticism, 1808–1831* (New York: Columbia University Press, 1949), p. 314.

70. The *Sun* reported (14 Apr. 1817): "All here is terrible, obscure, and
undefined—our blood absolutely runs cold. Never do we recollect any such
impression produced from a combination of musical sounds" (Arundell,
Critic, p. 294). Stendhal appreciated "l'accompagement terrible de la ré-
ponse de la statue, absolument pur de toute fausse grandeur, de toute
enflure: c'est, pour l'oreille, de la terreur à la Shakspeare" (*Vies de Haydn*,
xxxix).

71. Hogarth (*Memoirs*, II, 253), noting a similarity of elements in *Così*
and *Don Giovanni*, declared that Mozart, by treating the plot situation
seriously, has made "a matter of mere badinage disagreeable and revolting."
But Peacock, who regarded both operas as "romantic," found nothing but
perfection. He wrote in the *Examiner* (2 June 1833; *Works*, I, 430): "As
wide a distinction is to be marked between the gaiety of *Figaro* and of *Così
fan tutte*; the first is of enjoyment, the other the light laugh of the world
coming more from the brain than the blood." Kerman (*Opera As Drama*,
pp. 109, 115) states that the "Romantic critics" (presumably later ones) have
considered *Così* as "outrageous, improbable, immoral, frivolous"; he concludes that "Mozart's music clarifies and damns da Ponte's cynicism, and so
spoils his immaculate play."

72. The *British Stage* (July, 1819), pp. 203–4, predicting that the opera
would not be popular despite the "scientific musician," declared that "the
piece has been greatly curtailed since the first representation. . . . This
expedient has made it pass off less heavily; but a sense of weariness appears
frequently to pervade . . . [a] great part of the audience." John Ebers, in
Seven Years of the King's Theatre (London, 1828), p. 78, thought that even
Figaro was much too long, "it having been composed for a theatre, where
the opera alone forms the business of the evening." Despite the various

objections, the opera was presented fourteen times in 1819—one of the most popular attractions of the season. But its popularity quickly waned in subsequent seasons.

73. Dent has observed, in *Mozart's Operas,* p. 363: "With Mozart the opera is going all the time; if the singers are resting the orchestra is acting, the dramatic imagination is never relaxed for an instant until the movement comes, often reluctantly, to an end. This was new to his audiences. . . . The result was that Mozart's music was respected, but not enjoyed." Even von Dittersdorf could say of him, "He leaves his hearer out of breath . . . [and] in the end it is impossible to retain any of these beautiful melodies"!

74. Hunt was particularly fascinated by oriental tales (Landré, II, 373). Hogarth *(Memoirs,* II, 257) regarded the subject to be "of that fantastic and mystical stamp which is congenial to the German mind" though unintelligible elsewhere. Besides, there were mutilations—"in the Italian version the allegorical matter is got rid of, and the piece reduced to a childish and insipid fairy tale"—apparently introduced in subsequent productions. Even Peacock *(Works,* IX, 240) called the story "too mystical to be interesting, or even generally intelligible." Donald F. Tovey, in *The Main Stream of Music and Other Essays* (Cleveland, Ohio: World Publishing Co., 1959), p. 355, overstates in claiming that "nobody wants to make sense of the story of *Die Zauberflöte";* nevertheless, as Grout has observed *(Short History,* p. 294): "One cannot hope to understand entirely the libretto of *The Magic Flute* unless he is willing to accept its externals as in some sense symbolical of profounder meanings."

75. Hunt would have learned this from "Bombet's" *Haydn and Mozart* (p. 384), though he would not then have known the author's identity. Stendhal, of course, got the story (which is authentic) from Schlichtergrall.

76. Cf. Kerman, *Opera As Drama,* p. 124: "Unlike *Don Giovanni, The Magic Flute* is unified in conception, and everything about it matches the temper of Mozart's genius. All the diversities—of musical style, action, tone, and mood—are perfectly controlled to a single dramatic end." Cf. also Peacock's distinction between these operas *(Works,* IX, 430).

77. Edward D. Mackerness writes in "Leigh Hunt's Musical Journalism," *The Monthly Musical Record,* LXXXVI (Nov.–Dec., 1956), 216: "It was not the mysterious, introspective Mozart (as conceived by some of Hunt's contemporaries) who was [Hunt's] hero; it was rather the Italianate buffo-like genius—the composer of *Figaro."* But where is a more "introspective" view of Mozart to be found in the English journalism of the period? Jones ("Opera House," pp. 13–15) reflects Mackerness's opinion when he links Hunt's "doubts" about *The Magic Flute* with objections to the ghost in *Don Giovanni* and when he links Hunt with Hazlitt in admiring the "lighter" Mozart, although he admits that Hunt found more psychological realism in Mozart than Hazlitt did. But Hunt's "doubts" with respect to *The Magic*

Flute have no relevance to his protests over the ghost; indeed, they do not even refer to that opera but only to the critic's previous "misconceptions" about the composer. Nor does Hunt reject a "somber" view of Mozart. It is precisely this aspect of the composer that he finds most poetic, and it is the poetry of *The Magic Flute* that challenges the perfect gaiety of *Figaro*.

78. Several misconceptions concerning the origin of Rossini's opera are discussed by Francis Toye, *Rossini: A Study in Tragi-Comedy* (London: William Heinemann Ltd., 1934), pp. 54–60. First produced in Rome, 20 Feb. 1816, the opera was a failure, not just because of Paesiello's partisans but also because of rival managements. At the London première the *Sun* critic took a position similar to Hunt's; the *Times* and *Observer* offered favorable though trite observations (Arundell, *Critic,* pp. 298–300).

79. How much further Hunt's views were to change may be observed in a disclaimer he recorded in "Words for Composers," *The Musical World,* New Series IV (10 Jan. 1839), 19: "Not that the present writer holds poetry, in its integrity, or in most of its particulars, to be inferior to music"!

80. The *True Sun* (30 Apr. 1832); see also the *Tatler* (24 Feb. 1831).

81. In *Rome, Naples, and Florence in 1817* . . . (London: Henry Colburn, 1818; first published in Paris, 1817), Stendhal recounts a chance meeting with the composer on which he bases his comments, though the interview was a pure fabrication. According to J. Dechamps in "Leigh Hunt et Stendhal," *Stendhal Club,* I, No. 4 (15 July 1959), 273–79, the French took little notice of the book and regarded the author as frivolous, pretentious, and ignorant. He further points out the considerable intellectual sympathy Hunt shared with the French author (their views on ballet were particularly close) and notes the perspicacity of Hunt in this review and elsewhere. (On 25 Nov. 1821, the *Examiner* published a letter from Stendhal to the editor protesting the DL production of *Richard III.*)

82. Cf. Stendhal: "Light, lively, amusing, never wearisome but seldom exalted—Rossini would appear to have been brought into this world for the express purpose of conjuring up visions of ecstatic delight in the commonplace soul of the Average Man"; he called Rossini "never boring . . . [and] very, *very* rarely sublime" (Coe, trans., *Rossini,* pp. 407–8).

83. Hunt was fairly active at the English theatres that season, but they made less claim on his energy. He refers to his illness in letters to his nephew Henry Hunt (25 Nov. 1820) and to Shelley (1 Mar. 1821). The 1820 season at KT was poor, owing to the imminent bankruptcy of the management, though the *Examiner* missed Rossini's *Tancredi,* which saw its London première on 4 May; it was repeated eleven times that season.

84. Of the sixty performances in 1819, eighteen were operas by Rossini, thirty-one by Mozart, and eleven by other composers. Within two or three years the Rossini fever was to sweep even Mozart off the boards for a time, despite Peacock's assertion, referring to the première of the *Barber,* when

he wrote (*Works,* IX, 244): "We saw at once that there was a great revolution in dramatic music. Rossini burst on the stage like a torrent, and swept everything before him except Mozart, who stood, and will stand, alone and unshaken, like the Rock of Ages, because his art is like Shakspeare's."

85. It seems odd that Rossini's music should have been regarded as "heavy," particularly after a diet of Mozart, yet Hunt's contemporaries shared his fears. Hogarth (*Memoirs,* II, 186–87) complained: "If Rossini's singers have only lungs strong enough to make themselves heard through the noise of the orchestra, they are as free from restraint as their predecessors were a century ago." He refers to the florid bel canto in many Rossini arias; but the singers were not free from restraint, for Rossini wrote notes for passages that would have been improvised by earlier singers. Even Stendhal felt that this restraint would be harmful to the art of singing.

86. Perhaps Hunt "met with" the opera at some amateur performance. The usual authorities agree with "Chronicles" in listing 16 May 1822 as the London première of *Otello* (Naples, 1816). This is the first Rossini opera in which the *secco* recitative was accompanied by the orchestra rather than the harpsichord.

87. "When men are sweet, they seem feeble and without passion" (*Autobiography,* p. 128).

88. Cf. Hunt's remarks in an "oratorio" review, 20 Feb. 1812. He recalled him as an "elegant" singer in his *Autobiography* as well as in a line (80) of his poem "The Fancy Concert," *Ainsworth's Magazine,* VII (Jan., 1845), 93, which line, however, he dropped in his 1857 edition of *Poetical Works* (Milford, ed., pp. 374 ff.). Mount-Edgcumbe, *Reminiscences* (pp. 102–3), found Tramezzani's appearance agreeable and his voice full of sweetness and elegance.

89. Hogarth (*Memoirs,* II, 383) agreed that Ambrogetti had great dramatic talent but not a superior voice.

90. Probably the carillon on which Burney heard excellent performances in Amsterdam. "But surely this was a barbarous invention," Burney asserted, noting that the performer perspired profusely after fifteen minutes at the instrument. "He stripped to his shirt, put on his night-cap, and trussed up his sleeves for this *execution*; and he said he was forced to go to bed the instant it is over, in order to prevent his catching cold" (Burney, *An 18th Century Musical Tour,* Vol. II: *Dr. Burney's Musical Tours in Europe,* Percy A. Scholes, ed. [London: Oxford University Press, 1959], II, 288).

91. Cf. "Sketches of Music in London," *Quarterly Musical,* 1820, p. 375. "Chronicles" (p. 286) also called Albert "totally unfit."

92. Though Hunt had no palate for food, he was fond of music-and-food analogies. In *Foliage* (p. 39) he wrote: "The body of the German people, though it had a good shake given it by the French revolution, and produced

some sprightly children in Wieland and others, does not seem to have recovered yet from the nightmares of it's old eating and drinking habits, and
it's sedentary school-divinity." In "Miscellaneous Sketches: Dead Alive"
(31 Apr. 1809) he reported: "Some men, who are called dead, enjoy a much
better existence in the world than ever they did when they were said to be
alive,—as Handel for instance, who from being a gross feeder now lives
entirely upon sound, and leads a very sublime kind of existence." In *A Jar
of Honey from Mount Hybla* (London: Smith, Elder and Co., 1847), chap.
five, he compared Beethoven, and even Mozart, to a liking for olives on
their first appearance in the orchestral world; he stated that he liked their
music *and* olives. (Cf. Stendhal's "peaches-to-brandy" theory in Coe, trans.,
Rossini, p. 115: music appreciation proceeds from sweets to spices, or, more
specifically, from peaches for the taste of the child, beer for the young man,
sauerkraut for the adult, to brandy for the cultivated adult taste, just as in
music taste begins with a simple melody and moves toward an appreciation
of complex harmony.)

93. "Chronicles" (p. 247) reported that her vocal execution was undistinguished and that she had no genius but "expressed feelings as her education
told her they ought to be expressed." Mount-Edgcumbe (*Reminiscences,*
pp. 139–43) thought her the best singer of her time, even though her voice
was not of the finest quality; but Peacock regarded Mount-Edgcumbe as
partial to "thin, shrill tones" like hers (*Works,* IX, 246).

94. In his *Autobiography* (p. 127) Hunt observed: "Her nature was so
truthful, that, having as yet no acquirements to display, it would appear
that she did not pretend she had. She must either have been prematurely
put forward by others, or, with an instinct of her future greatness, supposed
that the instinct itself would be recognized." He praised her highly in
Mayr's *Medea* (*Tatler,* II [13 May 1831], 863).

95. "Chronicles" ranks her "unhesitatingly" among the first—with Billington and Catalani—as *prima donna assoluta.*

96. As M. Buxton Forman thought, in citing Hunt's review. His articles
(*Athenaeum,* 31 Aug. and 2 Nov. 1907) discuss the origin of Shelley's "I
arise from dreams of thee," which was apparently inspired by an adaptation
of Metastasio's "Ah! Perdona," as sung by Fodor in *Tito.* On this question
see also B. A. Parks, "The Indian Elements of the 'Indian Serenade,' "
Keats-Shelley Journal, X (Winter, 1961), 8–12, and Dent, *Mozart's Operas,*
p. 219.

97. Ayrton ran into difficulties with the company almost from the beginning of the season. "Chronicles" (p. 246) reports that "intrigues of every
kind were resorted to" in an effort to forestall production of *Don Giovanni,*
and that the manager, "honestly supported alone by Ambrogetti," won
against the cabal. Later "Fodor discovered that Mozart did not know where
to place the grand aria of the prima donna [in *Tito*], and insisted on singing

the scena 'Non più di fiori' at the commencement of the second act, instead of the end, where the story of the drama demanded it. [The singer] Crivelli found out that the songs which Mozart had written for the Roman emperor were not of importance enough for a 'primo tenore assoluto,' and demanded to introduce others. The manager remained firm; not so the proprietor: at the last rehearsal, his written permission was produced. . . . Mr. Ayrton bowed and retired; responsibility without power came not within his bargain." Hogarth (*Memoirs*, II, 384) adds that the singers were "too often supported by their aristocratic patrons" and that Ayrton "was forced to have recourse at law for the remuneration due to himself for his services." "Chronicles" also states that the 1821 season did not go much better for Ayrton in this respect. Mazzolà, not da Ponte, was Mozart's librettist.

98. Commissioned to do an opera in one month, Mozart produced the music for *Tito* in eighteen days, leaving to his pupil Süssmayr the task of writing out the *seccos*, a rather common practice at the time though unusual with Mozart. The arias, as Dent observes (*Mozart's Operas*, p. 318), "instead of being placed in the most salient positions, were left wherever they chanced to come."

99. In a letter to Shelley (July, 1819), Hunt was a good deal less complimentary, calling Bellochi "coarse in every other respect except her voice, and that is too sharp at top. She is the oddest little heyday lump you ever saw, fantastically dressed, and looking alternately good-humoured and sulky to an excess" (*Correspondence*, I, 134). "Chronicles" agreed that she in no way measured up to Fodor. Though improved in 1820, she left the company at the end of that season.

100. In the play she administers no fewer than nine "slaps"—only slightly reduced in the libretto. Beaumarchais, the first playwright to provide full stage directions, characterized Susanna as: "A clever girl, full of wit and laughter, but displaying nothing of the impudent frivolity of our corruptive chambermaids" (*Phaedra and Figaro,* trans. respectively by Robert Lowell and Jacques Barzun [New York: Farrar, Strauss and Cudahy, 1961], pp. 97–100). Speaking of Hunt's translations of poetry, Blunden in *Leigh Hunt, a Biography* (London: Cobden-Sanderson Ltd., 1928), p. 136, cites his ability to bring "foreign beauty home to us without spoiling its native difference."

101. Hogarth (*Memoirs*, II, 380) called Vestris's singing at KT "characterised by truth of expression and Italian purity of style." Mount-Edgcumbe (*Reminiscences*, p. 155) found Vestris a pleasing singer who did not live up to her original promise—referring, presumably, to her desertion of Italian opera. "Chronicles," too, regretted that desertion. She "has gained wealth," but "the art has lost incalculably" (p. 198).

102. Cf. Hunt's "Longus" in the *Liberal,* I (1822), 361: "We must be content . . . to suppose that the hero of an opera is soliloquizing in perfect solitude, although every word gives praeternatural activity to the elbows of

fifty fiddlers; and, in spite of ourselves, to feel drowsy during the ballet, in sympathy with the heroine, who, by a fiction of the theatre, sleeps soundly in a horn-pipe."

REPRISE

1. Herschel Baker, *William Hazlitt* (Cambridge, Mass.: Belknap Press of Harvard University Press, 1962), p. 297.

2. Alvin Whitley, in "Hazlitt and the Theatre," *Studies in English, The University of Texas,* XXXIV (1955), 67–68, asserts that Hazlitt gets to the heart of his subject, relating cause to effect and theory to practice. "Hazlitt excelled in style and analysis; Hunt did little more than describe and record." Jeffrey A. Fleece, in "Leigh Hunt's Theatrical Criticism" (unpublished Ph.D. dissertation, State University of Iowa, 1952), pp. 60–70, 123, 156–57, finds Hunt's lack of a systematic method and a unifying philosophy his "most obvious fault"; Hazlitt was not an "impressionist" like Hunt but was "grounded in theory"; Hazlitt's style is "brutally straightforward, clear and modern," while Hunt's is "somewhat ornate and fluid." Although Landré (II, 111–18, 130–31) tends to overemphasize the importance of Hunt's failure to systematize, his comparative evaluations of Hunt and Hazlitt are accurate.

3. See Baker, pp. 302, 473; Kathleen Coburn, "Hazlitt on the Disinterested Imagination," in *Some British Romantics: A Collection of Essays,* J. V. Logan, J. E. Jordan, and N. Frye, eds. (Columbus, Ohio: Ohio State University Press, 1966), pp. 185–88; M. H. Abrams, *The Mirror and the Lamp* (New York: W. W. Norton and Co., Inc., 1958), p. 135.

4. Kenneth N. Cameron, *Shelley and his Circle, 1773–1822* (2 vols.; Cambridge, Mass.: Harvard University Press, 1961), I, 270.

5. Abrams, *Mirror and Lamp,* p. 319.

6. Cf. J. C. Trewin, "Leigh Hunt as Drama Critic," *Keats-Shelley Memorial Bulletin,* X (1959), 18.

7. Young, "Leigh Hunt—Music Critic," *Music and Letters,* XXV, No. 2 (1944), 87. Hunt anticipated Heinrich Heine, whom Max Graf calls "the first to write about music and musicians not as an expert but as a journalist," citing his Paris reviews from 1830 to 1840 (*Composer and Critic: Two Hundred Years of Musical Criticism* [New York: W. W. Norton and Co., Inc., 1946], p. 280).

8. Hunt no doubt had Montaigne in mind. Cf. "On the Education of Children," *The Complete Essays of Montaigne,* trans. Donald M. Frame (3 vols.; Garden City, N.Y.: Doubleday & Co., Inc., Anchor Books, 1960), I, 178.

Select Bibliography

Abrams, M. H. *The Mirror and the Lamp: Romantic Theory and the Critical Tradition.* New York: W. W. Norton and Co., Inc., 1958.

Addison, Joseph, and Steele, Richard. *The Spectator.* Edited with introductory notes by Donald F. Bond. 5 vols. London: Oxford University Press, 1965.

Altick, Richard D. *The Cowden Clarkes.* London: Oxford University Press, 1948.

————. *The English Common Reader.* Chicago: University of Chicago Press, 1957.

Andrews, Alexander. *The History of British Journalism, from the Foundation of the Newspaper Press in England, to the Repeal of the Stamp Act in 1855, with sketches of Press Celebrities.* 2 vols. London: Richard Bentley, 1859.

Arundell, Dennis. *The Critic at the Opera.* London: Ernest Benn Ltd., 1957.

Aspinall, Arthur. "The Social Status of Journalists at the Beginning of the Nineteenth Century," *Review of English Studies,* XXI (1945), 216–32.

"Autobiography of an Amateur Singer," *Harmonicon,* II (1831), 106–7, 135–37.

Bagster-Collins, Jeremu Felix. *George Colman the Younger, 1762–1836.* New York: Kings Crown Press, 1946.

Baker, David Erskine. *Biographia Dramatica.* 4 vols. London: Longman, Hurst, Rees, Orme and Brown, 1812.

Baker, Henry Barton. *The London Stage: Its History and Tradition, 1576–1888.* 2 vols. London: W. H. Allen and Co., 1889.

Baker, Herschel. *William Hazlitt.* Cambridge, Mass.: Belknap Press of Harvard University Press, 1962.

Barnet, Sylvan. "Lamb's Contribution to the Theory of Dramatic Illusion," *PMLA,* LXIX (Dec., 1954), 1150–59.

Barzun, Jacques. Preface to "Figaro's Marriage" by Beaumarchais in *Phaedra and Figaro.* Translated respectively by Robert Lowell and Jacques Barzun. New York: Farrar, Strauss and Cudahy, 1961.

———— (ed.). *Pleasures of Music.* New York: Viking Press, 1951.

Bate, Walter Jackson (ed.). *Criticism: The Major Texts.* New York: Harcourt, Brace and World, 1952.

————. *John Keats.* Cambridge, Mass.: Harvard University Press, 1963.

Berlioz, Hector. *Evenings in the Orchestra.* Translated by C. R. Fortescue. Baltimore: Penguin Books, 1963.

Beyle, Henri. *Vies de Haydn, de Mozart, et de Métastase.* Daniel Muller, editeur; Préface de Romain Rolland. Paris: Librarie Ancienne Honoré Champion, 1914. (Centenary of initial publication, Paris, 1814: *Lettres écrites de Vienne en Autriche, sur le célèbre compositeur, Jh. Haydn, suivies d'une vie de Mozart, et de considérations sur Métastase et l'état présent de la musique en France et en Italie.* Par Louis-Alexandré César Bombet.)

———— [M. Bombet, pseud.]. *The lives of Haydn and Mozart, with observations on Metastasio, and on the present state of music in France and Italy.* [Translated by Rev. C. Berry and R. Brewin.] Annotations by William Gardiner. 2nd ed. London: J. Murray, 1818. (First edition, London: Henry Colburn, 1817.)

———— [The Count de Stendhal, pseud.]. *Rome, Naples and Florence, in 1817: Sketches of the present state of society, manners, arts, and literature, &c. in these celebrated cities.* London: Henry Colburn, 1818. (First edition. Paris, 1817.)

————. *Life of Rossini.* Translated by Richard N. Coe. New York: Criterion Books, 1957. (First edition. Paris, 1823.)

Blom, Eric. *Mozart.* Revised edition. London: J. M. Dent and Sons, Ltd., 1952.

Blunden, Edmund C. *Leigh Hunt, A Biography.* London: Cobden-Sanderson Ltd., 1930.

————. *Leigh Hunt's "Examiner" Examined.* London: Cobden-Sanderson Ltd., 1928.

Bourne, H. R. Fox. *English Newspapers: Chapters in the History of Journalism.* 2 vols. London: Chatto and Windus, 1887.

Brayley, Edward W. *Historical and Descriptive Accounts of the Theatres of London.* London: J. Taylor, 1826.

Brewer, Luther A. *My Leigh Hunt Library.* Vol. I: *First Editions.* Vol. II: *The Holograph Letters.* Cedar Rapids, Iowa: Privately printed, 1932 (I), 1938 (II).

Brightfield, Myron F. "Leigh Hunt—American," *University of California Essays in Criticism.* Vol. 4. Second Series. Berkeley: University of California, 1934.

The British Stage, and Literary Cabinet. Edited by Thomas Kenrick. 3 vols. London: J. Chappell, 1817–1819.

Bulletin of the American Musicological Society. 1948.

Bunn, Alfred. *The Stage: Both Before and Behind the Curtain.* 3 vols. London: R. Bentley, 1840.

Burney, Charles. *An 18th Century Musical Tour.* Vol. II: *Dr. Burney's Musical Tours in Europe.* Edited by Percy A. Scholes. London: Oxford University Press, 1959. (First edition. London, 1775.)

————. *General History of Music.* 4 vols. Edited by Frank Mercer. New York: Dover Publications, 1957. (First edition. London, 1776–1789.)

————. *Memoirs of the Life and Writings of Abate Métastasio.* 2 vols. London: G. G. and J. Robinson, 1796.

————. *The Present State of Music in Germany, the Netherlands and United Provinces, &c.* 2 vols. London: T. Becket and Company, 1773.

Cameron, Kenneth N. *Shelley and His Circle, 1773–1822.* 2 vols. Cambridge, Mass.: Harvard University Press, 1961.

Campbell, Olwen W. *Thomas Love Peacock.* London: Arthur Barker, Ltd., 1953.

Charms, Desiree, and Breed, Paul F. *Songs in Collection: An Index.* Detroit, Mich.: Information Service Inc., 1966.

"Chronicles of the Italian Opera in England." *Harmonicon,* I (1830), 10–338 passim.

Clarke, Charles and Mary Cowden. *Recollections of Writers.* London: Sampson, Low, Marston, Searle and Rivington, 1878.

Clarke, Mary Cowden. *The Life and Labours of Vincent Novello.* London: Novello and Co., [1864].

————. *My Long Life.* New York: Dodd, Mead and Co., 1896.

Coburn, Kathleen. "Hazlitt on the Disinterested Imagination." *Some British Romantics: A Collection of Essays.* Edited by James V. Logan, John E. Jordan, and Northrop Frye. Columbus, Ohio: Ohio State University Press, 1966.

Dean, Winton. "Shakespeare in the Opera House," *Shakespeare Survey,* XVIII (1965), 75–93.

Dechamps [sic], J. "Leigh Hunt et Stendhal," *Stendhal Club,* I (July, 1959), 273–79.

Demuth, Norman (ed.). *An Anthology of Musical Criticism from the 15th to the 20th Century.* London: Eyre and Spottiswoode, 1947.

Dent, Edward J. *Foundations of English Opera.* Cambridge: The University Press, 1928.

————. *Mozart's Operas: A Critical Study.* London: Chatto and Windus, 1913.

Dibdin, Charles. *Professional and Literary Memoirs of Charles Dibdin the Younger.* Edited by George Speaight. London: The Society for Theatre Research, 1956.

Ebers, John. *Seven Years of the King's Theatre.* London: n.p., 1828.

Einstein, Alfred. *Essays on Music.* New York: W. W. Norton and Co., Inc., 1956.

————. *Mozart: His Character, His Work.* Translated by Arthur Mendel and Nathan Broder. London: Oxford University Press, 1945.

————. *Music in the Romantic Era.* New York: W. W. Norton and Co., Inc., 1947.

Escott, Thomas H. *Masters of English Journalism.* London: T. Fisher Unwin, 1911.

Fleece, Jeffrey A. "Leigh Hunt's Theatrical Criticism." Ph.D. dissertation, State University of Iowa, 1952.

Foster, Myles B. *History of the Philharmonic Society of London, 1813–1912.* London: John Love, 1912.

Fuller-Maitland, J. A. *English Music in the XIXth Century.* New York: E. P. Dutton and Co., 1902.

Gagey, Edmond M. *Ballad Opera.* N.Y.: Columbia University Press, 1937.

Gay, John. *The Beggar's Opera.* Edited by Max Goberman and Louis Kronenberger. Larchmont, N.Y.: Argonaut Books, 1961.

Genest, John. *Some Account of the English Stage.* 9 vols. Bath: T. Rodd, 1832.

Graf, Max. *Composer and Critic: Two Hundred Years of Musical Criticism.* New York: W. W. Norton and Co., Inc., 1946.

Gray, Charles H. *Theatrical Criticism in London to 1795.* New York: Columbia University Press, 1931.

Grout, Donald J. *A Short History of Opera.* New York: Columbia University Press, 1947.

Grove, Sir George. *Grove's Dictionary of Music and Musicians.* 5th ed. Edited by Eric Blom. New York: St. Martin's Press, 1954.

Hawkins, Sir John. *A General History of the Science and Practice of Music.* New York: Dover Publications, 1963. (Reprint of 1853 edition. First edition. London, 1776.)

Haydon, Benjamin Robert. *The Autobiography and Memoirs of Benjamin Robert Haydon.* Edited by Tom Taylor. New York: Harcourt Brace and Co., [1926].

————. *The Diary of Benjamin Robert Haydon.* Edited by Willard B. Pope. Cambridge, Mass.: Harvard University Press. Vols. 1 and 2, 1960. Vols. 3–5, 1963.

Hazlitt, William. *The Complete Works of William Hazlitt.* Edited by P. P. Howe. 21 vols. London and Toronto: J. M. Dent and Sons, 1930–1934.

————. *Literary Remains of the late William Hazlitt.* Edited by E. L. Bulwer and Thomas N. Talfourd. 2 vols. London: Saunders and Otley, 1836.

Hertzman, Erich. "Mozart's Creative Process," *The Creative World of Mozart*. Edited by Paul Henry Lang. New York: W. W. Norton and Co., Inc., 1963.

The History of "The Times." Vol. I: *The Thunderer in the Making, 1785–1841*. New York: The Macmillan Co., 1935.

Hoffman, D. S. "Some Shakespearian Music, 1660–1900," *Shakespeare Survey*, XVIII (1965), 94–101.

Hogan, Charles Beecher (ed.). *The London Stage: 1660–1800. Part 5: 1776–1800.* 2 vols. With introduction by the editor. Carbondale, Ill.: Southern Illinois University Press, 1968.

Hogarth, George. *Memoirs of the Musical Drama.* 2 vols. London: Richard Bentley, 1838.

Hudson, Derek. *Thomas Barnes of "The Times."* London: Cambridge University Press, 1944.

Hughes, Patrick C. *Famous Mozart Operas.* New York: The Citadel Press, 1958.

Hughes, Rosemary. *Haydn in London.* London: J. M. Dent and Sons, Ltd., 1950.

Hunt, Leigh. *The Autobiography of Leigh Hunt.* Edited by Jack E. Morpurgo. London: Cresset Press, Ltd., 1948.

————. *The Correspondence of Leigh Hunt.* Edited by his eldest son [Thornton L. Hunt]. 2 vols. London: Elder and Co., 1862.

————. *Critical Essays on the performers of the London Theatres, including general observations on the practise and genius of the stage by the author of the theatrical criticism in the weekly paper called the News.* London: John Hunt, 1808.

————. *Dramatic Essays of Leigh Hunt.* Introduction by William Archer. Selected and edited with notes by William Archer and Robert W. Lowe. London: W. Scott, Ltd., 1894.

———— (ed.). *The Examiner, a Sunday Paper on Politics, Domestic Economy and Theatricals.* London, 1808–1822.

————. *Foliage: or, poems original and translated.* London: C. and J. Ollier, 1818.

———— (ed.). *The Indicator.* (Weekly.) London, 1819–1821.

————. *A Jar of Honey from Mount Hybla.* London: Smith, Elder and Co., 1847.

————. *Leigh Hunt's Autobiography: The Earliest Sketches.* Edited with introduction and notes by Stephen Fogle. Gainesville, Fla.: University of Florida Press, 1959.

————. *Leigh Hunt's Dramatic Criticism, 1808–1831.* Edited by Lawrence H. and Carolyn W. Houtchens. New York: Columbia University Press, 1949.

————. *Leigh Hunt's Literary Criticism.* Edited by Lawrence H. and Carolyn W. Houtchens. Introduction by Clarence DeWitt Thorpe. New York: Columbia University Press, 1956.

———— (ed.). *Leigh Hunt's London Journal.* (Weekly.) 2 vols. London: Charles Knight, 1835.

————. *Leigh Hunt's Political and Occasional Essays.* Edited by Lawrence H. and Carolyn W. Houtchens. Introduction by Carl R. Woodring. New York: Columbia University Press, 1962.

————. *Letters of Leigh Hunt in the Luther A. Brewer Collection: 1816–1825.* Edited by Hunter P. McCartney. Microfilmed Ph.D. dissertation, University of Pennsylvania, 1958.

———— (ed.). *The Liberal: Verse and Prose from the South.* (Quarterly.) 2 vols. London, 1822–1823.

————. *Musical Copyright.* London: G. Richards, [1816].

————. *Musical Evenings, or Selections Vocal and Instrumental.* Edited from MS. with introduction by David R. Cheney. Columbia, Mo.: University of Missouri Press, 1964.

————. *The Poetical Works of Leigh Hunt.* Edited by H. S. Milford. London and New York: Oxford University Press, 1923.

————. *Prefaces by Leigh Hunt.* Edited by R. Brimley Johnson. London: T. Hollings, 1927.

———— (ed.). *The Reflector, a Quarterly Magazine.* 2 vols. London: J. Hunt, 1811–1812.

————. *Table Talk.* London: Smith, Elder and Co., 1882.

———— (ed.). *The Tatler.* (Daily.) London, 1830–1832.

Hunt, Thornton. "Introduction by the author's eldest son" to *The Autobiography of Leigh Hunt.* New York and London: Smith, Elder and Co., 1891. (This edition first published 1860.)

————. "A Man of Letters of the Last Generation," *The Cornhill Magazine,* I (Jan., 1860), 85–95.

Jones, David L. "Hazlitt and Leigh Hunt at the Opera House," *Symposium,* XVI (Spring, 1962), 5–16.

Keats, John. *The Letters of John Keats, 1814–1821.* Edited by Hyder E. Rollins. 2 vols. Cambridge, Mass.: Harvard University Press, 1958.

Kelly, Michael. *Reminiscences of Michael Kelly, of the King's Theatre, and Theatre Royal Drury Lane, including a period of nearly half a century; with original anecdotes of many distinguished persons, political, literary, and musical.* [Written for Kelly by Theodore Hook.] 2nd ed. 2 vols. London: Henry Colburn, 1826.

Kerman, Joseph. *Opera As Drama.* New York: Alfred A. Knopf, 1956.

Lamb, Charles. *Works of Charles Lamb.* Vol. I: *Miscellaneous Prose.* Edited by E. V. Lucas. New York: Macmillan and Co., 1913.

Lamb, Charles and Mary. *The Letters of Charles Lamb and Mary Lamb*. Edited by E. V. Lucas. 3 vols. New Haven: Yale University Press, 1935.

Landré, Louis. *Leigh Hunt. Contribution à l'histoire de Romantisme anglais*. 2 vols. Paris: Société d'edition "Les Belles-lettres," 1935–1936.

————. "Leigh Hunt: His Contribution to English Romanticism," *Keats-Shelley Journal*, VIII, pt. 2 (Autumn, 1959), 133–44.

Lang, Paul Henry. *George Frideric Handel*. New York: W. W. Norton and Co., Inc., 1966.

Loewenberg, Alfred (comp.). *Annals of Opera: 1597–1940*. Introduction by Edward J. Dent. 2nd ed. 2 vols. Geneva: Societas Bibliographica, 1955.

Lucas, E. V. *Life of Charles Lamb*. 3rd ed. 2 vols. New York: P. Putnam's Sons, 1907.

Mackerness, Edward D. "Leigh Hunt's Musical Journalism," *The Monthly Musical Record*, LXXXVI (Nov.–Dec., 1956), 212–22.

Mandel, Oscar (ed.). *The Theatre of Don Juan: A Collection of Plays and Views, 1630–1963*. With commentary by the editor. Lincoln, Nebr.: University of Nebraska Press, 1963.

Mellers, Wilfred. *Music and Society*. 2nd ed. New York: Roy Publishers, 1950.

Mount-Edgcumbe, Richard, Earl of. *Musical Reminiscences, containing an account of Italian opera in England, from 1773*. 4th ed. London: John Andrews, 1834.

Naylor, Edward W. *Shakespeare and Music*. London: J. M. Dent and Sons, Ltd., 1931.

Nettel, Reginald. *The Orchestra in England: A Social History*. London, Jonathan Cape, 1946.

————. *Sing a Song of England: A Social History of Traditional Song*. London: Phoenix House, Ltd., 1954.

Nicholson, Watson. *The Struggle for a Free Stage in London*. London: Archibald Constable, and Co., Ltd., 1906.

Nicoll, Allardyce. *A History of English Drama, 1660–1900*. 6 vols. London: Cambridge University Press, 1952 (4th ed., I–III), 1955 (2nd ed., IV), 1959 (2nd ed., V; 1st ed., VI).

Novello, Vincent and Mary. *A Mozart Pilgrimage, Being the Travel Diaries of Vincent and Mary Novello in the year 1829*. Transcribed and compiled by Nerini M. di Marignano. Edited with introduction by Rosemary Hughes. London: Novello and Co., Ltd., 1955.

Park, B. A. "The Indian Elements of the 'Indian Serenade,'" *Keats-Shelley Journal*, X (Winter, 1961), 8–12.

Peacock, Thomas Love. *The Works of Thomas Love Peacock*. Edited by

H. F. B. Brett-Smith and C. E. Jones. 10 vols. London: Constable and Co., Ltd., 1924–1934.

Pearson, Hesketh. *G.B.S.: A Full Length Portrait*. New York: Harper, 1952.

Planché, J. R. *The Recollections and Reflections of J. R. Planché*. 2 vols. London: Tinsley Brothers, 1872.

Pohl, C. F. *Mozart und Haydn in London*. 2 vols. Vienna: Druck und Verlag von Carl Gerold's Sohn, 1867.

Pope, Willard B. "Leigh Hunt & His Companions," *Keats-Shelley Journal*, VIII, pt. 2 (Autumn, 1959), 89–91.

The Quarterly Musical Magazine and Review. Edited by R. M. Bacon. 3 vols. London, 1818–1820.

Quinlan, Maurice J. *Victorian Prelude: A History of English Manners, 1700–1830*. New York: Columbia University Press, 1941.

[Reynolds, Frederic.] *The Life and Times of Frederick* [sic] *Reynolds, written by himself*. 2 vols. London: H. Colburn, 1826.

Rhodes, R. Crompton. *Harlequin Sheridan: The Man and the Legends*. Oxford: Basil Blackwell, 1933.

Rubsamen, Walter H. "The Ballad Burlesques and Extravaganzas," *Musical Quarterly*, XXXVI (1950), 551–61; XXXVII (1951), 144.

Schlegel, Augustus William. *A Course of Lectures on Dramatic Art and Literature*. Translated by John Black. Revised by the Rev. A. J. W. Morrison. London: Henry G. Bohn, 1846.

Scholes, Percy A. *Concise Oxford Dictionary of Music*. 2nd ed. Edited by John Owen Ward. London: Oxford University Press, 1964.

Schultz, William E. *Gay's Beggar's Opera: Its Content, History and Influence*. New Haven, Conn.: Yale University Press, 1923.

Sears, Minnie E. *Song Index*. New York: H. W. Wilson Co., 1926.

————. *Song Index Supplement*. New York: H. W. Wilson Co., 1934.

Shelley, Percy Bysshe. *The Letters of Percy Bysshe Shelley*. Edited by Frederick L. Jones. 2 vols. London: Oxford University Press, 1964.

Southworth, James S. *Vauxhall Gardens: A Chapter in the Social History of London*. New York: Columbia University Press, 1941.

Spettacolo, Enciclopedia dello. 9 vols. Rome: Casa Editrice le Maschere, 1954–1962.

Staël, Madame de. *Considérations sur les principaux événements de la révolution française*. 3rd ed. Paris: Delaunay, 1820.

Stone, George W., Jr. (ed.). *The London Stage: 1660–1800. Part 4: 1747–1776*. 3 vols. With introduction by the editor. Carbondale, Ill.: Southern Illinois University Press, 1962.

Stout, George D. "Political History of Leigh Hunt's *Examiner*," *Washington University Studies*, New Series, No. 19, 1949.

Strunk, William O. (ed.). *Source Readings in Music History*. New York: W. W. Norton and Co., 1950.

Tovey, Donald F. *The Main Stream of Music and Other Essays*. Cleveland, Ohio: World Publishing Co., Meridian Books, 1959.

Toye, Francis. *Rossini: A Study in Tragi-Comedy*. London: William Heinemann Ltd., 1934.

Trewin, J. C. "Leigh Hunt as Drama Critic," *Keats-Shelley Memorial Bulletin*, X (1959), 14–19.

Walker, Ernest. *A History of Music in England*. 2nd ed. London: Oxford University Press, 1924.

Ward, Aileen. *John Keats*. New York: The Viking Press, 1963.

Ward, William S. "Periodical Literature," *Some British Romantics: A Collection of Essays*. Edited by James V. Logan, John E. Jordan, and Northrop Frye. Columbus, Ohio: Ohio State University Press, 1966.

Watson, Ernest B. *Sheridan to Robertson: A Study of the Nineteenth-Century London Stage*. Cambridge, Mass.: Harvard University Press, 1926.

Watson, Melvin R. "The *Spectator* Tradition and the Development of the Familiar Essay," *English Literary History*, XIII (1946), 189–205.

Werkmeister, Lucyle. *A Newspaper History of England, 1792–1793*. Lincoln, Nebr.: University of Nebraska Press, 1967.

White, Eric W. *The Rise of English Opera*. New York: Philosophical Library, 1951.

White, Newman I. *Shelley*. 2 vols. New York: Alfred A. Knopf, 1940.

Whitley, Alvin. "Hazlitt and the Theatre," *Studies in English, The University of Texas*, XXXIV (1955), 67–100.

Williams, Raymond. *The Long Revolution*. London: Chatto and Windus, 1961.

Winisanker, Michael. "Musico-Dramatic Criticism of English Comic Opera, 1750–1800," *Bulletin of American Musicological Society*, Nov., 1948, pp. 82–83.

Woodring, Carl R. *Prose of the Romantic Period*. Boston: Houghton Mifflin Co., 1961.

Wyndham, Henry Saxe. *The Annals of Covent Garden Theatre from 1732 to 1897*. 2 vols. London: Chatto and Windus, 1906.

Young, Percy M. "Leigh Hunt—Music Critic," *Music and Letters*, XXV, No. 2 (Apr., 1944), 86–94.

Index

THIS INDEX has three sections: General, Operas (English and Italian), and Performers. Under the names of composers, dramatists, and librettists in the General section of the index, there are cross-references to the Operas section for entries on specific operas the criticism of which is relevant to those individuals; other references to specific operas are to their first listings in the appendixes. In the Operas section, the boldface page numbers that follow the names of operas refer to their first listings in the appendixes. In the General section and in the Performers section, the boldface page numbers that follow the names of individuals refer to biographical information about them in the appendixes or in the notes. The numbers of *notes* are set in italics.

Abbreviations for critics that appear in the index are:
LH—Leigh Hunt
WH—William Hazlitt
HR—Henry Robertson
TB—Thomas Barnes
CL—Charles Lamb

Abbreviations for theatres that appear in the index are:
CG—Covent Garden
DL—Drury Lane
HY—the Haymarket
KT—the King's Theatre
LY—the Lyceum
OLY—the Olympic

Other abbreviations that are used in the index are:
EO—English Opera
IO—Italian Opera

GENERAL

Cross-references to "Operas" are to entries in the Operas section of the index. Boldface numbers that follow the names of individuals refer to biographical information about them in the appendixes or in the notes. The numbers of *notes* are set in italics.

OPERAS

Boldface page numbers refer to the first listings of operas in the appendixes. The numbers of *notes* are set in italics.

English Operas

Artaxerxes, **241, 242, 245**; "true" opera seria in English, 14; music and lib. (Arne): LH: lasting composition in songs, 92, and best things in it admired by public, 124–25, but public prefers "The Soldier Tired" for difficulty of execution, not merits, 125; recitative: usually cut, 134; restored, 137; LH argues for naturalness of, 134–35; airs curtailed by Braham, WH, *295n78;* WH on, *294–95n77;* LH and Barnett on, *294–95n77;* Walker on, *294–95n77;* performers, 96–97, 102, 111

Barber of Seville, **243**; managers credited for making IO music better known, LH, 119; music (Bishop, with borrowings from Mozart, Rossini): well adapted, LH, 119; performers: LH: unsuitableness of, 105, and unable to cope with music, 119; 98

Beggar's Opera, The, **241, 243, 245**; first ballad opera, 10; EO influence of, 10–11; early views on morality of, 10–11; LH and WH on, 230; LH mentions, 234; drama (Gay): public enjoys gross scenes, LH, 143; vulgarity converted to refinement, a corrective to vice, WH, 143–45; LH: public's appreciation due perhaps to WH, 145; music (Gay's ballad airs arranged by Pepusch): charm and simplicity of, is work's greatest appeal, LH, 91–92; Colman's transvestite productions, *290n54;* many alterations of, 295–*96n82;* morality of, Schultz and Hogarth on, *296n83;* performers, 94–95, 96, 97, 98, 105, 106, 107, 132, *290n54*

Belles without Beaux, **244**

Bonifacio and Brigetina . . . , **240**; drama (T. Dibdin): wretched burlesque, disgrace to stage, LH, 80; music (unidentified, probably traditional airs): good music "dishonoured" by vehicle, LH, 84; mentioned, 115

Brown Man, The, **244**

Cabinet, The, **239, 242**; drama (T. Dibdin): LH enjoys this cut-down version, 81–82; performers, 138

Castle of Andalusia, The, **241**; performers: 107

Comedy of Errors, **245**; drama (Reynolds): unsuitable for opera, LH, 118; music (Bishop adaptations from Arne, Stevenson, others): on songs and glees, LH, 129; performers, 93, 125

Devil's Bridge, The, **241**

Don Giovanni; or, A Spectre on Horseback, **243**; drama (T. Dibdin?): CL prefers this "make-believe" Giovanni and an English Leporello, 146–47

Duenna, The, **244**; drama (Sheridan): public's expectation of "mere singing" hurts wit, LH, 126; performers, 108

Duke of Savoy, **243**; drama (Reynolds); music (Bishop): more worthy of his promise but wasted on vehicle, LH, 87

Exile, The, **240**; drama (Reynolds, based on Cottin): good source turned into pretentious melodrama, LH, 79; music (Bishop and Mazzinghi): mentioned, 87; performers, 98; mentioned, 120

Fortune Teller, The, **240**; drama (author unknown): amateurish lyrics in, LH, 76–77; music (Reeve): pleasing but unoriginal, LH, 89–90

Gentle Shepherd, The, **242**; drama (Ramsay): avoids all affectation, LH, 83; music (folk tunes): LH enjoys the few Scots airs retained, 90; production: mutilations and interpolations, LH, 117

Giovanni in London, **245**; drama (Moncrieff): good-humored plot contrasts with Mozart's, LH, 148–49; music (arranger unknown): list of songs in, 8–9; performers, 111, *297n91*

Italian Operas

mental and absurd, HR, 162; Catalani in breeches, HR, 160

L'Eroina di Raab, 259; music (Ferrari): indifferent, HR, 164; lib. (unknown): "old recipe of chains and dungeons," HR, 164; and Catalani, 302n*31*

Le Nozze di Figaro, 259, 260, 261; Peacock on, 310n*71*; Ebers on length of, 310–11n*72*; LH mentions, 210; music (Mozart): finest of his works, HR, 171, has novelty, surprise, charming melody, 171; better than *Don Giovanni*, a complete delight, LH, 206; lib. (da Ponte, based on Beaumarchais): quick succession of incidents, abounds in vigor, HR, 171; role of Susanna needs vivacity, LH, 223; performers, 160–61, 171–72, 217–18, 219, 220, 221, 222, 223, 302n*27*, 302n*28*

Le Semiramide, 258; music (Portugal): unimpressive, HR, 162; performers, 299n*11*

L'Inganno Felice, 261; music (Rossini): early work but worth hearing, LH, 213

L'Italiana in Algeri, **260**; better than *Il Barbiere*, LH, 213; music (Rossini): more animal spirits than intellectual, LH, 213, and cites overture, 214; lib. (Anelli): poor, LH, 213; performers, 216–17, 222

Penelope, **260**; mentioned, 184; performers, 184

Romeo e Giulietta, 258; music (Guglielmi "*le fils*"), lib. (Buonaiuti): music and language "contemptible," HR, 162

Sidagero, 258; performers, 161

Teresa e Claudio, 258; music (Farinelli): excessively sentimental, HR, 162

Zaira, 258; music (Federici): at disadvantage with Winter's *Zaira* but new style welcome, HR, 166; performers, 166

PERFORMERS

Boldface page numbers refer to biographical information in the appendixes or in the notes. The numbers of *notes* are set in italics.

Albert (German singer): as Figaro, not well received by public, 219; unsuited to role, LH, 219; "Chronicles" on, 313n*91*

Ambrogetti, Giuseppe, **261**; as the Don, WH on, 199, LH on, 200; LH: despite his acting, dislikes the Don, 148; CL on, 146–47; Shelley on, 307n*58*; LH: a posturing actor in *La Molinara*, disappointing as Papageno, ill-costumed in *Il Matrimonio Segreto*, excelled as Don Giovanni, as Figaro, and in *Fanatico per la Musica*, 218–19; Hogarth on, 313n*89*; and Ayrton, 314–15n*97*; mentioned, 219

Angrisani, Carlo, **261**; LH: versatile actor, noble bass but upper tones fail him, 217–18; excellent as Sarastro, 218

Bannister, John, **246**; young LH enjoys portrayals of, 30

Barrymore, William: LH on, 112

Begrez, Pierre Ignace, **261**; LH mentions, 220

Bellamy, Thomas L., **246**; rare as "gentlemanly" singer, LH, 137

Belloc (Bellochi), Teresa Giorgi Trombetta, **261**; *L'Inganno Felice* written for her, 261; LH: as Zerlina has vivacity but lacks pathos of Fodor, 222; in debut showed mannerisms but gave promise as actress, 222; admirable in *La Modista Raggiratrice*, 222; best role as Susanna in *Figaro*, 222–23; LH on voice, appearance, 315n*99*; "Chronicles" on, 315n*99*; mentioned, 220

Bellochi. *See* Belloc

Beridino, Sig.: inadequate in *Il Flauto Magico*, HR, 168

Bertinotti (Radicati), Teresa, **261**; influence on operas at KT, 21; in debut, fine voice but no actress, HR, 166; in *Così* best singing at KT for years, HR, 167; proves public taste by success of *Così*, HR, 168; sang well as Pamina, HR, 169; as Fiordiligi in